BERLITZ®
TRAVEL GUIDE

PARIS

NEW!
with
restaurant and hotel
recommendations

Copyright © 1978,1987 by Berlitz Guides, a division of Macmillan S.A., Avenue d'Ouchy 61, 1000 Lausanne 6, Switzerland.

All rights reserved. No part of this book may be reproduced or transmitted in any form or by any means, electronic or mechanical, including photocopying, recording or by any information storage and retrieval system without permission in writing from the publisher.

Berlitz Trademark Reg. U.S. Patent Office and other countries. Marca Registrada. Library of Congress Catalog Card No. 78-70369.

Printed in Hong Kong by Mandarin Offset.

Deluxe Guide
1988/1989 Edition

By the staff of Berlitz Guides

How to use our guide

- All the practical information, hints and tips that you will need before and during the trip start on page 100.
- For general background, see the sections Paris and the Parisians, p. 6, and A Brief History, p. 12.
- All the sights to see are listed between pages 22 and 76. Our own choice of sights most highly recommended is pinpointed by the Berlitz traveller symbol.
- Entertainment, nightlife and all other leisure activities are described between pages 76 and 91, while information on restaurants and cuisine is to be found on pages 93 to 99.
- Finally, there is an index at the back of the book, pp. 125–127.

Found an error or an omission in this Berlitz Guide? Or a change or new feature we should know about? Our editor would be happy to hear from you, and a postcard would do. Be sure to include your name and address, since in appreciation for a useful suggestion, we'd like to send you a free travel guide.

Although we make every effort to ensure the accuracy of all the information in this book, changes occur incessantly. We cannot therefore take responsibility for facts, prices, addresses and circumstances in general that are constantly subject to alteration.

Text: Jack Altman
Photography: cover, pp. 4–5, 6, 7, 13, 21, 34, 39, 45, 62, 69, 71, 72, 85 Monique Jacot; pp. 9, 15, 22, 31, 33, 53, 59, 60, 75, 81, 82, 87, 88, 89, 91 Loomis Dean; pp. 10, 36, 43, 47, 49, 54, 57, 65, 66, 79, 92, 97 Erling Mandelmann; p. 19 A. Held; pp. 28, 77 PRISMA
We wish to thank Suzanne Patterson and Claire Teeuwissen for their help with this guide, and we're also grateful to the Office de Tourisme de Paris and the Office national français du Tourisme for their valuable assistance.
 Cartography: Falk-Verlag, Hamburg

Contents

Maps

Paris and the Parisians

The city and the people of Paris share a boundless self-confidence that exudes from every stone in its monuments and museums, bistrots and and boutiques, from every chestnut tree along its avenues and boulevards, from every little street-urchin, fashion model, butcher and baker, from every irate motorist and every charming maître d'hôtel. It is a self-confidence that will exhilarate anyone open to the breathless adventure of Paris, though it may intimidate people who dislike the light, movement and noise of life itself.

Some see it spilling over into arrogance—in the bombast of monumental architecture or in the overbearing attitudes of know-it-all street-philosophers. But looking around, you must admit they have something to be arrogant about. Stand on the

Pont Royal in the late afternoon and gaze down the Seine to the glass-panelled Grand Palais, bathed in the pink-and-blue glow of the river's never tranquil waters. Already you sense that the light in this City of Light is of a very special kind, bringing phosphorescence to the most commonplace little square or side-street. In case the message is not clear, Paris offers unparalleled night-time illumination of its major historic buildings, avenues and squares, underscored by the ongoing battle between the city's monument-cleaners and automobile pollution.

Despite inevitable erosions of social change, Paris manages to sustain most of its myths and legends. Take the jargon of its topography, for example,

Something old, something new, something borrowed—and something blue.

names that evoke not just a place but a state of mind.

The Right Bank conjures up an image of bourgeois respectability. Historically the stronghold of merchants and royalty, it remains today the home of commerce and government. Faubourg Saint-Honoré offers the luxury of *haute couture* and jewellery shops and the authority of the president's palace (and the British embassy), while the Champs-Elysées claims the first-run cinemas, airline companies and car showrooms.

The Left Bank, on the other hand, has always had a bohemian and intellectual image, dating back to the founding of the university and the monasteries. Today the Sorbonne, the Académie française, the publishing houses and myriad bookshops continue to exert an intellectual magnetism. Left Bank theatres typically prefer avant-garde drama to the boulevard comedy of the Right Bank.

The art galleries, doubtless needing the sustenance both of business and the intelligentsia, are about equally divided between Right and Left Banks, though the establishment-oriented galleries seem to be more in evidence on the Right Bank. The artists themselves remain characteristically on the periphery of both Right and Left Banks, in Montmartre and Montparnasse respectively.

A constant flow and interchange of citizenry from one bank to the other takes place over the bridges of the Seine, a very accessible river well integrated into the town's life.

Paris is a city of people constantly on the move, at all hours of day and night—inevitable, really, since it's one of the most densely populated urban centres in the world. In nearly every one of Paris's 20 *arrondissements,* or districts, you will find shops, offices and apartments side by side and on top of each other, which makes the city's streets exceedingly lively. Don't be surprised if you become addicted to Paris's most marvellous sport—watching the world from a café table.

From that vantage point you can easily check on another of the town's legends—that of the good-looking women. The emphasis is not so much on "beautiful" or "pretty" but quite simply "good-looking". You may note that Parisian women are by and large *not* more or less pretty than elsewhere,

Hunting for bargains—whether in fashions, antiques, prints or stamps —is an absorbing Paris pastime.

but somehow they manage, with a colour combination, a hairstyle, a scarf tied in a particular way, but above all in the way they sit, stand or walk, to just *look* good. Drawing on that communal self-confidence, they convince themselves—and nearly everybody else.

The key to the joy of just sitting and watching Paris go by is in the endless variety of the people. There is no "Parisian" type, physically speaking. The town's 2 million population is drawn from every region in France—Brittany, Alsace, Burgundy, Provence, for example—and the Parisian's traditional contempt for the "provinces"

is matched only by his fierce regional loyalty to the distant home of his ancestors, most often just one generation removed.

However dominant Paris may be in French art, literature, music, fashion, education, scientific research, commerce and politics, one area has been denied it—cuisine. There is no such thing as Parisian cuisine. This has the advantage, if you are a first-time visitor to France, of letting you come to the capital and sample each of the country's regional cuisines as you pick your way among the 11,000 or more bistrots and restaurants around town. Often a region's representative restaurants cluster around the railway station serving that area—like the Breton restaurants around the Gare Montparnasse—for that is where yesterday's "provincials" stopped off and set up home as Parisians.

These "provincials" were drawn, like people the world over, to a city conceived and evolved on the grand scale but offering at the same time an intimacy on the neighbourhood level. While avenues and boulevards sweep up to monumental vistas, the narrow streets around the church of Saint-Séverin lead back to medieval times and the Rue de Varenne to the gracious classicism of the 18th century. In the same way, the Parisian has an imposing, sometimes forbidding reputation, but also wit, style and charm in his personal dealings that make him much more accessible than you would expect.

Paris has the astounding treasures of the Louvre and the ambitious Beaubourg cultural centre. But it also offers those tiny storefronts on the Rue Jacob for collections of old artistic playing cards and Napoleonic tin soldiers. You can spend a small fortune on the most fabulous evening dress or buy the most stylish tee-shirt—for a thousand times less.

Don't expect to find any amazing bargains in the City of Light. Paris has been around long enough to learn the correct price for everything. The nightlife of the cabarets, theatres, opera, discotheques and nightclubs is *not* cheap, but it *is* still gay, and it is still an adventure. The real bargain is the magic of that light, movement and noise around the Paris streets. That costs just a little shoe leather.

Pigalle, with famed Moulin Rouge, lives on in round-the-clock whirl.

A Brief History

It all began in the middle of the river. Some Celtic fishermen and boatmen called Parisii set up their homes on an island in the Seine—the Ile de la Cité of today. The swiftly flowing waters provided good protection against invaders until the Romans conquered the town in 52 B.C. It was known as Lutetia or Lutèce, meaning marshland.

In Roman times the right bank of the river was too marshy to live on—so the town expanded to the Left Bank. Excavations have revealed the Roman arena, popular for the usual fights between gladiators, lions and Christians, and the public baths (see p. 73), dating from the 2nd and 3rd centuries A.D.

St. Denis brought Christianity to the city and was rewarded by decapitation on the hill of Montmartre. Legend and popular depictions of the event have Denis picking up his head and walking away with it.

Towards the end of the 3rd century Lutetia was overrun by barbarians, mostly Huns and Franks, and the town's inhabitants moved back to the fortified Ile de la Cité. Attila headed this way in 451 but the fervour of St. Geneviève's prayers is said to have persuaded him to spare the city. Clovis, King of the Franks, who showed good faith by converting to Christianity, arrived in 508 and settled down in the Palais de la Cité (now Palais de Justice). People moved back to the Left Bank and the church of Saint-Germain-des-Prés was built in the 6th century.

The Middle Ages

But Paris remained a backwater of the European scene until Hugues Capet established himself there in 987 and made Paris the economic and political capital of France for the Capetian dynasty. Under Louis VI (1108–37) Paris enjoyed its "agricultural age", when enclosed farms, *clos*, flourished. But the strength of Paris was its merchants who exploited the commerce of the Seine by collecting duties and taxes from ships passing through Paris, making the town rich under the motto: *Fluctuat nec mergitur* (It floats but it doesn't sink).

These revenues enabled Philippe Auguste (1180–1223) to construct Notre-Dame cathedral, a fortress named the Louvre, aqueducts, fresh-water fountains and some paved streets. To protect his investment while away on the Third Crusade, he surrounded the growing city with walls.

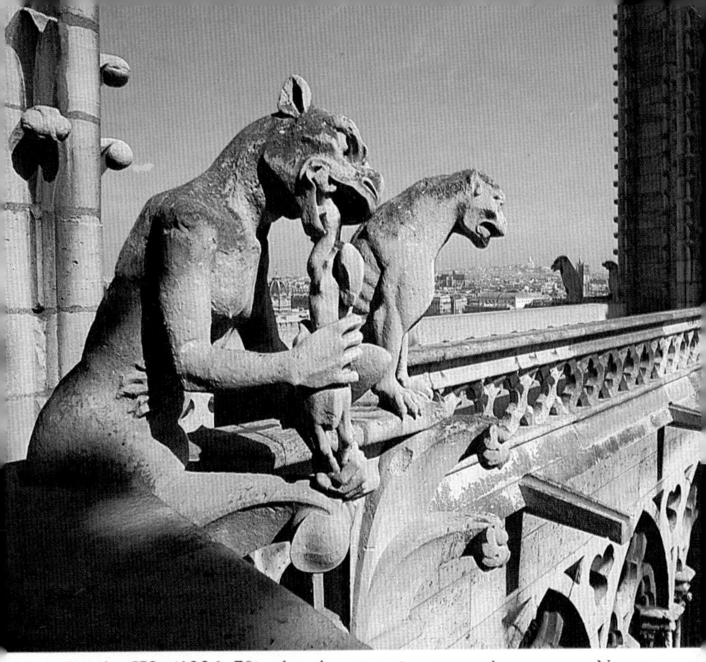

Leering gargoyles roost on Notre-Dame, keeping Evil at bay.

Louis IX (1226–70) developed the spiritual and intellectual side of Paris life by building the Gothic masterpiece, the Sainte-Chapelle, and many colleges on the Left Bank, including that of Robert de Sorbon (see p. 54). With a population of 100,000, Paris was the largest city in Western Christendom.

The mercantile backbone of the city proved itself in the 14th century when plague and the Hundred Years' War devastated France, leaving Paris at the mercy of the English. In 1356, with King Jean le Bon taken prisoner at Poitiers, the provost of the city merchants, Etienne Marcel, profited from the confusion and set up a municipal dictatorship. Though assassinated a year later, Marcel had showed that the Parisians themselves were a force to be reckoned with in France's history. The next king, Charles V, ever wary of Parisian militancy, built the Bastille fortress.

If the strife of the 14th century had been unsettling for Paris, that of the 15th was positively disastrous. In 1407, the Duke of Burgundy had the Duke of Orleans murdered on Rue Barbette, which led to 12 years of strife between the Burgundians and Armagnacs. The carnage ended only with the capture of Paris by the English in 1420. Ten years later Joan of Arc tried and failed to liberate the town. The next year came the ultimate humiliation with the crowning of the young English King Henry VI at Notre-Dame as King of France. In case that was not enough, the plague of 1466 felled thousands of Parisians.

Paris Takes Shape

Nonetheless the city remained resilient. With François Ier (1515–47), Paris learned to thrive under an absolutist and absentee monarch, busy with wars in Italy and even a year's imprisonment in Spain. The arts, sciences and literature flourished. Much of the Louvre was torn down and rebuilt along its present lines. A new Hôtel de Ville (town hall) was begun, as well as the superb Saint-Eustache church. The Parisians were already assuming that distinctive pride over the uniqueness of their town. Poet Pierre de Ronsard saw Paris as "the city imbued with the discipline and glory of the Muses".

The religious wars wreaked havoc and mayhem in Paris, starting in 1572 with the Massacre of St. Bartholomew—3,000 Protestants were killed—and culminating in the siege of the city by Henri de Navarre

in 1589. Before the Catholic League capitulated, 13,000 Parisians had died of starvation. Henri was crowned at Chartres and finally entered the city in 1594—but not before he had turned Catholic. His famous words, "Paris is well worth a mass", have remained an ambiguous comment on the merely political value attached to religion and the special desirability of the French capital. Paris's myth was growing.

Henri IV did Paris proud once he was its master. He built the beautiful Place des Vosges and Place Dauphine, embellished the river banks with the Quais de l'Arsenal, de l'Horloge and des Orfèvres and constructed the Samaritaine hydraulic machine that pumped

The Conciergerie was the last stop for many on their way to the guillotine.

fresh water to Right Bank households till 1813. By far the most popular of France's monarchs, Henri IV was a notorious ladies' man and was known to his subjects as the Vert Galant. He completed the Pont-Neuf (despite its name, the city's oldest standing bridge) and the adjacent gardens, where he had been known to dally with his ladies. Young lovers carry on the tradition there today.

Under Louis XIII (1610–43), Paris began to take on the "fashionable" aspect that has become its mark. The Cours-la-Reine, precursor of the Champs-Elysées, was built for Henri's widow Marie de Médicis. Elegant houses went up along the Faubourg Saint-Honoré, and tree-lined boulevards stretched clear across the city over to the Bastille, creating the airy sweep of modern Paris. The capital also consolidated its position as the hub of the country—with the establishment of the royal printing press, Cardinal Richelieu's Académie française and other scientific institutions such as the botanical gardens, and Paris's new ecclesiastical status as an archbishopric. The cardinal also deserves credit for the splendid Palais-Royal. With the Ile Saint-Louis—formed from two separate islands in 1614 by engineer Christophe Marie—and the residential development of the Marais and Saint-Germain-des-Prés districts, Paris was becoming an increasingly attractive place for nobles from the provinces.

Too much so for the liking of Louis XIV (1643–1715). To bring his overly powerful and independent aristocrats back into line he decided to move the court to Versailles, where palace life was ruinously expensive.

Paris continued to flourish with the landscaping (by Louis' counsellor Jean-Baptiste Colbert) of the Tuileries Gardens, the Champs-Elysées, the construction of the Louvre's great colonnade, the triumphal arches of Saint-Antoine, Saint-Denis and Saint-Martin and the Invalides hospital for soldiers wounded in Louis' wars. The Sun King's fears about Parisian talent for trouble-making led to the innovation of street-lighting (on moonless nights only). The city now numbered 560,000 inhabitants, almost six times as many as in the 13th century under Louis IX.

Paris asserted its cultural ascendancy in Europe with the organization of the academies of the arts, literature and sciences and the founding of the Comédie-Française (1680) and other theatres under Louis XV. Cafés sprang up around the Palais-Royal, and the boulevard life was the animated focus of European intellectual ferment as the Revolution approached.

One of the last constructions of the Ancien Régime, begun in 1784, was a new wall around the city. This became a major factor in the revolutionary unrest, for it was there that the *fermiers-généraux* (financiers) collected taxes from merchants and artisans coming to do business in Paris.

Revolution and Empire

The Revolution of 1789 was more notable for its destruction than for additions to Parisian landmarks—though the removal of the Bastille and the monasteries and convents did create more open spaces. The Revolutionaries made special use of the stronghold of the Capetian dynasty: the Conciergerie in the Palais de Justice, the heart of the medieval kings' palace, became a prison for those condemned by Revolutionary tribunals. And Dr Joseph Guillotin, a member of parliament, who said the times demanded something more humane than the Ancien Régime's hanging, drawing and quartering, developed a new gadget to chop heads off.

With the advent of Napoleon, the city's development resumed. The emperor's frequent absences on foreign business did not hinder his projects for making Paris the capital of Europe. Detailed maps of the city and architectural plans for new buildings were always part of his baggage. Typically he found time during his stop-over in Moscow to work on the reorganization of the Comédie-Française back home. While most visitors see Napoleon's mark in spectacular monuments—the Arc de Triomphe, the 12 avenues of the Etoile, the column of the Grande Armée on Place Vendôme—the emperor himself regarded his most important achievements as those more appropriate to a mayor than a world conqueror: increased supplies of fresh water for the city, the new food-markets, the five slaughter houses and the wine-market. His streamlined municipal administration and police force became a model for modern European urban government.

The centralization of power in the capital also made Paris a potential threat to the government—the concentration of aggressively ambitious bourgeois, dissatisfied workers and an intellectual class eager to try out its radical ideas. Typically, the Revolution of 1830 came from an alliance of liberal bourgeois Parisian intellectuals, denied the right to publish their newspapers, and the printing-workers thrown into unemployment by the closing of the papers. The 1848 Revolution which ended Louis-Philippe's "bourgeois" monarchy also originated in Paris when the government tried to forbid banquets held in the capital in support of electoral and parliamentary reform. Building Paris up as a great, lively, volatile capital of cultural, social and political innovation automatically turned it into a hotbed of trouble for its rulers.

Modernizing the City

Napoleon III, the great one's nephew, was literally scared into modernizing Paris. He had seen the popular uprisings of 1830 and 1848 flare up in the capital's densely populated working-class neighbourhoods around the city centre and wanted to prevent a recurrence. He commissioned Baron Georges Haussmann to do away with the clusters of narrow streets and alleyways that nurtured discontent and barricades. The baron razed them and moved the occupants out to the suburbs, creating the "red belt" which makes Paris one of the few Western capitals whose suburbia is not predominantly conservative.

The city was opened up by wide boulevards and avenues, giving Paris its modern airy look and highlighting the city's monumental churches and other public buildings. Furthermore, as the baron explained to his emperor, these avenues gave the artillery a clear line of fire in case of revolt.

But this Second Empire was also a time of gaiety and boisterous expansion, emphasized by world fairs in 1855 and 1867, attracting royalty from England, Austria, Russia and Prussia to look at the sparkling new city of Offenbach's operettas and the comedies of Labiche. This was the beginning of "gay Paree".

Then came war, the Franco-Prussian War, with a crippling siege of Paris in 1870 and another uprising, barricades and all. The Paris Commune—self-government of the workers—lasted 10 weeks (March 18

La Belle Epoque—when you could hear Bruant sing at the Chat Noir.

BRUAN
et

to May 29, 1871), until Adolphe Thiers, first president of the Third Republic, sent in troops from Versailles to crush the revolt.

Into the 20th Century

The Third Republic brought unparalleled prosperity to Paris. Projects begun under Napoleon III, such as the new opera house and the gigantic Halles market (today moved out to the suburbs) were completed in the construction boom that followed the capital's triumphant resurrection after its defeat by the Prussians. By the 1890s Paris had risen to the fore as a cultural magnet. Artists, writers and revolutionaries flocked to this hub of creative activity. Picasso arrived from Barcelona in 1900, followed by Modigliani from Livorno, Soutine from Minsk, Stravinsky from St. Petersburg, Gertrude Stein from San Francisco, and then the long stream of American writers and artists led by Ernest Hemingway and F. Scott Fitzgerald. Paris was Mecca, the myth so powerful that detractors of the Belle Epoque and the Gay Twenties were drowned out by the true believers raising another glass at La Coupole *brasserie* and dancing another foxtrot at Maxim's.

Two wars, of course, took their toll. Though the Germans did not make it to Paris during the First World War, they occupied the city for four drab years (June 1940 to August 1944) in the Second. It took Paris some time to recover. Typically, what the French remember best was the august parade of General de Gaulle and his fellow Resistance fighters down the Champs-Elysées; the expatriates' fondest memory, on the other hand, is of Ernest Hemingway "liberating" the bar of the Ritz Hotel. While much of the cultural magnetism had moved from Paris to New York, the French capital retained some of its mythic character with Jean-Paul Sartre holding existentialist court on the Left Bank and Juliette Greco singing all in black in the jazz-cellars of Saint-Germain-des-Prés.

Students recaptured some of the capital's old revolutionary spirit in May 1968 by hurling the Latin Quarter's paving stones against the smugly entrenched Establishment of de Gaulle's Fifth Republic. President Georges Pompidou affirmed the new prosperity with riverside expressways and skyscrapers, but his crowning achievement was the once controversial, now hugely successful, Beaubourg Cultural Centre.

In 1977, Jacques Chirac became the first democratically elected mayor of Paris. (For over a century, since the turbulent days of the Commune, the national government controlled the city with its own appointed officials.) Now, in a country where politicians can double as mayor and prime minister, Parisians benefit from a leader eager to further national political ambitions with a dynamic municipal performance: cleaner streets, more sports stadiums, tennis courts and swimming pools. Meanwhile, President François Mitterrand has made his own mark with a grand programme, among others, to reorganize the Louvre around a monumental glass pyramid. Paris emerges the winner from these eternal political rivalries.

Left, right or centre, French politicians are a knockout.

What to See

The Seine

The river is by far the best place to begin to take the measure of Paris. Its mixture of grandeur and intimacy is the very essence of the city.

Stand on the Right Bank by the Pont Mirabeau, facing east. Upriver you'll see the Statue of Liberty (a scale-model of the New York original) on the next bridge, framed against the Eiffel Tower over on the Left Bank. This visual melding of the Old and New Worlds prepares you well for the cosmopolitan experience of Paris.

Again and again the Seine provides a spectacular vantage-point for the city's great landmarks. The Eiffel Tower itself, the Palais de Chaillot and Trocadéro Gardens, the Grand and Petit Palais, the Palais-Bourbon, Louvre Museum and Notre-Dame all take on a more enchanting, even dream-like quality if you see them first when floating by in a boat. This is of course even more true of the river's bridges, many of them also monuments to the capital's history.

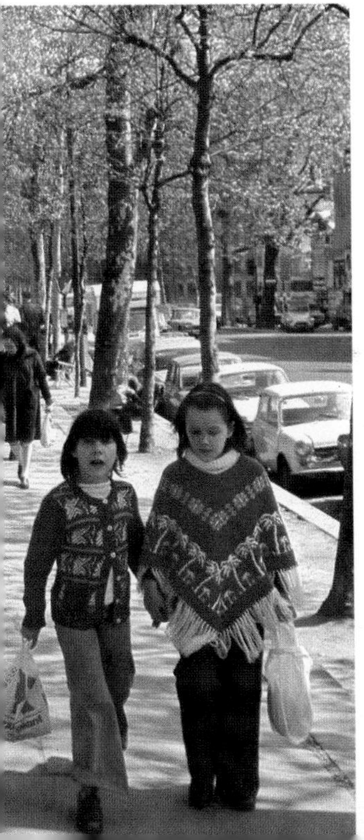

For that all-important first impression, a **guided boat-trip** on the Seine is unbeatable (see page 27). But this also remains a river to be walked along, despite the encroachments of cars on rapid *voies express* along the banks. You can take delightful strolls right down by the river between the Pont Sully at the eastern end of the Ile Saint-Louis and the Pont de la Concorde and around the two river-islands. Nothing is more restful—and the excitement of Paris demands an occasional rest—than an hour on a bench beneath the poplars and plane trees along the Seine, especially in early morning and late afternoon when that pink Paris light is at its best.

If you want to see the river from its bridges, there are four especially worthy of your attention.

The **Pont-Neuf** (*neuf* means "new") is in fact the oldest stand-

Old prints, magazines and books line stalls on the quais *of the Seine.*

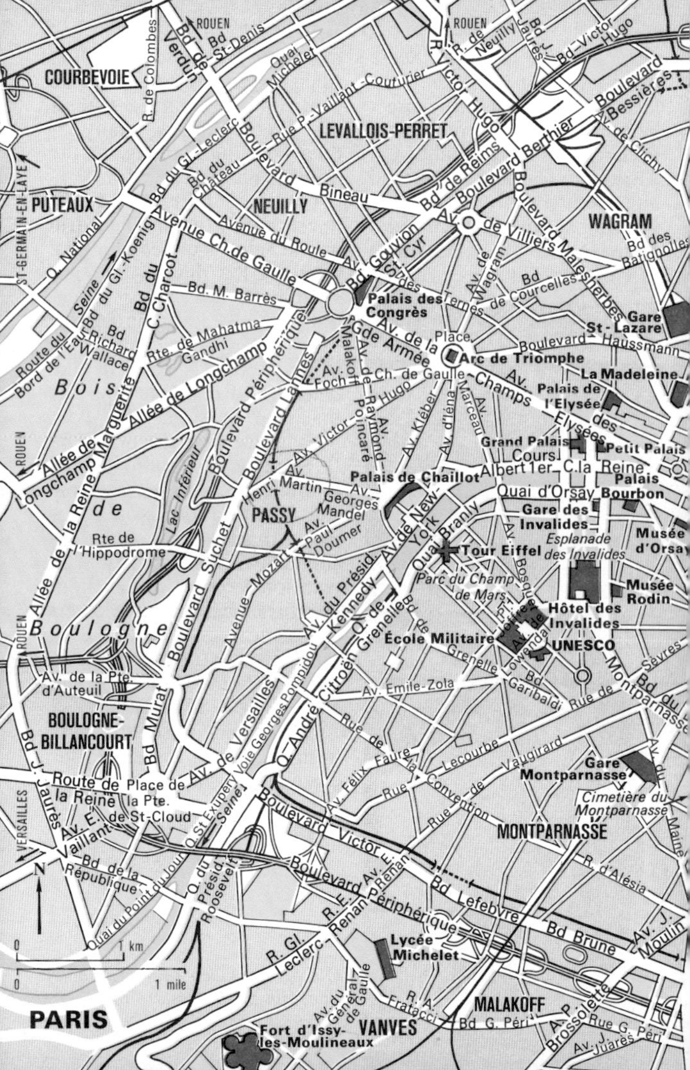

ROUEN
Bd de Verdun
Bd St-Denis
R. de Colombes
COURBEVOIE
Quai Michelet
ROUEN
R. de Neuilly
Bd J. Jaurès
Bd Victor Hugo
R. Victor Hugo
Rue P.-Vaillant-Couturier
Boulevard Bessières
Bd du Gl. Leclerc
LEVALLOIS-PERRET
Boulevard Berthier
R. de Clichy
ST-GERMAIN-EN-LAYE
Bd du Château
Boulevard Bineau
Bd de Reims
PUTEAUX
NEUILLY
Boulevard Malesherbes
WAGRAM
Q. National
Avenue du Roule
Bd Gouvion St Cyr
Av. de Villiers
Bd des Batignolles
Avenue Ch. de Gaulle
Seine
Bd du Gl. Koenig
Bd du C. Charcot
Av. de Wagram
Bd. M. Barrès
Av. des Ternes
Bd de Courcelles
Palais des Congrès
Gare St-Lazare
Route du Bord de l'Eau
Bd Richard Wallace
Rte. de Mahatma Gandhi
Av. de la Gde Armée
Place
Boulevard Haussmann
Arc de Triomphe
Av. Malakoff
Av. Foch
Ch. de Gaulle
La Madeleine
Bois de Boulogne
Allée de Longchamp
Av. Raymond Poincaré
Av. Victor-Hugo
Av. des Champs Elysées
Palais de l'Elysée
ROUEN
Allée de Longchamp
Allée de la Reine Marguerite
Boulevard Périphérique
Boulevard Lannes
Av. Kléber
Av. d'Iéna
Av. Marceau
Grand Palais
Petit Palais
Cours Albert 1er
C. la Reine
Lac Inférieur
Av. Henri Martin
Palais de Chaillot
Palais Bourbon
Quai d'Orsay
Av. Georges Mandel
PASSY
Gare des Invalides
Musée d'Orsay
Rte de l'Hippodrome
Av. Paul Doumer
Av. de New-York
Quai Branly
Esplanade des Invalides
Tour Eiffel
Av. Bosquet
Boulevard Suchet
Avenue Mozart
Av. du Présid. Kennedy
Parc du Champ de Mars
Musée Rodin
Hôtel des Invalides
Av. de Lowendal
UNESCO
ROUEN
Bd de Grenelle
Q. de Grenelle
École Militaire
Bd Garibaldi
Bd du Montparnasse
Rue de Sèvres
Av. de la Pte. d'Auteuil
Av. Emile-Zola
Bd Murat
Voie Georges Pompidou
Q. André Citroën
Av. de Versailles
BOULOGNE-BILLANCOURT
Rue de la Convention
Rue Lecourbe
Rue de Vaugirard
Gare Montparnasse
Av. Félix Faure
Bd J. Jaurès
Route de la Reine
Place de la Pte. de St-Cloud
Q. St Exupéry
Seine
Cimetière du Montparnasse
VERSAILLES
Av. E. Vaillant
Boulevard Victor
MONTPARNASSE
Av. du Maine
Bd de la République
Quai du Point du Jour
Q. du Présid. Roosevelt
Av. Renan
Boulevard Périphérique
R. d'Alésia
Bd Lefebvre
Bd Brune
Av. J. Moulin
N
0 1 km
0 1 mile
R. Gl. Leclerc
R. E. Renan
Lycée Michelet
Av. du Général de Gaulle
R. A. Fratacci
MALAKOFF
Bd G. Péri
Rue G. Péri
A. P. Brossolette
PARIS
Fort d'Issy-les-Moulineaux
VANVES
Av. J. Jaurès

LILLE
Boulevard Périphérique
LILLE
LILLE
Boulevard Ney
Bd Ney
Boulevard Macdonald
Av. E. Vaillant
Gl. Leclerc
PANTIN
Cité des sciences et de l'industrie
LA VILLETTE
Avenue Jean Lolive
REIMS
MONTMARTRE
Bd Ornano
Bd Barbès
R. Chapelle
R. de la R. M. Dormoy
Rue de Flandre
Boulevard
Cimetière de Montmartre
Sacré Cœur
LE PRÉ-ST-GERVAIS
R. J. Auffret
Avenue Jean Jaurès
Moulin Rouge
Pl. Pigalle
Bd de Rochechouart
Bd de la Chapelle
Gare du Nord
Pl. de Stalingrad
Rue de Crimée
Parc des Buttes Chaumont
Av. Secrétan
Sérurier
R. de Paris
Trinité
Rue La Fayette
Bd de Magenta
Gare de l'Est
Bd de la Villette
Av. S. Bolivar
Rue de Belleville
BELLEVILLE
Bd Mortier
Musée Grévin
Opéra
R. des Pyrénées
R. du Faubourg du Temple
Bd de Belleville
Av. Gambetta
Bd Saint-Martin
Pl. de la République
Bd de Sébastopol
Av. de la République
Rue Belgrand
Jardin des Tuileries
Palais Royal
Centre Pompidou
Av. Gambetta
Forum des Halles
Bd Beaumarchais
Bd de Ménilmontant
Cimetière du Père-Lachaise
REIMS
R. de Rivoli
Musée et Palais du Louvre
Boulevard Voltaire
Boulevard Davout
Place des Vosges
R. des Pyrénées
Q. de Conti
Palais de Justice
Sainte-Chapelle
Hôtel-de-Ville
R. Saint-Antoine
Pl. de la Bastille
Colonne de Juillet
Av. Philippe Auguste
R. de Paris
Bd Montebello
Q. de Montebello
Notre-Dame
Bd Henri IV
Rue d'Avron
Bd St-Germain
R. du Faubourg St-Antoine
Pl. de la Nation
C. de Vincennes
Palais de Luxembourg
Sorbonne
Q. St-Bernard
Q. Henri IV
Bd Diderot
Jardin du Luxembourg
Panthéon
Gare de Lyon
Avenue
REIMS
Bd Saint-Michel
Rue Monge
Q. de la Rapée
Quai d'Austerlitz
Quai Seine
Bd de Picpus
Gl-M. Bizot
Boulevard Soult
Bd de Port Royal
Bd St-Marcel
Bd de l'Hôpital
Gare d'Austerlitz
Bd de Bercy
Pl. Félix Éboué
Palais omnisports de Paris-Bercy
Daumesnil
Observatoire
Av. des Gobelins
Quai de Bercy
Quai de la Gare
Rte. de Ceinture du L. Daumesnil
Bd St-Jacques
Bd V. Auriol
Pl. d'Italie
Place J. d'Arc
Av. du
Boulevard Poniatowski
Rue de Tolbiac
Bois de Vincennes
R. d'Alésia
R. de Tolbiac
Avenue d'Italie
Av. de Choisy
Boulevard Masséna
Q. d'Ivry
Rue de Paris
Av. de la Liberté
Q. de Bercy
Bd Jourdan
Bd Kellermann
Boulevard Périphérique
R. Boyer
Q. M.
CHARENTON
DIJON
Q. des Carrières
IVRY
R. Lénine
AÉROPORT D'ORLY
FONTAINEBLEAU

ing bridge in Paris, completed by Henri IV in 1606. It was the first one built without houses: Parisians were pleased to walk across and see their river. It soon became a favourite spot for promenades, for street-singers, charlatans, amateur dentists, professional ladies, pickpockets and above all for the *bouquinistes* selling their old books and pamphlets out of boxes. Established booksellers on the Ile de la Cité were enraged and drove them off to the banks of the Seine, where they have remained ever since.

The **Pont Royal,** built for Louis XIV in 1685, commands a splendid panorama of the Tuileries Gardens and the Louvre. It is the capital's most central bridge in the sense that it offers good views of the Grand and Petit Palais of the *grand-bourgeois* and the Ecole des Beaux-Arts and Institut de France of the intellectual community.

The **Pont de la Concorde,** truly the bridge of the French Revolution, went up between 1787 and 1790. Its support structure used stones from the demolished Bastille prison—especially galling for Royalists in that it was originally Pont Louis XVI. The name was duly changed to Pont de la Révolution the year before Louis was guillotined a couple of hundred yards from the bridge on the Place de la Concorde.

The **Pont Alexandre III,** distinguished architecturally by its single steel arch, represents the final flowering of that bumptiously proud 19th-century industrial spirit exemplified by the Eiffel Tower. The tsar of Russia, Nicholas II, laid the first stone in 1896; the bridge was completed at the turn of the century. The purists find its statues to Fame and Pegasus insufferably bombastic, but lovers view them as an appropriately melodramatic touch to a moonlit stroll beneath the bridge's Belle-Epoque lanterns.

Getting your Bearings

Your orientation in Paris on foot or by car will be simplified by reference to five easily visible landmarks—the Arc de Triomphe and Sacré-Cœur basilica on the Right Bank; the Eiffel Tower and (jarring but nonetheless conveniently visible) Tour Maine-Montparnasse skyscraper on the Left Bank; and Notre-Dame Cathedral in the middle of the Ile de la Cité. Whenever you get lost, you should normally not have to go more than a couple of hundred yards before sighting one of these monuments on the horizon.

Paris by Boat

You can see Paris (and more) from the river and hear multilingual commentaries on all the landmarks.

The **Bateaux-Mouches** have open-air or covered seating according to the weather. The standard 75-minute tour starts by the Pont de l'Alma going west to the Pont Mirabeau and turning back upriver to the Pont Sully at the far end of the Ile Saint-Louis. Lunch and dinner cruises (no anoraks or blue jeans, ties obligatory) last 150 minutes (tel. 42.25.22.55).

The **Vedette** or motorboat tours take 60 minutes. Vedettes Paris-Tour Eiffel start at the Pont d'Iéna (Left Bank) and the Quai de Montebello, going west to the Pont de Bir-Hakeim and east to the Pont Sully and back. Vedettes du Pont-Neuf leave from the Pont-Neuf ("illuminated" cruises every evening from May 1 to Oct. 15) to the Eiffel Tower and back (tel. 46.33.98.38).

Leaving from the Quai Anatole France, the **Patache Eautobus** offers half-day cruises to Parc de la Villette north-east of the city via the Seine and the Canal Saint-Martin. Or you could try a one-day cruise up the Seine and the Marne to Nogent (tel. 48.74.75.30).

Right Bank

(Rive Droite)

L'Etoile–Concorde–Palais-Royal

Any tour of the Right Bank should begin at the **Place de l'Etoile** (officially, Place Charles-de-Gaulle), preferably on top of the **Arc de Triomphe.** One reason for climbing up Napoleon's gigantic triumphal arch (164 feet high, 148 feet wide) is to get a good view of the 12-pointed star, formed by 12 avenues radiating from the arch in a *tour de force* of geometric planning. The *place,* a vast sloping mound, cannot really be taken in at ground level. The monumental ensemble, conceived by Napoleon as a tribute to France's military glories and heroes, was completed by Baron Haussmann. Over the years the arch has taken on a mythic quality as succeeding régimes have invested it with the spirit of the nation, republican or imperial.

Napoleon himself saw only a life-size wooden and canvas model. Louis-Philippe inaugurated the final version in 1836, complete with bas-reliefs and statuary celebrating victories of the Revolution and Napoleonic empire. It became the tradi-

BRASSERIE
à toute heure...
Salade Niçoise 28
Poulet froid garni 35
Assiette des Champs 35
Assiette jambon de Paris 20
Assiette jambon de pays 31
Terrine du Quercy 19
Rillettes 24
Spécial lunch 31
Roquefort aux noix 24
Assiette de gruyère 19
Faux filet Béarnaise
Confit de canard
6 escargots
Quiche Paysanne 23
Tourte Provençale 25
Croque-monsieur 20
Croque-madame 24
Omelette nature 20
Omelette jambon 24
Omelette gruyère 24
Omelette mixte 28
Potage de légumes 18
Gratinée 24
HOT-DOG · SANDWICHES
PATISSERIES

tional focus for state funerals of national political, military and even literary heroes—Victor Hugo was given a positively pharaonic tribute here after his death in 1885. In 1920, the Unknown Soldier of World War I was buried at the arch, and three years later the Eternal Flame was lit.

When Hitler came to Paris as a conqueror in 1940, this was the first thing he wanted to see; and, of course, General de Gaulle's triumphant march of Liberation in 1944 started from here.

Avenue Foch, leading away from the Etoile, is the most majestic of the city's residential avenues and the best of the Baron Haussmann's grandiose conceptions. The **Champs-Elysées,** despite extensive commercialization, still deserves the title of the world's most celebrated avenue. It stretches in an absolutely straight line from the Arc de Triomphe to the Place de la Concorde, lined with chestnut trees all the way. The first two-thirds, as you walk down, are devoted to cinemas, shops and café terraces; you'll find the best people-watching

Champs-Elysées or Elysian Fields—abode of the blessed people-watchers.

points at the corner of the Avenue George-V on the "shady" side and at Rue du Colisée on the "sunny" side. After the Rond-Point, a pleasant park takes you down to the Place de la Concorde. An interesting theory about the special appeal of the Champs-Elysées is that people look more relaxed and attractive when walking downhill—so ignore the ones going in the other direction.

The **Place de la Concorde** has had a hard time earning its name. More than 1,000 people were guillotined here during the Revolution, the drums rolling to drown out any incendiary words the condemned might utter. In 1934, bloody rioting against the government took place here. Ten years later it was the Germans' last hold in Paris. Today, with floodlit fountains and elegant lamps it is a night-time romance and a daytime adventure, both for the pedestrian pausing to enjoy the vast opening of the Paris sky and for the driver daring to make his way around it. Along with the Etoile, it ranks as one of Europe's greatest challenges to the motorist's ability to survive the centrifugal force that hopefully flings him out to his destination. Smack in the centre you'll see Paris's oldest monument, the 75-foot pink syenite-granite obelisk of Luxor from the temple of Ramses II, dating back to 1300 B.C. For a change it's not something Napoleon brought back from his campaigns but a gift from Mohammed Ali, the viceroy of Egypt, erected in 1836.

After the bustle of the Champs-Elysées and the Place de la Concorde, you'll appreciate the cool, peaceful park, the **Jardin des Tuileries,** named after 13th-century tile works. Its spaciousness is due in large part to the destruction of the Palais des Tuileries during the 1871 Commune (fragments can still be seen by the Jeu de Paume museum in the northwest corner). Children will enjoy the circular ponds on which boats are sailed and sunk almost all year round and the marionette shows in spring and summer.

At the eastern end of the Tuileries stands the **arc de triomphe du Carrousel,** built about the same time as its big brother at the Etoile, visible in a straight line beyond the Luxor Obelisk. This imposing effect

Driving round the Place de la Concorde is one of life's great adventures, especially at rush hour.

was originally planned for Napoleon to see from his bedroom in the Louvre. Today the vista is somewhat spoiled by the skyscrapers of La Défense looming on the horizon.

Leaving the Louvre Museum for a separate visit (see p. 66), cross the Rue de Rivoli to the **Palais-Royal.** There are few pleasanter places to dip back into the history of Paris. Completed in 1639 for the Cardinal Richelieu (after whom it was originally named the Palais-Cardinal), this serene arcaded palace with its garden of limes and beeches and a pond where the young Louis XIV nearly drowned has always been a colourful centre of more or less respectable activity. In the days of Philippe d'Orléans, Regent of France during Louis XV's minority, the Palais-Royal was the scene of notorious orgies. To meet the family's extravagant debts, the ground-floor rooms were turned into boutiques—the last of which still sell old coins, medals, engravings and antiques—and cafés that attracted a fashionable society.

But in Paris the beau monde and demi-monde have always lived off each other, and the Palais-Royal soon took over from the Pont-Neuf as the meeting-place of artists, intellectuals, charlatans, prostitutes and pickpockets. On July 13, 1789, a young firebrand orator, Camille Desmoulins, stood on a table at the Palais-Royal's Café de Foy and made the call to arms that set off the French Revolution the next day. At the other end of that era, Prussian General Blücher came to the Palais-Royal after Waterloo to

J. KLEIN, LAUSANNE

Peaceful area around the Palais-Royal recalls a more elegant age.

squander 1,500,000 francs in one night at one of the many rambunctious gambling dens.

East of the Palais-Royal, the old food markets of les Halles (moved to the more hygienic, inevitably less colourful suburb of Rungis) have been replaced by gardens, new apartment buildings and the **Forum des Halles,** a rather garish shopping centre. Around it, the lively neighbourhood of cafés, boutiques and art galleries linking up with the Centre Pompidou (Beaubourg, see p. 68) is very popular with the young crowd. The liveliest meeting-place is around the handsome Renaissance **Fontaine des Innocents** (once part of a cemetery).

On the north side of les Halles, another monument of the Renaissance period, but decidedly Gothic in silhouette, is the church of **Saint-Eustache,** remarkable for its 17th-century stained-glass windows over the choir, crafted according to medieval traditions.

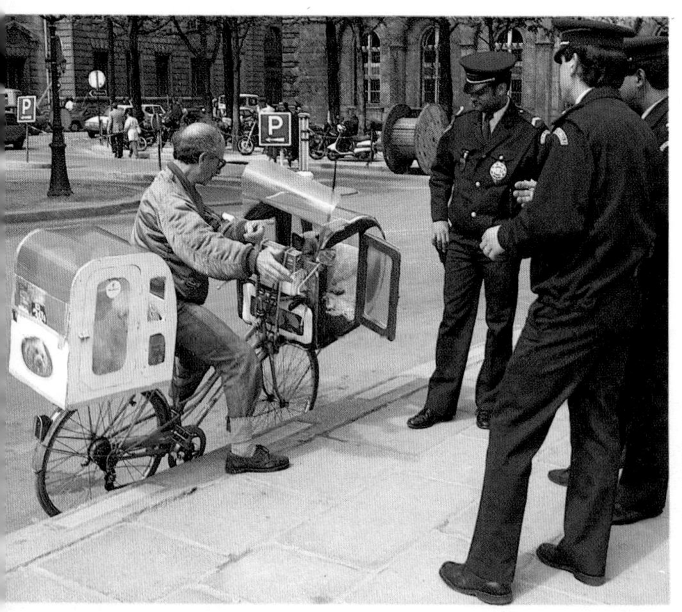

Place Vendôme–Opéra–Madeleine

It's hard to find a more elegant place to work in than the **Place Vendôme,** an airy gracious octagon designed to provide an imposing setting for a statue of Louis XIV. Only his financiers could afford the rents here, and nearly 300 years later the situation has not changed much: there are 19 banks (as well as world-famous jewellers, the Ministry of Justice and the Ritz Hotel) encircling the column with which Napoleon replaced the Sun King. The spiral of bronze bas-reliefs depicting scenes from the Great Battles, topped by a statue of Napoleon himself, was cast from 1,250 cannons captured from the Austrians and Russians at Austerlitz.

A quick walk up the Rue de la Paix—a slow one might prove ruinous to your budget—takes you past jewellers, goldsmiths and furriers to the

Opéra, the massive epitome of the pretensions of Napoleon III's Second Empire. Started at the height of his power in 1862 (by architect Charles Garnier), when Paris claimed to be Europe's most glamorous capital, the Opéra was not completed until 1875. Its neo-baroque style is less of an aesthetic joy than a splendid act of conspicuous consumption proclaiming the triumph of the French bourgeoisie. It takes honours as the world's largest theatre, though it seats only 2,000 people.

The **grands boulevards** leading from the Opéra to the Madeleine are perhaps less fashionable than in their heyday at the turn of the century, but their bustle and great open sweep make it easy to recapture the atmosphere. On the Boulevard des Capucines you will be retracing the footsteps of Renoir, Manet and Pis-

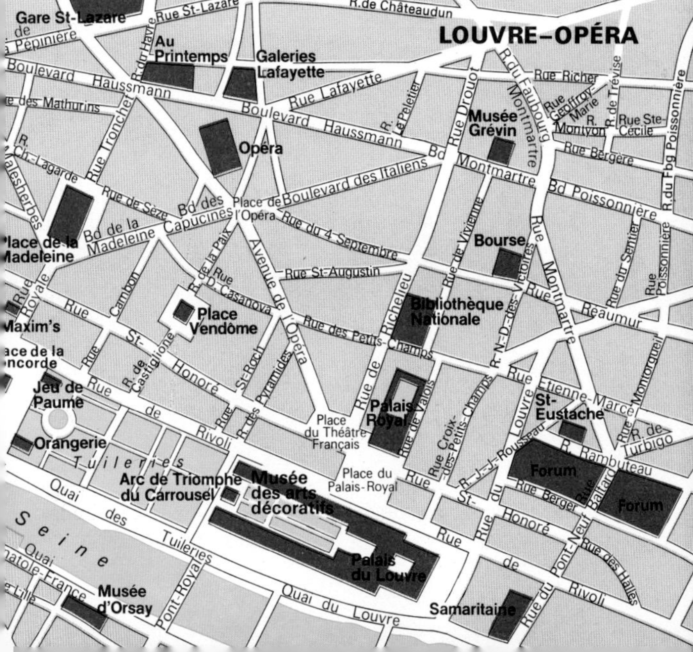

sarro, who took their paintings to the house of photographer Nadar, at number 35, for the first exhibition of Impressionist painting in 1874. The boulevards are now appropriately the home of the town's most popular cinemas—appropriately because it was here at the Hôtel Scribe, that the Lumière brothers staged the first public moving-picture show in 1895.

Many people are surprised to learn that the **Madeleine** is a church—and, in fact, it did not start out as one. Originally there *was* going to be a church here, and Louis XV even laid its first stone in 1764, but the Revolution halted construction. Then Napoleon decided to put up a huge temple-like structure, Greek on the outside and Roman on the inside. It

In Montmartre, the artist must also be adept at making a deal.

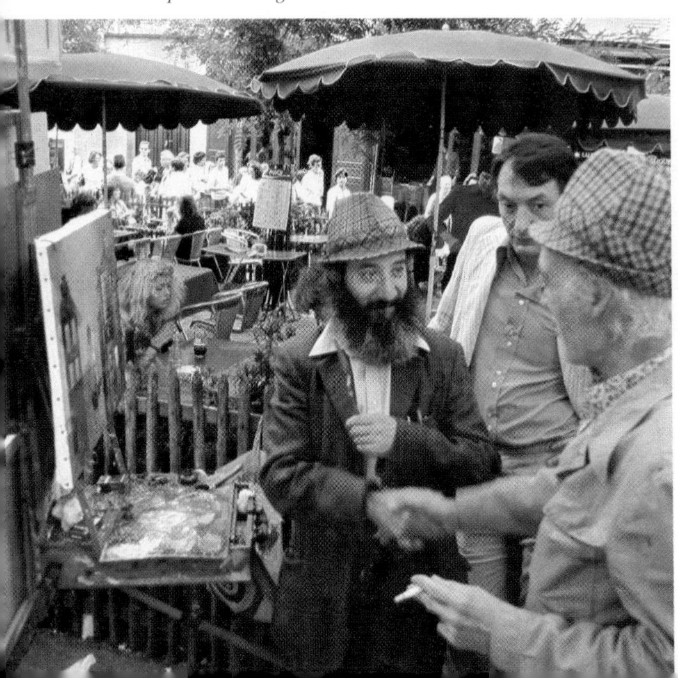

was variously projected as a stock exchange, the Bank of France, a theatre or a state banquet hall. Napoleon himself saw it as a Temple de la Gloire for his military victories until the architect persuaded him to build the Arc de Triomphe instead. After Waterloo Louis XVIII reverted to the plan for a church, but with no transept, aisles or bell-tower, or even a cross on the roof. It remains an awe-inspiring monument embellished on most days by the flower market at its base.

From the Madeleine you can either return to the Place de la Concorde by taking the grand Rue Royale past Maxim's restaurant, a monument no less awesome than the Madeleine, or go up towards the Etoile along the city's most opulent shopping street, the **Rue du Faubourg Saint-Honoré,** with a peek through the gates of the French president's Elysée Palace at number 55. But two other, entirely different neighbourhoods belong to and enrich the Right Bank: Montmartre and the Marais. Each deserves at least a day.

Montmartre

If Paris more than most places thrives on its mythology, few quarters have contributed more than Montmartre, known locally as "La Butte". Long famous as the home of artists and bohemian crazies, it is also a focus of the city's spiritual sources. The pagan and religious aspects of Montmartre's personality begin with the etymology of its name. Scholars still argue whether the popularly accepted derivation of Mons Martyrum, referring to the site of St. Denis's decapitation, is not a pious misconception of the true origins—Mons Mercurii, site of a pagan Roman temple.

A walk around Montmartre will help you make up your own mind. Still topographically the little country village of 400 years ago, it is impossible to drive a car around this area. Take the Métro, Porte de la Chapelle line, that goes from Concorde to Abbesses. (Do *not* get off at Pigalle; however attractive you may find its lurid glitter at night, by day it might depress you into not visiting the rest of Montmartre.)

From the Place des Abbesses, take Rue Ravignan to number 13, Place Emile-Goudeau. This was the site of the Bateau-Lavoir studio, an unprepossessing glass-roofed loft that burned down in 1970. Here—if in any one place—modern art was born: Picasso, Braque and Juan Gris developed Cubism, while Modigliani worked his mysteries and Apollinaire sang it all in the first surrealistic verses.

Properly respectful of the spirits of the past, make your way around the neighbourhood where the illustrious predecessors of these "upstarts" lived and worked—Renoir, Van Gogh, Gauguin—in the Rue Cortot, Rue de l'Abreuvoir, Rue Saint-Rustique (with the restaurant A La Bonne Franquette where Van Gogh painted his famous *La Guinguette*). In artistic terms you move from the sublime to the ludicrous with the street-painters of the old **Place du Tertre.** Too rich a spot to be spoiled by the daubers, this is the very centre of Montmartre's village life, its original public square where marriages were announced, militiamen enlisted and criminals hanged. You should also visit the Rue Saint-Vincent, site of Paris's own vineyard, the Clos de Montmartre at the corner of the Rue des Saules, where they produce a wine that reputedly "makes you jump like a goat".

At the other end of Rue Saint-Vincent you come around the back of the basilica of the **Sacré-Cœur.** You have probably spotted it a hundred times during the day so its back view will make a welcome change. This weird Romano-Byzantine church enjoys a dubious reputation in the city. The aesthetes quite simply hate its over-ornate exterior and extravagant interior mosaics, or at best find it grotesquely amusing; working-class people of the neighbourhood resent the way it was put up as a symbol of penitence for the insurrection of the 1871 Commune and defeat in the war against the Prussians. The Sacré-Cœur's miraculously white façade derives from the special quality of the Château-Landon stone that whitens and hardens with age. For many its most attractive feature is the view from the dome, which can be visited, covering a radius of 30 miles on a clear day.

Just down the hill from the Sacré-Cœur is **Saint-Pierre-de-Montmartre,** one of Paris's oldest churches. Consecrated in 1147, 16 years before Saint-Germain-des-Prés, it represents a significant work of early Gothic art, belied by its 18th-century façade. The Sacré-Cœur's architect, Paul Abadie, wanted to demolish Saint-Pierre, but he was overruled, and a group of artists succeeded in having it restored, "as a worthy riposte to the Sacré-Cœur".

Every day's walk should end with a good rest, and you should not be put off by the idea of going to the **Cimetière de Montmartre** off the Rue Caulaincourt, a place of delightful tranquillity often neglected for the more illustrious cemetery of Père-Lachaise (see p. 42). You can visit the tombs of Degas, Berlioz, Offenbach, Stendhal, Nijinski and Heine and try to find the excellent bronze sculpture by François Rude at the grave of Godefroy Cavaignac.

Marais

The Marais district, north of the two river-islands, has bravely withstood the onslaught of real estate developers over the years, providing a remarkably authentic record of Paris's development from Henri IV at the end of the 16th century up to the Revolution. Built on land

Crowds flock to the Sacré-Cœur, mainly for its great view of Paris.

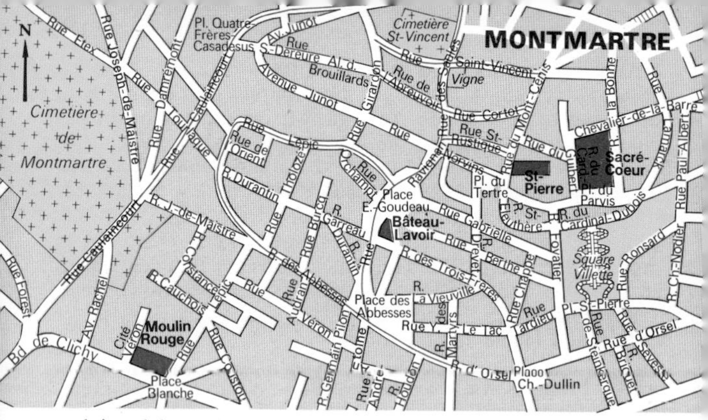

reclaimed from the swamps, as the name suggests, it contains some of Europe's most elegant Renaissance-style houses *(hôtels)*, now serving as museums and libraries.

Start at the corner of Rue des Archives and **Rue des Francs-Bourgeois,** named after the poor people allowed to live there tax-free in the 14th century. (Métro line Mairie des Lilas to Rambuteau.) The National Archives are kept here in a magnificent 18th-century mansion, the **Hôtel de Soubise.** The beautiful horseshoe-shaped *cour d'honneur* leads you into an exquisite rococo world: the apartments of the Prince and Princess of Soubise, the high point of Louis XV decor, contain the Musée de l'Histoire de France.

A garden (not always open to the public) connects the Soubise with its twin, the **Hôtel de Rohan** on Rue Vieille-du-Temple. Be sure to look for Robert Le Lorrain's magnificent stone sculpture, *Chevaux d'Apollon,* over the old stables in the second courtyard. A few steps away, on Rue de Thorigny, you'll find the Hôtel Salé which houses the **Musée Picasso** (see p. 71).

Two other architectural jewels grace the Rue des Francs-Bourgeois—the **Hôtel Lamoignon** at the corner of Rue Pavée and the **Hôtel Carnavalet,** once the home of the illustrious lady of letters Madame de Sévigné and now the Musée Historique de la Ville de Paris (see p. 73).

With a fine dramatic sense, the Rue des Francs-Bourgeois ends at what many consider to be the city's most picturesque square, **Place des Vosges.** Its classical harmony is achieved by a subtle diversity of detail in the gables, windows and archways of its red-brick façades. When Henri IV had the square built in 1605, on the site of a horse-market, it consisted of 36 homes or *pavillons,* each encompassing four arches, nine *pavillons* on each side. But these have since expanded or contracted according to the means of the owners. Place des Vosges remains one of the most luxurious residential areas of Paris. The gardens of the square, now a peaceful playground for children, were a favourite spot for the aristocratic duel and, after Louis XIII's wedding festivities here, the town's most fashionable promenade.

In those days it was known as the Place Royale. It received its current name for the prosaic reason that the department of the Vosges was the first to pay up all its taxes to the Revolutionary Government. If you are a fan of Victor Hugo, stop by the fascinating **museum** of his manuscripts, artefacts and 350 of his drawings at number 6.

You can finish your visit to the Marais with a walk around the old **Jewish quarter.** Jews have lived continuously on the Rue des Rosiers since 1230,

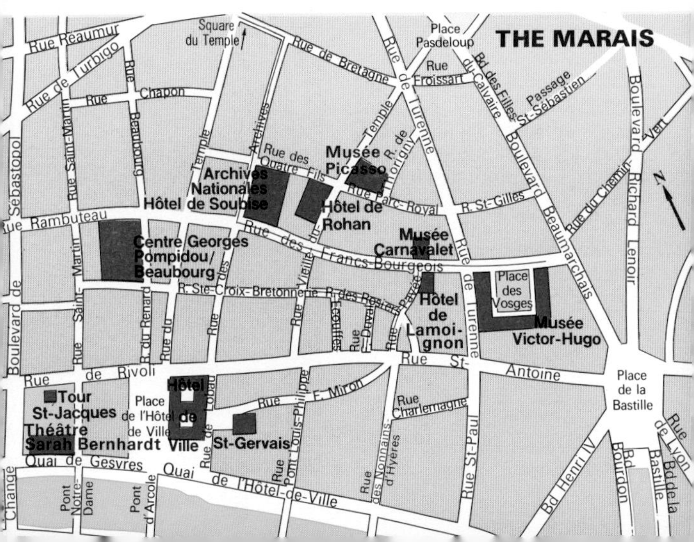

and Rue Ferdinand-Duval was known until 1900 as the Rue des Juifs. Rue des Ecouffes is a lively shopping street, with Jews from North Africa gradually replacing the Ashkenzani of Poland and Hungary who themselves took over from the original Sephardim.

Père-Lachaise

Such is Paris's perpetual homage to the great of its past that the Cimetière Père-Lachaise manages to be an inspiring and quite undepressing pilgrimage for tourists and Parisians alike. This vast "City of the Dead" has a population estimated at 1,350,000 buried since its foundation in 1804. Named after Louis XIV's confessor, a member of the Jesuits who previously owned the land, the cemetery has long been renowned as the resting place for the heroes of the country's revolutions. It even served as a battleground on May 28, 1871, for the last stand of the Communards and a "Mur des Fédérés" marks the place where they were executed by firing-squads at the south-east corner. In this pantheon of the city's artistic heritage, you will find writers Colette and Alfred de Musset and Italian composer Rossini at lot No. 4, Chopin (11), philosopher Auguste Comte (17), painters Ingres (23), Corot and Daumier (24), La Fontaine and Molière (25), Sarah Bernhardt (44), Bal-

Henri IV made Place des Vosges a lovely place to live. It still is.

zac (48), Delacroix (49), Bizet (68), Proust (85), Apollinaire (86), Isadora Duncan (87), Oscar Wilde (89) (with a fine monument by sculptor Jacob Epstein) and Gertrude Stein (94). Napoleon's emancipation of the Jews meant that they could have their own section, and Napoleon III's deference to the Turkish ambassador for his Eastern foreign policy led to an area for Moslems. Presidents of the Third Republic like Adolphe Thiers and Félix Faure lay just a stone's throw from the radicals they bitterly opposed. Père-Lachaise remains a unique site of national unity and reconciliation.

The Islands

Ile de la Cité

Shaped like a boat with the Square du Vert-Galant as its prow, the Ile de la Cité is the veritable cradle of the city of Paris, the original dwelling place of the fishermen and bargees of early Lutetia. The island also exemplifies what over-ambitious, wilful urban planning can do to charming neighbourhoods. In the middle of the 19th century, the much praised but often insensitive Baron Haussmann swept away nearly all of the medieval and 17th-century structures, leaving only the Place Dauphine and the Rue Chanoinesse (ancient home of the cathedral canons) as evidence of the island's rich residential life.

The baron was also thinking of replacing the triangular **Place Dauphine's** gracious red-brick, gabled and arcaded architecture with a neo-Grecian colonnaded square. But, fortunately, he was forced out of office for juggling his books before the wreckers could move in. The *place*, close by the lively Pont-Neuf, was built in 1607 by Henri IV in honour of his son the *dauphin* (later Louis XIII). Sadly only the houses at number 14 and 26 are still in their original state since 18th-century property developers found it more profitable to remodel the premises.

The massive **Palais de Justice,** today a complex of buildings encompassing the centralized legal machinery of modern France, holds echoes of the nation's earliest kings, who dwelt here, and of the later nobility, aristocracy and Revolutionary leaders, who were imprisoned here before execution. It also conceals a Gothic masterpiece, the **Sainte-Chapelle.** With its walls of stained-glass and its harmonious proportions (nearly equal height and length), the chapel has an ethereal quality—in startling counterpoint to the ponderous surrounding palace. It was built in 1248 by the pious King Louis IX (known as St. Louis) for the relics obtained from the emperor of Constantinople. There are in fact two chapels, the lower for the canons, chaplains and other dignitaries of the church, and the upper one for the king and his retinue. The 15 **stained-glass windows** include 1,134 different pieces depicting mainly Old Testament scenes; 720 of them are 13th-century originals.

Between 1789 and 1815, the chapel served variously as a flour warehouse during the

Some of the Métro entrances are masterpieces of Art-Nouveau design.

Revolution, a clubhouse for high-ranking dandies and finally as an archive for Napoleon's Consulate. It was this latter role that saved the chapel from projected destruction, because the bureaucrats did not know where else to put their mountains of paperwork.

These days they find space in the endless corridors of offices in the Palais de Justice and the nearby Préfecture de Police. What started off in 360 as the site of Julian's coronation as Emperor of Rome, later housing Merovingian kings Clovis, Childebert, Chilpéric and Dagobert, is now strictly "Maigret" country. The great Salle des Pas-Perdus is worth a visit for a glimpse of the lawyers, plaintiffs, witnesses, court-reporters and hangers-on waiting nervously for the wheels of French justice to grind into action.

But their anxiety is nothing compared with those who were condemned to bide their time in the prison of the **Conciergerie** (reached from the Quai de l'Horloge). After April 6, 1793, when the Revolutionary Terror was in full swing, the Conciergerie (named after the royally appointed *concierge* in charge of common-law criminals) truly became the "antechamber of the guillotine". In the Galerie des Prisonniers, Marie-Antoinette, Robespierre, Saint-Just and Danton all spent their last nights after the Revolutionary tribunals had pronounced sentence. The Salle des Girondins displays one of the guillotine blades, the crucifix to which Marie-Antoinette prayed before execution and the lock from Robespierre's cell. Look out on the Cour des Femmes and see where husbands, lovers, wives and mistresses were allowed one last tryst before the tumbrels came. About 2,500 victims of the Revolutionary guillotine passed their final hours in the Conciergerie.

The site of the cathedral of **Notre-Dame de Paris** has had a religious significance for at least 2,000 years. In Roman times a temple to Jupiter stood here; some stone fragments of the early structure, unearthed in 1711, can be seen in the Cluny Museum (see p. 73). In the 4th century the first Christian church, Saint-Etienne, was built here, joined two centuries later by a second church, dedicated to Notre Dame. Norman invasions of Paris left the two edifices in a sorry state and the Bishop Maurice de Sully authorized construction of a cathedral to replace them in 1163. The main part of Notre-Dame took 167 years to complete and the transition it represented from Romanesque to Gothic has been called a perfect expression of medieval architecture. One dissenting voice was that of St. Bernard, who protested that the godly virtue of poverty would be insulted by the erection of such a sumptuous structure. And some architectural purists today find Notre-Dame a bit "too much". But it was built to inspire awe.

Old Baron Haussmann comes in for criticism again, because he greatly enlarged the *parvis*, or square, in front of the cathedral, thereby diminishing, it is said, the grandiose impact of the western façade. Others argue this brought back the animated street-life of the square, recapturing some of the gaiety of the Middle Ages when the *parvis* was used for public executions and the populace was invited to throw old fruit and rotten eggs provided by the authorities.

The cathedral remains an

In Paris's old quartiers, *a bike is often the best way to get around.*

4e Arr.
RUE
DU
ROI DE SICILE
ACHAT DE CHEVAUX

impressive monument, truly the nation's parish church. It has witnessed, in 1239, Louis IX walking barefoot with his holy treasure, Christ's crown of thorns (before the Sainte-Chapelle was built); in 1430, the humiliation of having Henry VI of England crowned King of France; in 1594, Henri IV attending the mass which sealed his conversion to Catholicism and reinforced his hold on the French throne; in 1804, Napoleon's coronation as emperor, attended by the pope but climaxed by Napoleon crowning himself; and in our own day, the state funerals of military heroes such as Foch, Joffre, Leclerc and de Gaulle.

Given the cathedral's gigantic size, the balance of its proportions and the harmony of its façade are nothing short of miraculous. The superb central **rose window,** encircling the statue of the *Madonna and Child,* depicts the Redemption after the Fall. Look for the **Galerie des Rois** across the top of the three doorways. These 28 statues representing the kings of Judah and Israel were pulled down during the Revolution because they were thought to be the kings of France (later restored).

Inside, the marvellous lighting is due in large part to two more outsize rose windows dominating the transept. Don't miss the lovely 14th-century **Virgin and Child** that bears the cathedral's name, Notre-Dame de Paris, to the right of the choir entrance.

The original architect is anonymous but the renowned Pierre de Montreuil was

responsible for much of the 13th-century work. For the present structure with its majestic towers, spire and breathtaking flying-buttresses, we must be grateful to Eugène Viollet-le-Duc, who worked centimetre by centimetre over the whole edifice between 1845 and 1863, restoring the cathe-

Notre-Dame cathedral, a national shrine of incomparable beauty, sits proudly on the island in the middle of the Seine where Paris was born.

dral after the ravages of the 18th century. For once, it was pre-Revolutionary meddlers—who tried to redecorate and improve—more than the Revolutionaries who where to blame. In 1831, Victor Hugo's novel, *Notre-Dame de Paris* started a public outcry that led to the restoration of the national shrine.

All the original bells have disappeared except for the *bourdon,* dating from 1400, in the South Tower. Its much admired purity of tone was achieved in the 1680s when the bronze bell was melted down and mixed with the gold and silver jewellery donated by Louis XIV's aristocracy. Today it is no longer operated by a hunchback but by an electric system installed in 1953.

Ile Saint-Louis

Very much a world apart, the Ile Saint-Louis is an enchanted, self-contained island of gracious living, long popular with Paris's affluent gentry. President Georges Pompidou lived here (on the Quai de Béthune) and loved to come here from the Elysée Palace as often as possible.

Appropriate to the island's stylish reputation, its church, the **Saint-Louis-en-l'Ile,** is as elegant as one of its great mansions, bright and airy with a golden light illuminating a veritable museum of Dutch, Flemish and Italian 16th- and 17th-century art and some splendid tapestries from the 12th century.

The most striking of the mansions, the **Hôtel Lauzun** at 17 Quai d'Anjou, was built in the 1650s by the great architect Louis Le Vau, who also worked on the Seine façade of the Louvre and Versailles. The Hôtel Lauzun's opulently ornamental decor was to provide a perfect setting for the Club des Haschischins frequented by Théophile Gautier and Charles Baudelaire.

The **Hôtel Lambert,** another impressive 17th-century mansion designed by Le Vau, stands on the corner of Rue Saint-Louis-en-l'Ile. Voltaire once enjoyed a tempestuous love affair here with the lady of the house, the Marquise du Châtelet.

But perhaps the island's greatest pleasure consists in walking along the poplar-shaded streets to the western end of Quai d'Orléans. There you have the most magnificent **view** of the apse of Notre-Dame, which incorrigible romantics much prefer to the cathedral's "front".

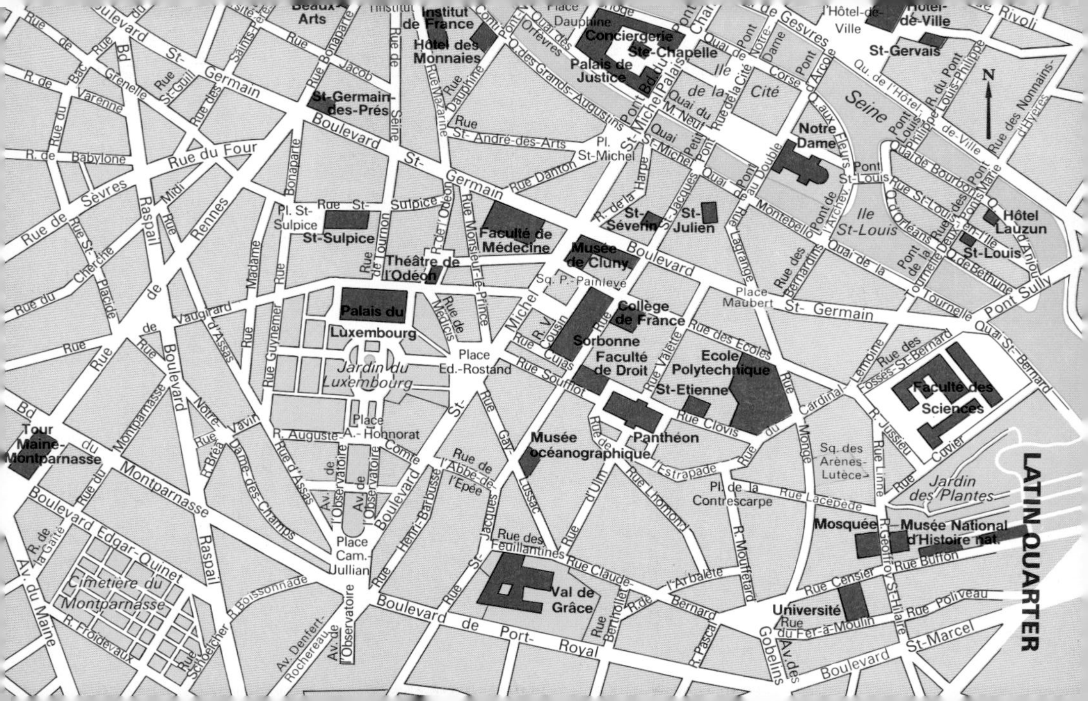

LATIN QUARTER
N
Beaux-Arts
Institut de France
Hôtel des Monnaies
Place Dauphine
Conciergerie
Ste-Chapelle
Palais de Justice
Quai des Orfèvres
Q. des Grands-Augustins
Bd du Palais
Rue de Gesvres
Quai de Pont Notre-Dame
Ile de la Cité
Cité
Rue de la Cité
Corse
Pont d'Arcole
l'Hôtel-de-Ville
Hôtel-de-Ville
St-Gervais
Rivoli
Qu. de l'Hôtel-de-Ville
R. du Pont Louis-Philippe
Rue des Nonnains-d'Hyères
Seine
Q. aux Fleurs
Notre Dame
Pont Louis-Philippe
Quai de Bourbon
Pont Marie
Pont St-Louis
Rue St-Louis-en-l'Ile
Hôtel Lauzun
Q. d'Orléans
Rue des Deux-Ponts
St-Louis
d'Anjou
Ile St-Louis
Pont de l'Archev.
Pont de la Tournelle
Q. de Béthune
Quai de la Tournelle
Pont Sully
Quai St-Bernard
Rue Jacob
Rue Bonaparte
Rue des Saints-Pères
Bd St-Germain
St-Germain-des-Prés
Rue de Seine
Rue Mazarine
Rue Dauphine
Rue St-André-des-Arts
Pl. St-Michel
Pont St-Michel
Quai St-Michel
Quai du M. Neuf
Petit Pont
Pont au Double
Quai de Montebello
Rue des Bernardins
R. de Bac
R. de Varenne
Rue de Grenelle
Rue St-Guill.
Rue des
Boulevard St-Germain
Rue du Four
R. de Babylone
Rue de Sèvres
Rue du Cherche-Midi
Rue St-Placide
Raspail
Rue du Midi
Rennes
Rue Danton
R. de la Harpe
St-Séverin
St-Julien
Rue St-Jacques
Rue Lagrange
Pl. St-Sulpice
Rue St-Sulpice
St-Sulpice
R. de l'Odéon
Rue Monsieur-le-Prince
Faculté de Médecine
Musée de Cluny
Rue de Tournon
Théâtre de l'Odéon
Sq. P.-Painlevé
Place Maubert
St-Germain
Rue Madame
Rue Bonaparte
Rue de Vaugirard
Palais du Luxembourg
Rue de Médicis
Michel
Collège de France
Rue des Ecoles
R. V. Cousin
Rue Cujas
Sorbonne
Rue Valette
Faculté de Droit
Ecole Polytechnique
Rue Lemoine
Rue des Fossés-St-Bernard
Faculté des Sciences
Rue Guynemer
Rue d'Assas
Jardin du Luxembourg
Place Ed.-Rostand
Rue Soufflot
St-Etienne
Rue Clovis
Rue du Cardinal
Rue Monge
R. Jussieu
Cuvier
Bd du Montparnasse
Tour Maine-Montparnasse
Notre-Dame-des-Champs
Rue Vavin
Rue Bréa
Place A.-Honnorat
R. Auguste-Comte
Panthéon
Musée océanographique
Rue Gay-Lussac
Rue de l'Abbé-de-l'Epée
Rue d'Ulm
Rue Lhomond
Rue de l'Estrapade
Sq. des Arènes-Lutèce
Rue Linné
Jardin des Plantes
Av. de l'Observatoire
Pl. de la Contrescarpe
Rue Lacépède
Boulevard Raspail
Rue du Montparnasse
Boulevard Edgar-Quinet
R. de la Gaîté
Av. du Maine
Cimetière du Montparnasse
R. Froidevaux
Rue Schoelcher
R. Boissonnade
Av. Denfert-Rochereau
Place Cam.-Jullian
Rue Henri-Barbusse
Rue St-Jacques
Rue des Feuillantines
Val de Grâce
Rue Claude-Bernard
Rue de l'Arbalète
R. Mouffetard
Rue Berthollet
R. Pascal
Mosquée
R. Geoffroy St-Hilaire
Musée National d'Histoire nat.
Rue Buffon
Rue Censier
Université
Rue du Fer-à-Moulin
Rue Poliveau
St-Marcel
Boulevard
Av. des Gobelins
Boulevard de Port-Royal

Left Bank

(Rive Gauche)

Latin Quarter

To get an idea of what the Left Bank is all about, start at the Quartier Latin. Here, facing Notre-Dame, the spirit of inquiry has traditionally been nurtured into protest and outright revolt before subsiding into a lifelong scepticism, as the rebels graduate from the university and move west to the more genteel Faubourg Saint-Germain. Starting in the 13th century, when the city's first "university" moved from the cloisters of Notre-Dame to the Left Bank, the young came to the *quartier* to learn Latin.

In those days *l'université* meant merely a collection of people—students who met on a street corner, in a public square or a courtyard to hear a teacher, standing on a bench or at an upstairs window or balcony, lecture them. Today there are classrooms, overcrowded, but the tradition of open-air discussion continues, often over an endlessly nursed coffee or glass of wine at a café terrace on the Boulevard Saint-Michel or in the streets around the faculty buildings, or in the ever-present cinema queues.

Begin at the **Place Saint-Michel,** where the Paris students come to buy their textbooks and stationery but the young of other countries come to sniff the Latin Quarter's mystique around the bombastic 1860s fountain by Davioud. Plunge into the narrow streets of the Saint-Séverin quarter—to the east Rue

Advocating a Left Bank revolution doesn't rule out getting a suntan.

Saint-Séverin, Rue de la Harpe, Rue Galande—into a medieval world updated by the varied exotica of Tunisian pastry shops, smoky Greek barbecue and stuffy little cinemas. A moment's meditation in the exquisite 13th–15th-century Flamboyant Gothic church of Saint-Séverin, where Dante is said to have prayed, and you are ready to confront the Latin Quarter's citadel, the **Sorbonne.**

Founded in 1253 as a college for poor theological students by

Robert de Sorbon, Louis IX's chaplain, the university was taken in hand by Cardinal Richelieu, who financed its reconstruction (1624–42). The Sorbonne's church houses the cardinal's tomb, and a memorial service is held for him every December 4 on the anniversary of his death. Visit the Grand Amphithéâtre, which seats 2,700, with its statues of Sorbon, Richelieu, Descartes, Pascal and Lavoisier, the great chemist. As you look at Puvis de Chavannes' monumental painting covering the back wall, *Le Bois Sacré*—allegorising Poetry, Philosophy, History, Geology,

Physiology and the rest—try to imagine 4,000 students packed into that hall in May 1968, arguing whether to have the whole thing plastered over. The student revolt against overcrowding, antiquated teaching and bureaucracy and the very basis of the social system made the Sorbonne the focal point of the movement. When police invaded the sanctuary—which for centuries had guaranteed student immunity—the rebellion was on.

Around the corner, as a kind of didactic inspiration for the students on what hard work can achieve, stands the gigantic Neo-classic **Panthéon,** resting place of the nation's military, political and literary heroes. Originally designed as the church of Sainte-Geneviève for Louis XV (1755), it was secularized during the Revolution as a vast mausoleum with the inscription "To our great men, the Fatherland's gratitude". But the Revolutionaries had a hard time deciding who merited the honour. Mirabeau and then Marat were interred and subsequently expelled. Napoleon ended the controversy by turning the Panthéon back into a church. Throughout the 19th century it went back and forth between secular and consecrated status, according to the regime's political colour. Finally Victor Hugo's funeral in 1885, the biggest the capital had seen, settled the Panthéon's status as a secular mausoleum. Hugo was buried there, followed (retroactively) by Voltaire and Rousseau, and then by prime minister Léon Gambetta, socialist leader Jean Jaurès, Emile Zola, inventor of the blind-alphabet Louis Braille, President Raymond Poincaré and many others.

After which, take a break in the **Jardin du Luxembourg.** If you want to picnic in the park (not on the grass), make a detour first to the old street-market behind the Panthéon on the bustling Rue Mouffetard by the tiny Place de la Contrescarpe, old hunting-ground of Rabelais and his spiritual descendants. Despite their 17th-century origins, the Luxembourg Gardens avoid the rigid geometry of the Tuileries and Versailles. The horse chestnuts, beeches and plane trees, the orangery and ornamental pond, best viewed from the east terrace near the Place Edmond Rostand entrance, were a major in-

Life's problems seem less arduous in a café on Boulevard St-Michel.

spiration for the bucolic paintings of 18th-century master Antoine Watteau.

Montparnasse

Montparnasse is where they invented the cancan in 1845, at the now defunct Grande Chaumière dancehall. In the twenties it took over from Montmartre as the stomping ground of Paris's artistic colony, or at least of its avant-garde. American expatriates like Hemingway, Gertrude Stein, F. Scott Fitzgerald, John Dos Passos and Theodore Dreiser also liked the free-living atmosphere and greatly added to the mystique themselves. Today French as well as American tourists point out the places where the Lost Generation found themselves.

Other quarters are known for their palaces and churches; Montparnasse (named after a 17th-century gravel mound since removed) has cafés and bars for landmarks. The Closerie des Lilas, a centre for French Symbolist poets at the turn of the century, served as a meeting-place for Trotsky and Lenin before World War I and for Hemingway and his friends after the war; the Select, first all-night bar to open in Montparnasse, in 1925, quickly became a Henry Miller hang-out; La Coupole, favourite of Sartre and Simone de Beauvoir, is still going strong, more living theatre than restaurant; breakfast was taken at the Dôme for a change of air; the Rotonde, favoured by Picasso, André Derain, Maurice Vlaminck, Modigliani and Max Jacob, after a spell as a cinema, is now

back as a restaurant, so that just about all, in one way or another, survive along the bustling **Boulevard du Montparnasse.**

The strength of Montparnasse's myth is such that habitués can pretend not to see the 58-floor Tour Maine-Montparnasse office-skyscraper by the railway station.

Names of fame (Baudelaire, Maupassant, Sartre) haunt the **Cimetière du Montparnasse** just behind.

There's always something astir in relaxed Jardin du Luxembourg.

Saint-Germain-des-Prés

Saint-Germain-des-Prés is the literary quarter par excellence, home of the major publishing houses, the Académie française, bookshops and literary cafés, but also a charming neighbourhood for round-the-clock people-watching. In the years following the Liberation it was known as headquarters for Jean-Paul Sartre and his existentialist acolytes, who were dressed, winter and summer, in black corduroy and long woollen scarves. Foreign students abroad would flock here in the 1950s hoping to see the master at work or at least at play. Failing that, there were always the nightclubs off the Boulevard Saint-Germain, where you could listen to "le jazz hot" and smoke your lungs out.

Today the discotheques have replaced the jazz-cellars and existentialism has had its day, if that is not a contradiction in terms. But the easy-going atmosphere of the outdoor cafés continues around the Place Saint-Germain-des-Prés. On the north side you'll find the Café Bonaparte, on the west the famous Les Deux Magots. Both provide ring-side seats for the street-theatre of mimes, musicians and fire-eaters, who collect money in hats, and for the neighbourhood eccentrics who offer their show for nothing. The Café de Flore up the boulevard has remained more relentlessly "intellectual" in atmosphere, perhaps because of its intense, ideologically confusing history. It has successively been the home of the extreme right-wing Action Française group under Charles Maurras in 1899, the Surrealists of Apollinaire and André Salmon in 1914 (they liked to provoke brawls), and then Sartre's existentialists, a peaceful bunch who never got enough sleep to have the energy for fighting.

Saint-Germain also has its more formal monuments. The church of **Saint-Germain-des-Prés,** a mixture of Romanesque and Gothic styles restored last century, has a clock-tower dating back to about 1000. A 17th-century porch shelters 12th-century doorposts.

To the north of the square runs the Rue Bonaparte, past the prestigious **Ecole des Beaux-Arts.** Incorporated in its structure are fragments of medieval and Renaissance architecture and sculpture that

Parisian hardware store is a veritable goldmine for all manner of off-beat kitchen gadgets.

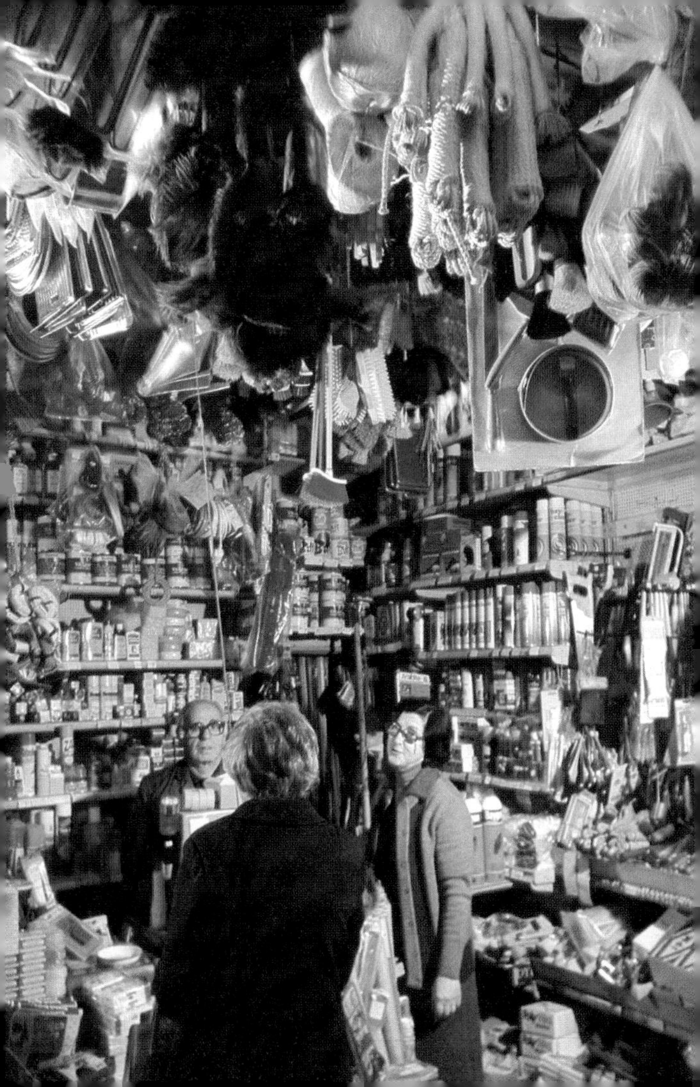

make it a living museum. More recently, in May 1968, it turned into a poster-factory when taken over by the students.

On the Rue des Beaux-Arts is the hotel where Oscar Wilde died in 1900, under the assumed name of Melmoth. He used to complain about the "horrible magenta flowers" of the room's wallpaper, saying "one of us has to go"—and now both have. The hotel has redone Oscar's room in what they consider a more fitting style.

The august **Palais de l'Institut de France,** home of the Académie française, is on the Quai de Conti by the Pont des Arts. Designed by Louis Le Vau in 1668 to harmonize with the Louvre across the river, the Institut began as a school for the sons of provincial gentry, financed by a legacy of Cardinal Mazarin. In 1805 the building was turned over to the Institut, which is comprised of the Académie française, the supreme arbiter of the French language founded by Richelieu in 1635, plus the Académie des Belles Lettres, Sciences, Beaux Arts and Sciences Morales et Politiques. The admission of a new member to the Académie française, an honour more exclusive than a British peerage, is the occasion of a great ceremony. Guides to the Institut like to point out the east pavilion, site of the old 14th-century Tour de Nesle. They say that Queen Jeanne de Bourgogne used to watch from there for likely young lovers whom she summoned for the night and then had thrown into the Seine.

L'Institut de France, prime show-place for intellectual pyrotechnics.

The **Palais-Bourbon,** seat of the National Assembly, provides a rather formidable riverside façade for the Left Bank's most stately district—the elegant 7th *arrondissement* with its 18th-century foreign embassies, ministries and noble residences *(hôtels particuliers).* The Grecian columns facing the Pont de la Concorde were added under Napoleon and belie the more graceful character of the Palais-Bourbon as seen from its real entrance on the south side. Designed as a residence for a daughter of Louis XIV in 1722, this government building can be visited only on written request or as the guest of a deputy. If you do get in, look for the Delacroix paintings on the history of civilization in the library.

The Foreign Ministry next to the *palais,* better known as the

Quai d'Orsay, is more distinguished for its diplomatic language than its architecture (nondescript Louis-Philippe).

If you are more interested in gracious living than supreme power, you will probably agree with those who feel it's better to be prime minister and live at the **Hôtel Matignon** than be president at the Elysée Palace. The prime minister's magnificent residence at 57 Rue de Varenne is just a short walk from the National Assembly. Its huge private park has a delightful music pavilion much favoured for secret strategy sessions. The same tranquil street, a veritable museum of 18th-century elegance, contains the Italian Embassy, known as the **Hôtel de La Rochefoucauld - Doudeauville** (No. 47), and the Rodin Museum (see p. 74) in the **Hôtel Biron,** No. 77, which served as the home of Rodin, of poet Rainer Maria Rilke and dancer Isadora Duncan.

Invalides–Tour Eiffel

From the quiet intimacy of this area we return to the massively monumental with the **Hôtel des Invalides,** Louis XIV's first vision of grandeur before Versailles and the work of the same architect, Jules Hardouin-Mansart. Picking up an idea from Henri IV, Louis XIV founded the first national hospital for soldiers wounded in the service of their country. In Napoleon's hands it also became an army museum, another celebration of his victories, and still later the supreme celebration of Napoleon himself, when his body was brought back from the island of St. Helena for burial in the chapel.

The awesomely elaborate tomb, set directly under an open space in the Invalides' golden dome, bears Napoleon's body dressed in the green uniform of the Chasseurs de la Garde. It is encased in six coffins, Chinese-box-fashion one inside the other, the first of iron, the second mahogany, then two of lead, one of ebony and the outer one of oak. The monument of red porphyry from Finland rests on a pedestal of green granite from the Vosges. Twelve colossal statues of Victories by Pradier frame the tomb.

The church of **Saint-Louis-des-Invalides** is decorated with the flags taken by French armies in battle since Waterloo. At the entrance to the Invalides are two German Panther tanks captured by General Leclerc

Only pedestrians can appreciate the all-embracing view from the Pont des Arts.

Romance

A bewitching conspiracy that began with the 15th-century poet François Villon and continued with Maurice Chevalier, Gene Kelly and Edith Piaf has made Paris the supreme city of romance. This is the town, they say, where broken hearts come to mend, where faltering marriages perk up and casual friendships grow brighter with the city's enchanted light. There are places ideally suited for a kiss, a poem, an engagement ring, or whatever other madness this town may drive you to.

Ideal places for whispered tenderness include the Rue Berton, a country lane behind Balzac's house that seems a million miles away from the 16th *arrondissement*. No kiss ever failed here. The Jardin du Vert Galant, at the tip of the Ile de la Cité, is imbued with the lusty spirit of Henri IV. On a moonlit night, the view of the Seine from this tree-enclosed triangle is the stuff dreams are made of. A few steps from the bustle of Saint-Germain-des-Prés is Rue Furstenberg's tiny square. Let the gentle lamplight, softened by the shadows of exotic paulownia trees, work its magic.

How can you miss in a city that is love's open and unashamed accomplice?

in the Vosges. The main courtyard contains the 18 cannons of the *batterie triomphale*, including eight taken from Vienna, which Napoleon ordered fired on momentous occasions, which included the birth of his son in 1811. The cannons sounded again for the Armistice of 1918 and the funeral of Marshal Foch in 1929.

The military complex continues with the **Ecole Militaire** and the vast **Champ-de-Mars** where officers have trained and performed military exercises since the middle of the 18th century. In its heyday, 10,000 soldiers passed in review on this expansive parade ground. Horse-races were held here in the 1780s and five world's fairs between 1867 and 1937. In this century it has been a park for the Left Bank's most luxurious residences.

There are monuments and there is the **Eiffel Tower.** Some celebrate heroes, commemorate victories, honour kings or saints. The Eiffel Tower is a monument for its own sake, a proud gesture to the world, a witty structure that makes aesthetics irrelevant. Its construction for the World's Fair of 1889 was an astounding engineering achievement—15,000 pieces of metal joined together by 2,500,000 rivets, soaring 984 feet into the air on a base of only 1,400 square feet. At the time, it was the tallest structure in the world.

At its inauguration the lifts were not yet operating and Prime Minister Pierre-Emmanuel Tirard, aged 62, stopped at the first platform (187 feet high), leaving his Minister of Commerce to go all the way up to the top to present Gustave Eiffel with the Legion of Honour medal. The tower was slated for destruction in 1910 but nobody had the heart to go through with it.

The critics hated it. Guy de Maupassant signed a manifesto against "this vertiginously ridiculous tower," and Verlaine rerouted his journeys around Paris to avoid seeing it (difficult now, almost impossible then). But today it has

The nation's military tradition is on view at the Invalides museum.

become so totally the symbol of Paris that to dislike the Eiffel Tower is to dislike Paris.

The first platform has a restaurant, the second and third, bars. From the top platform you can theoretically see about 40 miles on a pollution-free day. The best time for the **view** is one hour before sunset.

Museums

The Louvre

The collections of the world's most famous museum are housed in the former royal palace. Open from 9.45 until 5 p.m. Closed Tuesdays.

The Louvre is so huge that people are sometimes frightened of going in at all. But you do not have to be an art fanatic to realize that to come to Paris without setting foot inside this great and truly beautiful palace would be a crime. If you do it right, it can be an exhilarating pleasure. First of all, get up very early on a sunny day and walk around its gardens in the Place du Carrousel. Admire the sensual Maillol statuary and then sit on a bench to take in the sheer immensity of this home of France's kings and storehouse of a world's treasures. At the east end is the Cour Carrée, covering the original fortress built by Philippe Auguste in 1190 to protect Paris from river attack while he was away on a crusade. Stretching out from the Cour Carrée (of which you should see Perrault's marvellous colonnade on the east façade) are the additions of François Ier, Henri IV, Catherine de Médicis, Louis XIV, Napoleon and Napoleon III. President Mitterrand's great glass pyramid in the Cour Napoléon completes eight centuries of construction.

Louvre visitors debate merits of famous 16th-century French work.

The latest addition is designed by American architect I.M. Pei to provide a spectacular modern entrance, together with underground bookshops and cafés, at the centre of corridors leading to the various wings of the museum.

François Ier, the Louvre's first major art collector, acquired four Raphaels, three Leonardo da Vincis and one Titian (portrait of the king himself). By 1793, when the leaders of the Revolution declared the palace a national museum, there were 650 works of art in the collection; at the last inventory, in 1933, there were 173,000. So don't be depressed if you don't see everything.

If you're planning several visits, you might like to concentrate on just one section at a time—the Italian, the French, the Spanish, the Flemish and Dutch, but also the ancient Egyptian, the Greek and Roman.

For an overall view of the collections, we've attempted a first selection:

Egyptian: lion-headed goddess *Sekhmet* (1400 B.C.) and the colossal *Amenophis IV* (1370 B.C.).

Greek: the winged *Victory of Samothrace* and the beautifully proportioned *Venus de Milo.*

Italian: the sculpture of

Two Slaves by Michelangelo; Leonardo da Vinci's fabled *Mona Lisa (La Joconde),* but also his sublime *Virgin of the Rocks;* Titian's voluptuous *Woman at Her Toilet* and sombre *Entombment of Christ;* the poignant *Old Man and His Grandson* of Ghirlandaio.

French: Poussin's bittersweet *Arcadian Shepherds;* Watteau's hypnotically melancholy *Gilles* and graceful *Embarkation for Cythera;* Delacroix's *Liberty Guiding the People* and Courbet's piercing study of provincial bourgeoisie, *Funeral at Ornans.*

Dutch and Flemish: Rembrandt's cheerful *Self-Portrait with a Toque,* his beloved *Hendrickje Stoffels,* also portrayed nude in *Bathsheba Bathing;* Van Dyck's gracious, dignified *Charles I* of England; among the scores of "official" Rubens, his tenderly personal *Helena Fourment;* Jordaens' *Four Evangelists* as diligent Dutchmen.

German: a gripping *Self-Portrait* by Dürer; Holbein's *Erasmus.*

Spanish: the uncompromising Velázquez portrait of ugly *Queen Marianna of Austria;* El Greco's powerfully mystic *Christ on the Cross;* Ribera's gruesomely goodhumoured *The Club Foot.*

English: Gainsborough's exquisite *Conversation in a Park;* Turner's *Landscape with River and Bay;* and **Americans** will be delighted to contemplate Whistler's *Mother.*

Beaubourg

The official name of Europe's most spectacular cultural centre is Centre d'art et de culture Georges-Pompidou, shortened to Centre Pompidou (after the French president whose pet project it was). But somehow Parisians have an aversion to naming their major monuments after their political leaders, and so this bright and dynamic monster will probably always be known quite simply as Beaubourg, after the 13th-century neighbourhood surrounding it.

The combination of public library, modern art museum, children's workshop, *cinémathèque,* industrial design centre, experimental music laboratory and open-air circus on the front plaza is the most popular show in town.

After an initial reaction similar to the delight and rage originally provoked by the Eiffel

Beaubourg's avant-garde sculpture continues the Paris tradition of playful fountains.

Tower, people have grown accustomed to the construction's resemblance to a multicoloured oil refinery. The comparison is readily accepted by its architects, Italians Renzo Piano and Gianfranco Franchi and Englishman Richard Rogers, who deliberately left the building's service system visible and colour-coded: red for the transportation, green for the water pipes, blue for the air-conditioning ducts and yellow for the electrical system.

One of Beaubourg's simplest pleasures is just going up the escalators in the long glass tubes that run diagonally from the bottom-left to the top-right-hand corner. Watch Paris unfold in front of your eyes with a stunning view of the city's rooftops—best on the *fourth,* not the fifth floor.

The **Fontaine Tinguely** on the Place Igor Stravinsky evokes the work of the composer, with moving machines by Tinguely and sculptures by Saint-Phalle.

And More Museums*

Though physically part of the Louvre, the **Musée des Arts décoratifs** is a separate museum with its own entrance at 107 Rue de Rivoli. The rich permanent collection includes tapestries, furniture and porcelain, but look out for the fascinating temporary exhibitions featuring great styles and eras of design history such as Jugendstil, Bauhaus and the American fifties. Next door is the new **Musée national des Arts de la mode,** devoted to the decorative art of which Paris is still the world capital, high fashion.

Right across the river, the 19th-century Orsay railway station has been transformed into the **Musée d'Orsay.** This exciting new museum embraces France's tremendous creativity from 1848 to 1914 in the domains of painting, sculpture, architecture and industrial design, advertising, newspapers, book publishing, photography and the early years of the cinema. It also displays the collection of Impressionists and their followers transferred from the Jeu de Paume museum, now used for temporary exhibitions.

On the river side of the Tuileries, the **Orangerie** is best known for its ground-floor rooms decorated with Monet's beautiful *Nymphéas* murals, offering a moment of repose after a hard day's sightseeing. But you should also take a look upstairs at the excellent Walter-Guillaume collection of Cézanne, Renoir, Utrillo, Douanier Rousseau and Picasso.

*Almost all museums close on Tuesdays.

Another recent addition is the long-awaited **Musée Picasso** (5 Rue de Thorigny in the Marais, Métro Saint-Paul). From the private collections of Picasso's heirs, the museum has received over 200 paintings and 158 sculptures, in addition to hundreds of drawings, engravings, ceramics and models for theatre décors and costumes. It also exhibits the artist's personal collection of masterworks by fellow painters Braque, Matisse, Miró, Degas, Renoir and Rousseau.

Housed in the beautifully restored 17th-century mansion, Hôtel Salé, the museum offers a moving portrait of the man, his family, his mistresses and friends, with letters, manuscripts, photo albums, notebooks, his French Communist Party membership card, bull-

Picasso portrayed the turbulence of his private life in the most enigmatic of expressions.

Time for reflection beneath the deflecting facets of the Géode sphere.

fight tickets and holiday post-cards.

The **Grand Palais** and **Petit Palais** (between the Champs-Elysées and the Seine) were both built for the World's Fair of 1900 and are now devoted to large-scale exhibitions of the great masters, though the Petit Palais does have some private collections donated to the state, most notably, the Dutuit that includes paintings by Rubens, Teniers and Ruysdael and superb engravings by Rembrandt and Dürer.

The **Musée Guimet,** 6 Place d'Iéna, houses a magnificent collection of Oriental art from India, Indochina, Tibet, Indonesia, Japan and China.

At the **Musée de l'Homme,** devoted as the name implies to man himself, in the Palais de Chaillot, you can look upon the skull of Descartes, inside which

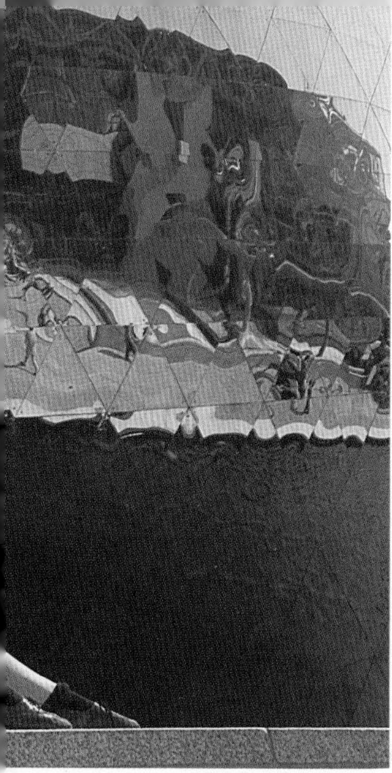

the great thinker proved our existence.

The **Musée de Cluny,** 6 Place Paul-Painlevé in the Latin Quarter, is the best place to see the very beginnings of Paris as well as being the city's finest example of Gothic civic architecture. Within its grounds are the remains of the Roman public baths, the **Thermes de Cluny** dating from A.D. 200–300. You can still see the large arched room of the *frigidarium* or cold baths with a swimming pool on the north side, the *tepidarium* or luke-warm baths on the west side and the *caldarium* or steam room on the south-west side. Even older are the fragments of a monument to Jupiter (probably 1st century A.D.) found near Notre-Dame cathedral. The fine Flamboyant chapel has an admirable Saint-Etienne tapestry, but the most celebrated tapestry in the museum is the world-renowned, 16th-century Boussac series, **The Lady with the Unicorn.**

The later history of Paris is charted in splendid detail at the **Hôtel Carnavalet** located at the corner of Rue des Francs-Bourgeois and Rue de Sévigné (closed on Mondays). This elegant 16th-century mansion —a joy to visit for itself— has a fascinating collection of documents, engravings and paintings of the pomp, circumstance and drama of Paris's history. The outstanding exhibit devoted to the Revolution includes a letter from Robespierre dramatically stained with the author's blood: he was arrested and wounded while signing it.

There are also three delightful small museums devoted respectively to **Balzac** (47 Rue Raynouard), **Delacroix** (6 Rue de Furstenberg) and

Rodin (77 Rue de Varenne), where you can see how these artists lived as well as admire their work. You'll find the *Thinker* and a bust of *Victor Hugo* in the garden of the Musée Rodin; the house contains the sculptor's private collection of Renoirs, Monets and Van Goghs.

Parc de la Villette

La Villette (on the north-east corner of town, Métro Porte de la Villette) has been converted from the world's biggest slaughterhouse to a striking futuristic complex of cultural and scientific activities.

Refusing to call itself a museum, La Villette's **Cité des sciences et de l'industrie** puts the accent on public participation in all phases of space technology, computers, astronomy and marine biology. The unabashed functionalism of its architecture carries the Beaubourg principle to a logical conclusion. Its most attractive symbol is the shining stainless steel **Géode** sphere containing a revolutionary cinema with a hemispheric screen 36 metres (118 feet) in diameter. There's also a giant rock-concert hall, **le Zénith,** alongside a projected avant-garde musical counterpart to the scientific museum, sorry, city: **Cité de la musique.**

Bois de Boulogne and Bois de Vincennes

To the east and west of the city, but incorporated now into its limits, are the two woods where Parisians take a breather. The **Bois de Boulogne,** more blithely known by residents of western parts of the city as *le Bois,* is the 2,224-acre remainder of the old Rouvray forest left completely wild until 1852. Napoleon III turned it into a place of recreation and relax-

ation for the people of Paris.

The transformations executed by Baron Haussmann were among his happier achievements, and the closest thing Paris has to a London-style park—with roads and paths for cycling and rambles, horse-trails, boating lakes, restaurants and open-air cafés.

One of the main attractions is the Parc de Bagatelle, a walled English garden with the city's most magnificent display of flowers.

Children enjoy the Jardin d'Acclimatation with its miniature train, Punch and Judy show, house of distorting mirrors, pony-rides and a miniature farm of pigs, goats and chickens.

The equally spacious **Bois de Vincennes** on the east offers much of the same attractions, together with France's largest zoo. This former royal hunting-ground has a more popular atmosphere than the Bois de Boulogne.

Paris Underground

One of the most fascinating tours offered by the municipality is through the **sewers.** In perfectly hygienic conditions you can take a guided boat tour underneath the streets (beginning by the Pont d'Alma), while the guide explains how the sewage has been chemically treated and distributed to fields outside Paris for the preparation of fertilizer—ever since 1868. You will notice the network of telegraph and telephone cables, and the old system of compressed-air tubes that was used for sending letters rapidly across Paris.

Another weird underground attraction, for those with a taste for the spooky, is the **Catacombs** (entrance, 2 Place Denfert-Rochereau), a vast network of corridors scooped out under the city to provide building-materials above ground and a mass burial-place down below. The remains of 6 million unidentified dead lay here, transferred from overcrowded cemeteries across the city or buried here in times of mass deaths —like the Revolutionary Terror. Often the bones and skulls are laid out in gruesomely decorative arrangements. Over the entrance to this *ossuaire* are the words of poet Jacques Delille: "Stop, this is the Empire of Death".

What to Do

Shopping

Shopping in Paris is a seductive, exotic adventure that turns adults into children and makes the children wish they had the adults' money. The choice of goods can be overwhelming and the attitude of salesmen and women sometimes forbidding, but if you go into the shop with a clear idea of what you want and a determined air, the aloof stares will melt into charming smiles. A cast-iron rule: never ask for what you want until you have said "Bonjour". (Don't worry if your French is not up to continuing the conversation beyond "Bonjour"; the new generation of sales people in Paris have a good command of English.)

The Big Stores

The department stores best equipped for dealing with foreigners are **Galeries Lafayette** and **Le Printemps,** next door to each other on the Boulevard Haussmann. Both have hostesses to help non-French-speaking customers, as well as the convenience of grouping selections from the major boutiques in their clothes departments. The Galeries has

LES ROUGES BICOLORES DE GUERLAIN

lost its great central staircase, but the circular galleries soaring above you still provide the most startling décor of Paris's big stores. They have an enormous chinaware department and excellent perfume and luggage sections. Le Printemps is famous for its lingerie and vast toy department.

For those who like the French habit of dressing up in baker's overalls, waiter's jackets, butcher's aprons, plumber's pants or sewer-worker's wadders, the **Samaritaine** department store at Pont-Neuf has an enormous selection of professional uniforms—52 different types representing 52 professions. It also offers a splendid view of the city from its 10th-floor bar.

FNAC, in the younger generation of Parisian department stores (at the Etoile, Montparnasse and the Forum des Halles), has the city's largest selection of books and records.

A strange Parisian phenomenon is **Le Drugstore,** the Frenchman's conception of the American institution of an all-night pharmacy and soda-counter. In French hands it has become a go-go paradise of grocery store, luxury gifts, newsstand, records, books, perfume, electronic gadgets, expensive luggage, car rental, theatre agency—and even a pharmacy—open till 2 a.m. (in Saint-Germain-des-Prés, on Avenue Matignon and the Champs-Elysées). Americans scarcely recognize it.

Fashion

These days, the fashion pendulum occasionally swings to New York, Rome or Tokyo, but the capital for all of them, the showplace for their talent, remains Paris. From the Right Bank, around the Rue du Faubourg-Saint-Honoré, the avenues Montaigne and George-V and over to Place des Victoires and les Halles, the *haute couture* houses and their *prêt-à-porter* (ready-to-wear) boutiques have spilled over to the Left Bank, around Saint-Germain-des-Prés.

Look out not only for the "old school" of Dior, Givenchy, Lanvin, Saint-Laurent, Ungaro and Louis Féraud, but the new generation of Gaultier, Mugler, Montana and their foreign competitors, Yamamoto, Issey Miyake, Valentino and Missoni—as well as the scores of cheaper satellite boutiques that turn out clever variations on the innovators' designs.

For leatherware, Hermès (Rue du Faubourg Saint-Honoré) is an institution all on its own, with high-quality luggage, saddles, stirrups and boots and a much sought-after address-book.

Paris seems to make a great appeal to one's vanity and even visitors get caught up with the desire to look a little better and celebrate with a Parisian hair-do. You can find hairdressing with great flair and style at Alexandre, Carita, Maniatis, Jean-Louis David and Jacques Dessange, most of them with branches on both sides of the river.

Bargains galore in Paris flea-markets, from superb antiques to delightful junk.

Old and Not-So-Old

Antique-hunting in Paris takes place on two levels—the high-priced shops grouped mainly in the 6th and 7th *arrondissements* on the Left Bank and the flea markets around the city limits. Antiques from ancient Egyptian and Chinese through pre-Columbian to Louis XV, Second Empire, Art Nouveau and Art Déco can be found in elegant or poky little shops between the Quai Voltaire and Boulevard Saint-Germain, on the Rue Bonaparte, Rue des Saints-Pères, Rue de Beaune and Rue du Bac as you walk away from the river and then zigzag the cross-streets of Rue de Lille, de Verneuil, de l'Université and Jacob. You'll find the biggest collection of antique shops in Europe (250 boutiques) at the Louvre des Antiquaires, 2, Place du Palais Royal, open every day except Monday.

The week-end **flea markets** are a well-established Parisian institution. The Marché aux Puces de Saint-Ouen at the Porte de Clignancourt groups half a dozen markets (also open Monday). Vernaison specializes in musical instruments, lead soldiers, old toys, buttons, brass and tinware; Biron has mostly antiques, not differing greatly in price from the Left Bank antique shops; Malik is a great favourite with the young for its Belle Epoque dresses, First World War military uniforms, 1920s hats, and an amazing assortment of Americana; Paul Bert might have that undiscovered masterpiece every flea market goer dreams of—but get there early, practically at dawn, before the professional antique dealers begin rummaging among the unloading trucks; Jules Vallès is the smallest and cosiest, especially good for Art Nouveau lamps, military souvenirs, theatre costumes and old dolls.

The **bouquinistes** (second-hand book sellers) along the Seine—principally from the Place Saint-Michel to the Pont des Arts—are better now for old periodicals than for old books, with a strange nostalgia in the latter for the period of the German Occupation. If you are looking for old books on Paris itself, your best bet is Francis Dasté, Rue de Tournon. For the homesick, a good selection English and American books can be found at Galignani and W.H. Smith on the Rue de Rivoli and at Brentano's on the Avenue de l'Opéra.

Modern Art lovers will find galleries to their hearts' content in Boulevard Saint-Germain and the streets off it.

For a whiff of the country, drop by the Ile de la Cité's flower market.

Gourmet Shops

Paris, more than most cities, is a place from which to take **food** home as a souvenir. Modern packaging makes it easier to transport goods that previously spoiled en route and many stores are equipped to export your purchases for you. The most famous luxury grocery shop is Fauchon, Place de la Madeleine. Despite the aristocratic reputation of these shops, the service is friendly, courteous and multilingual. Salespeople only become (mild-

OULANGERIE
PAINS
SEIGLE
GRUAU
ANGLAIS

ly) annoyed if you suggest they might not have what you are looking for. Of equally high standard but less comprehensive is Hédiard, on the other side of the Place de la Madeleine, which some people prefer for its more intimate, almost 19th-century atmosphere. For the best *foie gras,* perfectly canned for transportation, and for marvellous sausages, hams and other *charcuterie,* try Coesnon, Rue Dauphine.

You may also want to take home some **wine.** The best bargains are at the Nicolas chainstores—150 branches in Paris. The greatest selection is at Legrand, Rue de la Banque (bankers and stockbrokers are notorious connoisseurs). The most intriguing wine-shop is perhaps Caves de la Madeleine, 24 Rue Boissy d'Anglas, where an Englishman holds wine-tasting sessions.

Finally there are the markets—all over town—but particularly colourful on the Rue Mouffetard, Place Maubert and Rue de Seine on the Left Bank and Rue des Martyrs and Avenue du Président-Wilson on the Right Bank.

Man cannot live by bread alone—but a baguette *is more than bread.*

Sports

As the back-to-nature movement gains ground, hitherto blasé Parisians are increasing their interest in sports and *le jogging* or *le footing, le squash* and *le bowling* are winning new adherents. The Bois de Boulogne and de Vincennes are favourite spots for **joggers;** more challenging is the hilly Parc Montsouris. Others trot along the Seine on the non-highway stretches of the Left Bank between Pont-Neuf and Pont Royal.

You can play **tennis** on public courts by contacting the Fédération Française de Tennis (Stade Roland Garros, 2 Av. Gordon-Bennett), or resorting to the jungle law of first-come-first-served at the Luxembourg Gardens' public courts. There are also over 400 clubs to which some hotels have access for their guests.

Swimming is a pleasant joke at the Piscine Deligny, a fresh-water pool on the Seine near the Palais-Bourbon, where sunbathers go in minimal costume. More serious action takes place at the Olympic-size indoor pool of the Centre de Natation, 34 Boulevard Carnot, or in one of the 30 other good municipal facilities.

Skating is possible from

September until May at the Palais de Glace, Rond-Point des Champs-Elysées; Patinoire Olympique, Rue du Commandant-Mouchotte; and Patinoire Molitor, Avenue de la Porte-Molitor.

In spectator sports, pride of place goes to **horse racing.** Longchamp and Auteuil in summer are every bit as elegant as Britain's Ascot. The serious punter who wants to avoid the frills and champagne can have a very good time at Vincennes at the trotting races. Betting also takes place in town at the Pari-Mutuel desks of the corner *café-tabac*.

Football and rugby can be seen at the modern flying-saucer-like stadium of Parc-des-Princes and tennis at Roland-Garros, both in the Bois de Boulogne. The palatial Palais Omnisports de Paris-Bercy was designed for a variety of sports.

Excursions

Any excursion outside Paris must include **Versailles** (21 km.), where Louis XIV created the most sumptuous royal court Europe had ever seen, partly for his own glory and partly to keep his nobles in impoverished dependency and away from the intrigues of that trouble-making city of Paris. Architects Louis Le Vau and Jules Hardouin-Mansart and landscape-designer André Le Nôtre began their huge undertaking in 1661. It was completed 21 years later. After the Revolutionary ravages, it became a historic museum in 1832 and was restored in this century. (Closed on Mondays.)

One of the principal attractions of the château is the **Galerie des Glaces.** Here the peace treaty of World War I was signed in 1919. The most impressive façade is in the west, facing the gardens. Try to be there at 3.30 p.m. when the fountains begin to play (three Sundays a month from May to September). You should also see the **Grand Trianon,** the little palace that Louis XIV used to get away from the château, the **Petit Trianon** that Louis XV preferred, and the **Hameau** or "cottages" where Marie-Antoinette went to get away from everything.

You might like to venture further afield to the magnificent Gothic cathedral at **Chartres** (95 km. from Paris), which has the finest stained-

Chartres stained-glass windows: a symphony in blue.

glass windows in France, or to the château at **Rambouillet** (54 km.), the summer residence of the French president, where heads of state get together to lament the price of petrol in the beautiful park. An hour's drive north of Paris is the lovely **Forêt de Compiègne** (76 km.), perfect for a cool walk and picnic. You can rent horses at the village of SAINT-JEAN-AUX-BOIS in the middle of the forest and visit the famous clearing in the north-east corner where the armistice was signed in a sleeping-car in 1918—the same sleeping-car that Hitler forced the French to use to sign their capitulation in 1940. A replica of it stands there with a little museum marking the events.

Other nearby sights include the early Gothic basilica of **Saint-Denis** (4 km. from Paris) with royal tombs from the Middle Ages and Renaissance, the national ceramic workshops and museum of **Sèvres** (12 km.), the elegant château and racing course of **Chantilly** (42 km.), **Senlis** (44 km.), where you will find yet another beautiful Gothic cathedral, and the famous forest and château of **Fontainebleau** (65 km.).

The château gardens at Versailles are a miracle of French precision.

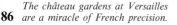

Entertainment

The Paris night-scene has lost none of the glitter and bounce that Toulouse-Lautrec made famous at the turn of the century. The myth he created in that Belle Epoque has sustained itself over the years, and visitors are surprised to discover that his Moulin Rouge, on Place Blanche, still puts on one of the great, boisterous **floor shows** of Europe. The rest of Pigalle is indeed sleazy, but it always was. Taste may have changed over the years but Pigalle has always managed to plumb its lower depths with a certain glee that continues to hold an almost anthropological fascination for visitors. Bright exceptions remain Chez Michou (Rue des Martyrs), a witty cabaret of talented transvestite impersonators, and two music-halls that launched the careers of Josephine Baker, Maurice Chevalier, Fernandel and Mistinguett—the Folies-Bergère (Rue Richer) and the Casino de Paris (Rue de Clichy). The other floor-show in the grand tradition of girls with feathers, balloons and little else takes place in the Lido over on the Champs-Elysées. But perhaps the most famous modern-day girl-show, conceived with great choreographic talent and de-

You pay a bit more than the bare minimum to see showgirls of Paris.

cors in which the girls are dressed only in cunning patterns of light, is in the Crazy Horse Saloon (Avenue George-V).

On the Left Bank there are two floor-shows that combine pretty girls and transvestites in a nonstop riot of pastiche, satire and surprisingly wholesome entertainment at the Alcazar (Rue Mazarine) and Paradis Latin (Rue du Cardinal-Lemoine).

If you would rather do the dancing yourself, a plethora of **discotheques** awaits you—either massive New York-style or chic Parisian. And Paris has some 15 **jazz** clubs, the French taking their jazz seriously. The New Morning (Rue des Petites-Ecuries) attracts all the major American and European musicians, while Le Dunois (Rue Dunois) is a modest, intimate place cultivating the avant-garde. You can hear good mainstream jazz at the Bilboquet (Rue Saint-Benoît), Le Furstenberg (Rue de Buci) and the bars of the Méridien hotel Boulevard Gouvion-Saint-Cyr) and Concorde-Lafayette (Place du Général-Koenig).

Those seeking more serious fare will be delighted by the great revival of the **Opéra.** The Orchestre de Paris has also improved its reputation since the advent of musical director Daniel Barenboim. It is worth going to the hall itself for tickets since agencies add at least 20 per cent to the price and cancellations are returned directly to the hall.

The classical **theatre** maintains its exacting standards for Molière, Racine and Corneille at the Comédie-Française (Rue de Richelieu) and more international works at the Odéon on the Left Bank. Drawing-room comedies and the like find a happy long-running home in the theatres around the *grands boulevards*.

If you feel your French is up to it, visit the tiny *café-théâtres* at which you can sip a drink while watching *chansonniers* in satirical cabaret or an avant-garde play. They are centred around the Marais or Montparnasse. For all of these it is a good idea to consult the excellent weekly entertainment-guides, *Pariscope* and *L'Officiel du Spectacle.*

For many, Paris's most important artistic attraction is not the opera, concerts, theatre or cabaret but the **cinema.** On a typical week you will find over 250 different films playing in town, a record that cineasts claim unequalled elsewhere. Paris is a film-crazy town where directors and even screenplay writers achieve a celebrity equal to that of the stars. To enjoy Paris's cinematic riches you should learn: a) not to be intimidated by queues—there

An Opéra gala—one of the truly great moments of the Paris season.

are always queues and you nearly always get in; b) the ushers expect to be tipped, it is their only income—one franc minimum; c) not to be surprised by applause, even in the middle of the film—cinema is not just an art here, it is a spectator sport; d) the one franc more for tickets on the Champs-Elysées is often for the air conditioning; e) never overdress in the Latin Quarter.

Perhaps from an excess of civilization or sophistication, for a long time Paris has not been a town to celebrate national or religious holidays in any grand style, but there are two days worth noting: **Bastille Day** (July 14) when you can still find a *bal populaire* in the Marais and working-class *arrondissements* (9th, 10th, 11th, 12th, 13th, 18th, 19th and 20th), usually around the fire-station; and **Assumption Day** (August 15) when Paris is totally empty and a sudden quiet heaven.

Wining and Dining

There are some tourists who come to Paris without visiting a single museum or church and who would not dream of "wasting" their time shopping. And yet, they come away with tales of adventure, excitement, poetry and romance—and the feeling they know the city inside out. They have spent their time wining and dining and sleeping in between meals. The onslaught of fast food and snack bars has not staled the infinite variety of Paris's restaurants, *bistrots* and cafés, at which anything from a gorgeous feast to a piquant regional sausage is served in the knowledge that eating and drinking are not just a means of satisfying hunger and thirst.

You can best enter into the spirit of this by devoting one, two or even all your evenings to the delights of good food. Go all the way: aperitif, hors d'œuvre, fish course, meat course, cheese, dessert, brandy and coffee. Back home, weddings and anniversaries may be your only occasion. Here, all you have to celebrate is the city itself. Not to dine well in Paris is not to have been there.*

The only thing that's better than a dozen oysters... is two dozen.

A Primer for Novice Gourmets
Paris has everything except a cuisine of its own. Instead, you can sample food from almost every region of France. But before sitting down to eat, it's useful to have a few basic notions of French cuisine.

First things first. Forgoing the hors d'œuvre does not necessarily mean that the main course will be served more quickly. Besides, it's worth trying some of the simplest dishes that do work genuinely as appetizers: *crudités*—a plate of fresh raw vegetables, tomatoes, carrots, celery, cucumber; or just radishes by themselves, served with salt and butter; *charcuterie*—various kinds of sausage or other cold meats, notably the *rosette* sausage from Lyon, *rillettes* (like a soft pâté) and *jambon* from Bayonne or Dijon; or *potage*—rich vegetable soup, with a base of leek and potato, or perhaps a *bisque de homard* (lobster).

Fish comes fresh to Paris every day. The trout *(truite)* is delicious *au bleu* (poached ab-

* For more about wining and dining in France, consult the Berlitz EUROPEAN MENU READER.

Handling the Waiter

Because French restaurants are regarded as secular temples, tourists sometimes feel they must treat waiters and maîtres d'hôtel like high priests and cardinals. First rule: never be in awe of them. They will not bite. If they bark, bark back. These people are not ogres by nature. They grow testy only when you show you are frightened or aggressive—much like the rest of us, really. You must remember that being a waiter is a respected profession in France, and they like nothing better than for you to call on their expertise.

If you are not satisfied with the wine or the meat is too rare, say so. If you do it with a smile, the waiter will be too surprised to argue. In any decent restaurant, surreptitious tipping to get a table when you have not made a reservation is rarely a good idea. But an extra tip (on top of the 15% in the bill) *after* the meal if you are pleased with your service will be greatly appreciated and get you good service if you return. Amazing how human Parisians can be.

solutely fresh), *meunière* (sautéed in butter) or *aux amandes* (sautéed with almonds). At their best, *quenelles de brochet* (dumplings of ground pike) are simply heavenly—light and airy. The sole and turbot take on a new meaning when served with a *sauce hollandaise,* that miraculous blend of egg yolks, butter and lemon juice with which the Dutch have only the most nominal connection.

For your main dish, expect your meat to be less well-done than in most countries—extra-rare is *bleu;* rare, *saignant;* medium, *à point;* well done, *bien cuit* (and frowned upon). Steaks *(entrecôtes* or *tournedos)* are often served with a wine sauce *(marchand de vin* or *bordelaise)* or with shallots *(échalotes).*

General de Gaulle once asked how one could possibly govern a country with 400 different cheeses. Most of them are to be found in Paris and it would be a crime, in the mere name of your sacred diet, not to try at least the most famous of them—the blue *Roquefort,* the soft yellow-white, crusted *Camembert* or *Brie* (the crust of which you can safely remove without offending true connoisseurs), and the myriad of goat cheeses *(fromage de chèvre).*

Desserts are perhaps the most personal of choices at a meal but you should not miss the chance of a *tarte Tatin* of hot caramelized apples, said to have been invented by mistake by a lady named Tatin who dropped an apple pie upside down on the hotplate when taking it out of the oven. Or *profiteroles,* delicate ball-shaped éclairs filled with vanilla ice-cream and covered with hot chocolate sauce.

If a restaurant offers a *menu* (meaning a special fixed-price meal with appetizer, main course and dessert—not the *carte,* which lists all the establishment's dishes), you can usually save quite a bit by taking it. Look, too, for house wine *(vin ouvert)* served by the *quart* (quarter) and *demi* (half) litre, or bottled by the restaurant. It's always cheaper.

Regional Cuisine

With these pointers as a basic gastronomic "vocabulary", you can begin to try out the various regional cuisines to be found around the capital.

Burgundy, the historic cradle of French culinary art, is ideal for those with robust appetites. This wine-growing region produces the world's greatest beef stew, *bœuf bourguignon,* beef simmered in red wine for at least four hours with mushrooms, small white onions and chunks of bacon. Its Bresse poultry is considered France's finest, and the Charolais beef provides the tenderest of steaks. The freshwater fish benefits from another great sauce, Nantua, made with the stock of crayfish *(écrevisses)* and cream. And don't be afraid of the *escargots* (snails). Start with half a dozen and you may find the chewy texture and garlic butter sauce addictive.

Lyon—the gastronomic capital of France, renowned for the quality of its pork, wild game, vegetables and fruit. If you are adventurous, try one of the rich peasant dishes like *gras-double à la lyonnaise,* tripe with onions and vinegar, the famous *saucisson de Lyon* or a succulent chicken *à la crème.*

Bordeaux—the second great wine-growing region and also justly famous for its *bordelaise* sauce, made with white or red wine, shallots and beef marrow, served variously with *entrecôte* steaks, *cèpe* mushrooms or (why not?) lamprey eels *(lamproie).* A surfeit of them may have killed a few medieval kings but the right amount never hurt anyone. The region's Pauillac lamb *à la persillade* (with parsley) is best eaten pink *(rose).*

Provence—the home of garlic, olives, tomatoes and the country's most fragrant herbs. From the coast between Marseille and Toulon comes the celebrated *bouillabaisse*, a Mediterranean fish stew that might contain rascasse, chapon, saint-pierre, eel, red mullet, whiting, perch, spiny lobster, crabs and other shellfish, seasoned with garlic, olive oil, tomatoes, bay leaf, parsley, pepper and (not authentic without it) saffron. It is also the home of frog's legs, *cuisses de grenouille,* much easier to digest, with garlic, parsley and butter, than you might think.

Landes, Languedoc, Périgord—the south-west famous for *pâté de foie gras* (goose-liver pâté) and truffles, and for all the richness of the goose and duck, especially the *confit d'oie* or *confit de canard,* made by cooking the bird slowly in its own fat and then keeping it for days, weeks and even months in earthenware jars. This is the base of the *cassoulet* with haricot beans, pork, mutton, small sausages, or whatever, one of the heartiest cold-weather meals imaginable.

Ethnic Restaurants

Like other capitals of the old colonial powers, Paris gives a prominent place to the cuisine of its empire: spicy stews from the Caribbean Antilles, savoury *couscous* from North Africa, and the delicate rice dishes of Indochina.

As a variation on the ubiquitous Chinese restaurants—many of them now quite luxurious establishments around the Champs-Elysées and Les Halles—try the little Vietnamese, Cambodian and Laotian places in the Latin Quarter and the 13th *arrondissement* behind Place de l'Italie. Since the immigration of the "boat people" of the 1970s, this quarter has become a haven for South-East Asians. Their cuisine uses distinctive touches of mint, lemon-grass *(citronnelle)* and ginger, and a great variety of seafoods. Thai restaurants, serving more highly spiced food, are growing in popularity.

The Indians have also made a strong assault on the Parisian palate, going beyond simple curries and tandoori to the grander subtleties of Mughal and Kashmiri cuisine.

To serve Japanese businessmen and tourists—and discerning Parisians—the neighbourhood between the Opera and Rue de Rivoli has filled with expensive high-class restaurants and more moderate, but excellent snack-bars serving *sushi* (raw fish and rice) and *yakitori* barbecue.

Wine

What is for many people the most intimidating of experiences—ordering a French wine—has in fact far fewer rules than you think. If you happen to like red wine more than white, you can safely and acceptably order red with fish; a light Beaujolais, Morgon or Brouilly chilled goes with both fish and meat. And if you prefer white, you can drink dry Burgundy with fish and Alsatian wine with everything, with impunity. Remember, in a Paris restaurant *you* are king. You prefer beer? Go ahead, it goes especially well with Toulouse sausage and Alsatian *choucroute.*

But if you do want a few basic pointers about the classic wines, the Burgundy reds divide easily into two categories, those that can more safely be drunk relatively young—the supple *Côte de Beaune* wines of *Aloxe-Corton, Pommard* and *Volnay*—and those that need to

age a little, the full-bodied *Côte de Nuits* wines of *Vougeot, Gevrey-Chambertin* and *Chambolle-Musigny*. The great Burgundy whites include *Meursault* and *Puligny-Montrachet*.

Bordeaux wines have four main regional divisions: *Médoc*, aromatic, mellow red with a slight edge to it; *Graves*, a soft, easy-to-drink red, both dry and vigorous like the Burgundies; *Saint-Emilion*, dark strong and full-bodied; and the pale golden *Sauternes*, sweet and fragrant, the most distinctive of the soft, aromatic whites. The lesser Bordeaux can all be drunk a couple of years old but good ones need five years.

The Loire Valley produces fine dry white wines, such as *Vouvray* and *Sancerre*, and robust reds like *Bourgueil* and *Chinon*. Perhaps the best-known red wine outside Bordeaux and Burgundy is the *Châteauneuf-du-Pape*, produced in the Rhone Valley and truly magnificent when mature. Other very drinkable regional wines include *Côtes du Rhône*, *Cahors* and the *Riesling*, *Traminer* and *Sylvaner* of Alsace.

And for a sparkling finish, the nation's pride and joy, from that little area east of Paris between Reims and Epernay: *Champagne*, which they describe as *aimable, fin et élégant*, "friendly, refined and elegant".

A votre santé!

To Help You Order...

Do you have a table?	**Avez-vous une table?**
Do you have a set-price menu?	**Avez-vous un menu à prix fixe?**
I'd like a/an/some...	**J'aimerais...**

beer	**une bière**	menu	**la carte**
butter	**du beurre**	milk	**du lait**
bread	**du pain**	mineral water	**de l'eau minérale**
cheese	**du fromage**	potatoes	**des pommes de terre**
coffee	**un café**	salad	**une salade**
dessert	**un dessert**	sandwich	**un sandwich**
egg	**un œuf**	soup	**de la soupe**
fish	**du poisson**	sugar	**du sucre**
glass	**un verre**	tea	**du thé**
ice-cream	**une glace**	wine	**du vin**
lemon	**du citron**		
meat	**de la viande**		

... and Read the Menu

agneau lamb
ail garlic
anchois anchovy
andouillette tripe sausage
artichaut artichoke
asperges asparagus
aubergine eggplant
bar sea-bass
bifteck steak
blanquette de veau white veal stew
bœuf beef
cabri baby goat
caille quail
canard, caneton duck, duckling
cervelle brains
champignons mushrooms
chou cabbage
chou-fleur cauliflower
concombre cucumber
côte, côtelette chop, cutlet
courgettes baby marrow (zucchini)
coquelet baby chicken
coquilles Saint-Jacques scallops
crevettes shrimps
daurade sea bream
écrevisse crayfish
endive chicory (endive)
épinards spinach
flageolets dried beans
foie liver
fraises strawberries
framboises raspberries
frites chips (French fries)
fruits de mer seafood
gigot (d'agneau) leg (of lamb)
haricots verts green beans
homard lobster
huîtres oysters
jambon ham
langouste spiny lobster
langue tongue
lapin rabbit
loup de mer sea-bass
macédoine de fruits fruit salad
médaillon tenderloin
moules mussels
moutarde mustard
mulet grey mullet
navarin lamb stew
nouilles noodles
oignons onions
oseille sorrel
petits pois peas
pintade guinea fowl
poisson fish
poire pear
poireaux leeks
pomme apple
porc pork
potage soup
poulet chicken
radis radishes
raisins grapes
ris de veau sweetbreads
riz rice
rognons kidneys
rouget red mullet
saucisse/ saucisson sausage/dried sausage
saumon salmon
sole sole
sorbet water-ice (sherbet)
thon tunny (tuna)
truffes truffles
veau veal
volaille poultry

How to Get There

If the choice of ways to go is bewildering, the complexity of fares and regulations can be downright stupefying. A reliable travel agent, up to date on the latest zigs and zags, can suggest which plan is best for your timetable and budget.

BY AIR

Scheduled flights

Paris is served by two intercontinental airports, Roissy-Charles-de-Gaulle and Orly (see also p. 104). Average journey time between Paris and Johannesburg is 14 hours, London 1 hour, New York 7 hours (less than 4 hours by Concorde), Toronto 9 hours.

Charter flights and package tours

From the U.K. and Eire: Most tour operators charter seats on scheduled flights at a reduced price as part of a package deal which could include a weekend or a couple of weeks' stay, a simple bed and breakfast arrangement or a combined "wine tour" and visit to Paris. Among the inclusive holiday packages are special tours for visitors with a common interest such as cookery courses, school trips or art.

However, most visitors from the U.K. travel to France individually, either by booking directly with a ferry operator and taking the car, or signing up for inclusive holidays which offer fly-drive and touring or self-catering arrangements.

From North America: ABC (Advance Booking Charters) provide air passage only (from New York, Chicago, Los Angeles and San Francisco to Paris), but OTC (One Stop Inclusive Tour Charter) package deals include airport transfers, hotel, some sightseeing and meals.

Paris is the starting point for many tours of France. Wine tasting, gourmet and cooking tours, as well as tours of the château country are included in package deals leaving from over a dozen major American and Canadian cities, usually on a seasonal basis (April to October) and for periods of from one to three weeks. You can also choose from fly-drive and fly-rail schemes.

From Australia and New Zealand: Package deals for Paris are offered by certain airlines. You can also travel by independent arrangement (the usual direct economy flight with unrestricted stopovers) or go on an air-and-car-hire arrangement.

From South Africa: There are both excursion fares and numerous package deals including Paris among other European sights.

BY CAR

Cross-channel operators offer plenty of special deals at competitive prices; a good travel agent will help you to find the suitable ferry for your destination.

BY BUS

Numerous lines serve Paris from regional cities like Bordeaux, Lyons, or Nice. Regular services also operate from London to Paris (via Calais).

BY RAIL

All the main lines converge on Paris. There is an excellent network of ultra-rapid express trains, TGVs (1st and 2nd class, advance booking compulsory, certain trains with supplement). Auto-train services *(Trains Autos Couchettes)* are also available from all major towns.

The journey from London to Paris takes from 6 to 11 hours by train. British and French railways offer London-to-Paris services with the possibility of overnight carriages from London. From Boulogne hoverport, there's a 2-hour, 20-minute turbo-train service to Paris (Gare du Nord).

Tickets. Visitors from abroad can buy a *France-Vacances Spécial* pass, valid for specified periods of unlimited travel on first or second class, with reductions on the Paris transport network and one or two days free car rental (with first class only), depending on type of card.

The *Rail Europ S* (senior) card, obtainable before departure only, entitles senior citizens to purchase train tickets for European destinations at reduced prices.

Any family of at least 3 people can buy a *Rail-Europ F* (family) card: the holder pays full price, the rest of the family obtain a 50% reduction in France, Switzerland and 13 other European countries; the whole family is also entitled to a 30% reduction on Sealink and Hoverspeed Channel crossings.

Anyone under 26 years of age can purchase an *Inter-Rail* card which allows one month's unlimited 2nd-class travel.

People living outside Europe and North Africa can purchase a *Eurailpass* for unlimited rail travel in 16 European countries including France. This pass must be obtained before leaving home.

When to Go

Paris enjoys a mild Continental climate without extremes of hot and cold. From mid-July to the end of August there seem to be more foreign than French people in Paris and shopkeepers and restaurant owners often close up and go on holiday themselves. The best seasons to visit Paris are spring and autumn. The following chart gives an idea of the average monthly temperature in Paris:

	J	F	M	A	M	J	J	A	S	O	N	D
°C	3	4	7	10	14	16	19	18	15	11	6	4
°F	37	39	45	50	57	61	66	64	59	52	43	39

Planning Your Budget

The following are some prices in French francs (F). However, they must be regarded as approximate and taken as broad guidelines; inflation in France, as elsewhere, rises steadily.

Airport transfers. Bus to Orly 27 F, to Charles-de-Gaulle 34 F. Train (2nd class) to Orly 17.30 F, to Charles-de-Gaulle 23 F. Taxi to Orly approx. 150 F, to Charles-de-Gaulle approx. 200 F.

Baby-sitters. 22–25 F per hour.

Bicycle hire. 190–300 F per week, plus 500–700 F refundable deposit.

Car hire (international company). *Renault 5 GTL* 200 F per day, 2.67 F per km., 2,212 F per week with unlimited mileage. *Renault 11* 244 F per day, 3.69 F per km., 2,996 F per week with unlimited mileage. *BMW 520* 457 F per day, 5.20 F per km., 7,168 F per week with unlimited mileage. Add insurance. Tax included.

Cigarettes. French 4.50–7 F, foreign 7–13 F, cigars 17–48 F per piece.

Entertainment. Discotheque (admission and first drink) 60–110 F, nightclub with dinner and floor show 250–485 F, cinema 30–37 F. Special rates for students/groups/Mondays 20–25 F.

Guides. 525–650 F for half-day.

Hairdressers. *Man's* haircut 80–180 F. *Woman's* cut 80 F and up, shampoo and set/blow-dry 90–150 F, colour rinse / dye 80–220 F.

Hotels (double room with bath). ****L 1,000–1,500 F, **** 600–900 F, *** 350–500 F, ** 250–350 F, * 150–250 F (* without bath, 80–120 F).

Meals and drinks. Continental breakfast, hotel 15–60 F, café 15–28 F. Lunch or dinner (in fairly good establishment) 80–200 F, coffee 5–8 F, beer 8–20 F, bottle of wine 30 F and up, cocktail 30–60 F, whisky 28–60 F, cognac 25–60 F.

Métro. 2nd-class ticket 4.60 F, 10 tickets *(carnet)* 27.50 F for 2nd class, 42 F for 1st class, weekly *carte orange (hebdomadaire)* bought for each Monday through Sunday only (valid on buses and Métro) 43 F (2nd class), monthly *carte orange* (2nd class) 152 F (also valid on buses). "Paris Sésame" card (bus or 2nd-class Métro) 55 F for two days, 83 F for four days, 138 F for seven days.

Sightseeing. Boats 23–25 F, museums 8–25 F.

Taxis. Start at 8.50 F (3.80 F extra at stations and terminals), 2.44 F per kilometre. Night rates are higher.

BLUEPRINT for a Perfect Trip

An A-Z Summary of Practical Information and Facts

Contents

Listed after most main entries is an appropriate French translation, usually in the singular. You'll find this vocabulary useful when asking for information or assistance.

A

AIRPORTS *(aéroport).* Paris is served by two main airports, Roissy-Charles-de-Gaulle, about 15 miles north-east of the city, with two terminals (C.D.G. 2 essentially for Air France flights), and Orly, about 9 miles to the south, with its two buildings, Orly-Sud and Orly-Ouest. Most intercontinental flights use Charles-de-Gaulle, a space-age modular construction. Both airports have currency-exchange banks, excellent restaurants, snack bars, post offices and well-stocked duty-free shops.

There is regular and comfortable bus service between airports and between the airports and Paris. The buses leave every twenty minutes from about 6.00 a.m. to 11.00 p.m. There's service outside of those hours from the terminals in Paris to the airport 45 minutes before airport check-in time. The terminal *(aérogare)* for Charles-de-Gaulle airport is at Porte Maillot, near the Etoile. Orly is served by the Invalides terminal. Average time to the airports from these terminals is around 40 minutes; it takes an hour and a quarter to get from one airport to the other by bus. You should plan to leave early if you travel during peak traffic hours.

You can also reach the airports by rail at a very modest price. Trains leave every 15 minutes from about 5 a.m. to 11 p.m. and take 45–75 minutes from the Gare du Nord to Charles-de-Gaulle. From Quai d'Orsay, Saint-Michel or Austerlitz stations to Orly the trip takes 40–60 minutes. Trains leave frequently from early morning to late at night. See p. 103 for rates.

There is also a regular helicopter service between airports and Paris. The Héliport de Paris is situated at 4, avenue de la Porte de Sèvres in the south-west (Métro Balard).

From the arrivals hall of Charles-de-Gaulle airport, you can contact free a broad selection of hotels throughout the city. By pressing a button, a lamp lights on a map showing position of hotel and prices; by pressing a second one, you get into direct telephone contact with the hotel. The reservation will be kept for you for up to two hours following your call.

Where's the bus/train for...? **D'où part le bus/le train pour...?**

B **BANKS and CURRENCY-EXCHANGE OFFICES** *(banque; bureau de change)*. Hours vary, but most Paris bank are open from 9 a.m. to 4.30 p.m., Mondays to Fridays. A few banks and currency-exchange offices operate later and on weekends. The Paris Tourist Information Office can provide a list of these.

Your hotel will usually change currency or traveller's cheques into francs, but the rate is not favourable. Always take your passport when you change money.

I want to change some pounds/dollars.	**Je voudrais changer des livres sterling/dollars.**

BUS SERVICE *(autobus)*. Bus transport around Paris and the suburbs is efficient, though not always fast. Stops are marked by red and yellow signs, with bus numbers posted. Most buses run from 7 a.m. to 8.30 p.m., some to 12.30. Service is reduced on Sundays and holidays. You use one, two or three tickets depending on the distance. You can buy a ticket as you board the bus. But for frequent bus travel it's less expensive to use one or two tickets from a series *(carnet)* purchased in Métro stations, special two-, four- or seven-day tourist passes or the *carte orange* (see MÉTRO). Bus and Métro tickets are interchangeable.

Do you go to...?	**Est-ce que vous allez à...?**

C **CAR HIRE** *(location de voitures)*. All car-hire firms in Paris handle French-made cars and often foreign makes. Local firms sometimes offer lower prices than the big international companies, but you may have to turn the car in at the same place, rather than dropping it off in another town. See sample rates on p. 103. Ask for any available seasonal deals.

To hire a car you must furnish a valid driving licence (held for at least one year) and your passport. Depending on the model you rent and the hiring firm, minimum age for renting a car varies from 21 to 25. Holders of major credit cards are normally exempt from advance deposit payments; otherwise you must pay a substantial (refundable) deposit for a car.

I'd like to hire a car tomorrow.	**Je voudrais louer une voiture demain.**
for one day/a week	**pour une journée/une semaine**
Please include full insurance.	**Avec assurance tous risques, s'il vous plaît.**

CHILDREN. The younger set will find a lot to do in Paris. The Eiffel Tower and boat trips are good fun for everyone. Paris's main zoo (open daily from 9 to 5.30) is in the Bois de Vincennes, easily reached by Métro. The Jardin d'Acclimatation of the Bois de Boulogne is a very special games-and-zoo park, complete with pony rides, marionette shows and other diversions. Prices are reasonable, and children love it (open from 9.30 to 6.30 every day). There are also art workshops for kids on Wednesday and Saturday afternoons in the Centre Georges Pompidou, Plateau Beaubourg (tel. 42.77.12.33). Ask for the Atelier des Enfants.

Reputable student and service organizations can provide babysitters *(babysitter, garde d'enfant)*. Ask at your hotel or the tourist office. You should try to request a sitter at least a day ahead. For prices, see p. 103.

Can you get me a babysitter for tonight/tomorrow night?	**Pouvez-vous me trouver une baby-sitter pour ce soir / demain soir?**

CIGARETTES, CIGARS, TOBACCO *(cigarettes; cigares; tabac)*. Tobacco is a state monopoly in France, and the best place to buy your cigarettes is at an official *débit de tabac* (licensed tobacconist). There are plenty of these—cafés and bars and many newsagents—bearing the conspicuous double red cone.

French cigarettes include brands with dark or light tobacco, with or without filter. Dozens of foreign brands are also available at higher prices (see p. 103).

A packet of.../A box of matches please.	**Un paquet de.../Une boîte d'allumettes, s'il vous plaît.**
filter-tipped/without filter	**avec/sans filtre**
light/dark tobacco	**du tabac blond/brun**

CLOTHING *(habillement)*. The world's fashion capital is a varied show on the streets. Women feel at home in anything from classic suits to the latest zany mode or jeans. Discretion and practicality are the rule. Paris women don't dress up much in the evening, though you'll want a cocktail dress or dressy slacks and blouses for better restaurants, nightclubs and discothèques.

Some restaurants require jacket and tie for men; and you'll probably get better service at most hotels and restaurants in conservative dress.

Unpredictable continental weather requires a versatile wardrobe, though neither in summer or winter are you likely to meet extremes. For

C

summer a good rule is lightweight clothing with a warm sweater or blazer and a raincoat. In winter, too, a raincoat is sometimes necessary, plus light woollen clothes and a warm coat and boots for the coldest days.

COMPLAINTS *(réclamation)*

Hotels and restaurants: Complaints should be referred to the owner or manager of the establishment in question. Try a firm attitude, and if this doesn't work you can take more serious steps. In the case of a hotel, you can consult the trade organization, the Syndicat Général de l'Industrie Hôtelière, 22, av. de la Grande-Armée, 75016 Paris; tel. 43.80.08.29.

Serious complaints may also be taken to the Préfecture de Police de Paris, 7–9, bd du Palais, 75004 Paris; tel. 42.60.33.22.

Bad merchandise: Within about 10 days of purchase a store will usually exchange faulty merchandise (if you have the receipt), but you will hardly ever get your money back.

Prices: If you wish to complain about a price you consider exorbitant, phone the Service de la Concurrence et de la Consommation,

8, rue Froissard, tel. 42.71.23.10

I'd like to make a complaint. **J'ai une réclamation à faire.**

CONVERTER CHARTS.

For fluid and distance measures, see p. 111. France uses the metric system.

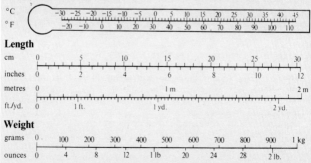

Temperature

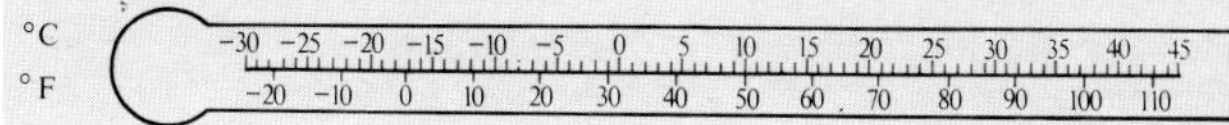

Length

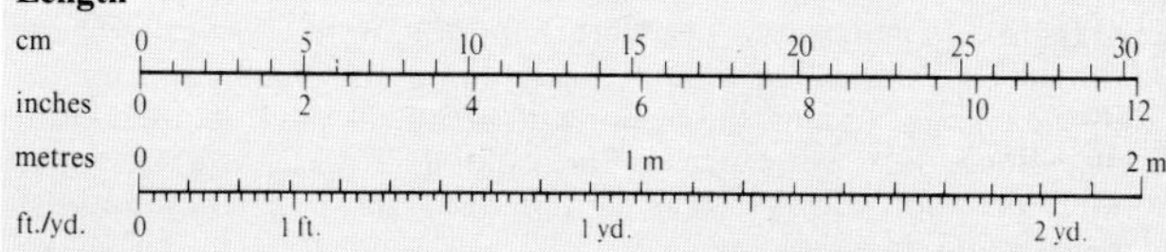

Weight

grams 0 100 200 300 400 500 600 700 800 900 1 kg

ounces 0 4 8 12 1 lb 20 24 28 2 lb.

CREDIT CARDS and TRAVELLER'S CHEQUES *(carte de crédit; chèque de voyage, traveller's cheque)*

C

Credit cards. Most hotels, smarter restaurants, some boutiques, carhire firms and tourist-related businesses accept certain credit cards.

Traveller's cheques. Hotels, travel agents and many shops accept them, although the exchange rate is invariably better at a bank. Don't forget to take your passport when going to cash a traveller's cheque.

Paying cash. Some shops or hotels may accept payment in sterling or dollars but the exchange rate will not be advantageous.

Do you accept traveller's cheques?	**Acceptez-vous les chèques de voyage?**
Can I pay with this credit card?	**Puis-je payer avec cette carte de crédit?**

CRIME and THEFT *(délit; vol).* Paris has its share of pickpockets, so watch your wallet and handbag, especially in crowds. Keep items of value in your hotel safe and obtain a receipt for them. It's a good idea to leave large amounts of money there as well.

Lock your car at all times and leave nothing valuable inside, or put what you're leaving in the locked boot(trunk). Any loss or theft should be reported at once to the nearest *commissariat de police* (see POLICE).

I want to report a theft.	**Je veux signaler un vol.**
My ticket/wallet/passport/handbag/credit card has been stolen.	**On a volé mon billet/portefeuille/passeport/sac à main/(ma) carte de crédit.**

CURRENCY *(monnaie).* For currency restrictions, see CUSTOMS CONTROLS. The French *franc* (abbreviated F or FF) is divided into 100 *centimes*. Current coins include 5-, 10-, 20- and 50-centime pieces as well as 1-, 2-, 5- and 10-franc pieces. Banknotes come in denominations of 20, 50, 100, 200 and 500 francs.

Could you give me some (small) change?	**Pouvez-vous me donner de la (petite) monnaie?**

CUSTOMS CONTROLS *(douane).* There's no limit on the importation of local or foreign currencies or traveller's cheques. Unless a declaration was made on entry, non-residents are allowed to reconvert no more than 12,000 French francs into foreign currency when leaving the country.

C The following chart shows some main items you may take into France:

Cigarettes	Cigars	Tobacco	Spirits	Wine
1) 400	100	500 g.	1 l.	2 l.
2) 300 or	75 or	400 g.	1½ l. and	5 l.
3) 200	50	250 g.	1 l.	2 l.

1) Visitors arriving from outside Europe
2) Visitors arriving from E.E.C. countries with non-duty-free items
3) Visitors arriving from E.E.C. countries with duty-free items, or from other European countries

For what you can bring back home, ask before leaving home for the customs notice setting out allowances. See also ENTRY FORMALITIES.

I've nothing to declare.	**Je n'ai rien à déclarer.**
It's for my own use.	**C'est pour mon usage personnel.**

D **DRIVING IN FRANCE.** To take a car into France, you will need:

- A valid driving licence
- Car registration papers
- A red warning triangle and a set of spare bulbs

The green card is no longer obligatory, but full insurance coverage is strongly recommended.

Drivers and front-seat passengers are required by law to wear seat belts. Children under 10 may not travel in the front (unless the car has no back seat). Driving on a provisional licence is not permitted in France. Minimum age is 18.

Driving regulations: As elsewhere on the Continent, drive on the right, overtake on the left, yield right-of-way to all vehicles coming from the right (except on roundabouts), unless otherwise indicated. Speed limits are 45 or 60 kph (kilometres per hour) in residential areas of Paris and its suburbs, 90 kph on through roads, 110 kph on dual carriageways (divided highways) and 130 kph on motorways (expressways) called *autoroutes*. When roads are wet, all limits are reduced by 10 kph. The word *rappel* means a restriction is continued.

Driving in Paris is hectic. Stick to your own pace and keep a safe distance between you and the vehicle in front. Be especially wary of vehicles coming from the right.

Road conditions: Beware of traffic jams on the major roads and motorways as you enter and leave Paris, especially on long weekends and around the summer dates of July 1 and 15, August 1 and 15 and September 1. Paris traffic police *(Gardiens de la Paix)* direct traffic and are helpful in giving directions (see POLICE).

Parking: This is a major problem in the capital, which authorities are trying to solve by building new underground parking lots, indicated by a large blue "P". In the centre most street parking is metered. The blue zones require the *disque de stationnement* (obtainable from petrol stations or stationers), which you set to show when you arrived and when you must leave.

Some streets have alternate parking on either side of the street according to which part of the month it is (the dates are marked on the signs). Fines for parking violations can be heavy, and in serious cases your car may be towed away or have a wheel clamp attached until you pay up at the local *commissariat*, or police station.

Breakdowns: It's wise to have internationally valid breakdown insurance, and to ask for an estimate *before* undertaking repairs. Two companies which offer 24-hour breakdown service are Service Dépannage Automobiles, tel. 42.36.10.00 and SOS Dépannage, tel. 47.07.99.99.

Fuel and oil: Fuel is available in super (98 octane), normal (90 octane), lead-free (still rare; 95 octane), and diesel *(gas-oil)*. All grades of motor oils are on sale. Service-station attendants are tipped for any additional services rendered.

Fluid measures

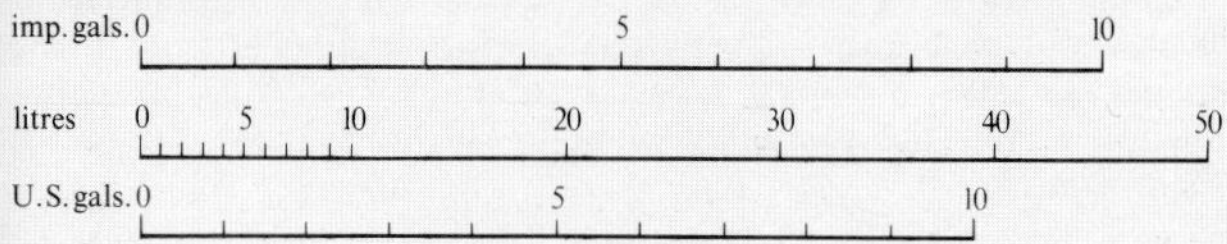

Distance

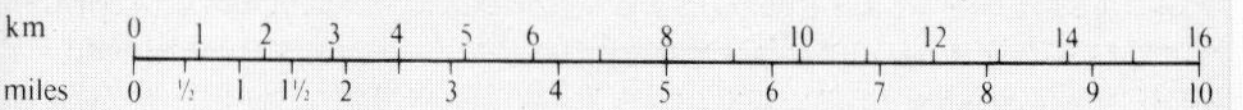

D

Road signs: Most road signs are the standard pictographs used throughout Europe, but you may encounter these written signs as well:

Accotements non stabilisés	Soft shoulders
Chaussée déformée	Bad road surface
Déviation	Diversion (detour)
Douane	Customs
Gravillons	Loose gravel
Impasse	Cul-de-sac (dead-end)
Péage	Toll
Priorité à droite	Yield to traffic from right
Ralentir	Slow
Sauf riverains	Entry prohibited except for inhabitants of street
Sens unique	One-way street
Serrez à droite/gauche	Keep right/left
Sortie de camions	Lorry (truck) exit
Stationnement interdit	No parking
Véhicules lents	Slow vehicles

(international) driving licence	**permis de conduire (international)**
car registration papers	**carte grise**
Are we on the right road for...?	**Sommes-nous sur la route de...?**
Fill the tank, please.	**Le plein, s'il vous plaît.**
normal / super / lead-free	**normale / super / sans plomb**
Check the oil / tires / battery.	**Veuillez contrôler l'huile / les pneus / la batterie.**
I've had a breakdown.	**Ma voiture est en panne.**
There's been an accident.	**Il y a eu un accident.**

E

ELECTRIC CURRENT. You will probably only find 220-volt, 50-cycle A.C. in Paris although some of the oldest hotels may still have 110 volts. British and American visitors using electric appliances from home should remember to buy the necessary adaptors. For razors, just about all hotels have the possibility of both 110 and 220, or the razors themselves do.

EMBASSIES and CONSULATES *(ambassade; consulat).* Contact your embassy or consulate when in trouble (loss of passport, theft or loss of all your money, problems with the police, serious accident).

Australia	embassy and consulate, 4, rue Jean-Rey, 75015 Paris; tel. 45.75.62.00
Canada	consulate, 35, av. Montaigne, 75008 Paris; tel. 47.23.01.01
Eire	consulate, 12, avenue Foch (enter from 4, rue Rude), 75016 Paris; tel. 45.00.20.87
New Zealand	embassy-chancellery, 9, rue Léonard-de-Vinci, 75016 Paris; tel. 45.00.24.11
South Africa	chancellery-consulate, 59, quai d'Orsay, 75007 Paris; tel. 45.55.92.37
United Kingdom	consulate, 35, rue du Faubourg Saint-Honoré, 75008 Paris; tel. 42.66.91.42
U.S.A.	consulate, 2, rue St-Florentin, 75008 Paris; tel. 42.96.12.02

Where's the... embassy/consulate?	**Où se trouve l'ambassade/ le consulat...?**
I'd like to phone the... embassy.	**Je voudrais téléphoner à l'ambassade...**
American/British	**américaine/britannique**
Canadian/Irish	**canadienne/irlandaise**

EMERGENCIES *(urgence).* You can get assistance anywhere in France by dialling the number 17 for the police *(Police-Secours);* 18 for the fire brigade *(pompiers).* Paris has an efficient anti-poison centre (tel. 42.05.63.29). You can get advice for other urgent medical problems by dialling S.O.S. Médecins: 47.07.77.77.

Careful!	**Attention!**	Police!	**Police!**
Fire!	**Au feu!**	Stop, thief!	**Au voleur!**
Help!	**Au secours!**		

Can you help me?	**Pouvez-vous m'aider?**

ENTRY FORMALITIES. See also CUSTOMS CONTROLS and DRIVING IN FRANCE. Visitors from E.E.C. countries and Switzerland need only a valid passport to enter France. If you come from another country, check with the nearest French embassy first to see if you need a visa. Though Europeans and North American residents are not subject to any health requirements, visitors from further afield may require a smallpox vaccination. Check with your travel agent before departure.

G

GUIDES and INTERPRETERS *(guide; interprète).* The Tourist Information Office provides a list of official guides. The Agence Nationale pour l'Emploi, a public placement service, can usually find you a guide-interpreter at the lowest prices. Telephone 43.55.44.05. "Meet the French" (182, bd Pereire; tel. 45.74.77.12) offers car with chauffeur-guide at a fixed price (excluding museum entry tickets).

Reputable travel agencies also furnish guides and cars, and the larger hotels have lists of chauffeur-guides. For prices see p. 103.

H

HAIRDRESSERS *(coiffeur).* Prices vary widely according to the class of establishment, but rates are often displayed in the window.

Most *coiffeurs* include service charges in the price, but it's customary to give something. See p. 103 for prices.

Not too much off (here).	**Pas trop court (ici).**
Trim the fringe (bangs)/nape of the neck.	**Coupez un peu la frange/sur la nuque.**
I'd like a perm/blow-dry.	**J'aimerais une permanente/un brushing.**

HEALTH *(santé).* Fatigue, change of diet and over-indulgence (especially in wine) are the main culprits causing the common "tourist's complaint". Watch the drinking and try French mineral water, which helps to digest meals. Serious gastro-intestinal problems lasting more than a day or two should be looked after by a doctor. See MEDICAL CARE.

HOTELS and ACCOMMODATION *(hôtel; logement).* Paris offers a wide range of hotels to suit every taste and budget. Advance bookings are highly recommended, since during holiday season and commercial exhibition weeks, rooms can be almost impossible to find.

Officially, hotels are classified into five categories; a booklet is available at the Paris Tourist Information Office. Rates, fixed according to amenities and the hotel's location, should be posted visibly at reception desks and behind each room door. See page 103 for rates.

Newspapers such as *Figaro* and the *International Herald Tribune* list available accommodation for rent. Most houses and flats are available for long lease only, though some can be let for a month or less. Agencies take large fees, but some flats can be rented from the owner or subleased from the tenant without a fee.

H

See also YOUTH HOSTELS and under AIRPORTS.

a double/single room with/without bath/toilet	**une chambre à deux lits/un lit avec/sans bains/toilettes**
What's the rate per night?	**Quel est le prix pour une nuit?**
I'm looking for a flat to rent for a month.	**Je cherche un appartement à louer pour un mois.**

HOURS *(heures d'ouverture).* Although you'll find tobacconists or small shops which sell food and wine open as early as 7 a.m. and as late as midnight, department stores and most shops do business from 9.30 a.m. to 6.30 p.m., Mondays through Saturdays. Boutiques and art galleries often stay open a bit later, especially in the summer.

Watch out for variable lunch hours; businesses and smaller shops close for an hour or so. Banks and some offices close at noon on the day before public holidays. Most museums and monuments open around 10 a.m. and close about 5 p.m. Virtually all are closed on Tuesdays.

See also sections on POST OFFICE, BANKS AND CURRENCY EXCHANGE.

L

LANGUAGE. You'll usually hear well-enunciated French in Paris, spoken quite quickly. But there are myriad accents, since many Parisians come from the provinces, North Africa or further afield.

Although many Frenchmen speak some English, the French really appreciate a tourist making an effort to speak French, even if it's only the odd word.

The Berlitz phrase book FRENCH FOR TRAVELLERS covers almost all situations you're likely to encounter in your travels in France. In addition, the Berlitz French-English/English-French pocket dictionary contains a glossary of 12,500 terms, plus a menu-reader supplement.

Good morning/Good afternoon	**Bonjour**
Good afternoon/Good evening	**Bonsoir**
Thank you	**Merci**
Please	**S'il vous plaît**
Goodbye	**Au revoir**
You're welcome.	**Je vous en prie.**
Speak slowly, please.	**Doucement, s'il vous plaît.**
I didn't understand.	**Je n'ai pas compris.**

L **LAUNDRY and DRY CLEANING** *(blanchisserie; nettoyage à sec).* If your hotel will not take care of laundry or cleaning, you can have clothes cleaned quickly and cheaply in chain dry cleaners (not recommended, however, for fragile fabrics or difficult spots). Better care takes longer and is more expensive; prices vary according to fabric and cut.

When will it be ready?	**Quand est-ce que ce sera prêt?**
I must have it tomorrow morning.	**Il me le faut pour demain matin.**

LOST PROPERTY *(objets trouvés).* If loss or suspected theft occurs in your hotel, check first at the desk. They may suggest you report the loss to the local police station *(commissariat).* Restaurant and café personnel are quite honest about returning objects left behind; they turn valuables over to the police.

Lost objects usually end up at the Bureau des Objets Trouvés, 36, rue des Morillons, 75015 Paris. If you've lost a passport, check first with your embassy, as the Bureau des Objets Trouvés would transfer it there first. Forms must be filled out in French, though there are usually English-speakers on hand.

I've lost my wallet/handbag/ passport.	**J'ai perdu mon portefeuille/sac/ passeport.**

M **MAIL** *(courrier).* See also Post Offices. If you don't know ahead of time where you'll stay in Paris, you can have mail addressed to you c/o Poste Restante, 52, rue du Louvre, 75001 Paris, which is Paris's main post office open 24 hours a day, every day.

The American Express at 11, rue Scribe, 75009 Paris, also holds mail. Take your passport with you to claim it.

Have you any mail for...?	**Avez-vous du courrier pour...?**

MAPS. Small maps of the city *(plan)* are given away at tourist offices, banks and hotels. More detailed maps are sold in bookshops and at newsstands. A good investment is the compact map book "Plan de Paris" put out by A. Leconte. It contains a large fold-out map and small detailed ones of each *arrondissement,* with useful addresses. Falk-Verlag, Hamburg (the map producer for this book) also publishes a good map of Paris.

MEDICAL CARE. See also EMERGENCIES and HEALTH. To be at ease, make sure your health insurance policy covers any illness or accident while on holiday. If not, ask your insurance representative, automobile association or travel agent for details of special travel insurance.

Visitors from E.E.C. countries with corresponding health insurance facilities are entitled to medical and hospital treatment under the French social security system. Before leaving home, make sure you find out about necessary formalities and forms.

Paris has excellent doctors, surgeons and medical facilities. Most better hotels and the consulates have a list of English-speaking doctors and dentists. Doctors who belong to the French social security system *(médecins conventionnés)* charge the minimum.

Two private hospitals serve the Anglo-American community: American Hospital of Paris, 63, bd Victor-Hugo, 92202 Neuilly, tel. 47.47.53.00; Hôpital Franco-Britannique, 48, rue de Villiers, Levallois-Perret; tel. 47.58.13.12.

Chemists *(pharmacies)* with green crosses are helpful in dealing with minor ailments or in finding a nurse *(infirmière)* if you need injections or other special care. The Pharmacie des Champs-Elysées, 84, av. des Champs-Elysées, tel. 45.62.02.41, is open 24 hours a day.

Where's the chemist on duty?	**Où est la pharmacie de garde?**
I need a doctor/dentist.	**Il me faut un médecin/dentiste.**
I've a pain here.	**J'ai mal ici.**
an upset stomach	**mal à l'estomac**
a fever	**de la fièvre**
headache	**mal à la tête**

MEETING PEOPLE. Cafés are a source of casual encounters and sometimes friendship, especially among the younger crowd in the Latin Quarter. You can also meet French people through a programme called Meet the French, a private organization which proposes personalized guide service (see GUIDES AND INTERPRETERS).

French people always kiss very close friends on both cheeks (sometimes more than once) and shake hands to greet or say goodbye to old and new friends and acquaintances.

Hello.	**Bonjour.**
I'm glad to meet you.	**Enchanté.**
How are you?	**Comment allez-vous?**

METRO. Paris's underground transport is possibly the world's most efficient, fastest and cleanest. It's also cheaper than most. Express

M lines (R.E.R.) get you into town in about 15 minutes, with a few stops in between.

You should buy a book of tickets *(carnet)*, available for first or second class, if you plan to take the Métro more than a few times.

For longer stays and lots of travel, you can buy an orange identity card *(carte orange)* valid for a week or a month on buses and the Métro. There are also special tourist tickets, called "Paris Sésame", for two, four or seven days, allowing unlimited travel on bus or Métro. For prices, see p. 103.

Big maps in every Métro station make the system easy to use. The service starts at 5.30 a.m. and ends around 1 a.m. See map on p. 128.

R.A.T.P., the Paris Transport Authority, has an information office at 53ter, quai des Grands-Augustins, 75271 Paris, Cedex 6. You can call them at 43.46.14.14, round the clock, for information on public transport in Paris.

Which line should I take for...?	**Quelle direction dois-je prendre pour...?**

N **NEWSPAPERS and MAGAZINES** *(journal; revue)*. In addition to the local French dailies, you'll find the Paris-based *International Herald Tribune* almost everywhere and several English newspapers at many news-stands. *Pariscope* is the best known of the weekly information magazines on sale. A wide range of magazines in English and other languages is available at larger news-stands.

P **PHOTOGRAPHY** *(photographie)*. Beautiful shots to be taken at so many street corners make Paris a photographer's dream. The city's hazy atmosphere and soft colours still inspire artists and photographers as they did the Impressionist painters.

All popular film makes and sizes are available; rapid development is possible, though sometimes expensive.

I'd like a film for this camera.	**J'aimerais un film pour cet appareil.**
a black-and-white film	**un film noir et blanc**
a film for colour prints	**un film couleurs**
a colour-slide film	**un film pour diapositives**
How long will it take to develop this film?	**Combien de temps faut-il pour développer ce film?**
May I take a picture?	**Puis-je prendre une photo?**

POLICE *(police).* In Paris you'll normally see the Police municipale wearing blue uniforms. Also known as Gardiens de la Paix, they direct traffic, help tourists with directions, investigate violations and make arrests.

The C.R.S. police *(Compagnies républicaines de Sécurité)* are responsible to the Ministry of the Interior and often appear *en masse* around the French President's Elysée Palace (usually in dark-blue buses) during important political visits or when demonstrations take place.

The elegantly dressed *Garde républicaine,* often on horse-back and accompanied by a very good band, turn out for ceremonies and parades.

In case of need, you can dial 17 in Paris and all over France for police help.

Where's the nearest police station?	**Où est le commissariat de police le plus proche?**

POST OFFICE and TELEGRAMS *(poste; télégramme).* See also MAIL and TELEPHONE. You can identify post offices by a sign with a stylized blue bird and the words Postes et Télécommunications (*P & T* or *PTT*). Paris post offices are open from 8 a.m. to 7 p.m. Mondays to Fridays and 8 a.m. to noon on Saturdays. Stamps may also be bought at tobacconists.

In addition to normal mail service, you can make local or long-distance telephone calls, send telegrams and receive or send money through the post office. The Paris Tourist Information Office has a list of post offices open on Sundays and holidays for telephone and telegraph services. You can send telegrams in English by telephoning 42.33.21.11.

Letters may be delivered within hours in the Paris district by sending them *postexpress* from the post office. Another quick and even cheaper system for delivering a message is the *message téléphoné.* Inquire at the post office of your hotel.

A stamp for this letter/postcard, please.	**Un timbre pour cette lettre/carte postale, s'il vous plaît.**
I want to send a telegram to…	**J'aimerais envoyer un télégramme à...**

PUBLIC HOLIDAYS *(jour férié).* Following are the French national holidays. Remember that traffic is especially heavy on summer vacation dates. Public offices and banks, as well as shops, are closed on holidays, although you may find an occasional bakery or small food shop open.

P

January 1	*Jour de l'An*	New Year's Day
May 1	*Fête du Travail*	Labour Day
May 8	*Fête de la Libération*	Victory Day (1945)
July 14	*Fête Nationale*	Bastille Day
August 15	*Assomption*	Assumption
November 1	*Toussaint*	All Saints' Day
November 11	*Anniversaire de l'Armistice*	Armistice Day
December 25	*Noël*	Christmas Day
Movable dates:	*Lundi de Pâques*	Easter Monday
	Ascension	Ascension
	Lundi de Pentecôte	Whit Monday

Are you open tomorrow? **Etes-vous ouvert demain?**

R

RADIO and TV *(radio; télévision)*. There are three main state-run TV channels in France. Some hotels have television in the lounges, many in the top categories have sets in the rooms.

BBC programmes can be heard on short or medium-wave radios. In summer the French radio broadcasts news and information in English.

RELIGIOUS SERVICES *(offices religieux)*. France is a predominantly Roman Catholic country. Mass *(la messe)* in English is said at St. Joseph's Roman Catholic Church, 50, av. Hoche; tel. 45.63.20.61.

There are three principal Anglo-American Protestant churches where services *(le culte)* are held in English:

The American Cathedral (Episcopal), 23, av. George-V; tel. 47.20.17.92

The American Church (interdenominational), 65, quai d'Orsay; tel. 47.05.97.99

St. Michael's Anglican Church, 5, rue d'Aguesseau; tel. 47.42.70.88

The main synagogue in Paris is at 44, rue de la Victoire; tel. 45.26.91.89

T

TAXIS *(taxi)*. You can find taxis cruising around or at the many stands all over town. You can also ring for radio-taxis, though they charge meter-fare for the trip to pick you up. For fares, see p. 103. You'll pay according to rates posted on the cab window, not just the price indicated on the meter (for example, extra charges for luggage).

TELEPHONE *(téléphone)*. Long-distance and international calls can be made from any phone box, but if you need assistance in placing the call, go to the post office or get your hotel to do it. (If you make a call from your hotel, a café or a restaurant, you are likely to be charged a little extra.)

There are two types of payphones. One takes a range of coins, the other is card operated. Telecards are sold at post offices, railway ticket counters and shops recognized by a "Télécarte" sign, and are available for 40 or 120 charge units.

For long-distance calls within France, there are no area codes (just dial the 8-digit number of the person you want to call), *except* when telephoning from Paris or the Paris region to the provinces (dial 16 and wait for the dialling tone, then dial the 8-digit number of the subscriber) and from the provinces to Paris or the Paris region (dial 16, wait for the dialling tone, then dial 1 followed by the 8-digit number). If you need the assistance of an operator, dial 36.10.

To ring abroad from France, dial 19 followed, after the change of tone, by the country's number (listed in all boxes), the area code and the subscriber's number. If direct dialling is not available to that country or if you don't know the telephone number of the subscriber, dial 19 and wait for the tone, then dial 33 followed by the code number of the country in question to reach the operator (UK 44, U.S.A. and Canada 1). If you do not know the number of the country, call the international information, 19.33.33.

It's cheaper to make long-distance trunk calls after 8 p.m.

TIME DIFFERENCES. France follows Greenwich Mean Time + 1, and in summer the clocks are put forward one hour.

Summer chart:

New York	London	**Paris**	Sydney	Auckland
6 a.m.	11 a.m.	**noon**	8 p.m.	10 p.m.

TIPPING *(pourboire)*. A 10 to 15 per cent service charge is generally included automatically in hotel and restaurant bills. Rounding off the overall bill helps round off friendships with waiters, too. It is also in order to hand the bellboys, doormen, filling station attendants, etc., a coin or two for their service.

T

Some suggestions:

Hotel porter, per bag	4–5 F
Hotel maid, per week	20–40 F
Lavatory attendant	2 F
Waiter	5–10% (optional)
Taxi driver	10–15%
Hairdresser/Barber	15% (gen. incl.)
Tour guide	10%

TOILETS *(toilettes)*. Paris is improving its public toilets, though sanitary standards are still far from perfect. Those near important Métro stops are generally modern and quite clean. Café W.C.'s are usually free, but you should order at least a coffee if you use the toilet. A saucer with small change on it means a tip is expected. If the toilet has no light-switch, the light will go on when you lock the door. The women's toilets may be marked *Dames*, the men's either *Messieurs* or *Hommes*.

Where are the toilets, please? **Où sont les toilettes, s'il vous plaît?**

TOURIST INFORMATION OFFICES *(office du tourisme)*. Paris's main Tourist Information Office is extremely efficient: 127, Champs-Elysées, 75008 Paris; tel. 47.23.61.72. They offer abundant documentation and a currency-exchange office. Other branches of the tourist office are located in major stations, airports and terminals.

For a selection of the principal weekly events in English, call 47.20.88.98.

For detailed information on Paris and surrounding *départements*, you can also contact the C.R.T.L., Loisirs en Ile-de-France, 19, rue Barbet Jouy, 75007 Paris; tel. 45.51.71.28.

French tourist offices abroad:

Australia BNP House, 12 Castlereagh Street, Sydney N.S.W. 2000; tel. (612) 231.52.44

Canada 1840 Ouest, rue Sherbrooke, Montreal, Que. H3H 1E4, P.Q.; tel. (514) 931-3855
1 Dundas Street W, Suite 2405, P.O. Box 8, Toronto, Ont. M5G 1Z3; tel. (416) 361-1605

U.K.	178, Piccadilly, London W1V 0AL; tel. (01) 493 6594
U.S.A.	645 N. Michigan Avenue, Suite 430, Chicago, IL 60611; tel. (312) 337-6301 9401 Wilshire Boulevard, Room 840, Beverly Hills, CA 90212; tel. (213) 271-6665 610 Fifth Avenue, New York, NY 10020; tel. (212) 757-1125 Post Street, Suite 601, San Francisco, CA 94108; tel. (415) 982-7272

T

TRAINS *(train).* The French National Railways (*Société des Chemins de Fer Français* or S.N.C.F.) run fast, punctual and comfortable trains. Excellent high-speed services (TGV—*train à grande vitesse*) operate on selected routes.

The main stations in Paris are Gare du Nord (for British connections), Gare de l'Est, Gare d'Austerlitz, Gare Saint-Lazare and Gare de Lyon (for links with the Riviera, Spain and Italy). Various categories of tickets are available (see p. 101). Make sure to get your ticket punched *before* getting on board, by inserting it in one of the orange machines (called a *machine à composter* or *composteur*) on the way to the platform. If it is not clipped and dated, the conductor *(contrôleur)* is entitled to fine you on the train. Tickets purchased abroad need not be punched.

W

WATER *(eau).* Tap water is safe in Paris and all over the country, except when marked *eau non potable* (unsafe for drinking). Several kinds of mineral water are sold everywhere. See also HEALTH.

a bottle of mineral water	**une bouteille d'eau minérale**
fizzy (carbonated)/still	**gazeuse/non gazeuse**

Y

YOUTH HOSTELS *(auberge de jeunesse).* For visitors between 16 and 30, a pamphlet "Youth Welcome" lists more than 20 centres, accommodation and prices. Write to the tourist office asking for this list, then reserve in advance at the hostel of your choice.

Other useful addresses are:

Fédération Unie des Auberges de Jeunesse, 6, rue Mesnil, 75116 Paris; tel. 42.61.84.03

Centre d'information et de documentation de la jeunesse, 101, quai Branly, 75015 Paris; tel. 45.66.40.20

SOME USEFUL EXPRESSIONS

yes/no	**oui/non**
please/thank you	**s'il vous plaît/merci**
excuse me	**excusez-moi**
you're welcome	**je vous en prie**
where/when/how	**où/quand/comment**
how long/how far	**combien de temps/à quelle distance**
yesterday/today/tomorrow	**hier/aujourd'hui/demain**
day/week/month/year	**jour/semaine/mois/année**
left/right	**gauche/droite**
up/down	**en haut/en bas**
good/bad	**bon/mauvais**
big/small	**grand/petit**
cheap/expensive	**bon marché/cher**
hot/cold	**chaud/froid**
old/new	**vieux/neuf**
open/closed	**ouvert/fermé**
Where are the toilets?	**Où sont les toilettes?**
Does anyone here speak English?	**Y a-t-il quelqu'un ici qui parle anglais?**
I don't understand.	**Je ne comprends pas.**
Please write it down.	**Veuillez bien me l'écrire.**
What does this mean?	**Que signifie ceci?**
Waiter/Waitress!	**S'il vous plaît!**
Help me, please.	**Aidez-moi, s'il vous plaît.**
Get a doctor—quickly!	**Un médecin, vite!**
What time is it?	**Quelle heure est-il?**
I'd like…	**J'aimerais...**
How much is that?	**C'est combien?**

DAYS OF THE WEEK

Sunday	**dimanche**	Thursday	**jeudi**
Monday	**lundi**	Friday	**vendredi**
Tuesday	**mardi**	Saturday	**samedi**
Wednesday	**mercredi**		

Index

An asterisk (*) next to a page number indicates a map reference. Page numbers in bold face refer to the main entry.

188/801 RP

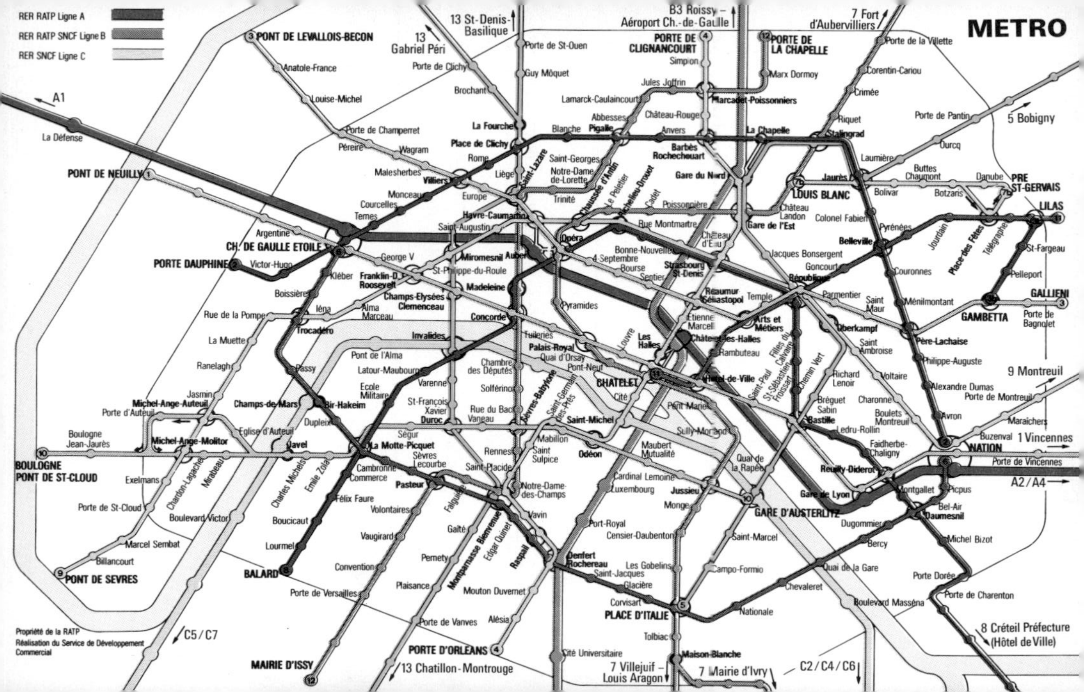
METRO
RER RATP Ligne A
RER RATP SNCF Ligne B
RER SNCF Ligne C
A1
La Défense
PONT DE NEUILLY
PONT DE LEVALLOIS-BECON
Anatole-France
Louise-Michel
13 Gabriel Péri
13 St-Denis-Basilique
B3 Roissy – Aéroport Ch.-de-Gaulle
7 Fort d'Aubervilliers
5 Bobigny
9 Montreuil
1 Vincennes
A2/A4
8 Créteil Préfecture (Hôtel de Ville)
C2/C4/C6
7 Mairie d'Ivry
7 Villejuif – Louis Aragon
13 Chatillon-Montrouge
C5/C7
Porte de St-Ouen
Guy Môquet
Porte de Clichy
Brochant
La Fourche
Place de Clichy
Porte de Champerret
Pereire
Wagram
Malesherbes
Villiers
Rome
Liège
Saint-Lazare
Monceau
Courcelles
Ternes
Europe
Havre-Caumartin
Saint-Augustin
Argentine
CH. DE GAULLE ETOILE
PORTE DAUPHINE
Victor-Hugo
Kléber
George V
Franklin-D. Roosevelt
St-Philippe-du-Roule
Miromesnil
Madeleine
Champs-Elysées Clemenceau
Concorde
Boissière
Iéna
Alma Marceau
Rue de la Pompe
Trocadéro
La Muette
Ranelagh
Passy
Pont de l'Alma
Invalides
Latour-Maubourg
Ecole Militaire
Varenne
Jasmin
Michel-Ange-Auteuil
Porte d'Auteuil
Champs-de-Mars
Bir-Hakeim
Dupleix
Eglise d'Auteuil
Michel-Ange-Molitor
Boulogne Jean-Jaurès
BOULOGNE PONT DE ST-CLOUD
Exelmans
Chardon-Lagache
Mirabeau
Javel
Charles Michels
Emile Zola
La Motte-Picquet
Cambronne
Commerce
Félix Faure
Boucicaut
Lourmel
BALARD
Porte de St-Cloud
Boulevard Victor
Marcel Sembat
Billancourt
PONT DE SEVRES
Porte de Versailles
Convention
Vaugirard
Volontaires
Pasteur
Sèvres Lecourbe
Ségur
Duroc
St-François Xavier
Rue du Bac
Vaneau
Sèvres-Babylone
Solférino
Chambre des Députés
Rennes
Saint-Placide
Falguière
Gaîté
Pernety
Plaisance
Porte de Vanves
Montparnasse Bienvenüe
Edgar Quinet
Raspail
Mouton Duvernet
Alésia
PORTE D'ORLEANS
MAIRIE D'ISSY
Notre-Dame-des-Champs
Vavin
Denfert Rochereau
Saint-Jacques
Glacière
Corvisart
PLACE D'ITALIE
Tolbiac
Maison-Blanche
Cité Universitaire
Les Gobelins
Censier-Daubenton
Port-Royal
Luxembourg
Cardinal Lemoine
Maubert Mutualité
Jussieu
Monge
Saint-Michel
Odéon
Mabillon
Saint Sulpice
Saint-Germain-des-Prés
Cité
CHATELET
Pont-Neuf
Quai d'Orsay
Palais-Royal
Tuileries
Louvre
Les Halles
Pyramides
Opéra
Auber
Quatre-Septembre
Bourse
Sentier
Bonne-Nouvelle
Rue Montmartre
Richelieu-Drouot
Chaussée d'Antin
Le Peletier
Cadet
Poissonnière
Trinité
Notre-Dame-de-Lorette
Saint-Georges
Blanche
Pigalle
Abbesses
Lamarck-Caulaincourt
Jules Joffrin
Simplon
PORTE DE CLIGNANCOURT
Marcadet-Poissonniers
Château-Rouge
Anvers
Barbès Rochechouart
Gare du Nord
La Chapelle
PORTE DE LA CHAPELLE
Marx Dormoy
Stalingrad
Riquet
Crimée
Corentin-Cariou
Porte de la Villette
Porte de Pantin
Ourcq
Laumière
Jaurès
LOUIS BLANC
Château Landon
Gare de l'Est
Colonel Fabien
Bolivar
Buttes Chaumont
Botzaris
Danube
PRE ST-GERVAIS
Place des Fêtes
Télégraphe
LILAS
Jourdain
Pyrénées
Belleville
St-Fargeau
Pelleport
GAMBETTA
GALLIENI
Porte de Bagnolet
Couronnes
Ménilmontant
Père-Lachaise
Philippe-Auguste
Alexandre Dumas
Avron
Porte de Montreuil
Maraîchers
Buzenval
NATION
Porte de Vincennes
Jacques Bonsergent
Goncourt
République
Parmentier
Saint Maur
Oberkampf
Saint Ambroise
Château d'Eau
Strasbourg St-Denis
Réaumur Sébastopol
Temple
Arts et Métiers
Etienne Marcel
Châtelet-les-Halles
Rambuteau
Filles du Calvaire
Saint-Sébastien Froissart
Chemin Vert
Saint-Paul
Hôtel-de-Ville
Pont Marie
Sully-Morland
Quai de la Rapée
Richard Lenoir
Bréguet Sabin
Bastille
Ledru-Rollin
Voltaire
Charonne
Boulets Montreuil
Faidherbe-Chaligny
Reuilly-Diderot
Gare de Lyon
GARE D'AUSTERLITZ
Saint-Marcel
Campo-Formio
Nationale
Chevaleret
Quai de la Gare
Bercy
Dugommier
Montgallet
Picpus
Bel-Air
Daumesnil
Michel Bizot
Porte Dorée
Porte de Charenton
Boulevard Masséna
Propriété de la RATP
Réalisation du Service de Développement Commercial

Selection of Paris Hotels and Restaurants

Where do you start? Choosing a hotel or restaurant in a place you're not familiar with can be daunting. To help you find your way amid the bewildering variety, we have made a few selections from the *Red Guide to France 1986* published by Michelin, the recognized authority on gastronomy and accommodation throughout Europe.

Our own Berlitz criteria have been price and position. In the hotel section, for a single room without bath, Higher-priced means above 900 F, Medium-priced 400–900 F, Lower-priced below 400 F. Similarly, for the restaurants, Higher-priced means above 300 F, Medium-priced 200–300 F, Lower-priced below 200 F. Within each price category, hotels and restaurants are grouped alphabetically according to geographical location. Special features, where applicable, plus regular closing days are given. Annual closing dates may be subject to change, so it is best to check in advance.

For hotel bookings, the French Government Tourist Office at 127, Avenue des Champs-Elysées in Paris will help, and there are reservation desks at Roissy-Charles-de-Gaulle and Orly airports. For both hotels and restaurants, advance reservations are advised.

For a wider choice of hotels and restaurants, we strongly recommend you obtain the authoritative Michelin *Red Guide to France*, which gives a comprehensive and reliable picture of the situation throughout the country.

HOTELS

HIGHER-PRICED (above 900 F)

Inter-Continental,
3 rue de Castiglione
75001*
Tel. 42.60.37.80
Tlx. 220114
Rôtisserie Rivoli. Café Tuileries. Outdoor dining.

Lotti
7 rue de Castiglione
75001
Tel. 42.60.37.34
Tlx. 240066

Ritz
15 place Vendôme
75001
Tel. 42.60.38.30
Tlx. 220262
Ritz-Espadon restaurant. Delightful indoor garden.

Westminster
13 rue de la Paix
75002
Tel. 42.61.57.46
Tlx. 680035
Le Céladon restaurant.

Sofitel Bourbon
32 rue St-Dominique
75007
Tel. 45.55.91.80
Tlx. 250019
All modern comforts. Le Dauphin restaurant.

**Postal or zip code. The final one or two figures represent the arrondissement or district.*

Bristol
112 rue du Faubourg-St-Honoré
75008
Tel. 42.66.91.45
Tlx. 280961
Indoor swimming pool. Garden.

Concorde-St-Lazare
108 rue St-Lazare
75008
Tel. 42.94.22.22
Tlx. 650442
Café Terminus.

Crillon
10 place de la Concorde
75008
Tel. 42.65.24.24
Tlx. 290204
L'Obélisque and Les Ambassadeurs restaurants. Outdoor dining.

Elysées-Marignan
12 rue de Marignan
75008
Tel. 43.59.58.61
Tlx. 660018

George V
31 av. George-V
75008
Tel. 47.23.54.00
Tlx. 650082
Les Princes restaurant. Outdoor dining.

Lancaster
7 rue de Berri
75008
Tel. 43.59.90.43
Tlx. 640991
Outdoor dining.

Plaza-Athénée
25 av. Montaigne
75008
Tel. 47.23.78.33
Tlx. 650092
Régence et Relais Plaza restaurants.

Prince de Galles
33 av. George-V
75008
Tel. 47.23.55.11
Tlx. 280627
Outdoor dining.

Royal Monceau
37 av. Hoche
75008
Tel. 45.61.98.00
Tlx. 650361
Le Jardin and Le Carpaccio restaurants. Indoor swimming pool. Outdoor dining.

Warwick
5 rue de Berri
75008
Tel. 45.63.14.11
Tlx. 642295
La Couronne restaurant.

Le Grand Hôtel
2 rue Scribe
75009
Tel. 42.68.12.13
Tlx. 220875
Le Patio and Café de la Paix restaurants.

Scribe
1 rue Scribe
75009
Tel. 47.42.03.40,
Tlx. 214653
Le Jardin des Muses restaurant.

Hilton
18 av. de Suffren
75015
Tel. 42.73.92.00
Tlx. 200955
All modern comforts. Le Toit de Paris restaurant with lovely view over Paris. Western and La Terrasse restaurants. Outdoor dining.

Montparnasse Park Hôtel
19 rue Cdt-Mouchotte
75014
Tel. 43.20.15.51
Tlx. 200135
All modern comforts. View. Outdoor dining. Montparnasse 25 and La Ruche restaurants.

Nikko
61 quai de Grenelle
75015
Tel. 45.75.62.62
Tlx. 260012
All modern comforts. View. Indoor swimming pool. Les Célébrités and Brasserie Pont Mirabeau restaurants and Benkay Japanese restaurant.

Baltimore
88 bis av. Kléber
75116
Tel. 45.53.83.33
Tlx. 611591
All modern comforts. L'Estournel restaurant.

La Pérouse
40 rue La Pérouse
75116
Tel. 45.00.83.47
Tlx. 613420
All modern comforts. Restaurant l'Astrolabe.

Concorde Lafayette
3 pl. du Gén-Koenig
75017
Tel. 47.58.12.84
Tlx. 650892
L'Etoile d'Or, L'Arc-en-Ciel restaurants and Les Saisons coffee shop. Panoramic bar on 34th floor.

Méridien
81 bd. Gouvion-St-Cyr
75017
Tel. 47.58.12.30
Tlx. 290952
All modern comforts. Le Clos de Longchamp, Café l'Arlequin, Le Yamato (Japanese) and La Maison Beaujolaise restaurants.

MEDIUM-PRICED (400–900 F)

Duminy Vendôme
3 rue du Mont-Thabor
75001
Tel. 42.60.32.80
Tlx. 213492

France et Choiseul
239 rue St-Honoré
75001
Tel. 42.61.54.60
Tlx. 680959
Outdoor dining.

Louvre-Concorde
pl. A.-Malraux
75001
Tel. 42.61.56.01
Tlx. 220412

Mayfair
3 rue Rouget-de-Lisle
75001
Tel. 42.60.38.14
Tlx. 240037
All modern comforts.

Atlantide
114 bd. Richard-Lenoir
75011
Tel. 43.38.29.29
Tlx. 216907
All modern comforts.

Holiday Inn
10 pl. de la République
75011
Tel. 43.55.44.34
Tlx. 210651
All modern comforts. Belle Epoque restaurant and Le Jardin d'Hiver coffee shop. Outdoor dining.

Lutèce
65 rue St-Louis-en-l'Ile
75004
Tel. 43.26.23.52

Abbaye St-Germain
10 rue Cassette
75006
Tel. 45.44.38.11
All modern comforts. Quiet situation. Garden.

Littré
9 rue Littré
75006
Tel. 45.44.38.68
Tlx. 203852
Quiet situation.

Lutétia
45 bd. Raspail
75006
Tel. 45.44.38.10
Tlx. 270424
Le Paris restaurant and brasserie Lutétia.

Relais Christine
3 rue Christine
75006
Tel. 43.26.71.80
Tlx. 202606
All modern comforts. Quiet situation.

Victoria Palace
6 rue Blaise-Desgoffe
75006
Tel. 45.44.38.16
Tlx. 270557

Cayré-Copatel
4 bd. Raspail
75007
Tel. 45.44.38.88
Tlx. 270577
All modern comforts.

Pont Royal
7 rue de Montalembert
75007
Tel. 45.44.38.27
Tlx. 270113
Les Antiquaires restaurant.

Résidence Elysées Maubourg
35 bd. de La-Tour-Maubourg
75007
Tel. 45.56.10.78
Tlx. 206227
All modern comforts.

St-Simon
14 rue de St-Simon
75007
Tel. 45.48.35.66
Attractively furnished.

Château-Frontenac
54 rue P.-Charron
75008
Tel. 47.23.55.85
Tlx. 660994
Pavillon Russe restaurant.

Claridge Bellman
37 rue François-1er
75008
Tel. 47.23.90.03
Tlx. 641150
All modern comforts.

Frantel-Windsor
14 rue Beaujon
75008
Tel. 45.63.04.04
Tlx. 650902
All modern comforts. Le Clovis restaurant.

Napoléon
40 av. de Friedland
75008
Tel. 47.66.02.02
Tlx. 640609
Napoléon Baumann restaurant.

Royal Malesherbes
24 bd. Malesherbes
75008
Tel. 42.65.53.30
Tlx. 660190
All modern comforts.

Brébant
32 bd. Poissonnière
75009
Tel. 47.70.25.55
Tlx. 280127
All modern comforts.

Commodore
12 bd. Haussmann
75009
Tel. 42.46.72.82
Tlx. 280601

Mercure Paris Porte de Versailles
rue Moulin
92170 Vanves
Tel. 46.42.93.22
Tlx. 202195

P.L.M. St-Jacques
17 bd. St-Jacques
75014
Tel. 45.89.89.80
Tlx. 270740
All modern comforts. Café Français and Le Patio restaurants.

Sofitel Paris
8 rue L.-Armand
75015
Tel. 45.54.95.00
Tlx. 200432
All modern comforts. Indoor swimming pool with panoramic view. Le Relais de Sèvres restaurant and La Tonnelle brasserie.

Résidence du Bois
16 rue Chalgrin
75116
Tel. 45.00.50.59
Quiet situation. Attractive furnishings. Garden.

Rond-Point de Longchamp
86 rue de Longchamp
75116
Tel. 45.05.13.63
Tlx. 620653
All modern comforts. Belles Feuilles restaurant.

Union H. Etoile
44 rue Hamelin
75116
Tel. 45.53.14.95
Tlx. 611394
All modern comforts.

Mercure
27 av. des Ternes
75017
Tel. 47.66.49.18
Tlx. 650679
All modern comforts.

Regent's Garden
6 rue P.-Demours
75017
Tel. 45.74.07.30
Tlx. 640127
Quiet situation. Attractive garden.

Splendid Etoile
1 bis av. Carnot
75017
Tel. 47.66.41.41
Tlx. 280773
All modern comforts.

Mercure Paris Montmartre
1 rue Caulaincourt
75018
Tel. 42.94.17.17
Tlx. 640605
All modern comforts.

Mercure Porte de Pantin
25 rue Scandicci
93500 Pantin
Tel. 48.46.70.66
Tlx. 230742
All modern comforts.

Terrass'Hôtel
12 rue J.-de-Maistre
75018
Tel. 46.06.72.85
Tlx. 280830
All modern comforts. Le Guerlande and l'Albaron restaurants.

LOWER-PRICED (below 400 F)

Family
35 rue Cambon
75001
Tel. 42.61.54.84

Montana Tuileries
12 rue St-Roch
75001
Tel. 42.60.35.10
Tlx. 214404
All modern comforts.

Du Piémont
22 rue de Richelieu
75001
Tel. 42.96.44.50

Richepanse
14 rue Richepanse
75001
Tel. 42.60.36.00
Tlx. 210811

Bretonnerie
22 rue Ste-Croix-de-la-Bretonnerie
75004
Tel. 48.87.77.63

Deux Iles
59 rue St.-Louis-en-l'Ile
75004
Tel. 43.26.13.35

Méridional
36 bd. Richard-Lenoir
75011
Tel. 48.05.75.00
Tlx. 211324

Angleterre
11 rue Jacob
75006
Tel. 42.60.34.72

Madison Hôtel
143 bd. St-Germain
75006
Tel. 43.29.72.50
Tlx. 201628

Odéon Hôtel
3 rue de l'Odéon
75006
Tel. 43.25.90.67
Tlx. 206731
All modern comforts.

Scandinavia
27 rue de Tournon
75006
Tel. 43.29.67.20
In beautiful rustic setting.

Bersoly's
28 rue de Lille
75007
Tel. 42.60.73.79

La Bourdonnais
111 av. de La Bourdonnais
75007
Tel. 47.05.45.42
Tlx. 201416
La Cantine des Gourmets restaurant.

Derby Hôtel
5 av. Dusquesne
75007
Tel. 47.05.12.05
Tlx. 206236

Suède
31 rue Vaneau
75007
Tel. 47.05.00.08
Tlx. 200596

Elysées Ponthieu
24 rue de Ponthieu
75008
Tel. 42.25.68.70
Tlx. 640053
All modern comforts.

Lord Byron
5 rue Chateaubriand
75008
Tel. 43.59.89.98
Tlx. 649662
Garden.

Plaza Haussmann
177 bd. Haussmann
75008
Tel. 45.63.93.83
Tlx. 643716
All modern comforts.

Rond-Point des Champs-Elysées
10 rue de Ponthieu
75008
Tel. 43.59.55.58
Tlx. 642386

Blanche Fontaine
34 rue Fontaine
75009
Tel. 45.26.72.32
Tlx. 660311
Quiet situation.

Franklin et du Brésil
19 rue Buffault
75009
Tel. 42.80.27.27
Tlx. 640988
Les Années Folles restaurant.

Paris Est
Cour d'Honneur
75010
Tel. 42.41.00.33
Tlx. 217916
All modern comforts.

Terminus Nord
12 bd. Denain
75010
Tel. 42.80.20.00
Tlx. 660615

Equinoxe
40 rue Le-Brun
75013
Tel. 43.37.56.56
Tlx. 201476
All modern comforts.

Modern Hôtel Lyon
3 rue Parrot
75012
Tel. 43.43.41.52
Tlx. 230369

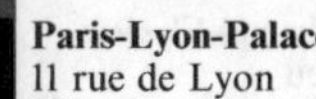

Paris-Lyon-Palace
11 rue de Lyon
75012
Tel. 43.07.29.49
Tlx. 213310

Relais de Lyon
64 rue Crozatier
75012
Tel. 43.44.22.50
Tlx. 216690
All modern comforts.

L'Aiglon
232 bd. Raspail
75014
Tel. 43.20.82.42

Waldorf
17 rue du Départ
75014
Tel. 43.20.64.79
Tlx. 201677
All modern comforts.

Wallace
89 rue Fondary
Tel. 45 78 83 30
Tlx. 205277
All modern comforts.

Fremiet
6 av. Fremiet
75016
Tel. 45.24.52.06
Tlx. 630329
Quiet situation.

Massenet
5 bis rue Massenet
75116
Tel. 45.24.43.03
Tlx. 620682

Régina de Passy
6 rue de la Tour
75116
Tel. 45.24.43.64
Tlx. 630004

Magellan
17 rue J.-B.-Dumas
75017,
Tel. 45.72.44.51
Tlx. 660728
Quiet situation.

Capucines Montmartre
5 rue A.-Bruant
75018
Tel. 42.52.89.80

Regyn's Montmartre
18 place des Abbesses
75018
Tel. 42.54.45.21

Airport

Hilton Orly
94396 Val-de-Marne
Tel. 46.87.33.88
Tlx. 250621
All modern comforts. Near airport railway station. View. Le Café du Marché and La Louisiane restaurants.

Holiday Inn
1 allée Verger
95500 Roissy-en-France
Tel. 49.88.00.22
Tlx. 695143
All modern comforts.

RESTAURANTS

HIGHER-PRICED (above 300 F)

Ritz-Espadon
15 place Vendôme
75001
Tel. 42.60.38.30
Outdoor dining.

Grand Vefour
17 rue de Beaujolais
75001
Tel. 42.96.56.27
Late 18th-century. Closed Saturday and Sunday.

Tour d'Argent (Terrail)
15 quai de Tournelle
75005
Tel. 43.54.23.31
Lovely view of Notre-Dame. In the cellars, a historical exhibit on wine. Closed Monday.

Les Ambassadeurs
10 place de la Concorde
75008
Tel. 42.65.24.24
18th-century setting. Outdoor dining.

Bristol
112 rue du Faubourg-St-Honoré
75008
Tel. 42.66.91.45

Lasserre
17 av. Franklin-D.-Roosevelt
75008
Tel. 43.59.53.43
Closed Sunday and Monday.

Laurent
41 av. Gabriel
75008
Tel. 47.23.79.18
Closed Saturday lunchtime, Sunday and public holidays.

Lucas-Carton (Senderens)
9 place de la Madeleine
75008
Tel. 42.65.22.90
Authentic early 1900s decor. Closed Saturday and Sunday.

Pavillon Elysée (Lenôtre)
10 av. des Champs-Elysées (1st floor)
75008
Tel. 42.65.85.10
Closed Saturday, Sunday and public holidays.

Régence
25 av. Montaigne
75008
Tel. 47.23.78.33
Outdoor dining.

Les Célébrités
61 quai de Grenelle
75015
Tel. 45.75.62.62
View.

Olympne
8 rue Nicolas-Charlet
75015
Tel. 47.34.86.08
Closed Mounday.

MEDIUM-PRICED (200–300 F)

Le Céladon
13 rue de la Paix
75002
Tel. 42.61.57.46
Closed Saturday and Sunday.

Carré des Feuillants (Dutournier)
14 rue fr Castiglione
75001
Tel. 42.86.82.82
Closed Saturday and Sunday.

Gérard Besson
5 rue du Coq-Héron
75001
Tel. 42.33.14.74
Closed Saturday, Sunday and public holidays.

Mercure Galant
15 rue des Petits-Champs
75001
Tel. 42.96.98.89
Closed Saturday lunchtime, Sunday and public holidays.

Quai des Ormes (4e) (Masraff)
72 quai de l'Hôtel de Ville
75004
Tel. 42.74.72.22
Closed Saturday and Sunday.

Benoît
20 rue St-Martin
75004
Tel. 42.72.25.76
Closed Saturday and Sunday.

Ambroisie (Pacaud)
65 quai de la Tournelle
75005
Tel. 46.33.18.65
Closed Sunday and Monday.

Duquesnoy
30 rue des Bernardins
75005
Tel. 43.54.21.13
Closed Saturday and Sunday.

Le Paris
45 bd. Raspail
75006
Tel. 45.44.38.10
Closed Sunday and Monday.

Relais Louis XIII
1 rue du Pont-de-Lodi
75006
Tel. 43.26.75.96
16th-century setting, with beautiful furnishings. Closed Monday lunchtime and Sunday.

Villars Palace
8 rue Descartes
75005
Tel. 43.26.39.08
Closed Saturday lunchtime.

L'Argonne
84 rue de Varenne
75007
Tel. 45.51.47.33
Closed Saturday lunchtime and Sunday.

Le Divellec
107 rue de l'Université
75007
Tel. 45.51.91.96
Closed Sunday and Monday.

La Flamberge (Albistur)
12 av. Rapp
75007
Tel. 47.05.91.37
Closed Saturday lunchtime and Sunday.

Jules Verne
2nd floor Eiffel Tower
Tel. 45.55.61.44
Tlx. 205789
View over Paris.

Chiberta
3 rue Arsène-Houssaye
75008
Tel. 45.63.77.90
Closed Saturday, Sunday and public holidays.

Fouquet's Elysées
99 av. des Champs-Elysées (1st floor)
75008
Tel. 47.23.70.60
Tlx. 648227
Closed Saturday and Sunday.

Lamazère
23 rue de Ponthieu
75008
Tel. 43.59.66.66
Closed Sunday.

Ledoyen
Carre Champs-Elysees
75008
Tel. 42.66.54.77
Closed Sunday.

La Marée
1 rue Daru
75008
Tel. 47.63.52.42
Closed Saturday and Sunday.

Taillevent
15 rue Lamennais
75008
Tel. 45.61.12.90
Closed Saturday, Sunday and public holidays.

Café de la Paix
Place de l'Opéra
75009
Tel. 47.42.97.02

Aquitaine (Mme. Massia)
54 rue de Dantzig
75015
Tel. 48.28.67.38
Closed Sunday and Monday. Outdoor dining.

Morot Gaudry
6 rue de la Cavalerie (8th floor)
75015
Tel. 45.67.06.85
View. Open-air terrace dining. Closed Saturday and Sunday.

Relais de Sèvres
8 rue L.-Armand
75015
Tel. 45.54.95.00
Closed Saturday and Sunday.

Faugeron
52 rue de Longchamp
75116
Tel. 47.04.24.53
Closed Saturday, Sunday and public holidays.

Michel Pasquet
59 rue LaFontaine
75016
Tel. 42.88.50.01
Saturday except 1 Sept.–30 Apr. and Sunday.

Toit de Passy (Jacquot)
94 av. P.-Doumer
75016
Tel. 45.24.55.37
Closed Saturday from 23 Aug.–20 Dec., Sunday and public holidays.

Vivarois (Peyrot)
192 av. V.-Hugo
75116
Tel. 45.04.04.31
Closed Saturday and Sunday.

Apicius (Vigato)
122 av. Villiers
75017
Tel. 43.80.19.66
Closed Saturday and Sunday.

Le Bernardin (Le Coze)
18 rue Troyon
75017
Tel. 43.80.40.61
Seafood specialities. Closed Sunday and Monday.

Etoile d'Or
3 place du Gén.-Koenig
75017
Tel. 47.58.12.84
Tlx. 650905

Manoir de Paris
6 rue Pierre-Demours
75017
Tel. 45.72.25.25
Closed Saturday and Sunday

Michel Rostang
20 rue Rennequin
75017
Tel. 47.63.40.77
Tlx. 649629
Closed Saturday (except evenings October to March), Sunday and public holidays.

Beauvilliers (Carlier)
52 rue Lamarck
75018
Tel. 42.54.54.42
Unusual decor. Terrace with outdoor dining. Closed Monday lunchtime and Sunday.

LOWER-PRICED (below 200 F)

Aux Petits Pères (Chez Yvonne)
8 rue N.-D.-des-Victoires
75002
Tel. 42.60.91.73
Closed Saturday and Sunday.

Chez Pauline (Génin)
5 rue Villedo
75001
Tel. 42.96.20.70
Closed Saturday evening and Sunday.

Pierre Traiteur
10 rue de Richelieu
75001
Tel. 42.96.09.17
Closed Saturday and Sunday.

Le Péché Mignon (Rousseau)
5 rue Guillaume-Bertrand
75011
Tel. 43.57.02.51
Closed Sunday and Monday.

Jacques Cagna
14 rue des Grands-Augustins
75006
Tel. 43.26.49.39
In old Parisian house. Closed Saturday and Sunday.

Bistrot de Paris
33 rue de Lille
75007
Tel. 42.61.16.83
1900s-style bistro. Closed Saturday lunchtime, Sunday and public holidays.

La Boule d'Or
13 bd de La-Tour-Maubourg
75007
Tel. 47.05.50.18
Closed Saturday lunchtime and Monday.

La Cantine des Gourmets
113 av. de La Bourdonnais
75007
Tel. 47.05.47.96
Closed Sunday and Monday.

Chez les Anges
54 bd de La-Tour-Maubourg
75007
Tel. 47.05.89.86
Closed Sunday evening, Monday.

Gildo (Bellini)
153 rue Grenelle
75007
Tel. 45.51.54.12
Italian. Closed Sunday, Monday.

Labrousse
4 rue Pierre-Leroux
75007
Tel. 43.06.99.39
Closed Sunday and Monday lunchtime.

Pantagruel (Israël)
20 rue de l'Exposition
75007
Tel. 45.51.79.96
Closed Saturday lunchtime and Sunday.

Récamier (Cantegrit)
4 rue Récamier
75007
Tel. 45.48.86.58
Closed Sunday.

Tan Dinh
60 rue Verneuil
75007
Tel. 45.44.04.84
Vietnamese. Closed Sunday.

Copenhague
142 av. des Champs-Elysées
75008
Outdoor dining. Closed Sunday and public holidays.

Les Jardins Lenôtre (ground floor)
10 av. des Champs-Elysées
75008
Tel. 42.65.85.10

Au Chateaubriant
23 rue Chabrol
75010
Tel. 48.24.58.94
Italian. Collection of paintings. Closed Sunday and Monday.

Chez Michel (Tounissoux)
10 rue de Belzunce
75010
Tel. 48.78.44.14
Closed Friday and Saturday.

Nicolas
12 rue de la Fidélité
75010
Tel. 42.46.84.74
Closed Saturday lunchtime.

Bistro 121
121 rue de Convention
75015
Tel. 45.57.52.90
Closed Sunday evening and Monday.

Pierre Vedel
19 rue Duranton
75015
Tel. 45.58.43.17
Closed Saturday and Sunday.

Guy Savoy
28 rue Duret
75116
Tel. 45.00.17.67
Closed Saturday and Sunday.

Le Petit Bedon (Ignace)
38 rue Pergolèse
75116
Tel. 45.00.23.66
Closed Saturday and Sunday.

Chez Augusta
98 rue de Tocqueville
75017
Tel. 47.63.39.97
Closed Sunday and public holidays.

Michel Comby
116 bd Périere
75017
Tel. 43.80.88.68
Closed Saturday and Sunday.

Le Petit Colombier (Fournier)
42 rue des Acacias
75017
Tel. 43.80.28.54
Closed Sunday lunchtime and Saturday.

Sormani
4 rue du Gén.-Lanrezac
75017
Tel. 43.80.13.91
Italian specialties. Closed Saturday, Sunday and public holidays.

Timgad (Laasri)
21 rue Brunel
75017
Tel. 45.74.23.70
North African specialities. Moorish decor.

Charlot 1er "Merveilles des Mers"
128 bis bd. de Clichy
75018
Tel. 45.22.47.08

Cochon d'Or
192 av. Jean-Jaurès
75019
Tel. 46.07.23.13

Relais Pyrénées (Marty)
1 rue du Jourdain
75020
Tel. 46.36.65.81
Closed Saturday.

Say BERLITZ®

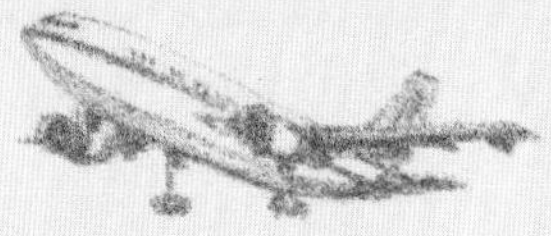

... and most people think of outstanding language schools. But Berlitz has also become the world's leading publisher of books for travellers – Travel Guides, Phrase Books, Dictionaries – plus Cassettes and Self-teaching courses.

Informative, accurate, up-to-date, Books from Berlitz are written with freshness and style. They also slip easily into pocket or purse – no need for bulky, old-fashioned volumes.

Join the millions who know how to travel. Whether for fun or business, put Berlitz in your pocket.

BERLITZ®

Leader in Books and Cassettes for Travellers

A Macmillan Company

BERLITZ® Books for travellers

TRAVEL GUIDES

They fit your pocket in both size and price. Modern, up-to-date, Berlitz gets all the information you need into 128 lively pages with colour maps and photos throughout. What to see and do, where to shop, what to eat and drink, how to save.

AFRICA	Kenya Morocco South Africa Tunisia
ASIA, MIDDLE EAST	China (256 pages) Hong Kong India (256 pages) Japan (256 pages) Nepal* Singapore Sri Lanka Thailand Egypt Jerusalem and the Holy Land Saudi Arabia
AUSTRAL-ASIA	Australia (256 pages) New Zealand
BRITISH ISLES	Channel Islands London Ireland Oxford and Stratford Scotland
BELGIUM	Brussels

*in preparation

PHRASE BOOKS

World's bestselling phrase books feature all the expressions and vocabulary you'll need, and pronunciation throughout. 192 pages, 2 colours.

Arabic	Hebrew	Russian
Chinese	Hungarian	Serbo-Croatian
Danish	Italian	Spanish (Castilian)
Dutch	Japanese	Spanish (Lat. Am.)
Finnish	Korean	Swahili
French	Norwegian	Swedish
German	Polish	Turkish
Greek	Portuguese	European Phrase Book
		European Menu Reader

FRANCE	Brittany France (256 pages) French Riviera Loire Valley Normandy Paris
GERMANY	Berlin Munich The Rhine Valley
AUSTRIA and SWITZER-LAND	Tyrol Vienna Switzerland (192 pages)
GREECE, CYPRUS & TURKEY	Athens Corfu Crete Rhodes Greek Islands of the Aegean Peloponnese Salonica and Northern Greece Cyprus Istanbul/Aegean Coast Turkey (192 pages)
ITALY and MALTA	Florence Italian Adriatic Italian Riviera Italy (256 pages) Rome Sicily Venice Malta
NETHER-LANDS and SCANDI-NAVIA	Amsterdam Copenhagen Helsinki Oslo and Bergen Stockholm
PORTUGAL	Algarve Lisbon Madeira
SPAIN	Barcelona and Costa Dorada Canary Islands Costa Blanca Costa Brava Costa del Sol and Andalusia Ibiza and Formentera Madrid Majorca and Minorca
EASTERN EUROPE	Budapest Dubrovnik and Southern Dalmatia Hungary (192 pages) Istria and Croatian Coast Moscow & Leningrad Split and Dalmatia Yugoslavia (256 pages)
NORTH AMERICA	U.S.A. (256 pages) California Florida Hawaii Miami New York Canada (256 pages) Toronto Montreal
CARIBBEAN, LATIN AMERICA	Puerto Rico Virgin Islands Bahamas Bermuda French West Indies Jamaica Southern Caribbean Mexico City Brazil (Highlights of) Rio de Janeiro
EUROPE	Business Travel Guide – Europe (368 pages) Pocket guide to Europe (480 pages) Cities of Europe (504 pages)
CRUISE GUIDES	Caribbean cruise guide (368 pages) Alaska cruise guide (168 p.) Handbook to Cruising (240 p.)

Most titles with British and U.S. destinations are available in French, German, Spanish and as many as 7 other languages.

DICTIONARIES

Bilingual with 12,500 concepts each way. Highly practical for travellers, with pronunciation shown plus menu reader, basic expressions and useful information. Over 330 pages.

Danish	Finnish	German	Norwegian	Spanish
Dutch	French	Italian	Portuguese	Swedish

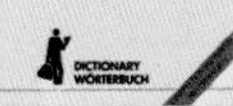

Berlitz Books, a world of information in your pocket! At all leading bookshops and airport newsstands.

BERLITZ CASSETTEPAKS

Together in one set, a phrase book and a hi-fi cassette. Here are just those expressions you need for your trip, plus a chance to improve your accent. Simply listen and repeat! Available in 24 different languages.
Each cassettepak includes a script giving tips on pronunciation and the complete text of the dual-language recording.

The most popular Berlitz cassettepaks have been completely revised and brought up to date with a 90-minute cassette and a newly revised phrase book containing a 2000 word dictionary, plus expanded colour coding and menu reader.

BERLITZ® GOES VIDEO – *FOR LANGUAGES*

Here's a brand new 90-minute video from Berlitz for learning key words and phrases for your trip. It's easy and fun. Berlitz language video combines computer graphics with live action and freeze frames. You see on your own TV screen the type of dialogue you will encounter abroad. You practice conversation by responding to questions put to you in the privacy of your own living room.

Shot on location for accuracy and realism, Berlitz gently leads you through travel situations towards language proficiency. Available from video stores and selected bookstores and Berlitz Language Centers everywhere.

To order by credit card, call 1-800-228-2028 Ext. 35.
Coming soon to the U.K.

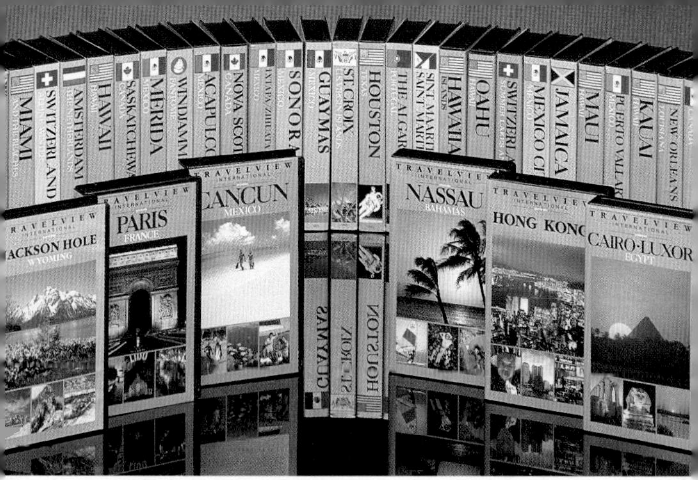

BERLITZ® GOES VIDEO – *FOR TRAVEL*

Travel Tips from Berlitz – now an invaluable part of the informative and colourful videocassette series of more than 50 popular destinations produced by Travelview International. Ideal for planning a trip or as a souvenir of your visit, Travelview videos provide 40 to 60 minutes of valuable information including a destination briefing, a Reference Guide to local hotels and tourist attractions plus practical Travel Tips from Berlitz.

Available from leading travel agencies and video stores everywhere in the U.S.A. and Canada or call 1-800-325-3108 (Texas, call (713) 975-7077; 1-800 661 9269 in Canada). Coming soon to the U.K.

5630 Beverly Hill
Houston, Texas 77057

BERLITZ®

NEW, REVISED!

FRENCH

for travellers

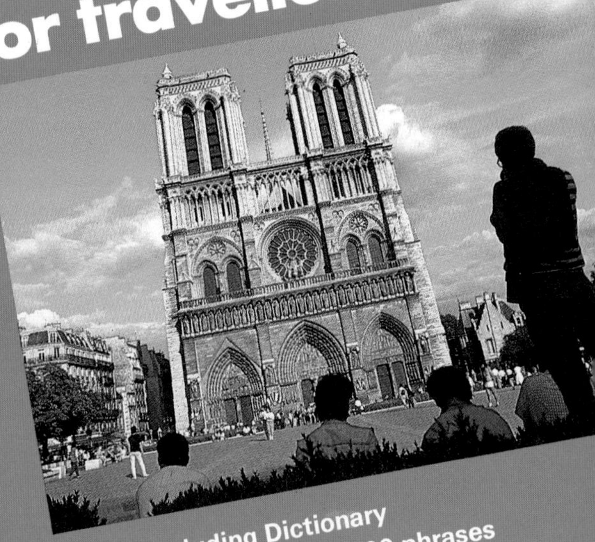

- Now including Dictionary
- 2400 useful words – 1200 phrases
- World's bestselling Phrase Book series

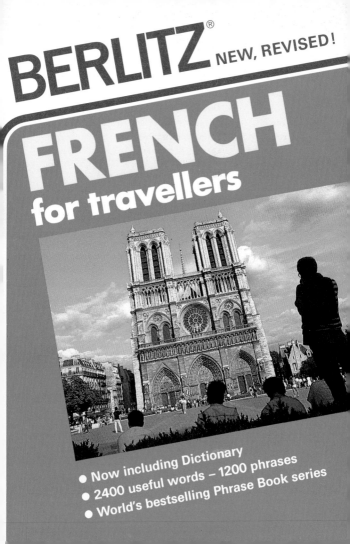

Quick reference page *Expressions indispensables*

Good morning/Good afternoon.	**Bonjour.**	bawngzhoor
Please ...	**S'il vous plaît ...**	seel voo pleh
Thank you.	**Merci.**	mehrssee
Yes/No.	**Oui/Non.**	wee/nawng
Excuse me.	**Excusez-moi.**	ehxkewzay mwah
Do you speak English?	**Parlez-vous anglais?**	pahrlay voo ahngglеh
Where can I find/ buy/hire (rent) ...?	**Où puis-je trouver/ acheter/louer ...?**	oo pweezh troovay/ ahshertay/looay
Where is ...?	**Où est ...?**	oo eh
How far?	**A quelle distance?**	ah kehl deestahngss
How long?	**Combien de temps?**	kawngbyang der tahng
How much is it?	**Combien est-ce?**	kawngbyang ehss
Waiter/Waitress, please.	**Garçon/Mademoiselle, s'il vous plaît!**	gahrsawng/mahdmwahzehl seel voo pleh
I'd like ...	**Je voudrais ...**	zher voodreh
What does this mean?	**Que veut dire ceci?**	ker vur deer serssee
I don't understand.	**Je ne comprends pas.**	zher ner kwangprahng pah
When does ... open/ close?	**A quelle heure ouvre/ferme ...?**	ah kehl urr oovr/fehrm
What time is it?	**Quelle heure est-il?**	kehl urr ehteel
Do you mind if I smoke?	**Est-ce que ça vous dérange que je fume?**	ehss ker sah voo dayrahngzh ker zher fewm
Would you mind not smoking, please.	**Pouvez-vous renoncer à fumer, s'il vous plaît.**	poovay voo rernawngssay ah fewmay seel voo pleh.
It's not permitted here.	**C'est interdit ici.**	seh angtehrdee eessee
Where are the toilets?	**Où sont les toilettes?**	oo sawng lay twahleht
Help me, please.	**Aidez-moi, s'il vous plaît.**	ehday mwah seel voo pleh
Where is the ... consulate?	**Où est le consulat ...?**	oo eh ler kawngsewlah
American	**américain**	ahmayreekang
British	**britannique**	breetahneek
Canadian	**canadien**	kahnahdyang

BERLITZ®

FRENCH

for travellers

By the staff of Berlitz Guides

How best to use this phrase book

● We suggest that you start with the **Guide to pronunciation** (pp. 6–9), then go on to **Some basic expressions** (pp. 10–15). This gives you not only a minimum vocabulary, but also helps you get used to pronouncing the language. The phonetic transcription throughout the book enables you to pronounce every word correctly.

● Consult the **Contents** pages (3–5) for the section you need. In each chapter you'll find travel facts, hints and useful information. Simple phrases are followed by a list of words applicable to the situation.

● Separate, detailed contents lists are included at the beginning of the extensive **Eating out** and **Shopping guide** sections (Menus, p. 39, Shops and services, p. 97).

● If you want to find out how to say something in French, your fastest look-up is via the **Dictionary** section (pp. 164–189). This not only gives you the word, but is also cross-referenced to its use in a phrase on a specific page.

● If you wish to learn more about constructing sentences, check the **Basic grammar** (pp. 159–163).

● Note the **colour margins** are indexed in French and English to help both listener and speaker. And, in addition, there is also an **index in French** for the use of your listener.

● Throughout the book, this symbol ☛ suggests phrases your listener can use to answer you. If you still can't understand, hand this phrase book to the French-speaker to encourage pointing to an appropriate answer. The English translation for you is just alongside the French.

Copyright © 1970, 1986 by Berlitz Guides, a division of Macmillan S.A., Avenue d'Ouchy 61, 1000 Lausanne 6, Switzerland. All rights reserved. No part of this book may be reproduced or transmitted in any form or by any means, electronic or mechanical, including photocopying, recording or by any information storage and retrieval system, without permission in writing from the publisher. Berlitz Trademark Reg. U.S. Patent Office and other countries—Marca Registrada.
Library of Congress Catalog Card No. 85-81370

Contents

Acknowledgments
We are particularly grateful to Gérard Chaillon for his help in the preparation of this book, and to Dr. T.J.A. Bennett who devised the phonetic transcription.

Guide to pronunciation

This and the following chapter are intended to make you familiar with the phonetic transcription we devised and to help you get used to the sounds of French.

As a minimum vocabulary for your trip, we've selected a number of basic words and phrases under the title "Some basic expressions" (pages 10–15).

An outline of the spelling and sounds of French

You'll find the pronunciation of the French letters and sounds explained below, as well as the symbols we're using for them in the transcriptions. Note that French has some diacritical marks—accents on letters, the cedilla—which we don't have in English.

The imitated pronunciation should be read as if it were English except for any special rules set out below. It is based on Standard British pronunciation, though we have tried to take into account General American pronunciation as well. Of course, the sounds of any two languages are never exactly the same; but if you follow carefully the indications supplied here, you'll have no difficulty in reading our transcriptions in such a way as to make yourself understood.

Consonants

Letter	Approximate pronunciation	Symbol	Example	
b, c, d, f, k, l, m, n, p, s, t, v, x, z	as in English			
ch	like **sh** in **shut**	sh	**chercher**	shehrshay

ç	like **s** in **sit**	s	**ça**	sah
g	1) before **e**, **i**, **y**, like **s** in pleasure 2) before **a**, **o**, **u**, like **g** in go	zh g	**manger** **garçon**	mahngzhay gahrsawng
gn	like **ni** in onion	ñ	**ligne**	leeñ
h	always silent		**homme**	om
j	like **s** in pleasure	zh	**jamais**	zhahmeh
qu	like **k** in **kill**	k	**qui**	kee
r	rolled in the back of the mouth, rather like gargling	r	**rouge**	roozh
w	usually like **v** in **voice**	v	**wagon**	vahgawng

Vowels

a, à or **â**	between the **a** in hat and the **a** in father	ah	**mari**	mahree
é, er, ez	like **a** in late, but a pure vowel, not a diphthong	ay	**été**	aytay
è, ê, e	like **e** in get	eh	**même**	mehm
e	sometimes (when at the end of a syllable or of a one-syllable word), like **er** in other (quite short)	er*	**je**	zher
i	like **ee** in meet	ee	**il**	eel
o	generally like **o** in hot but sometimes like **o** in wrote	o/ oa	**donner** **rose**	donnay roaz
ô	like **o** in wrote	oa	**Rhône**	roan
u	no equivalent in English. Round your lips and try to say **ee**; this should sound more or less correct	ew	**cru**	krew

* The **r** should not be pronounced when reading this transcription.

Sounds spelt with two or more letters

ai, ay	can be pronounced as **a** in late	ay	**j'ai**	zhay
aient, ais, ait, aî	like **e** in get	eh	**chaîne**	shehn
(e)au	similar to **o** in wrote	oa	**chaud**	shoa
ei	like **e** in get	eh	**peine**	pehn
eu	like **ur** in fur, but with lips rounded, not spread	ur*	**peu**	pur
oi	like **w** followed by the **a** in hat	wah	**moi**	mwah
ou	like **oo** in look	oo	**nouveau**	noovoa
ui	approximately like **wee** in between	wee	**traduire**	trahdweer

Nasal sounds

The following sounds are pronounced through the mouth and the nose at the same time.

an	something like **arn** in tarnish	ahng	**tante**	tahngt
en	generally like the previous sound	ahng	**enchanté**	ahngshahngtay
ien	sounds like **yan** in **yank**	yang	**bien**	byang
in, ain	approximately like **ang** in rang	ang	**instant**	angstahng
on	approximately like **ong** in song	awng	**maison**	mayzawng
un	approximately like **ang** in rang	ang	**brun**	brang

* The **r** should not be pronounced when reading this transcription.

Liaison

Normally, the final consonants are not pronounced in French. However, when a word ending in a consonant is followed by one beginning with a vowel, they are often run together, and the consonant is pronounced as if it began the following word. For instance, **nous** *(we)* is pronounced **noo,** but, in the sentence **"Nous avons un enfant"** *(We have a child),* the s of **nous** is pronounced, and the sentence sounds something like: **noo zahvawng zang nahngfahng.** Another example: **"comment"** is pronounced **kommahng,** but the **t** is pronounced in **"Comment allez-vous?"** *(How are you),* which sounds something like: **kommahng tahlay voo.**

Stress

Unlike English, all syllables in French have more or less the same degree of stress (loudness), although in some short and common words the vowel "e" tends to be pronounced only very weakly. For French ears, there is a slightly heavier stress on the last syllable of a word-group, but as this is a fine distinction, stress has not been indicated in the transcription of this book. Each syllable should be pronounced with equal stress.

Pronunciation of the French alphabet

A	ah	**H**	ahsh	**O**	oa	**V**	vay
B	bay	**I**	ee	**P**	pay	**W**	doobler vay
C	say	**J**	zhee	**Q**	kew	**X**	eex
D	day	**K**	kah	**R**	ehr	**Y**	ee grehk
E	er	**L**	ehl	**S**	ehss	**Z**	zehd
F	ehf	**M**	ehm	**T**	tay		
G	zhay	**N**	ehn	**U**	ew		

Some basic expressions

Yes.	**Oui.**	wee
No.	**Non.**	nawng
Please.	**S'il vous plaît.**	seel voo pleh
Thank you.	**Merci.**	mehrsee
Thank you very much.	**Merci beaucoup.**	mehrsee boakoo
You're welcome.	**De rien.**	der ryang
That's all right/ Don't mention it.	**Il n'y a pas de quoi.**	eel nee ah pah der kwah

Greetings *Salutations*

Good morning.	**Bonjour.**	bawngzhoor
Good afternoon.	**Bonjour.**	bawngzhoor
Good evening.	**Bonsoir.**	bawngsswahr
Good night.	**Bonne nuit.**	bon nwee
Good-bye.	**Au revoir.**	oa rervwahr
See you later.	**A tout à l'heure.**	ah too tah lurr
This is Mr./Mrs./ Miss ...	**Je vous présente Monsieur/Madame/ Mademoiselle ...**	zher voo prayzahngt mursyur/mahdahm/ mahdmwahzehl
How do you do? (Pleased to meet you.)	**Enchanté(e).***	ahngshahngtay
How are you?	**Comment allez-vous?**	kommahng tahlay voo
Very well, thanks. And you?	**Très bien, merci. Et vous?**	treh byang mehrsee. ay voo

* The final -e in the written form shows that the writer is a woman. Pronunciation remains the same, however, whether the speaker is a man or a woman.

How's life?	**Comment ça va?**	kommahng sah vah
Fine.	**Bien.**	byang
I beg your pardon?	**Pardon?**	pahrdawng
Excuse me. (May I get past?)	**Excusez-moi!/ Pardon!**	ehxkewzay mwah/ pahrdawng
Sorry!	**Désolé(e).**	dayzolay

Questions *Questions*

Where?	**Où?**	oo
How?	**Comment?**	kommahng
When?	**Quand?**	kahng
What?	**Quoi?**	kwah
Why?	**Pourquoi?**	poorkwah
Who?	**Qui?**	kee
Which?	**Lequel/Laquelle?**	lerkehl/lahkehl
Where is ...?	**Où est/ Où se trouve ...?**	oo eh/oo ser troov
Where are ...?	**Où sont/ Où se trouvent ...?**	oo sawng/oo ser troov
Where can I find/ get ...?	**Où puis-je trouver ...?**	oo pweezh troovay
How far?	**A quelle distance?**	ah kehl deestahngss
How long?	**Combien de temps?**	kawngbyang der tahng
How much/ How many?	**Combien?**	kawngbyang
How much does this cost?	**Combien coûte ceci?**	kawngbyang koot serssee
When does ... open/ close?	**A quelle heure ouvre/ ferme ...?**	ah kehl urr oovr/fehrm
What do you call this/that in French?	**Comment appelle-t-on ceci/cela en français?**	kommahng tahpehl tawng serssee/serlah ahng frahngsseh
What does this/that mean?	**Que veut dire ceci/ cela?**	ker vur deer serssee/ serlah

Do you speak ...? *Parlez-vous ...?*

Do you speak English?	**Parlez-vous anglais?**	pahrlay voo ahnggleh
Is there anyone here who speaks English?	**Y a-t-il quelqu'un qui parle anglais ici?**	ee ahteel kehlkang kee pahrl ahnggleh eessee
I don't speak (much) French.	**Je ne parle pas (bien) français.**	zher ner pahrl pah (byang) frahngsseh
Could you speak more slowly?	**Pourriez-vous parler plus lentement?**	pooryay voo pahrlay plew lahngtermahng
Could you repeat that?	**Pourriez-vous répéter?**	pooryay voo raypaytay
Could you spell it?	**Pourriez-vous me l'épeler?**	pooryay voo mer layperlay
Please write it down.	**Ecrivez-le, s'il vous plaît.**	aykreevay ler seel voo pleh
Can you translate this for me?	**Pouvez-vous me traduire ceci?**	poovay voo mer trahdweer serssee
Can you translate this for us?	**Pouvez-vous nous traduire ceci?**	poovay voo noo trahdweer serssee
Please point to the word/phrase/ sentence in the book.	**Montrez-moi le mot/ l'expression/la phrase dans le livre, s'il vous plaît.**	mawngtray mwah ler moa/ lehxprehssyawng/lah frahz dahng ler leevr seel voo pleh
Just a minute. I'll see if I can find it in this book.	**Un instant. Je vais voir si je la trouve dans ce livre.**	ang nangstahng. zher vay vwahr see zher lah troov dahng ser leevr
I understand.	**Je comprends.**	zher kawngprahng
I don't understand.	**Je ne comprends pas.**	zher ner kawngprahng pah
Do you understand?	**Comprenez-vous?**	kawngprernay voo

Can/May ...? *Puis-je ...?*

Can I have ...?	**Puis-je avoir ...?**	pweezh ahvwahr
Can we have ...?	**Pouvons-nous avoir ...?**	poovawng noo ahvwahr
Can you show me ...?	**Pouvez-vous m'indiquer ...?**	poovay voo mangdeekay

I can't.	**Je ne peux pas.**	zher ner pur pah
Can you tell me…?	**Pouvez-vous me dire …?**	poovay voo mer deer
Can you help me?	**Pouvez-vous m'aider?**	poovay voo mehday
Can I help you?	**Puis-je vous aider?**	pweezh voo zehday
Can you direct me to …?	**Pouvez-vous m'indiquer la direction de …?**	poovay voo mangdeekay lah deerehkssyawng der

Wanting … *Je voudrais …*

I'd like …	**Je voudrais …**	zher voodreh
We'd like …	**Nous voudrions …**	noo voodreeyawng
What do you want?	**Que désirez-vous?**	ker dayzeeray voo
Give me …	**Donnez-moi …**	donnay mwah
Give it to me.	**Donnez-le-moi.**	donnay ler mwah
Bring me …	**Apportez-moi …**	ahportay mwah
Bring it to me.	**Apportez-le-moi.**	ahportay ler mwah
Show me …	**Montrez-moi …**	mawngtray mwah
Show it to me.	**Montrez-le-moi.**	mawngtray ler mwah
I'm looking for …	**Je cherche …**	zher shehrsh
I'm hungry.	**J'ai faim.**	zhay fang
I'm thirsty.	**J'ai soif.**	zhay swahf
I'm tired.	**Je suis fatigué(e).**	zher swee fahteegay
I'm lost.	**Je me suis perdu(e).**	zher mer swee pehrdew
It's important.	**C'est important.**	seh tangportahng
It's urgent.	**C'est urgent.**	seh tewrzhahng
Hurry up!	**Dépêchez-vous.**	daypehshay voo

It is/There is … *C'est/Il y a …*

It is …	**C'est …**	seh
Is it …?	**Est-ce …?**	ehss
It isn't …	**Ce n'est pas …**	ser neh pah

Here it is.	**Le voici/La voici.**	ler vwahssee/lah vwahssee
Here they are.	**Les voici.**	lay vwahssee
There it is.	**Le voilà/La voilà.**	ler vwahlah/lah vwahlah
There they are.	**Les voilà.**	lay vwahlah
There is/There are ...	**Il y a ...**	eel ee ah
Is there/Are there ...?	**Y a-t-il ...?**	ee ahteel
There isn't/aren't ...	**Il n'y a pas ...**	eel nee ah pah
There isn't/aren't any.	**Il n'y en a pas.**	eel nee ahng nah pah

It's ... *C'est ...*

big/small	**grand/petit***	grahng/pertee
quick/slow	**rapide/lent**	rahpeed/lahng
hot/cold	**chaud/froid**	shoa/frwah
full/empty	**plein/vide**	plang/veed
easy/difficult	**facile/difficile**	fahsseel/deefeesseel
heavy/light	**lourd/léger**	loor/layzhay
open/shut	**ouvert/fermé**	oovehr/fehrmay
right/wrong	**juste/faux**	zhewst/foa
old/new	**ancien/nouveau (nouvelle)**	ahngssyang/noovoa (noovehl)
old/young	**vieux (vieille)/jeune**	vyur (vyehy)/zhurn
next/last	**prochain/dernier**	proshang/dehrnyay
beautiful/ugly	**beau (belle)/laid**	boa (behl)/leh
free (vacant)/ occupied	**libre/occupé**	leebr/okkewpay
good/bad	**bon/mauvais**	bawng/moaveh
better/worse	**meilleur/pire**	mehyurr/peer
early/late	**tôt/tard**	toa/tahr
cheap/expensive	**bon marché/cher**	bawng mahrshay/shehr
near/far	**près/loin**	preh/lwang
here/there	**ici/là**	eessee/lah

Quantities *Quantités*

a little/a lot	**un peu/beaucoup**	ang pur/boakoo
few/a few	**peu de/quelques**	pur der/kehlker
much	**beaucoup**	boakoo

* For feminine and plural forms, see grammar section page 160 (adjectives).

many	**beaucoup de**	boakoo der
more/less	**plus/moins**	plew(ss)/mwang
more than/less than	**plus que/moins que**	plewss ker/mwang ker
enough/too	**assez/trop**	ahssay/troa
some/any	**de, de la, du, des**	der der lah dew day

A few more useful words *Autres mots utiles*

at	**à**	ah
on	**sur**	sewr
in	**dans**	dahng
to	**à**	ah
after	**après**	ahpreh
before (time)	**avant**	ahvahng
before (place)	**devant**	dervahng
for	**pour**	poor
from	**de**	der
with/without	**avec/sans**	ahvehk/sahng
through	**à travers**	ah trahvehr
towards	**vers**	vehr
until	**jusqu'à**	zhewskah
during	**pendant**	pahngdahng
next to	**à côté de**	ah koatay der
near	**près de**	preh der
behind	**derrière**	dehryehr
between	**entre**	ahngtr
since	**depuis**	derpwee
above	**au-dessus (de)**	oa derssew (der)
below	**au-dessous (de)**	oa derssoo (der)
under	**sous**	soo
inside/outside	**dedans/dehors**	derdahng/deror
up/upstairs	**en haut**	ahng oa
down/downstairs	**en bas**	ahng bah
and	**et**	ay
or	**ou**	oo
not	**ne ... pas**	ner ... pah
never	**ne ... jamais**	ner ... zhahmeh
nothing	**rien**	ryang
none	**aucun, aucune**	oakang oakewn
very	**très**	treh
too (also)	**aussi**	oassee
yet	**encore**	ahngkor
soon	**bientôt**	byangtoa
now	**maintenant**	mangternahng
then	**ensuite**	ahngssweet
perhaps	**peut-être**	purtehtr

Arrival

CONTRÔLE DES PASSEPORTS
PASSPORT CONTROL

Here's my passport.	**Voici mon passeport.**	vwahssee mawng pahsspor
I'll be staying ...	**Je resterai ...**	zher rehsterray
a few days	**quelques jours**	kehlker zhoor
a week	**une semaine**	ewn sermehn
a month	**un mois**	ang mwah
I don't know yet.	**Je ne sais pas encore.**	zher ner seh pah zahngkor
I'm here on holiday.	**Je suis en vacances.**	zher swee zahng vahkahngss
I'm here on business.	**Je suis en voyage d'affaires.**	zher swee zahng vwahyahzh dahfehr
I'm just passing through.	**Je suis de passage.**	zher swee der pahssahzh

If things become difficult:

I'm sorry, I don't understand.	**Excusez-moi, je ne comprends pas.**	ehxkewzay mwah zher ner kawngprahng pah
Is there anyone here who speaks English?	**Y a-t-il quelqu'un qui parle anglais?**	ee ahteel kehlkang kee pahrl ahnggleh

DOUANE
CUSTOMS

After collecting your baggage at the airport (*l'aéroport* – lahayropor) you have a choice: follow the green arrow if you have nothing to declare. Or leave via a doorway marked with a red arrow if you have items to declare.

articles à déclarer
goods to declare

rien à déclarer
nothing to declare

The chart below shows what you can bring in duty-free (visitors from overseas are allowed greater concessions as regards duty-free cigarettes and tobacco).*

	Cigarettes	Cigars	Tobacco	Spirits (liquor)	Wine
France } Belgium }	[1]300 [2]200	or 75 or 50	or 400 gr. or 250 gr.	1½ l. 1 l.	and 5 l. and 2 l.
Switzerland	200	or 50	or 250 gr.	1 l.	and 2 l.

[1]Visitors arriving from EEC countries with non-tax-free items
[2]Visitors arriving from EEC countries with tax-free items

I've nothing to declare.	**Je n'ai rien à déclarer.**	zher nay ryang nah dayklahray
I've ...	**J'ai ...**	zhay
a carton of cigarettes	**une cartouche de cigarettes**	ewn kahrtoosh der seegahreht
a bottle of whisky	**une bouteille de whisky**	ewn bootehy der whisky
It's for my personal use.	**C'est pour mon usage personnel.**	seh poor mawng newzahzh pehrsonnehl

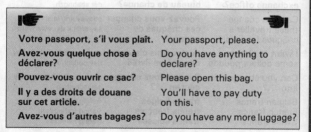

Votre passeport, s'il vous plaît.	Your passport, please.
Avez-vous quelque chose à déclarer?	Do you have anything to declare?
Pouvez-vous ouvrir ce sac?	Please open this bag.
Il y a des droits de douane sur cet article.	You'll have to pay duty on this.
Avez-vous d'autres bagages?	Do you have any more luggage?

* All allowances subject to change without notice.

Baggage—Porter *Bagages – Porteur*

These days porters are only available at airports or the railway stations of large cities. Where no porters are available you'll find luggage trolleys for the use of the passengers.

Porter!	**Porteur!**	porturr
Please take (this/ my) ...	**Prenez ..., s'il vous plaît.**	prernay ... seel voo pleh
luggage	**mes bagages**	may bahgahzh
suitcase	**ma valise**	mah vahleez
(travelling) bag	**mon sac (de voyage)**	mawng sahk (der vwahyahzh)
That's mine.	**C'est à moi.**	seh tah mwah
Take this luggage ...	**Portez ces bagages ...**	portay say bahgahzh
to the bus	**à l'arrêt du bus**	ah lahreh dew bewss
to the luggage lockers	**à la consigne automatique**	ah lah kawngseeñ oatomahteek
How much is that?	**C'est combien?**	seh kawngbyang
There's one piece missing.	**Il en manque un/une.**	eel ahng mahngk ang/ewn
Where are the luggage trolleys (carts)?	**Où sont les chariots à bagages?**	oo sawng lay shahryoa ah bahgahzh

Changing money *Change*

Where's the currency exchange office?	**Où se trouve le bureau de change?**	oo ser troov ler bewroa der shahngzh
Can you change these traveller's cheques (checks)?	**Pouvez-vous changer ces chèques de voyage?**	poovay voo shahngzhay say shehk der vwahyahzh
I want to change some dollars/pounds.	**Je voudrais changer des dollars/livres.**	zher voodreh shahngzhay day dollahr/leevr
Can you change this into ...?	**Pouvez-vous changer ceci en ...?**	poovay voo shahngszhay serssee ahng
Belgian francs	**francs belges**	frahng behlzh
French francs	**francs français**	frahng frahngsseh
Swiss francs	**francs suisses**	frahng sweess
What's the exchange rate?	**Quel est le cours du change?**	kehl eh ler koor dew shahngzh

BANK – CURRENCY, see page 129

Where is ...? *Où est ...?*

Where is the ...?	**Où est ...?**	oo eh
booking office	**le bureau de réservation**	ler bewroa der rayzehrvahssyawng
car hire	**l'agence de location de voitures**	lahzhahngss der lokahssyawng der vwahtewr
duty-free shop	**le magasin hors-taxe**	ler mahgahzang or tahks
newsstand	**le kiosque à journaux**	ler kyosk ah zhoornoa
restaurant	**le restaurant**	ler rehstoarahng
How do I get to ...?	**Comment puis-je aller à ...?**	kommahng pweezh ahlay ah
Is there a bus into town?	**Y a-t-il un bus pour aller en ville?**	ee ahteel ang bewss poor ahlay ahng veel
Where can I get a taxi?	**Où puis-je trouver un taxi?**	oo pweezh troovay ang taxi
Where can I hire a car?	**Où puis-je louer une voiture?**	oo pweezh looay ewn vwahtewr

Hotel reservation *Réservation d'hôtel*

Do you have a hotel guide?	**Avez-vous un guide des hôtels?**	ahvay voo ang geed day zoatehl
Could you reserve a room for me at a hotel/boarding house?	**Pourriez-vous me réserver une chambre dans un hôtel/une pension?**	pooryay voo mer rayzehrvay ewn shahngbr dahng zang noatehl/zewn pahngssyawng
in the centre	**dans le centre**	dahng ler sahngtr
near the railway station	**près de la gare**	preh der lah gahr
a single room	**une chambre pour une personne**	ewn shahngbr poor ewn pehrson
a double room	**une chambre pour deux personnes**	ewn shahngbr poor dur pehrson
not too expensive	**pas trop chère**	pah troa shehr
Where is the hotel/boarding house?	**Où est l'hôtel/la pension?**	oo eh loatehl/lah pahngssyawng
Do you have a street map?	**Avez-vous un plan de ville?**	ahvay voo ang plahng der veel

HOTEL/ACCOMMODATION, see page 22

Car hire (rental) *Location de voitures*

To hire a car you must produce a valid driving licence (held for at least one year) and your passport. Some firms set a minimum age at 21, other 25. Holders of major credit cards are normally exempt from deposit payments, otherwise you must pay a substantial (refundable) deposit for a car. Third-party insurance is usually automatically included.

I'd like to hire (rent) a car.	**Je voudrais louer une voiture.**	zher voodreh looay ewn vwahtewr
small car	**une petite voiture**	ewn perteet vwahtewr
medium-sized car	**une voiture moyenne**	ewn vwahtewr mwahyehn
large car	**une grande voiture**	ewn grahngd vwahtewr
automatic car	**une voiture automatique**	ewn vwahtewr oatomahteek
I'd like it for a day/ a week.	**Je l'utiliserai un jour/ une semaine.**	zher lewteeleezerray ang zhoor/ewn sermehn
Are there any week-end arrangements?	**Existe-t-il des forfaits de fin de semaine?**	ehxeest teel day forfeh der fang der sermehn
Do you have any special rates?	**Proposez-vous des tarifs spéciaux?**	propoazay voo day tahreef spayssyoa
What's the charge per day/week?	**Quel est le tarif par jour/semaine?**	kehl eh ler tahreef pahr zhoor/sermehn
Is mileage included?	**Le kilométrage est-il compris?**	ler keeloamehtrahzh ehteel kawngpree
What's the charge per kilometre?	**Quel est le tarif par kilomètre?**	kehl eh ler tahreef pahr keeloamehtr
I want to hire the car here and leave it in ...	**Je voudrais prendre la voiture ici et la rendre à ...**	zher voodreh prahngdr lah vwahtewr eessee ay lah rahngdr ah
I want full insurance.	**Je voudrais une assurance tous risques.**	zher voodreh zewn ahssewrahngss too reesk
What's the deposit?	**A combien s'élève la caution?**	ah kawngbyang saylehv lah koassyawng
I've a credit card.	**J'ai une carte de crédit.**	zhay ewn kahrt der kraydee
Here's my driving licence	**Voici mon permis de conduire.**	vwahssee mawng pehrmee der kawngdweer

CAR, see page 75

Taxi *Taxi*

Taxis are clearly marked and available in all the larger towns. If the cab is unmetered, or you have a fair distance to go, ask the fare beforehand. Special rates for night journeys, baggage etc. should be posted on an official fare chart.

Where can I get a taxi?	**Où puis-je trouver un taxi?**	oo pweezh troovay ang tahksee
Please get me a taxi.	**Appelez-moi un taxi, s'il vous plaît.**	ahperlay mwah ang tahksee seel voo pleh
What's the fare to ...?	**Quel est le tarif pour ...?**	kehl eh ler tahreef poor
How far is it to ...?	**A quelle distance se trouve ...?**	ah kehl deestahngss ser troov
Take me to ...	**Conduisez-moi ...**	kawngdweezay mwah
this address	**à cette adresse**	ah seht ahdrehss
the airport	**à l'aéroport**	ah lahayropor
the town centre	**au centre de la ville**	oa sahngtr der lah veel
the ... Hotel	**à l'hôtel ...**	ah loatehl
the railway station	**à la gare**	ah lah gahr
Turn ... at the next corner.	**Tournez ... au prochain coin de rue.**	toornay ... oa proshang kwang der rew
left/right	**à gauche/à droite**	ah goash/ah drwaht
Go straight ahead.	**Tout droit.**	too drwah
Please stop here.	**Arrêtez-vous ici, s'il vous plaît.**	ahrehtay voo eessee seel voo pleh
I'm in a hurry.	**Je suis pressé(e).**	zher swee prehssay
Could you drive more slowly?	**Pourriez-vous conduire moins vite, s'il vous plaît?**	pooryay voo kawngdweer mwang veet seel voo pleh
Could you help me carry my luggage?	**Pouvez-vous m'aider à porter mes bagages, s'il vous plaît?**	poovay voo mehday ah portay may bahgahzh seel voo pleh
Could you wait for me?	**Pourriez-vous m'attendre?**	pooryay voo mahtahngdr
I'll be back in 10 minutes.	**Je serai de retour dans 10 minutes.**	zher serray der rertoor dahng 10 meenewt

TIPPING, see inside back-cover

Hotel—Other accommodation

Early reservation and confirmation are essential in most major tourist centres during the high season. Most towns and arrival points have a tourist information office (*le syndicat d'initiative*—ler sangdeekah deeneessyahteev), and that's the place to go if you're stuck without a room.

Hôtel (oatehl)	Hotels are officially classified into five categories by the *Direction du Tourisme.* Room prices, fixed according to amenities, size and to the hotel's star rating, must be posted visibly at reception desks and behind each room door. *Hôtel garni* means that only a room and breakfast are offered. *Note: Hôtel de Ville* is not a hotel, but the town hall.
Château-Hôtel (shahtoa oatehl)	A chain of castles and mansions covering all of France and offering many tempting possibilities. All are four-star establishments.
Relais de campagne (rerleh der kahngpahñ)	A similar chain offering a wider variety of hotels in country settings, from two- to four-star establishments. Some are genuine, old-time stagecoach inns. Both *châteaux-hôtels* and *relais* are listed jointly in a free booklet published annually.
Logis de France/ Auberge rurale (lozhee der frahngss/ oabehrzh rewrahl)	Government-sponsored hotels, often on the outskirts or outside of towns. *Logis de France* are in the one- and two-star bracket; *auberges rurales* are three- or four-star establishments.
Motel (motehl)	Motels are being increasingly found near motorways (expressways) and other major roads.
Auberge (oabehrzh)	A country inn providing simple accommodation at economical boarding rates.
Pension (pahngssyawng)	Boarding house offering full or half board.
Auberge de jeunesse (oabehrzh der zhurnehss)	Youth hostel; in season, some local student associations operate dormitories to accommodate the influx of foreign students.

Checking in—Reception *A la réception*

My name is ...	**Je m'appelle ...**	zher mahpehl
I've a reservation.	**J'ai fait réserver.**	zhay feh rayzehrvay
We've reserved two rooms, a single and a double.	**Nous avons réservé deux chambres – une pour une personne, et l'autre pour deux.**	noo zahvawng rayzehrvay dur shahngbr – ewn poor ewn pehrson ay loatr poor dur
Here's the confirmation.	**Voici la confirmation.**	vwahssee lah kawngfeermahssyawng
Do you have any vacancies?	**Avez-vous des chambres disponibles?**	ahvay voo day shahngbr deesponeebl
I'd like a ... room ...	**Je voudrais une chambre ...**	zher voodreh ewn shahngbr
single	**pour une personne**	poor ewn pehrson
double	**pour deux personnes**	poor dur pehrson
with twin beds	**avec des lits jumeaux**	ahvehk day lee zhewmoa
with a double bed	**avec un grand lit**	ahvehk ang grahng lee
with a bath	**avec salle de bains**	ahvehk sahl der bang
with a shower	**avec douche**	ahvehk doosh
with a balcony	**avec balcon**	ahvehk bahlkawng
with a view	**avec vue**	ahvehk vew
We'd like a room ...	**Nous voudrions une chambre ...**	noo voodreeyawng ewn shahngbr
in the front	**qui donne sur la rue**	kee don sewr lah rew
at the back	**qui donne sur la cour**	kee don sewr lah koor
facing the sea	**qui donne sur la mer**	kee don sewr lah mehr
It must be quiet.	**Une chambre tranquille.**	ewn shahngbr trahngkeel
Is there ...?	**Y a-t-il ...?**	ee ahteel
air conditioning	**la climatisation**	lah kleemahteezahssyawng
heating	**le chauffage**	ler shoafahzh
a radio/television in the room	**un poste de radio/ télévision dans la chambre**	ang post der rahdyoa/ taylayveezyawng dahng lah shahngbr
a laundry service	**une blanchisserie**	ewn blahngsheesserree
room service	**le service d'étage**	ler sehrveess daytahzh
hot water	**l'eau chaude**	loa shoad
running water	**l'eau courante**	loa koorahngt
a private toilet	**des toilettes privées**	day twahleht preevay

CHECKING OUT, see page 31

Could you put an extra bed in the room?	**Pourriez-vous installer un autre lit dans la chambre?**	pooryay voo angstahllay ang noatr lee dahng lah shahngbr

How much? *Combien?*

What's the price ...?	**Quel est le prix ...?**	kehl eh ler pree
per night	**par nuit**	pahr nwee
per week	**par semaine**	pahr sermehn
for bed and breakfast	**avec petit déjeuner**	ahvehk pertee dayzhurnay
excluding meals	**sans les repas**	sahng lay rerpah
for full board (A.P.)	**en pension complète**	ahng pahngssyawng kawngpleht
for half board (M.A.P.)	**en demi-pension**	ahng dermee pahngssyawng
Does that include ...?	**Ce prix comprend-il ...?**	ser pree kawngprahng teel
breakfast	**le petit déjeuner**	ler pertee dayzhurnay
service	**le service**	ler sehrveess
value-added tax (VAT)*	**la T.V.A.**	lah tay-vay-ah
Is there any reduction for children?	**Y a-t-il une réduction pour les enfants?**	ee ahteel ewn raydewksyawng poor lay zahngfahng
Do you charge for the baby?	**Faut-il payer pour le bébé?**	foateel pehyay poor ler baybay
That's too expensive.	**C'est trop cher.**	seh troa shehr
Haven't you anything cheaper?	**N'avez-vous rien de meilleur marché?**	nahvay voo ryang der mehyurr mahrshay

How long? *Combien de temps?*

We'll be staying ...	**Nous resterons ...**	noo rehsterrawng
overnight only	**juste cette nuit**	zhewst seht nwee
a few days	**quelques jours**	kehlker zhoor
a week (at least)	**une semaine (au moins)**	ewn sermehn (oa mwang)
I don't know yet.	**Je ne sais pas encore.**	zher ner seh pah zahngkor

* Americans note: a type of sales tax in Belgium and France

NUMBERS, see page 147

Decision *Décision*

May I see the room?	**Puis-je voir la chambre?**	pweezh vwahr lah shahngbr
That's fine. I'll take it.	**D'accord. Je la prends.**	dahkor. zher lah prahng
No. I don't like it.	**Non, elle ne me plaît pas.**	nawng ehl ner mer pleh pah
It's too …	**Elle est trop …**	ehl eh troa
cold/hot dark/small noisy	**froide/chaude sombre/petite bruyante**	frwahd/shoad sawngbr/perteet brweeyahngt
I asked for a room with a bath.	**J'avais demandé une chambre avec salle de bains.**	zhahveh dermahngday ewn shahngbr ahvehk sahl der bang
Do you have anything …?	**Avez-vous quelque chose …?**	ahvay voo kehlker shoaz
better bigger cheaper quieter	**de mieux de plus grand de meilleur marché de plus tranquille**	der myur der plew grahng der mehyurr mahrshay der plew trahngkeel
Do you have a room with a better view?	**Auriez-vous une chambre avec une meilleure vue?**	oaryay voo ewn shahngbr ahvehk ewn mehyurr vew

Registration *Enregistrement*

Upon arrival at a hotel or boarding house you'll be asked to fill in a registration form (*une fiche*—ewn feesh).

Nom/Prénom	Name/First name
Lieu de domicile/Rue/N°	Home address/Street/Number
Nationalité/Profession	Nationality/Profession
Date/Lieu de naissance	Date/Place of birth
Venant de …/Allant à …	From …/To…
Numéro du passeport	Passport number
Lieu/Date	Place/Date
Signature	Signature

What does this mean?	**Que signifie ceci?**	ker seeñeefee serssee

Votre passeport, s'il vous plaît.	May I see your passport, please?
Voudriez-vous remplir cette fiche?	Would you mind filling in this registration form?
Signez ici, s'il vous plaît.	Please sign here.
Combien de temps resterez-vous?	How long will you be staying?

What's my room number?	**Quel est le numéro de ma chambre?**	kehl eh ler newmehroa der mah shahngbr
Will you have our luggage sent up?	**Pouvez-vous faire monter nos bagages?**	poovay voo fehr mawngtay noa bahgahzh
Where can I park my car?	**Où puis-je garer ma voiture?**	oo pweezh gahray mah vwahtewr
Does the hotel have a garage?	**L'hôtel a-t-il un garage?**	loatehl ahteel ang gahrahzh
I'd like to leave this in your safe.	**Je voudrais déposer ceci dans votre coffre-fort.**	zher voodreh daypoazay serssee dahng votr kofr for

Hotel staff *Personnel hôtelier*

hall porter	**le concierge**	ler kawngssyehrzh
maid	**la femme de chambre**	lah fahm der shahngbr
manager	**le directeur**	ler deerehkturr
page (bellboy)	**le chasseur**	ler shahssurr
porter	**le bagagiste**	ler bahgahzheest
receptionist	**le réceptionnaire**	ler rayssehpssyonnehr
switchboard operator	**la standardiste**	lah stahngdahrdeest
waiter	**le garçon**	ler gahrsawng
waitress	**la serveuse**	lah sehrvurz

Call the members of the staff *madame* (mahdahm), *mademoiselle* (mahdmwahzehl) or *monsieur* (mursyur). Address the waiter as *garçon* (gahrsawng) when calling for service.

TELLING THE TIME, see page 153

General requirements *Questions générales*

The key, please.	**La clé, s'il vous plaît.**	lah klay seel voo pleh
Will you please wake me at ...?	**Pourriez-vous me réveiller à ...?**	pooryay voo mer ray-vehyay ah
Is there a bath on this floor?	**Y a-t-il une salle de bains à cet étage?**	ee ahteel ewn sahl der bang ah seht aytahzh
What's the voltage here?	**Quel est le voltage?**	kehl eh ler voltahzh
Where's the socket (outlet) for the shaver?	**Où est la prise pour le rasoir?**	oo eh lah preez poor ler rahzwahr
Can you find me a ...?	**Pouvez-vous me procurer ...?**	poovay voo mer prokewray
babysitter	**une garde d'enfants**	ewn gahrd dahngfahng
secretary	**une secrétaire**	ewn serkraytehr
typewriter	**une machine à écrire**	ewn mahsheen ah aykreer
May I have a/an/ some ...?	**Puis-je avoir ...?**	pweezh ahvwahr
ashtray	**un cendrier**	ang sahngdryay
bath towel	**une serviette de bain**	ewn sehrvyeht der bang
extra blanket	**une couverture supplémentaire**	ewn koovehrtewr sewplay-mahngtehr
envelopes	**des enveloppes**	day zahngverlop
(more) hangers	**(d'autres) cintres**	(doatr) sangtr
hot-water bottle	**une bouillotte**	ewn booyot
ice cubes	**des glaçons**	day glahssawng
extra pillow	**encore un oreiller**	ahngkor ang norehyay
needle and thread	**une aiguille et du fil**	ewn aygweey ay dew feel
reading-lamp	**une lampe de chevet**	ewn lahngp der sherveh
soap	**du savon**	dew sahvawng
writing-paper	**du papier à lettres**	dew pahpyay ah lehtr
Where's the ...?	**Où est ...?**	oo eh
bathroom	**la salle de bains**	lah sahl der bang
dining-room	**la salle à manger**	lah sahl ah mahngzhay
emergency exit	**la sortie de secours**	lah sortee der serkoor
hairdresser's	**le salon de coiffure**	ler sahlawng der kwahfewr
lift (elevator)	**l'ascenseur**	lahssahngssurr
Where are the toilets?	**Où sont les toilettes?**	oo sawng lay twahleht

BREAKFAST, see page 38

Telephone—Post (mail) *Téléphone–Courrier*

Can you get me Paris 123-45-67?	**Passez-moi le 123-45-67 à Paris, s'il vous plaît.**	pahssay mwah ler 123-45-67 ah pahree seel voo pleh
Do you have stamps?	**Avez-vous des timbres?**	ahvay voo day tangbr
Would you please mail this for me?	**Pourriez-vous mettre ceci à la poste?**	pooryay voo mehtr ser-ssee ah lah post
Is there any mail for me?	**Y a-t-il du courrier pour moi?**	ee ahteel dew kooryay poor mwah
Are there any messages for me?	**Y a-t-il des messages pour moi?**	ee ahteel day mehssahzh poor mwah
How much are my telephone charges?	**A combien se monte ma note de téléphone?**	ah kawngbyang ser mawngt mah not der taylayfon

Difficulties *Difficultés*

The ... doesn't work.	**... ne fonctionne pas.**	ner fawngksyon pah
air conditioner	**le climatiseur**	ler kleemahteezurr
bidet	**le bidet**	ler beedeh
fan	**le ventilateur**	ler vahngteelahturr
heating	**le chauffage**	ler shoafahzh
light	**la lumière**	lah lewmyehr
radio	**la radio**	lah rahdyoa
television	**la télévision**	lah taylayveezyawng
The tap (faucet) is dripping.	**Le robinet fuit.**	ler robeeneh fwee
There's no hot water.	**Il n'y a pas d'eau chaude.**	eel nee ah pah doa shoad
The wash-basin is blocked.	**Le lavabo est bouché.**	ler lahvahboa eh booshay
The window is jammed.	**La fenêtre est coincée.**	lah fernehtr eh kwangssay
The curtains are stuck.	**Les rideaux sont coincés.**	lay reedoa sawng kwangssay
The bulb is burned out.	**L'ampoule a sauté.**	lahngpool ah soatay
My room has not been made up.	**Ma chambre n'a pas été faite.**	mah shahngbr nah pah aytay feht

POST OFFICE AND TELEPHONE, see page 132

The ... is broken.	**... est cassé(e).**	eh kahssay
blind	**le store**	ler stor
lamp	**la lampe**	lah lahngp
plug	**la fiche**	lah feesh
shutter	**le volet**	ler voleh
switch	**l'interrupteur**	langtehrewpturr
Can you get it repaired?	**Pouvez-vous le faire réparer?**	poovay voo ler fehr raypahray

Laundry – Dry cleaner's *Blanchisserie – Teinturerie*

I want these clothes ...	**Je voudrais faire ... ces vêtements.**	zher voodreh fehr ... say vehtermahng
cleaned	**nettoyer**	nehtwahyay
ironed	**repasser**	rerpahssay
pressed	**repasser à la vapeur**	rerpahssay ah lah vahpurr
washed	**laver**	lahvay
When will they be ready?	**Quand seront-ils prêts?**	kahng serrawng teel preh
I need them ...	**Il me les faut ...**	eel mer lay foa
today	**aujourd'hui**	oazhoordwee
tonight	**ce soir**	ser swahr
tomorrow	**demain**	dermang
before Friday	**avant vendredi**	ahvahng vahngdrerdee
Can you ... this?	**Pouvez-vous ... ceci?**	poovay voo ... serssee
mend	**raccommoder**	rahkommoday
patch	**rapiécer**	rahpyayssay
stitch	**recoudre**	rerkoodr
Can you sew on this button?	**Pouvez-vous coudre ce bouton?**	poovay voo koodr ser bootawng
Can you get this stain out?	**Pouvez-vous faire partir cette tache?**	poovay voo fehr pahrteer seht tahsh
Is my laundry ready?	**Mon linge est-il prêt?**	mawng langzh ehteel preh
This isn't mine.	**Ce n'est pas à moi.**	ser neh pah zah mwah
There's something missing.	**Il me manque quelque chose.**	eel mer mahngk kehlker shoaz
There's a hole in this.	**Ce vêtement a un trou.**	ser vehtermahng ah ang troo

Hairdresser—Barber *Coiffeur*

Is there a hairdresser/ beauty salon in the hotel?	**Y a-t-il un coiffeur/ salon de beauté à l'hôtel?**	ee ahteel ang kwahfurr/ salawng der boatay ah loatehl
Can I make an appointment for sometime on Thursday?	**Puis-je prendre rendez-vous pour jeudi?**	pweezh prahngdr rahngday voo poor zhurdee
I'd like it cut and shaped.	**Je voudrais une coupe et une mise en plis.**	zher voodreh ewn koop eh ewn meez ahng plee
I want a haircut, please.	**Une coupe de cheveux, s'il vous plaît.**	ewn koop der shervur seel voo pleh
bleach	**une décoloration**	ewn daykolorahssyawng
blow-dry	**un brushing**	ang "brushing"
colour rinse	**une coloration**	ewn kolorahssyawng
dye	**une teinture**	ewn tangtewr
face-pack	**un masque de beauté**	ang mahsk der boatay
manicure	**une manucure**	ewn mahnewkewr
permanent wave	**une permanente**	ewn pehrmahnahngt
setting lotion	**un fixatif**	ang feeksahteef
shampoo and set	**un shampooing et une mise en plis**	ang shahngpwang eh ewn meez ahng plee
with a fringe (bangs)	**avec une frange**	ahvehk ewn frahngzh
I'd like a shampoo for ... hair.	**Je voudrais un shampooing pour ...**	zher voodreh ang shahngpwang poor
normal/dry/ greasy (oily)	**cheveux normaux/ secs/gras**	shervur normoa/ sehk/grah
Do you have a colour chart?	**Avez-vous un nuancier?**	ahvay voo ang newahngssyay
Don't cut it too short.	**Pas trop court, s'il vous plaît.**	pah troa koor seel voo pleh
A little more off the ...	**Dégagez un peu plus ...**	daygahzhay ang pur plewss
back	**derrière**	dehryehr
neck	**la nuque**	lah newk
sides	**les côtés**	lay koatay
top	**le haut de la tête**	ler oa der lah teht
I don't want any hairspray.	**Je ne veux pas de laque.**	zher ner vur pah der lahk

DAYS OF THE WEEK, see page 151

I'd like a shave.	**Je voudrais me faire raser.**	zher voodreh mer fehr rahzay
Would you please trim my ...?	**Pourriez-vous me rafraîchir ...?**	pooryay voo mer rahfrehsheer
beard	**la barbe**	lah bahrb
moustache	**la moustache**	lah moostash
sideboards (sideburns)	**les favoris**	lay fahvorree

Checking out *Départ*

May I please have my bill?	**Puis-je avoir ma note, s'il vous plaît?**	pweezh ahvwahr mah not seel voo pleh
I'm leaving early in the morning. Please have my bill ready.	**Je pars demain de bonne heure. Veuillez préparer ma note.**	zher pahr dermang der bonurr. vuryay praypahray mah not
We'll be checking out around noon.	**Nous partirons vers midi.**	noo pahrteerawng vehr meedee
I must leave at once.	**Je dois partir immédiatement.**	zher dwah pahrteer eemaydyahtermahng
Is everything included?	**Tout est compris?**	too teh kawngpree
Can I pay by credit card?	**Puis-je payer avec une carte de crédit?**	pweezh pehyay ahvehk ewn kahrt der kraydee
You've made a mistake in this bill, I think.	**Je crois qu'il y a une erreur dans la note.**	zher krwah keel ee ah ewn ehrurr dahng lah not
Can you get us a taxi?	**Pouvez-vous nous appeler un taxi?**	poovay voo noo zahperlay ang tahksee
Would you send someone to bring down our luggage?	**Pourriez-vous faire descendre nos bagages?**	pooryay voo fehr dehssahngdr noa bahgahzh
Here's the forwarding address.	**Faites suivre mon courrier à cette adresse.**	feht sweevr mawng kooryay ah seht ahdrehss
You have my home address.	**Vous avez mon adresse habituelle.**	voo zahvay mawng nahdrehss ahbeetewehl
It's been a very enjoyable stay.	**Le séjour a été très agréable.**	ler sayzhoor ah aytay treh zahgrayahbl

TIPPING, see inside back-cover

Camping *Camping*

Camping is extremely popular and very well organized in France. The sites are classified from one to four stars depending on their amenities. In the summer season, it's important to book in advance. If you camp on private property, ask the landowner for permission. A *camping interdit* notice means the site is forbidden to campers.

Is there a camp site near here?	**Y a-t-il un camping près d'ici?**	ee ahteel ang kahngpeeng preh deessee
Can we camp here?	**Pouvons-nous camper ici?**	poovawng noo kahngpay eessee
Have you room for a tent/caravan (trailer)?	**Avez-vous de la place pour une tente/une caravane?**	ahvay voo der lah plahss poor ewn tahngt/ewn kahrahvahn
What's the charge ...?	**Quel est le tarif ...?**	kehl eh ler tahreef
per day	**par jour**	pahr zhoor
per person	**par personne**	pahr pehrson
for a car	**par voiture**	pahr vwahtewr
for a tent	**par tente**	pahr tahngt
for a caravan (trailer)	**par caravane**	pahr kahrahvahn
Is the tourist tax included?	**La taxe de séjour est-elle comprise?**	lah tahks der sayzhoor ehtehl kawngpreez
Is there/Are there (a) ...?	**Y a-t-il ...?**	ee ahteel
drinking water	**l'eau potable**	loa potahbl
electricity	**l'électricité**	laylehktreesseetay
playground	**un terrain de jeu**	ang tehrrang der zhur
restaurant	**un restaurant**	ang rehstoarahng
shopping facilities	**des commerces**	day kommehrs
swimming pool	**une piscine**	ewn peesseen
Where are the showers/toilets?	**Où sont les douches/ toilettes?**	oo sawng lay doosh/twahleht
Where can I get butane gas?	**Où puis-je trouver du butane?**	oo pweezh troovay dew bewtahn
Is there a youth hostel near here?	**Y a-t-il une auberge de jeunesse dans les environs?**	ee ahteel ewn oabehrzh der zhurnehss dahng lay zahngveerawng

CAMPING EQUIPMENT, see page 106

Eating out

There are many types of places where you can eat and drink.

Auberge (oabehrzh) An inn, often in the country; serves full meals and drink.

Bar (bahr) Bar; can be found on virtually every street corner; coffee and drinks served, sometimes light meals, too.

Bar à café (bahr ah kahfay) Coffee shop; alcoholic beverages aren't served, but light meals are (Switzerland).

Bistrot (beestroa) The nearest equivalent to an English pub or an American tavern though the atmosphere may be very different; usually only serves a few "dishes of the day", sometimes the choice is bigger.

Brasserie (brahsserree) A large café serving food and drink.

Buffet (bewfeh) A restaurant found in principal train stations; food is generally quite good.

Cabaret (kahbahreh) Features supper and show including song and dance acts, vaudeville patter and political satire.

Café (kahfay) Nowadays, a lot of cafés serve snacks and complete meals. At least you'll be able to get a crescent roll with your morning coffee. Cafés always serve beer, wine and liquor but don't ask for any fancy cocktails or highballs.

Carnotzet (kahrnotzeh) A cozy cellar restaurant found in French-speaking Switzerland; cheese specialities like *fondue* (fawngdew) and *raclette* (rahkleht) are the principal fare as well as locally produced cured, dried beef, sausages and the region's wine.

Hostellerie (ostehlerree) A handsome country restaurant furnished in a traditional style; the cuisine will usually please a gourmet's palate but the prices may be a bit steep.

Relais (de campagne) (rerleh [der kahngpahñ]) — A country inn; menus range from a snack to a banquet; food can be superb.

Restaurant (rehstoarahng) — These are rated by scores of professional and amateur gourmets. You'll encounter restaurants classified by stars, forks and knives and endorsed by everyone including travel agencies, automobile associations and gastronomic guilds. Bear in mind that any form of classification is relative.

Restoroute (rehstoaroot) — A large restaurant just off a motorway (expressway); table and/or cafeteria service is available.

Rôtisserie (roateesserree) — Originally, such restaurants specialized in grilled meats and chicken. Today the word is frequently used synonymously with *restaurant*. You can usually count on a *rôtisserie* being smart and a bit on the expensive side.

Routier (rootyay) — Roughly equivalent to a roadside diner; the food is simple but can be surprisingly good if you happen to hit upon the right place.

Salon de thé (sahlawng der tay) — (*Tea-Room,* in Switzerland). Serves ice-cream and pastries in addition to nonalcoholic beverages. Some even serve snacks and full meals.

Snack bar — The French have taken over the word though you may see *buffet-express* (bewfeh ehxprehss) which is the same type of place.

Meal times *Heures de repas*

Breakfast (*le petit déjeuner*—ler pertee dayzhurnay): from 7 to 10 a.m.

Lunch (*le déjeuner*—ler dayzhurnay) is generally served from noon until 2 p.m.

Dinner (*le dîner*—ler deenay) is usually served later than at home, seldom beginning before 8 p.m. and until around 10.

The French like to linger over a meal, so service may seem on the leisurely side.

French cuisine *Cuisine française*

In 1825, Brillat-Savarin, a well-known gastronomic writer, declared that "cookery is the oldest form of art"; this is truly illustrated by the French, who have developed their culinary skills with brio throughout the centuries. There are few countries in the world where you can spend more delightful hours just eating. For, apart from many regional specialities which do ample justice to the local produce, you can sample, among others, gastronomic *haute cuisine*—sophisticated dishes made according to time-honoured recipes—or *nouvelle cuisine,* where a more refined preparation enhances the delicate flavours of the food. But most restaurants offer homely cooking and well-balanced, tasty menus: *hors-d'œuvre,* main dish, cheese and/or dessert. As for the famous French wines—they certainly live up to their reputation!

Que prendrez-vous?	What would you like?
Je vous recommande ceci.	I recommend this.
Que boirez-vous?	What would you like to drink?
Nous n'avons pas ...	We haven't got ...
Voulez-vous ...?	Do you want ...?

Hungry? *Avez-vous faim?*

I'm hungry/I'm thirsty.	**J'ai faim/J'ai soif.**	zhay fang/zhay swahf
Can you recommend a good restaurant?	**Pouvez-vous m'indiquer un bon restaurant?**	poovay voo mangdeekay ang bawng rehstoarahng
Are there any inexpensive restaurants around here?	**Y a-t-il des restaurants bon marché dans les environs?**	ee ahteel day rehstoarahng bawng mahrshay dahng lay zahngveerawng

If you want to be sure of getting a table in well-known restaurants, it may be better to telephone in advance.

I'd like to reserve a table for 4.	**Je voudrais réserver une table pour 4 personnes.**	zher voodreh rayzehrvay ewn tahbl poor 4 pehrson
We'll come at 8.	**Nous viendrons à 8 heures.**	noo vyangdrawng ah 8 urr
Could we have a table ...?	**Pouvons-nous avoir une table ...?**	poovawng noo ahvwahr ewn tahbl
in the corner	**dans un angle**	dahng zang nahngl
by the window	**près de la fenêtre**	preh der lah fernehtr
outside	**dehors**	deror
on the terrace	**sur la terrasse**	sewr lah tehrahss
in a non-smoking area	**dans un endroit pour non-fumeurs**	dahng zang nahngdrwah poor nawng fewmurr

Asking and ordering *Demandes et commandes*

Waiter/Waitress!	**Garçon/ Mademoiselle!**	gahrsawng/ mahdmwahzehl
I'd like something to eat/drink.	**Je voudrais manger/ boire quelque chose.**	zher voodreh mahngzhay/ bwahr kehlker shoaz
May I have the menu, please?	**Puis-je avoir la carte?**	pweezh ahvwahr lah kahrt
Do you have a set menu/local dishes?	**Avez-vous un menu/ des spécialités locales?**	ahvay voo ang mernew/ day spayssyahleetay lokahl
What do you recommend?	**Que me recomman-dez-vous?**	ker mer rerkommahngday voo
I'd like ...	**Je voudrais ...**	zher voodreh
Could we have a/ an ..., please?	**Pourrions-nous avoir ...?**	pooryawng noo ahvwahr
ashtray	**un cendrier**	ang sahngdryay
cup	**une tasse**	ewn tahss
fork	**une fourchette**	ewn foorsheht
glass	**un verre**	ang vehr
knife	**un couteau**	ang kootoa
napkin (serviette)	**une serviette**	ewn sehrvyeht
plate	**une assiette**	ewn ahssyeht
spoon	**une cuillère**	ewn kweeyehr
May I have some ...?	**Pourrais-je avoir ...?**	poorehzh ahvwahr
bread	**du pain**	dew pang
butter	**du beurre**	dew burr

lemon	**du citron**	dew seetrawng
mustard	**de la moutarde**	der lah mootahrd
oil	**de l'huile**	der lweel
pepper	**du poivre**	dew pwahvr
salt	**du sel**	dew sehl
seasoning	**des condiments**	day kawngdeemahng
sugar	**du sucre**	dew sewkr
vinegar	**du vinaigre**	dew veenehgr

Some useful expressions for dieters and special requirements:

I have to live on a diet.	**Je suis au régime.**	zher swee oa rayzheem
I mustn't eat food containing …	**Je dois éviter les plats contenant …**	zher dwah ayveetay lay plah kawngternahng
flour/fat	**de la farine/du gras**	der lah fahreen/dew grah
salt/sugar	**du sel/du sucre**	dew sehl/dew sewkr
Do you have … for diabetics?	**Avez-vous … pour diabétiques?**	ahvay voo … poor dyahbayteek
cakes	**des gâteaux**	day gahtoa
fruit juice	**du jus de fruits**	dew zhew der frwee
special menu	**un menu spécial**	ang mernew spayssyahl
Do you have vegetarian dishes?	**Avez-vous des plats végétariens?**	ahvay voo day plah vayzhaytahryang
Could I have … instead of the dessert?	**Pourrais-je avoir … à la place du dessert?**	poorehzh avwahr … ah lah plahss dew dehssehr
Can I have an artificial sweetener?	**Puis-je avoir de l'édulcorant?**	pweezh avwahr der laydewlkorahng

And …

I'd like some more.	**J'en voudrais encore.**	zhahng voodreh ahngkor
Can I have more …, please.	**Puis-je avoir encore un peu de …**	pweezh avwahr ahngkor ang pur der
Just a small portion.	**Juste une petite portion.**	zhewst ewn perteet porsyawng
Nothing more, thanks.	**Je suis servi(e), merci.**	zher swee sehrvee mehrssee
Where are the toilets?	**Où sont les toilettes?**	oo sawng lay twahleht

Breakfast *Petit déjeuner*

The French breakfast consists of coffee, rolls (*petits pains*—pertee pang), *croissants* (krwahssahng—flaky pastry in the form of a crescent) and jam, seldom marmalade. Most of the larger hotels, however, are now used to providing an English or American breakfast.

I'd like breakfast, please.	**Je voudrais prendre mon petit déjeuner.**	zher voodreh prahngdr mawng pertee dayzhurnay
I'll have a/an/ some ...	**Je prendrai ...**	zher prahngdray
bacon and eggs	**des œufs au bacon**	day zur oa baykon
boiled egg	**un œuf à la coque**	ang nurf ah lah kok
soft/hard	**mollet/dur**	molleh/dewr
cereal	**des céréales**	day sayrayahl
eggs	**des œufs**	day zur
fried eggs	**des œufs au plat**	day zur oa plah
scrambled eggs	**des œufs brouillés**	day zur brooyay
fruit juice	**un jus de fruits**	ang zhew der frwee
grapefruit	**pamplemousse**	pahngplermooss
orange	**orange**	orahngzh
ham and eggs	**des œufs au jambon**	day zur oa zhahngbawng
jam	**de la confiture**	der lah kawngfeetewr
marmalade	**de la marmelade**	der lah mahrmerlahd
toast	**du pain grillé**	dew pang greeyay
yoghurt	**un yaourt/yoghourt**	ang yahoort/yogoort
May I have some ...?	**Pourrais-je avoir ...?**	poorehzh ahvwahr
bread	**du pain**	dew pang
butter	**du beurre**	dew burr
(hot) chocolate	**un chocolat (chaud)**	ang shokolah (shoa)
coffee	**un café**	ang kahfay
caffein-free	**décaféiné**	daykahfayeenay
black/with milk	**noir/au lait**	nwahr/oa leh
honey	**du miel**	dew myehl
milk	**du lait**	dew leh
cold/hot	**froid/chaud**	frwah/shoa
pepper	**du poivre**	dew pwahvr
rolls	**des petits pains**	day pertee pang
salt	**du sel**	dew sehl
tea	**du thé**	dew tay
with milk	**au lait**	oa leh
with lemon	**au citron**	oa seetrawng
(hot) water	**de l'eau (chaude)**	der loa (shoad)

What's on the menu? *Qu'y a-t-il au menu?*

Most restaurants display a menu *(la carte)* outside. Besides ordering à la carte, you can order a fixed-price menu *(le menu).* Cheaper meals often run to three courses, with or without wine, but service is always included. More expensive menus stretch to four or even five courses, but hardly ever include wine. Words like *maison* or *du chef* next to a dish listed on the menu are clues that the dish is a speciality of the restaurant.

Under the headings below you'll find alphabetical lists of dishes that might be offered on a French menu with their English equivalent. You can simply show the book to the waiter. If you want some fruit, for instance, let *him* point to what's available on the appropriate list. Use pages 36 and 37 for ordering in general.

	page	
Starters (Appetizers)	41	**Hors-d'œuvre**
Salads	42	**Salades**
Omelets	42	**Omelettes**
Soups	43	**Potages et soupes**
Fish and seafood	44	**Poissons et fruits de mer**
Meat	46	**Viandes**
Game and poultry	48	**Gibier et volailles**
Vegetables	49	**Légumes**
Potatoes, rice, noodles	51	**Pommes de terre, riz, pâtes**
Sauces	51	**Sauces**
Cheese	53	**Fromages**
Fruit	54	**Fruits**
Dessert	55	**Desserts**
Drinks	56	**Boissons**
Wine	57	**Vins**
Nonalcoholic drinks	60	**Boissons sans alcool**
Snacks—Picnic	63	**Casse-croûte – Pique-nique**

Reading the menu *Pour lire la carte*

Menu à prix fixe	Set menu
Plat du jour	Dish of the day
Boisson comprise	Drink included
Le chef vous propose ...	The chef proposes ...
Spécialités locales	Local specialities
Garniture au choix	Choice of vegetable accompaniment
Toutes nos viandes sont servies avec une garniture	All our meat dishes are accompanied by vegetables
Supplément pour changement de garniture	Extra charge for alternative vegetable accompaniment
Sur commande	Made to order
Supplément/En sus	Extra charge
En saison	In season
Selon arrivage	When available
Attente: 15 min	Waiting time: 15 minutes
Pour deux personnes	For two

boissons	bwahssawng	drinks
crustacés	krewstahssay	shellfish
desserts	dehssehr	desserts
entrées	ahngtray	first course
fromages	fromahzh	cheese
fruits	frwee	fruit
fruits de mer	frwee der mehr	seafood
gibier	zheebyay	game
glaces	glahss	ice-cream
grillades	greeyahd	grilled meat
légumes	laygewm	vegetables
pâtes	paht	pasta
pâtisseries	pahteesserree	pastries
poissons	pwahssahng	fish
potages	potahzh	soups
riz	ree	rice
salades	sahlahd	salads
viandes	vyahngd	meat
vins	vang	wine
volailles	volahy	poultry

Starters (Appetizers) *Hors-d'œuvre*

I'd like an appetizer.	**Je voudrais un hors-d'œuvre.**	zher voodreh ang ordurvr
What do you recommend?	**Que nous/me recommandez-vous?**	ker noo/mer rerkommahng-day voo
assiette anglaise	ahssyeht ahngglehz	assorted cold cuts
assiette de charcuterie	ahssyeht der shahrkewterree	assorted pork products
cervelas	sehrverlah	type of sausage
crudités	krewdeetay	mixed raw vegetable salad
hors-d'œuvre variés	ordurvr vahryay	assorted appetizers
jambon (de Bayonne)	zhahngbawng (der bahyon)	(Bayonne) ham
jambonneau	zhahngbonnoa	cured pig's knuckle
jus de tomate	zhew der tomaht	tomato juice
mortadelle	mortahdehl	Bologna sausage
œufs à la diable	ur ah lah dyahbl	devilled eggs
olives	oleev	olives
farcies/noires/ vertes	fahrsee/nwahr/ vehrt	stuffed/black/ green
saucisson	soasseessawng	cold sausage
viande séchée	vyahngd sayshay	cured dried beef

andouille(tte) (ahngdooy [eht]) — seasoned, aromatic sausage made from tripe, served grilled or fried

bouchée à la reine (booshay ah lah rehn) — pastry shell usually filled with creamed sweetbreads and mushrooms

crépinette (kraypeeneht) — small, flat sausage, highly seasoned

pâté (pahtay) — an exquisite liver purée which may be blended with other meat like a *pâté de campagne; pâté de fois gras* indicates a fine paste of duck or goose liver, often with truffles *(truffé)*; *pâté en croûte* would be enveloped in a pastry crust.

quenelles (kernehl) — light dumplings made of fish, fowl or meat, served with a velvety sauce. The best known are *quenelles de brochet,* made of pike.

quiche (keesh) — a flan or open-faced tart with a rich, creamy filling of cheese, vegetables, meat or sea-food; *quiche lorraine* (keesh lorehn), the best known of the *quiches*, is garnished with bacon.

rillettes de porc (reeyeht der por)	minced pork, cooked in its own fat and served chilled in earthenware pots
soufflé (sooflay)	a puffy, brown dish made of egg whites delicately flavoured with cheese, vegetables or seafood
terrine (tehreen)	the same as a *pâté* but sliced and served from its *terrine* (traditionally an earthenware pot). It may resemble a perfectly flavoured meat loaf and be made of any meat including game or fowl.

Salads *Salades*

A green or mixed salad is usually eaten after the main course—never with it. Other salads may be very well ordered as a first course.

What salads do you have?	**Quelles salades servez-vous?**	kehl sahlahd sehrvay voo
salade mêlée	sahlahd mehlay	mixed salad
salade de museau de bœuf	sahlahd der mewzoa der berf	marinated brawn (beef headcheese)
salade russe	sahlahd rewss	diced vegetable salad
salade de thon	sahlahd der tawng	tunny (tuna) salad
salade verte	sahlahd vehrt	green salad

salade niçoise (sahlahd neeswahz)	a Riviera combination salad which includes tuna, anchovies, olives and vegetables.

Omelets *Omelettes*

A classic French *omelette* isn't merely scrambled eggs but is shaped like a smooth, slightly swelling golden oval. It should be tender and creamy inside and served either plain or flavoured with one or more ingredients:

omelette (nature)	omerleht (nahtewr)	(plain) omelet
aux champignons	oa shahngpeeñawng	mushroom
aux fines herbes	oa feen zehrb	herb
au fromage	oa fromahzh	cheese
au jambon	oa zhahngbawng	ham

Soups *Potages et soupes*

You may see one of any number of words for a type of soup on the menu, some of which may be main-course fare.

aïgo bouïdo	aheegoa bweedoa	garlic soup (Provençal speciality)
bisque	beesk	seafood stew (chowder)
d'écrevisses	daykrerveess	crayfish
de homard	der omahr	lobster
bouillabaisse	booyahbehss	fish and seafood stew (Marseilles speciality)
bouillon	booyawng	bouillon
de poule	der pool	chicken
consommé	kawngssommay	consommé
à l'œuf	ah lurf	with a raw egg
au porto	oa portoa	with port wine
crème	krehm	cream of ...
d'asperges	dahspehrzh	asparagus
de bolets	der boleh	boletus mushrooms
de volaille	der volahy	chicken
garbure	gahrbewr	cabbage soup, often with salt pork or preserved goose
pot-au-feu	po toa fur	stew of meat and vegetables
potage	potahzh	soup
à l'ail	ah lahy	garlic
au cresson	oa krehssawng	watercress
bonne femme	bon fahm	potato, leek and sometimes bacon
Condé	kawngday	mashed red beans
julienne	zhewlyehn	shredded vegetables
Parmentier	pahrmahngtyay	potato
soupe	soop	soup
à l'ail	ah lahy	garlic
aux choux	oa shoo	cabbage
du jour	dew zhoor	day's soup
à l'oignon	ah lonyawng	French onion soup
au pistou	oa peestoo	Provençal vegetable soup
velouté	verlootay	cream of ...
de tomates	der tomaht	tomato
de volaille	der volahy	chicken

Fish and seafood *Poissons et fruits de mer*

Don't miss the opportunity to sample some of the wide variety of fresh fish and seafood in coastal areas. Fish is most commonly baked or poached until just done, then dressed with a delicate sauce. Trout are often made *au bleu* which means they're freshly poached in a simmering bouillon.

I'd like some fish.	**Je voudrais du poisson.**	zher voodreh dew pwahssawng
What kinds of seafood do you have?	**Quel genre de fruits de mer servez-vous?**	kehl zhahngr der frwee der mehr sehrvay voo
aiglefin (aigrefin)	ehglerfang	haddock
anchois	ahngshwah	anchovies
anguille	ahnggeey	eel
bar	bahr	bass
barbue	bahrbew	brill
baudroie	boadrwah	angler
blanchaille	blahngshahy	whitebait
brochet	brosheh	pike
cabillaud	kahbeeyoa	(fresh) cod
calmars	kahlmahr	squid
carpe	kahrp	carp
carrelet	kahrerleh	plaice
crabe	krahb	crab
crevettes	krerveht	shrimp
cuisses de grenouilles	kweess der grernooy	frog's legs
daurade	doarahd	sea bream
écrevisses	aykrerveess	crayfish
éperlans	aypehrlahng	smelt
escargots	ehskahrgoa	snails
féra	fayrah	lake salmon
goujons	goozhawng	gudgeon
grondin	grawngdang	gurnet
harengs	ahrahng	herring
homard	omahr	lobster
huîtres	weetr	oysters
lamproie	lahngprwah	lamprey
langouste	lahnggoost	spiny lobster
langoustines	lahnggoosteen	Dublin bay prawns, scampi
lotte	lot	burbot
lotte de mer	lot der mehr	angler

loup	loo	sea bass
maquereau	mahkerroa	mackerel
merlan	mehrlahng	whiting
morue	morew	cod
moules	mool	mussels
omble (chevalier)	awngbl (shervahlyay)	char
palourdes	pahloord	clams
perche	pehrsh	perch
plie	plee	plaice
poulpes	poolp	octopus
rascasse	rahskahss	fish used in *bouillabaisse*
rouget	roozheh	red mullet
sardines	sahrdeen	sardines
saumon	soamawng	salmon
scampi	skahngpee	prawns
sole	sol	sole
thon	tawng	tunny (tuna)
truite	trweet	trout
turbot	tewrboa	turbot

baked	**au four**	oa foor
fried	**frit**	free
grilled	**grillé**	greeyay
marinated	**mariné**	mahreenay
poached	**poché**	poshay
sautéed	**sauté**	soatay
smoked	**fumé**	fewmay
steamed	**cuit à la vapeur**	kwee ah lah vahpurr

bourride (boorreed)	fish stew (chowder) from Marseilles
brandade de morue (brahngdahd der morew)	creamed salt cod
coquilles St-Jacques (kokeey sang zhahk)	scallops served in a creamy sauce on the half shell
homard à l'américaine (omahr ah lahmayree-kehn)	sautéed diced lobster, flamed in cognac and then simmered in wine, aromatic vegetables, herbs and tomatoes
matelote (mahterlot)	fish (especially eel) stew with wine

Meat *Viandes*

I'd like some ...	**Je voudrais ...**	zher voodreh
beef/lamb pork/veal	**du bœuf/de l'agneau** **du porc/du veau**	dew burf/der lahñoa dew por/dew voa
boulettes	booleht	meatballs
carré d'agneau	kahray dahñoa	rack of lamb
cervelle	sehrvehl	brains
charcuterie	shahrkewterree	assorted pork products
cochon de lait	koshawng der leh	suck(l)ing pig
côte	koat	rib
côtelettes	koaterleht	chops
épaule	aypoal	shoulder
escalope	ehskahlop	cutlot, scallop
foie	fwah	liver
gigot	zheegoa	leg
jambon	zhahngbawng	ham
jambonneau	zhahngbonnoa	pig's knuckle
jarret	zhahreh	knuckle
langue	lahngg	tongue
lard	lahr	bacon
médaillon	maydahyawng	a tenderloin steak (lamb, pork or veal)
pieds	pyay	trotters (feet)
ris de veau	ree der voa	veal sweetbreads
rognons	roñawng	kidneys
rosbif	rosbeef	roast beef
saucisses	soasseess	sausages
selle	sehl	saddle
steak/steack	stehk	steak (always beef)

Meat is cut differently in France than at home. Here are the names of some commonly seen cuts of beef with their approximate English equivalents:

chateaubriand	shahtoabryahng	double fillet steak (tenderloin of porterhouse steak)
contre-filet	kawngtr feeleh	loin strip steak
côte de bœuf	koat der burf	T-bone steak
entrecôte	ahngtrerkoat	rib or rib-eye steak
filet	feeleh	fillet steak
tournedos	toornerdoa	tenderloin of T-bone steak

baked	**au four**	oa foor
baked in grease-proof paper	**en chemise**	ahng shermeez
boiled	**bouilli**	booyee
braised	**braisé**	brehzay
fried	**frit**	free
grilled	**grillé**	greeyay
roast	**rôti**	roatee
sautéed	**sauté**	soatay
stewed	**à l'étouffée**	ah laytoofay
very rare	**bleu**	blur
underdone (rare)	**saignant**	sehñahng
medium	**à point**	ah pwang
well-done	**bien cuit**	byang kwee

Meat dishes *Plats de viande*

In many restaurants, meat is dressed with some sort of creamy sauce or gravy—sometimes prepared at your table. Some establishments customarily serve low-calorie *nouvelle cuisine* sauces to go with their dishes.

bœuf bourguignon (burf boorgeeñawng)	a rich beef stew with vegetables, braised in red Burgundy wine
carbon(n)ade flamande (kahrbonnahd flahmahngd)	beef slices and onions braised in beer (a Belgian speciality)
cassoulet toulousain (kahssooleh tooloozang)	a casserole of white beans, mutton or salt pork, sausages and preserved goose
choucroute garnie (shookroot gahrnee)	a mound of sauerkraut served with sausages and cured pork
ragoût (rahgoo)	a meat stew, generally served in a delicate gravy with vegetables; *ragoût* will be followed by words like *de bœuf* which will tell you it's a beef stew
tripes à la mode de Caen (treep ah lah mod der kahng)	tripe baked with calf's trotters (calf's feet), vegetables, apple brandy or cider

Game and poultry *Gibier et volailles*

Chicken, duck and turkey can be found at any time of the year on a French menu. But the hunting season is a unique period in which to sample wild boar, venison or pheasant. Some game is roasted and braised with fruits and vegetables while other game is jugged and stewed. *Civet*—as in *civet de lièvre*—will tell you that the preparation has been jugged. *Terrines, pâtés* and *galantines* are often made of game or fowl. We've also listed below some other seasonal delicacies.

I'd like some game **Je voudrais du gibier.** zher voodreh dew zheebyay

alouette	ahlooeht	lark
bécasse	baykahss	woodcock
bécassine	baykahsseen	snipe
cabri	kahbree	kid goat
caille	kahy	quail
canard (sauvage)	kahnahr (soavahzh)	(wild) duck
caneton	kahnertawng	duckling
cerf	sehr	venison (red deer)
chapon	shahpawng	capon
chevreuil	shervrury	venison (roe deer)
coq de bruyère	kok der brweeyehr	woodgrouse
dinde	dangd	turkey
dindonneau	dangdonnoa	young turkey (cock)
faisan	fehzahng	pheasant
grive	greev	thrush
lapin	lahpang	rabbit
lièvre	lyehvr	wild hare
marcassin	mahrkahssang	young wild boar
oie	wah	goose
ortolan	ortolahng	ortolan bunting
perdreau	pehrdroa	young partridge
perdrix	pehrdree	partridge
pigeon	peezhawng	pigeon
pigeonneau	peezhonnoa	squab
pintade	pangtahd	guinea fowl
pintadeau	pangtahdoa	young guinea cock
poularde	poolahrd	fattened pullet
poule	pool	stewing fowl
poulet	pooleh	chicken
poussin	poossang	spring chicken
sanglier	sahngglyay	wild boar

sarcelle	sahrsehl	teal
suprême de volaille	sewprehm der volahy	chicken breast
volaille	volahy	fowl

canard (or **caneton**) **à l'orange** (kahnahr [kahnertawng] ah lorahngzh) — the best known of the French duck recipes; it's braised with oranges and orange liqueur

coq au vin (kok oa vang) — chicken stewed in red wine. Sometimes the menu will tell exactly what kind of wine was used, for instance, *coq au Chambertin*.

poule au pot (pool oa poa) — stewed chicken with vegetables

Vegetables *Légumes*

artichaut	ahrteeshoa	artichoke
asperges	ahspehrzh	asparagus
aubergines	oabehrzheen	aubergines (eggplant)
betterave	behterrahv	beet(root)
bolets	boleh	boletus mushrooms
cardon	kahrdawng	cardoon
carottes	kahrot	carrots
céleri (-rave)	sehlerree (rahv)	celery root
cèpes	sehp	flap mushrooms
champignons (de Paris)	shahngpeeñawng (der pahree)	mushrooms
chicorée	sheekoray	endive (Am. chicory)
chou (rouge)	shoo (roozh)	(red) cabbage
choucroute	shookroot	sauerkraut
chou-fleur	shoo flurr	cauliflower
choux de Bruxelles	shoo der brewssehl	Brussels sprouts
concombre	kawngkawngbr	cucumber
cornichons	korneeshawng	gherkins (pickles)
courgette	koorzheht	courgette (zucchini)
cresson	krehssawng	watercress
endives	ahngdeev	chicory (Am. endive)
épinards	aypeenahr	spinach
fenouil	fernooy	fennel
fèves	fehv	broad beans
flageolets	flahzholeh	small kidney beans
haricots blancs	ahreekoa blahng	haricot beans, white kidney beans
haricots verts	ahreekoa vehr	French (green) beans

laitue	lehtew	lettuce
lentilles	lahngteey	lentils
maïs	maheess	sweet corn (corn)
morilles	moreey	morels
navets	nahveh	turnips
oignons	oñawng	onions
petits pois	pertee pwah	peas
poireaux	pwahroa	leeks
pois mange-tout	pwah mahngzh too	string-peas
poivrons	pwahvrawng	sweet peppers
pommes (de terre)	pom (der tehr)	potatoes
potiron	poteerawng	pumpkin
radis	rahdee	radishes
raifort	rayfor	horseradish
tomates	tomaht	tomatoes
truffes	trewf	truffles

One popular vegetable dish comes from Provence:

ratatouille (rahtahtooy) a casserole of stewed eggplant, onions, green peppers and vegetable marrow (zucchini)

Spices and herbs *Epices et fines herbes*

ail	ahy	garlic
aneth	ahneht	dill
anis	ahneess	aniseed
basilic	bahzeeleek	basil
cannelle	kahnehl	cinnamon
câpres	kahpr	capers
cerfeuil	sehrfery	chervil
ciboulette	seebooleht	chives
clous de girofle	kloo der zheerofl	clove
cumin	kewmang	caraway
échalote	ayshahlot	shallot
estragon	ehstrahgawng	tarragon
fines herbes	feen zehrb	mixture of herbs
gingembre	zhangzhahngbr	ginger
laurier	loryay	bay leaf
marjolaine	mahrzholehn	marjoram
menthe	mahngt	mint
moutarde	mootahrd	mustard
noix (de) muscade	nwah (der) mewskahd	nutmeg
origan	oreegahng	oregano
persil	pehrsee	parsley
piment	peemahng	pimiento

poivre	pwahvr	pepper
romarin	roamahrang	rosemary
safran	sahfrahng	saffron
sauge	soazh	sage
thym	tang	thyme

Potatoes, rice and noodles *Pommes de terre, riz et pâtes*

pâtes	paht	pasta
nouilles	nooy	noodles
pommes (de terre)	pom (der tehr)	potatoes
allumettes	ahlewmeht	matchsticks
chips	"chips"	crisps (Am. potato chips)
dauphine	doafeen	mashed in butter and egg-yolks, mixed in seasoned flour and deep-fried
duchesse	dewshehss	mashed with butter and egg-yolks
en robe des champs	ahng rob day shahng	in their jackets
frites	freet	chips (french fries)
mousseline	moosserleen	mashed
nature	natewr	boiled, steamed
nouvelles	noovehl	new
vapeur	vahpurr	steamed, boiled
riz	ree	rice
pilaf	peelahf	rice boiled in a bouillon with onions

Sauces and preparations *Sauces et préparations*

What would French cuisine be without its infinite variety of sauces, dressings and gravies? Some of them are creamy and velvety with the delicate taste of herbs, wine and other flavourings. Others are tangy and spicy. Below are a few common names of sauces and garnishes with a hint as to what they're made of.

aïoli	garlic mayonnaise
américaine	white wine, brandy, garlic, shallots, tomatoes, shrimp or lobster flavouring
béarnaise	a creamy sauce flavoured with vinegar, egg yolks, white wine, shallots, tarragon

béchamel	white sauce
beurre blanc	butter, shallots, vinegar, white wine
beurre noir	browned butter, vinegar and/or lemon juice
bigarade	with oranges
bordelaise	boletus mushrooms, red wine, shallots, beef marrow
bourguignonne	red wine, herbs
café de Paris	a butter flavoured with cognac, herbs
chasseur	wine, mushrooms, onions, shallots, herbs
chaud-froid	dressing containing gelatine
diable	hot-pepper sauce
duxelles	with mushrooms
financière	Madeira wine, truffles, olives, mushrooms
fines herbes	with herbs
florentine	with spinach
forestière	with mushrooms
hollandaise	egg yolks, butter, vinegar
indienne	curry sauce
lyonnaise	with onions
madère	with Madeira wine
maître d'hôtel	butter, parsley, lemon juice
marchand de vin	red wine, shallots
marinière	white wine, mussel broth thickened with egg yolks
meunière	brown butter, parsley, lemon juice
Mornay	cheese sauce
mousseline	mayonnaise with cream
moutarde	mustard sauce
normande	mushrooms, eggs and cream
Parmentier	with potatoes
Périgueux	with a goose—or duck—liver purée and truffles
poivrade	pepper sauce
porto	with port wine
provençale	onions, tomatoes, garlic
rémoulade	sauce flavoured with mustard and herbs
Soubise	onion-cream sauce
suprême	thickened chicken broth
tartare	mayonnaise flavoured with mustard and herbs
veloutée	thickened chicken or meat stock
verte	mayonnaise with spinach, watercress and/or herbs
vinaigrette	vinegar dressing

Cheese *Fromages*

Below are the names of just a few of the most popular cheeses of France and Switzerland.

mild	beaufort, beaumont, belle étoile, boursin, brie, cantal, comté, coulommiers, mimolette, reblochon, saint-paulin, tomme de Savoie
sharp, tangy	bleu de Bresse, camembert, livarot, fromage au marc, munster, pont-l'évêque, roquefort
goat's milk cheese	st-marcellin, valençay
Swiss cheeses	emmenthal (which we call Swiss cheese), gruyère, vacherin; Swiss cheeses are almost all mild

The following dishes in French-speaking Switzerland make a meal in themselves:

fondue (fawngdew) a hot, bubbly mixture of melted cheese, white wine, a drop of kirsch and a hint of garlic; each guest dips a bite-size piece of bread on a fork into the pot of cheese.

raclette (rahkleht) a half round of a firm cheese which is heated against a fire or grilled until the surface begins to melt; the melting cheese is then scraped off onto a warmed plate and eaten with boiled potatoes, gherkins and pickled pearl onions.

And here are some cheese snacks which are favourites among the French and Swiss:

croque-monsieur (krok mersyur)	toasted ham and cheese sandwich
croûte au fromage (kroot oa fromahzh)	hot, melted cheese served over a slice of toast, sometimes with ham and topped by a fried egg
ramequin (rahmerkang)	cheese ramekin (small cheese tart)
tarte au fromage (tahrt oa fromahzh)	cheese tart

Fruit *Fruits*

Fruit is generally served after the cheese.

Do you have fresh fruit?	**Avez-vous des fruits frais?**	ahvay voo day frwee freh
I'd like a (fresh) fruit cocktail.	**Je voudrais une salade de fruits (frais).**	zher voodreh ewn sahlahd der frwee (freh)

abricot	ahbreekoa	apricot
amandes	ahmahngd	almonds
ananas	ahnahnahss	pineapple
banane	bahnahn	banana
brugnon	brewñawng	nectarine
cassis	kahsseess	blackcurrants
cerises (noires)	serreez (nwahr)	(black) cherries
citron	seetrawng	lemon
cacahouètes	kahkahooeht	peanuts
dattes	daht	dates
figues	feeg	figs
fraises	frehz	strawberries
framboises	frahngbwahz	raspberries
fruits secs	frwee sehk	dried fruit
groseilles	grozehy	redcurrants
à maquereau	ah mahkerroa	gooseberries
mandarine	mahngdahreen	tangerine
marrons	mahrawng	chestnuts
melon	merlawng	melon
mûres	mewr	mulberries blackberries
myrtilles	meerteey	bilberries, blueberries
noisettes	nwahzeht	hazelnuts
noix	nwah	walnuts
noix de coco	nwah der kokoa	coconut
orange	orahngzh	orange
pamplemousse	pahngplermooss	grapefruit
pastèque	pahstehk	watermelon
pêche	pehsh	peach
poire	pwahr	pear
pomme	pom	apple
pruneaux	prewnoa	prunes
prunes	prewn	plums
raisin	rehzang	grapes
blanc/noir	blahng/nwahr	green/blue
raisins secs	rehzang sehk	raisins
rhubarbe	rewbahrb	rhubarb

Dessert *Desserts*

I'd like a dessert, please.	**Je prendrai un dessert, s'il vous plaît.**	zher prahngdray ang dehssehr seel voo pleh
What do you recommend?	**Que me/nous recommandez-vous?**	ker mer/noo rerkommahngday voo
Something light, please.	**Quelque chose de léger, s'il vous plaît.**	kehlker shoaz der layzhay seel voo pleh
Just a small portion.	**Une petite portion, s'il vous plaît.**	ewn perteet porsyawng seel voo pleh

barquette (bahrkeht) small boat-shaped pastry shell garnished with fruit

crêpe suzette (krehp sewzeht) large, thin pancakes simmered in orange juice and flambéd with orange liqueur

poire Belle Hélène (pwahr behl aylehn) pear with vanilla ice-cream and chocolate sauce

profiterole (profeeterrol) puff pastry filled with whipped cream or custard

sabayon (sahbahyawng) creamy dessert of egg yolks, wine, sugar and flavouring

colonel	kolonehl	lemon (water ice) doused with vodka
coupe (glacée)	koop glahssay	often means a sundae
crème caramel	krehm kahrahmehl	caramel pudding
crème Chantilly	krehm shahngteeyee	whipped cream
flan	flahng	custard
gâteau au chocolat	gahtoa oa shokolah	chocolate cake
glace aux fraises/ à la vanille	glahss oa frehz/ah lah vahneey	strawberry/vanilla ice-cream
mousse au chocolat	mooss oa shokolah	chocolate pudding
omelette norvégienne	omerleht norvayzhyehn	baked Alaska
sorbet	sorbeh	water ice (Am. sherbet)
soufflé au Grand-Marnier	sooflay oa grahng mahrnyay	soufflé made of orange liqueur
tarte aux pommes	tahrt oa pom	apple tart (pie)
tartelette	tahrterleht	small tart
tourte	toort	layer cake
vacherin glacé	vahsherrang glahssay	ice-cream cake

Aperitifs *Apéritifs*

For most Frenchmen, the aperitif is just as important as our cocktail or highball. Often bittersweet, some aperitifs have a wine and brandy base with herbs and bitters (like Amer Picon, Byrrh, Dubonnet), others called *pastis* have an aniseed base (like Pernod, Ricard) or a vegetable base (like Cynar produced from artichoke). An aperitif may also be simply vermouth (like Noilly Prat) or a liqueur drink like *blanc-cassis* or *"kir"* (chilled white wine mixed with a black-currant syrup). An aperitif is rarely drunk neat (straight) but usually with ice or seltzer water.

I'd like a Cynar ...	**Je voudrais un Cynar ...**	zher voodreh ang seenahr
neat (straight)	**sec**	sehk
on the rocks	**avec des glaçons**	ahvehk day glahssawng
with (seltzer) water	**à l'eau (au siphon)**	ah loa (oa seefawng)

À VOTRE SANTÉ
(ah votr sahngtay)
YOUR HEALTH!/CHEERS!

Beer *Bières*

Beer is a popular drink in some French-speaking areas. You may like to sample some of the local brews, for instance *Kronenbourg* in France, *Stella Artois* in Belgium and *Cardinal* in Switzerland.

I'd like a beer, please.	**Je voudrais une bière, s'il vous plaît.**	zher voodreh ewn byehr seel voo pleh
Do you have ... beer?	**Avez-vous de la bière ...?**	ahvay voo der lah byehr
bottled	**en bouteilles**	ahng bootehy
draught	**pression**	prehssyawng
foreign	**étrangère**	aytrahngzhehr
light/dark	**blonde/brune**	blawngd/brewn

Wine *Vins*

France is the world's greatest producer of fine wine so naturally the matter is taken quite seriously. However, you needn't be frightened off by an impressive list of expensive wines. There are a few rules of thumb to bear in mind, and the rest is largely up to your personal taste.

French cuisine and wine are inseparable components. The one complements the other. The enjoyment of a delicately flavoured *pâte de foie gras,* for instance, can be all the more enhanced with the proper wine.

There are some dishes, however, with which no wine should be drunk. Don't drink wine with salads or other dishes with vinegar preparations. Combining the two could result in a strange taste. Wine doesn't necessarily accompany soup. But if wine is an ingredient in the soup, like *consommé au porto,* then you could have the same wine—port wine in that case—with your soup.

Otherwise, the time-honoured general guideline has it that white wine goes well with fish, fowl and light meats while dark meats call for a red wine. A good rosé or dry champagne goes well with almost anything and can accompany the whole meal.

Everyone's heard of *Bordeaux* (we call it claret) and *Bourgogne* (burgundy) wine. But France has hundreds of kinds of wine going all the way from its prestigious *premiers crus* to the more humble *vins ordinaires.* Don't miss the opportunity to sample local wine. Much of it doesn't travel well and is therefore never exported. The wine of each region is imbued with the character of that district.

The chart on the next page will help to identify some of the good regional wine. Fine provincial cooking is well accompanied by good local wine whereas exquisite cuisine calls for a noble wine.

Type of wine	Examples	Accompanies
sweet white wine	best known are those in the Sauternes family; the noblest is Château-Yquem	desserts, especially custard, pudding, cake, sweet soufflé, pâté—at one time popular with oysters
light, dry white wine	Alsatian, Muscadet, Riesling, Sancerre; some types of Pouilly fumé, Pouilly-Fuissé, Chablis; local white wine and Swiss wine often fall into this category	oysters, cold meat or shellfish, grilled fish, boiled meat, egg dishes, first courses, Swiss raclette and fondue
full-bodied, dry white wine	white Burgundy, dry Côtes-du-Rhône, Graves	fish, fowl, veal served in creamy sauces, *foie gras*
rosé	Rosé d'Anjou	goes with almost anything but especially cold dishes, pâtés, eggs, pork, lamb
light-bodied red wine	Bordeaux from Médoc or Graves districts; a Beaujolais, local or Swiss wine often fits into this selection	roast chicken, turkey, veal, lamb, beef fillet, ham, liver, quail, pheasant, *foie gras,* soft-textured cheeses, stews, steaks
full-bodied red wine	any of the fine Burgundies or Châteauneuf-du-Pape; certain Bordeaux	duck, goose, kidneys, most game, tangy cheese like *bleu*—in short, any strong-flavoured preparations
extra dry champagne	any of this category	goes with anything, may be drunk as an aperitif or as the climax to the dinner
dry champagne	any of this category	as an aperitif; shellfish, *foie gras,* nuts and dried fruit
sweet champagne	any of this category	dessert and pastry

I'd like ... of ...	**Je voudrais ... de ...**	zher voodreh ... der
a carafe	**une carafe**	ewn kahrahf
a half bottle	**une demi-bouteille**	ewn dermee bootehy
a glass	**un verre**	ang vehr
a litre	**un litre**	ang leetr
I want a bottle of white/red wine.	**J'aimerais une bouteille de vin blanc/rouge.**	zhehmerreh ewn bootehy der vang blahng/roozh
A bottle of champagne, please.	**Une bouteille de champagne, s'il vous plaît.**	ewn bootehy der shangpahñ seel voo pleh
Please bring me another ...	**Apportez-m'en encore ...**	ahportay mahng ahngkor
Where does this wine come from?	**De quelle région vient ce vin?**	der kehl rayzhyawng vyang ser vang

red	**rouge**	roozh
white	**blanc**	blahng
rosé	**rosé**	roazay
dry	**sec**	sehk
light	**léger**	layzhay
full-bodied	**corsé**	korsay
sparkling	**mousseux**	moossur
very dry	**brut**	brewt
sweet	**doux**	doo

Other alcoholic drinks *Autres boissons alcoolisées*

You'll certainly want to take the occasion to sip a fine cognac after a meal. We usually consider cognac and brandy as being synonymous. In the strict sense of the word, cognac is the famed wine-distilled brandy from the Charente-Maritime region. Try one of these: *Courvoisier, Hennessy, Rémy-Martin*. Other areas are noted for their fruit-distilled brandies like *quetsche* (plum), *marc* (grape), *calvados* (apple), *kirsch* (cherry), *poire Williams* (pear).

Are there any local specialities?	**Avez-vous des spécialités locales?**	ahvay voo day spayssyahleetay lokahl

I'd like to try a glass of ..., please.	**Je voudrais goûter un verre de ...**	zher voodreh gootay ang vehr der
A (double) whisky, please.	**Un whisky (double), s'il vous plaît.**	ang "whisky" (doobl) seel voo pleh
brandy	**un cognac**	ang koñyahk
gin and tonic	**un gin-tonic**	ang "gin-tonic"
liqueur	**une liqueur**	ewn leekurr
port	**un porto**	ang portoa
rum	**un rhum**	ang rom
sherry	**un sherry**	ang "sherry"
vermouth	**un vermouth**	ang vehrmoot
vodka	**une vodka**	ewn vodka
neat (straight)	**sec**	sehk
on the rocks	**avec des glaçons**	ahvehk day glahssawng

Nonalcoholic drinks — *Boissons sans alcool*

apple juice	**un jus de pomme**	ang zhew der pom
(hot) chocolate	**un chocolat (chaud)**	ang shokolah (shoa)
coffee	**un café**	ang kahfay
black	**noir**	nwahr
with cream	**crème**	krehm
with milk	**au lait**	oa leh
caffein-free	**décaféiné**	daykahfayeenay
espresso coffee	**un express**	ang nehxprehss
fruit juice	**un jus de fruits**	ang zhew der frwee
grapefruit juice	**un jus de pamplemousse**	ang zhew der pahngplermooss
herb tea	**une tisane**	ewn teezahn
lemon juice	**un citron pressé**	ang seetrawng prehssay
lemonade	**une limonade**	ewn leemonahd
milk	**un lait**	ang leh
milkshake	**un frappé**	ang frahpay
mineral water	**de l'eau minérale**	der loa meenayrahl
fizzy (carbonated)	**gazeuse**	gahzurz
still	**non gazeuse**	nawng gahzurz
orange juice	**un jus d'orange**	ang zhew dorahngzh
orangeade	**une orangeade**	ewn orahngzhahd
tea	**un thé**	ang tay
cup of tea	**une tasse de thé**	ewn tahss der tay
with milk/lemon	**crème/citron**	krehm/seetrawng
iced tea	**un thé glacé**	ang tay glahssay
tomato juice	**un jus de tomate**	ang zhew der tomaht
tonic water	**un Schweppes**	ang "Schweppes"

Complaints *Réclamations*

There is a plate/glass missing.	**Il manque une assiette/un verre.**	eel mahngk ewn ahssyeht/ ang vehr
I have no knive/fork/ spoon.	**Je n'ai pas de couteau/fourchette/ cuillère.**	zher nay pah der kootoa/ foorsheht/kweeyehr
That's not what I ordered.	**Ce n'est pas ce que j'ai commandé.**	ser neh pah ser ker zhay kommahngday
I asked for ...	**J'ai demandé ...**	zhay dermahngday
There must be some mistake.	**Il doit y avoir une erreur.**	eel dwah ee avwahr ewn ehrurr
May I change this?	**Pourriez-vous me changer ceci?**	pooryay voo mer shahngzhay serssee
I asked for a small portion (for the child).	**J'avais demandé une petite portion (pour cet enfant).**	zhahveh dermahngday ewn perteet porsyawng (poor seht ahngfahng)
The meat is ...	**La viande est ...**	lah vyahngd eh
overdone underdone too rare too tough	**trop cuite pas assez cuite trop saignante trop dure**	troa kweet pah zahssay kweet troa sehñahngt troa dewr
This is too ...	**C'est trop ...**	seh troa
bitter/salty/sweet	**amer/salé/sucré**	ahmehr/sahlay/sewkray
I don't like this.	**Je n'aime pas ceci.**	zher nehm pah serssee
The food is cold.	**C'est tout froid.**	seh too frwah
This isn't fresh.	**Ce n'est pas frais.**	ser neh pah freh
What's taking you so long?	**Pourquoi y a-t-il autant d'attente?**	poorkwah ee ahteel oatahng dahtahngt
Have you forgotten our drinks?	**Avez-vous oublié nos boissons?**	ahvay voo zoobleeyay noa bwahssawng
The wine tastes of cork.	**Ce vin a un goût de bouchon.**	ser vang ah ang goo der booshawng
This isn't clean.	**Ce n'est pas propre.**	ser neh pah propr
Would you ask the head waiter to come over?	**Envoyez-moi donc le maître d'hôtel.**	ahngvwahyay mwah dawngk ler mehtr doatehl

The bill (check) *L'addition*

A service charge is generally included automatically in restaurant bills. Anything extra for the waiter is optional. Credit cards may be used in an increasing number of restaurants. Signs are posted indicating which cards are accepted.

I'd like to pay.	**L'addition, s'il vous plaît.**	lahdeessyawng seel voo pleh
We'd like to pay separately.	**Nous voudrions payer chacun notre part.**	noo voodreeyawng pehyay shahkang notr pahr
I think you made a mistake in this bill.	**Je crois qu'il y a une erreur dans l'addition.**	zher krwah keel ee ah ewn ehrurr dahng lahdeessyawng
What is this amount for?	**Que représente ce montant?**	ker rerprayzahngt ser mawngtahng
Is service included?	**Est-ce que le service est compris?**	ehss ker ler sehrveess eh kawngpree
Is the cover charge included?	**Est-ce que le couvert est compris?**	ehss ker ler koovehr eh kawngpree
Is everything included?	**Est-ce que tout est compris?**	ehss ker too teh kawngpree
Do you accept traveller's cheques?	**Acceptez-vous les chèques de voyage?**	ahksehptay voo lay shehk der vwahyahzh
Can I pay with this credit card?	**Puis-je payer avec cette carte de crédit?**	pweezh pehyay ahvehk seht kahrt der kraydee
Thank you, this is for you.	**Merci. Voici pour vous.**	mehrsee. vwahssee poor voo
Keep the change.	**Gardez la monnaie.**	gahrday lah monneh
That was a delicious meal.	**Le repas était délicieux.**	ler rerpah ayteh dayleessyur
We enjoyed it, thank you.	**C'était très bon, merci.**	sayteh treh bawng mehrsee

SERVICE COMPRIS
SERVICE INCLUDED

TIPPING, see inside back-cover

Snacks – Picnic *Casse-croûte – Pique-nique*

Cafés serve hearty sandwiches of long hunks of French bread filled with ham, cheese, pâté, tomatoes, green salad or hardboiled eggs. Thin-sliced sandwich bread *(pain de mie)* is used for *croque-monsieur* (toasted ham-and-cheese sandwich). Omelettes are always reliable fare, and so are the excellent thin-crusted pizzas (all flavours). The delicious *crêpes,* paper-thin pancakes dusted with sugar or filled with jam, are sold at small street stands.

I'll have one of these, please.	**J'en voudrais un de ceux-ci, s'il vous plaît.**	zhahng voodreh ang der surssee seel voo pleh
Give me two of these and one of those.	**Donnez-moi deux de ceux-ci et un de ceux-là.**	donnay mwah dur der surssee ay ang der surlah
to the left/right	**à gauche/à droite**	ah goash/ah drwaht
above/below	**au-dessus/au-dessous**	oa derssew/oa derssoo
It's to take away.	**C'est pour emporter.**	seh poor ahngportay
I'd like a/some ...	**Je voudrais ...**	zher voodreh
chicken	**un poulet**	ang pooleh
half a roasted chicken	**un demi-poulet grillé**	ang dermee pooleh greeyay
chips (french fries)	**des frites**	day freet
pancake	**une crêpe**	ewn krehp
with sugar	**au sucre**	oa sewkr
with jam	**à la confiture**	ah lah kawngfeetewr
sandwich	**un sandwich**	ang "sandwich"
cheese	**au fromage**	oa fromahzh
ham	**au jambon**	oa zhahngbawng
vegetable salad	**des crudités**	day krewdeetay

Here's a basic list of food and drink that might come in useful when shopping for a picnic.

Please give me a/an/ some ...	**Donnez-moi ..., s'il vous plaît.**	donnay mwah ... seel voo pleh
apples	**des pommes**	day pom
bananas	**des bananes**	day bahnahn
biscuits (Br.)	**des biscuits**	day beeskwee
beer	**de la bière**	der lah byehr

bread	**du pain**	dew pang
butter	**du beurre**	dew burr
cake	**un gâteau**	ang gahtoa
cheese	**du fromage**	dew fromahzh
chips (Am.)	**des chips**	day "chips"
chocolate bar	**une plaque de chocolat**	ewn plahk der shokolah
coffee	**du café**	dew kahfay
cold cuts	**de la charcuterie**	der lah shahrkewterree
cookies	**des biscuits**	day beeskwee
crackers	**des biscuits salés**	day beeskwee sahlay
crisps	**des chips**	day "chips"
eggs	**des œufs**	day zur
gherkins (pickles)	**des cornichons**	day korneeshawng
grapes	**du raisin**	dew rehzang
ham	**du jambon**	dew zhahngbawng
ice-cream	**de la glace**	der lah glahss
lemon	**un citron**	ang seetrawng
milk	**du lait**	dew leh
mustard	**de la moutarde**	der lah mootahrd
oranges	**des oranges**	day zorahngzh
pastries	**des pâtisseries**	day pahteesserree
pepper	**du poivre**	dew pwahvr
roll	**un petit pain**	ang pertee pang
salt	**du sel**	dew sehl
sausage	**une saucisse**	ewn soasseess
soft drink	**une boisson non alcoolisée**	ewn bwahssawng nawng nahlkoleezay
sugar	**du sucre**	dew sewkr
tea	**du thé**	dew tay
yoghurt	**un yoghourt (yaourt)**	ang yogoort (yahoort)

… plus a choice of French bread:

baguette	bahgeht	long thin loaf of French bread
ficelle	feessehl	same as *baguette*, but thinner
pain	pang	bread
blanc/bis	blahng/bee	white/brown
complet	kawngpleh	wholemeal (whole-wheat)
de seigle	der sehgl	rye
petit pain	pertee pang	roll
au cumin	oa kewmang	with caraway seeds
aux pavots	oa pahvoa	with poppy seeds

Travelling around

Plane *Avion*

Is there a flight to Paris?	**Y a-t-il un vol pour Paris?**	ee ahteel ang vol poor pahree
Is it a direct flight?	**Est-ce un vol direct?**	ehss ang vol deerehkt
When's the next plane to Lyons?	**Quand part le prochain avion pour Lyon?**	kahng pahr ler proshang nahvyawng poor lyawng
Do I have to change planes?	**Est-ce que je dois changer d'avion?**	ehss ker zher dwah shahngzhay dahvyawng
Can I make a connection to Geneva?	**Puis-je avoir une correspondance pour Genève?**	pweezh ahvwahr ewn korrehspawngdahngss poor zhernehv
I'd like a ticket to Brussels.	**Je voudrais un billet pour Bruxelles.**	zher voodreh ang beeyeh poor brewssehl
single (one-way)	**aller**	ahlay
return (roundtrip)	**aller-retour**	ahlay rertoor
What time does the plane take off?	**A quelle heure part l'avion?**	ah kehl urr pahr lahvyawng
What time do I have to check in?	**A quelle heure est l'enregistrement?**	ah kehl urr eh lahngrerzheestrermahng
Is there a bus to the airport?	**Y a-t-il un bus pour l'aéroport?**	ee ahteel ang bewss poor lahayropor
What's the flight number?	**Quel est le numéro du vol?**	kehl eh ler newmayroa dew vol
What time do we arrive?	**A quelle heure arrivons-nous?**	ah kehl urr ahreevawng noo
I'd like to ... my reservation on flight no ...	**Je voudrais ... ma réservation sur le vol ...**	zher voodreh ... mah rayzehrvahssyawng sewr ler vol
cancel	**annuler**	ahnnewlay
change	**changer**	shahngzhay
confirm	**confirmer**	kawngfeermay

ARRIVÉE ARRIVAL	**DÉPART** DEPARTURE

Train *Train*

Rail travel in France is usually fast on the main lines, and the trains (diesel and electric) run on time. Unless otherwise indicated, the terms below apply equally to France, Belgium and Switzerland.

TGV (tay zhay vay)	Extra-high-speed train *(Train à Grande Vitesse)* operating on some routes; reservation compulsory, surcharge sometimes payable
TEE (tay ay ay)	Trans Europ Express; a luxury international service with first class only; reservation compulsory, surcharge payable
Rapide (rahpeed)	Long-distance express stopping only at main stations; luxury coaches; additional fare sometimes required (France)
Intercity (angtehrseetee)	Inter-city express with very few stops
Express (ehxprehss)	Ordinary long-distance train, stopping at main stations (France)
Direct (deerehkt)	The equivalent of the French *express* (Switzerland and Belgium)
Omnibus (omneebewss)	Local train stopping at all stations (France and Belgium)
Train régional (trang rayzhyonahl)	Local train stopping at all stations (Switzerland)
Autorail (oatorahy)	Small diesel used on short runs

Here are a few more useful terms which you may need:

Wagon-restaurant* (vahgawng rehstoarahng)	Dining-car
Wagon-lit* (vahgawng lee)	Sleeping-car with individual compartments (single or double) and washing facilities
Couchette (koosheht)	Berth (converted from seats) with blankets and pillows. You may want a *couchette supérieure* (koosheht sewpayryurr—upper berth) or a *couchette inférieure* (koosheht angfayryurr—lower berth)

* The term *voiture* (vwahtewr) is often used instead of *wagon*.

To the railway station *Pour aller à la gare*

Where's the railway station?	**Où se trouve la gare?**	oo ser troov lah gahr
Taxi!	**Taxi!**	tahksee
Take me to the railway station.	**Conduisez-moi à la gare.**	kawngdweezay mwah ah lah gahr
What's the fare?	**C'est combien?**	say kawngbyang

ENTRÉE	ENTRANCE
SORTIE	EXIT
ACCÈS AUX QUAIS	TO THE PLATFORMS
RENSEIGNEMENTS	INFORMATION

Where's the ...? *Où est ...?*

Where is/are the ...?	**Où est ...?**	oo eh
bar	**le bar**	ler bahr
booking office	**le bureau de réservation**	ler bewroa der rayzehrvahssyawng
currency exchange office	**le bureau de change**	ler bewroa der shahngzh
left-luggage office (baggage check)	**la consigne**	lah kawngsseeñ
lost property (lost and found) office	**le bureau des objets trouvés**	ler bewroa day zobzheh troovay
luggage lockers	**la consigne automatique**	lah kawngsseeñ oatomahteek
newsstand	**le kiosque à journaux**	ler kyosk ah zhoornoa
platform 7	**le quai 7**	ler kay 7
reservations office	**le bureau de réservation**	ler bewroa der rayzehrvahssyawng
restaurant	**le restaurant**	ler rehstoarahng
snack bar	**le buffet-express**	ler bewfeh exprehss
ticket office	**le guichet**	ler geesheh
waiting-room	**la salle d'attente**	lah sahl dahtahngt
Where are the toilets?	**Où sont les toilettes?**	oo sawng lay twahleht

TAXI, see page 21

Inquiries *Renseignements*

In Belgium, France and Switzerland [i] means information office.

When is the ... train to Nice?	**Quand part le ... train pour Nice?**	kahng pahr ler ... trang poor neess
first/last next	**premier/dernier prochain**	prermyay/dehrnyay proshang
What time does the train for Calais leave?	**A quelle heure part le train pour Calais?**	ah kehl urr pahr ler trang poor kahleh
What's the fare to Avignon?	**Quel est le prix du billet pour Avignon?**	kehl eh ler pree dew beeyeh poor ahveeñawng
Is it a through train?	**Est-ce un train direct?**	ehss ang trang deerehkt
Is there a connection to ...?	**Est-ce qu'il existe une correspondance pour ...?**	ehss keel ehxeest ewn korrehspawngdahngss poor
Do I have to change trains?	**Dois-je changer (de train)?**	dwahzh shahngzhay (der trang)
Is there sufficient time to change?	**A-t-on le temps de changer?**	ahtawng ler tahng der shahngzhay
Will the train leave on time?	**Est-ce que le train partira à l'heure?**	ehss ker ler trang pahrteerah ah lurr
What time does the train arrive at Bordeaux?	**A quelle heure le train arrive-t-il à Bordeaux?**	ah kehl urr ler trang ahreev teel ah bordoa
Is there a dining-car/ sleeping-car on the train?	**Y a-t-il un wagon-restaurant/un wagon-lit?**	ee ahteel ang vahgawng rehstoarahng/ang vahgawng lee
Does the train stop at Mâcon?	**Est-ce que le train s'arrête à Mâcon?**	ehss ker ler trang sahreht ah mahkawng
What platform does the train for Strasbourg leave from?	**De quel quai part le train pour Strasbourg?**	der kehl kay pahr ler trang poor strahsboor
What platform does the train from Geneva arrive at?	**Sur quel quai arrive le train de Genève?**	sewr kehl kay ahreev ler trang der zhernehv
I'd like to buy a timetable.	**Je voudrais acheter un horaire.**	zher voodreh ahshertay ang norrehr

C'est un train direct.	It's a through train.
Changez à ...	You have to change at ...
Changez à ... et prenez un omnibus.	Change at ... and get a local train.
Le quai 7 se trouve ...	Platform 7 is ...
là-bas/en haut **à gauche/à droite**	over there/upstairs on the left/on the right
Il y a un train pour ... **à ...**	There's a train to ... at ...
Votre train partira du quai 8.	Your train will leave from platform 8.
Le train a un retard de ... minutes.	There'll be a delay of ... minutes.
Première classe en tête/ au milieu/en queue.	First class at the front/in the middle/at the end.

Tickets *Billets*

I want a ticket to Nice.	**Je voudrais un billet pour Nice.**	zher voodreh ang beeyeh poor neess
single (one-way)	**aller**	ahlay
return (roundtrip)	**aller-retour**	ahlay rertoor
first/second class	**première/deuxième classe**	prermyehr/durzyehm klahss
half price	**demi-tarif**	dermee tahreef

Reservation *Réservation*

I want to book a ...	**Je voudrais réserver ...**	zher voodreh rayzehrvay
seat (by the window)	**une place (côté fenêtre)**	ewn plahss (koatay fernehtr)
berth	**une couchette**	ewn koosheht
upper	**supérieure**	sewpayryurr
middle	**au milieu**	oa meelyur
lower	**inférieure**	angfayryurr
berth in the sleeping car	**une place en wagon-lit**	ewn plahss ang vahgawng lee

All aboard *En voiture*

Is this the right platform for the train to Paris?	**Est-ce bien de ce quai que part le train pour Paris?**	ehss byang der ser kay ker pahr ler trang poor pahree
Is this the right train to Marseilles?	**C'est bien le train pour Marseille, n'est-ce pas?**	seh byang ler trang poor mahrsehy nehss pah
Excuse me. May I get by?	**Pardon. Puis-je passer?**	pahrdawng pweezh pahssay
Is this seat taken?	**Cette place est-elle occupée?**	seht plahss ehtehl okkewpay

FUMEURS
SMOKER

NON-FUMEURS
NONSMOKER

I think that's my seat.	**Je crois que c'est ma place.**	zher krwah ker seh mah plahss
Would you let me know before we get to Liège?	**Pourriez-vous m'avertir quand nous arriverons à Liège?**	pooryay voo mahvehrteer kahng noo zahreeverrawng ah lyehzh
What station is this?	**A quelle gare sommes-nous?**	ah kehl gahr som noo
How long does the train stop here?	**Combien de temps le train s'arrête-t-il ici?**	kawngbyang der tahng ler trang sahreht teel eessee
When do we get to Orleans?	**Quand arriverons-nous à Orléans?**	kahng tahreevrawng noo ah orlayahng

Sleeping *En wagon-lit*

Are there any free compartments in the sleeping-car?	**Y a-t-il des compartiments libres dans le wagon-lit?**	ee ahteel day kawngpahrteemahng leebr dahng ler vahgawng lee
Where's the sleeping-car?	**Où se trouve le wagon-lit?**	oo ser troov ler vahgawng lee
Where's my berth?	**Où est ma couchette?**	oo eh mah koosheht

I'd like a lower berth.	**Je voudrais une couchette inférieure.**	zher voodreh ewn koosheht angfayryurr
Would you make up our berths?	**Pourriez-vous installer nos couchettes?**	pooryay voo angstahlay noa koosheht
Would you wake me at 7 o'clock?	**Pourriez vous me réveiller à 7 heures?**	pooryay voo mer rayvehyay ah 7 urr

Eating *Au wagon-restaurant*

You can get snacks and drinks in the buffet-car and in the dining-car when it's not being used for main meals. On some trains an attendant comes around with snacks, coffee, tea, and soft drinks.

Where's the dining-car?	**Où est le wagon-restaurant?**	oo eh ler vahgawng rehstoarahng

Baggage and porters *Bagages et porteurs*

Porter!	**Porteur?**	porturr
Can you help me with my luggage?	**Pouvez-vous m'aider à porter mes bagages?**	poovay voo mehday ah portay may bahgahzh
Where are the luggage trolleys (carts)?	**Où sont les chariots à bagages?**	oo sawng lay shahryoa ah bahgahzh
Where are the luggage lockers?	**Où est la consigne automatique?**	oo eh lah kawngseeñ oatomahteek
Where's the left-luggage office (baggage check)?	**Où est la consigne?**	oo eh lah kawngseeñ
I'd like to leave my luggage, please.	**Je voudrais déposer mes bagages, s'il vous plaît.**	zher voodreh daypoazay may bahgahzh seel voo pleh
I'd like to register (check) my luggage.	**Je voudrais faire enregistrer mes bagages.**	zher voodreh fehr ahngrergeestray may bahgahzh

ENREGISTREMENT DES BAGAGES
REGISTERING (CHECKING) BAGGAGE

PORTERS, see also page 18

Coach (long-distance bus) *Car*

You'll find information on destinations and timetables at the coach terminals, usually situated near railway stations. Many companies offer coach tours, as do the French National Railways.

When's the next coach to ...?	**A quelle heure est le prochain car pour ...?**	ah kehl urr eh ler proshang kahr poor
Does this coach stop at ...?	**Ce car s'arrête-t-il à ...?**	ser kahr sahreht teel ah
How long does the journey (trip) take?	**Combien de temps dure le trajet?**	kawngbyang der tahng dowr lor trahzhoh

Note: Most of the phrases on the previous pages can be used or adapted for travelling on local transport.

Bus—Tram (streetcar) *Bus – Tram*

Many cities have introduced an automatic system of fare-paying whereby you insert the exact change into a ticket dispenser at the bus or tram stop or have the machine validate your prepaid ticket.

If you're planning to get around a lot in one city by bus, tram, or *métro* (see next page), enquire about a booklet of tickets or special runabout tickets, such as the *carte* or *abonnement d'un jour* (one-day ticket), *carte orange* (valid a week or a month, in Paris) or *billet touristique* (special tourist ticket for two or more days).

I'd like a booklet of tickets.	**J'aimerais un carnet de tickets.**	zhehmerreh ang kahrneh der teekeh
Where can I get a bus to the opera?	**Où puis-je prendre le bus pour l'Opéra?**	oo pweezh prahngdr ler bewss poor lopayrah
What bus do I take for Montmartre?	**Quel bus dois-je prendre pour aller à Montmartre?**	kehl bewss dwahzh prahngdr poor ahlay ah mawngmahrtr
Where's the bus stop?	**Où se trouve l'arrêt de bus?**	oo ser troov lahreh der bewss

When is the ... bus to St. Germain?	**Quand part le ... bus pour Saint-Germain?**	kawng pahr ler ... bewss poor sang zhehrmang
first/last/next	**premier/dernier/ prochain**	prermyay/dehrnyay/ proshang
How much is the fare to ...?	**Quel est le prix du trajet jusqu'à ...?**	kehl eh ler pree dew trahzheh zhewskah
Do I have to change buses?	**Dois-je changer de bus?**	dwahzh shahngzhay der bewss
How many bus stops are there to ...?	**Combien y a-t-il d'arrêts jusqu'à ...?**	kawngbyang ee ahteel dahreh zhewskah
Will you tell me when to get off?	**Pourriez-vous me dire quand je dois descendre?**	pooryay voo mer deer kahng zher dwah dehssahngdr
I want to get off at Notre-Dame	**Je voudrais descendre à Notre-Dame.**	zher voodreh dehssahngdr ah notrer dahm

ARRÊT FIXE	REGULAR BUS STOP
ARRÊT SUR DEMANDE	STOPS ON REQUEST

Underground (subway) *Métro*

The *métros* (maytroa) in Paris and Brussels correspond to the London underground or the New York subway. In both cities, the fare is always the same, irrespective of the distance you travel. There's first and second class. Big maps in every Métro station make the system easy to use.

Where's the nearest underground station?	**Où se trouve la station de métro la plus proche?**	oo ser troov lah stahssyawng der maytroa lah plew prosh
Does this train go to ...?	**Est-ce que cette rame va à ...?**	ehss ker seht rahm vah ah
Where do I change for ...?	**Où faut-il changer pour aller à ...?**	oo foateel shahngzhay poor ahlay ah
Is the next station ...?	**La prochaine gare est-elle bien ...?**	lah proshehn gahr ehtehl byang
Which line should I take for ...?	**Quelle ligne dois-je prendre pour ...?**	kehl leeñ dwahzh prahngdr poor

Boat service *Bateau*

When does the next boat for ... leave?	**A quelle heure part le prochain bateau pour ...?**	a kehl urr pahr ler proshang bahtoa poor ...
Where's the embarkation point?	**Où s'effectue l'embarquement?**	oo sehffehktew lahngbahrkermahng
How long does the crossing take?	**Combien de temps dure la traversée?**	kawngbyang der tahng dewr lah trahvehrsay
At which port(s) do we stop?	**Quel(s) port(s) dessert ce bateau?**	kehl por dehssehr ser bahtoa
I'd like to take a cruise.	**Je voudrais faire une croisière.**	zher voodreh fehr ewn krwahzyehr
boat	**le bateau**	ler bahtoa
cabin	**la cabine**	lah kahbeen
single/double	**pour une personne/ deux personnes**	poor ewn pehrson/ dur pehrson
deck	**le pont**	ler pawng
ferry	**le ferry**	ler ''ferry''
hovercraft	**l'aéroglisseur**	lahayrogleessurr
hydrofoil	**l'hydroptère**	leedroptehr
life belt/boat	**la ceinture/le canot de sauvetage**	la sangtewr/ler kahnoa der soavertahzh
ship	**le navire**	ler nahveer

Bicycle hire *Location de bicyclettes*

French National Railways operate a cycle-hire service at major stations. Bicycles may be hired at one station and returned at another.

I'd like to hire a bicycle.	**Je voudrais louer une bicyclette.**	zher voodreh looay ewn beesseekleht

Other means of transport *Autres moyens de transport*

cable car	**la télécabine**	lah taylaykahbeen
helicopter	**l'hélicoptère**	layleekoptehr
moped	**le vélomoteur**	ler vayloamoturr
motorbike/scooter	**la moto/le scooter**	lah moto/ler skootehr

Or perhaps you prefer:

to hitchhike	**faire de l'auto-stop**	fehr der loatostop
to walk	**marcher**	mahrshay

Car *Voiture*

In general roads are good in Belgium, France and Switzerland. Motorways (expressways) are subject to tolls *(le péage)* in France, they are free in Belgium. If you use the motorways in Switzerland you must purchase a sticker (valid for one year) to be displayed on the windscreen.

A red reflector warning triangle must be carried for use in case of a breakdown, and seat belts *(la ceinture de sécurité)* are obligatory.

Where's the nearest filling station?	**Où est la station-service la plus proche?**	oo eh lah stahssyawng sehrveess lah plew prosh
Full tank, please.	**Le plein, s'il vous plaît.**	ler plang seel voo pleh
Give me ... litres of petrol (gasoline).	**Donnez-moi ... litres d'essence.**	donnay mwah ... leetr dehssahngss
super (premium)/ regular/unleaded/ diesel	**du super/de la normale/sans plomb/ gas-oil**	dew sewpehr/der lah normahl/sahng plawng/ gahzoyl
Please check the ...	**Veuillez contrôler ...**	veryay kawngtroalay
battery	**la batterie**	lah bahterree
brake fluid	**le liquide des freins**	ler leekeed day frang
oil/water	**l'huile/l'eau**	lweel/loa
Would you check the tyre pressure?	**Pourriez-vous contrôler la pression des pneus?**	pooryay voo kawngtroalay lah prehssyawng day pnur
1.6 front, 1.8 rear.	**1,6 à l'avant, 1,8 à l'arrière.**	ang seess ah lahvahng ang weet ah lahryehr
Please check the spare tyre, too.	**Vérifiez aussi la roue de secours.**	vayreefyay oassee lah roo der serkoor
Can you mend this puncture (fix this flat)?	**Pourriez-vous réparer ce pneu?**	pooryay voo raypahray ser pnur
Would you please change the ...?	**Pourriez-vous changer ...?**	pooryay voo shahngzhay
bulb	**l'ampoule**	lahngpool
fan belt	**la courroie du ventilateur**	lah koorrwah dew vahngteelahturr

CAR HIRE, see page 20

spark(ing) plugs	**les bougies**	lay boozhee
tyre	**le pneu**	ler pnur
wipers	**les essuie-glace**	lay zehsswee glahss
Would you clean the windscreen (windshield)?	**Pourriez-vous nettoyer le pare-brise?**	pooryay voo nehtwahyay ler pahr breez

Asking the way—Street directions *Pour demander son chemin*

Can you tell me the way to ...?	**Pourriez-vous m'indiquer la route de ...?**	pooryay voo mangdeekay lah root der
How do I get to ...?	**Comment-puis-je aller à ...?**	kommahng pweezh ahlay ah
Are we on the right road for ...?	**Sommes-nous bien sur la route pour ...?**	som noo byang sewr lah root poor
How far is the next village?	**A quelle distance se trouve le prochain village?**	ah kehl deestahngss ser troov ler proshang veelahzh
How far is it to ... from here?	**A quelle distance sommes-nous de ...?**	ah kehl deestahngss som noo der
Is there a motorway (expressway)?	**Y a-t-il une autoroute?**	ee ahteel ewn oatoroot
How long does it take by car/on foot?	**Combien de temps est-ce que cela prend en voiture/à pied?**	kawngbyang der tahng ehss ker serlah prahng ahng vwahtewr/ah pyay
Can I drive to the centre of town?	**Puis-je gagner le centre-ville en voiture?**	pweezh gahñay ler sahngtr veel ahng vwahtewr
Can you tell me, where ... is?	**Pourriez-vous me dire où se trouve ...?**	pooryay voo mer deer oo ser troov
How can I find this place?	**Comment puis-je trouver cet endroit?**	kommahng pweezh troovay seh tahngdrwah
Where can I find this address?	**Où puis-je trouver cette adresse?**	oo pweezh troovay seht ahdrehss
Where's this?	**Où est-ce?**	oo ehss
Can you show me on the map where I am?	**Pouvez-vous me montrer sur la carte où je suis?**	poovay voo mer mawngtray sewr lah kahrt oo zher swee

Vous êtes sur la mauvaise route.	You're on the wrong road.
Allez tout droit.	Go straight ahead.
C'est là-bas à ...	It's down there on the ...
gauche/droite	left/right
en face de/derrière ... **à côté de/au-delà de ...**	opposite/behind ... next to/after ...
nord/sud **est/ouest**	north/south east/west
Allez jusqu'au premier/ deuxième carrefour.	Go to the first/second crossroads (intersection).
Tournez à gauche après les feux.	Turn left at the traffic lights.
Tournez à droite au prochain coin de rue.	Turn right at the next corner.
Prenez la route de ...	Take the road for ...
Vous devez revenir jusqu'à ...	You have to go back to ...
Suivez la direction "Nice".	Follow signs for Nice.

Parking *Stationnement*

In town centres, most street parking is metered. The blue zones require the *disque de stationnement* or parking disc (obtainable from petrol stations), which you set to show when you arrived and when you must leave.

Where can I park?	**Où puis-je me garer?**	oo pweezh mer gahray
Is there a car park nearby?	**Y a-t-il un parking à proximité?**	ee ahteel ang pahrkeeng ah proxeemeetay
May I park here?	**Puis-je me garer ici?**	pweezh mer gahray eessee
How long can I park here?	**Combien de temps puis-je rester ici?**	kawngbyang der tahng pweezh rehstay eessee
What's the charge per hour?	**Quel est le tarif horaire?**	kehl eh ler tahreef orehr
Do you have some change for the parking meter?	**Avez-vous de la monnaie pour le parcomètre?**	ahvay voo der lah monneh poor ler pahrkommehtr

Breakdown—Road assistance *Pannes – Assistance routière*

Where's the nearest garage?	**Où se trouve le garage le plus proche?**	oo ser troov ler gahrahzh ler plew prosh
Excuse me. My car has broken down.	**Excusez-moi. Ma voiture est en panne.**	ehxkewzay mwah. mah vwahtewr eh tahng pahn
May I use your phone?	**Puis-je me servir de votre téléphone?**	pweezh mer sehrveer der votr taylayfon
I've had a breakdown at ...	**Je suis tombé en panne à ...**	zher swee tawngbay ahng pahn ah
Can you send a mechanic?	**Pouvez-vous envoyer un mécanicien?**	poovay voo ahngvwahyay ang maykahneessyang
My car won't start.	**Je n'arrive pas à démarrer.**	zher nahreev pah ah daymahray
The battery is dead.	**La batterie est à plat.**	lah bahterree eh ah plah
I've run out of petrol (gasoline).	**Je suis en panne d'essence.**	zher swee ahng pahn dehssahngss
I have a flat tyre.	**J'ai un pneu à plat.**	zhay ang pnur ah plah
The engine is overheating.	**Le moteur chauffe.**	ler moturr shoaf
There is something wrong with ...	**J'ai un problème avec ...**	zhay ang problehm ahvehk
brakes	**les freins**	lay frang
carburetor	**le carburateur**	ler kahrbewrahturr
exhaust pipe	**le pot d'échappement**	ler poa dayshahpmahng
radiator	**le radiateur**	ler rahdyahturr
wheel	**une roue**	ewn roo
Can you send a breakdown van (tow truck)?	**Pouvez-vous envoyer une dépanneuse?**	poovay voo ahngvwahyay ewn daypahnurz
How long will you be?	**Combien de temps faut-il compter?**	kawngbyang der tahng foateel kawngtay

Accident—Police *Accident – Police*

Please call the police.	**Appelez la police, s'il vous plaît.**	ahperlay lah poleess seel voo pleh
There's been an accident. It's about 2 km. from ...	**Il y a eu un accident à environ 2 km de ...**	eel ee ah ew ang nahksseedahng ah ahngveerawng 2 keelomehtr der

Where is there a telephone?	**Où y a-t-il un téléphone?**	oo ee ahteel ang taylayfon
Call a doctor/an ambulance quickly.	**Appelez d'urgence un médecin/une ambulance.**	ahperlay dewrzhahngss ang maydsang/ewn ahngbewlahngss
There are people injured.	**Il y a des blessés.**	eel ee ah day blehssay
Here's my driving licence.	**Voici mon permis de conduire.**	vwahssee mawng pehrmee der kawngdweer
What's your name and address?	**Quels sont vos nom et adresse?**	kehl sawng voa nawng ay ahdrehss
What's your insurance company?	**Auprès de quelle compagnie êtes-vous assuré?**	oapreh der kehl kawngpahñee eht voo ahssewray

Road signs *Panneaux routiers*

ALLUMEZ VOS PHARES	Switch on headlights
ATTENTION	Caution
ATTENTION ÉCOLE	Caution, school
ATTENTION TRAVAUX	Road works ahead (men working)
CÉDER LE PASSAGE	Give way (Yield)
CIRCULATION DIFFICILE	Slow traffic
CHAUSSÉE DÉFORMÉE	Poor road surface
CHUTES DE PIERRES	Falling rocks
DÉVIATION	Diversion/detour
FIN DE L'INTERDICTION DE ...	End of no ... zone
FORTE DÉCLIVITÉ	Steep hill
INTERDICTION DE DOUBLER	No overtaking (no passing)
NIDS DE POULE	Potholes
PASSAGE À NIVEAU	Level (railroad) crossing
PÉAGE	Toll
PISTE RÉSERVÉE AUX TRANSPORTS PUBLICS	Lane reserved for public transport
POIDS LOURDS	Heavy vehicles
RALENTIR	Slow down
RÉSERVÉ AUX PIÉTONS	Pedestrians only
SERREZ À DROITE	Keep right
SORTIE DE CAMIONS	Lorry (truck) exit
STATIONNEMENT AUTORISÉ	Parking allowed
STATIONNEMENT INTERDIT	No parking
VERGLAS	Icy road
VIRAGES	Bends/curves

Sightseeing

Where's the tourist office?	**Où se trouve le syndicat d'initiative (l'office du tourisme)?**	oo ser troov ler sangdeekah deeneessyahteev (loffeess dew tooreezm)
What are the main points of interest?	**Qu'y a-t-il de plus intéressant?**	kee ahteel der plew zangtayrehssahng
We're here for ...	**Nous sommes ici pour ...**	noo som zeessee poor
only a few hours	**quelques heures seulement**	kehlker zurr surlermahng
a day	**un jour**	ang zhoor
a week	**une semaine**	ewn sermehn
Can you recommend a sightseeing tour/ an excursion?	**Pourriez-vous me conseiller une visite guidée/une excursion?**	pooryay voo mer kawngssehyay ewn veezeet geeday/ewn ehxkewrsyawng
What's the point of departure?	**D'où part-on?**	doo pahrtawng
Will the bus pick us up at the hotel?	**Le bus nous prendra-t-il à l'hôtel?**	ler bewss noo prahngdrah teel ah loatehl
How much does the tour cost?	**A combien revient l'excursion?**	ah kawngbyang rervyang lehxkewrsyawng
What time does the tour start?	**A quelle heure commence l'excursion?**	ah kehl urr kommahngss lehxkewrsyawng
Is lunch included?	**Le déjeuner est-il compris?**	ler dayzhurnay ehteel kawngpree
What time do we get back?	**A quelle heure serons-nous de retour?**	ah kehl urr serrawng noo der rertoor
Do we have free time in ...?	**Aurons-nous un peu de temps libre à ...?**	oarawng noo ang pur der tahng leebr a
Is there an English-speaking guide?	**Y a-t-il un guide qui parle anglais?**	ee ahteel ang geed kee pahrl ahnggleh
I'd like to hire a private guide for ...	**Je voudrais retenir un guide pour ...**	zher voodreh rerterneer ang geed poor
half a day	**une demi-journée**	ewn dermee zhoornay
a full day	**toute une journée**	too tewn zhoornay

Where is/Where are the ...?	**Où se trouve/ Où se trouvent ...?**	oo ser troov/ oo ser troov
abbey	**l'abbaye**	lahbayee
art gallery	**la galerie d'art**	lah gahlerree dahr
artists' quarter	**le quartier des artistes**	ler kahrtyay day zahrteest
botanical gardens	**le jardin botanique**	ler zhahrdang bottahneek
building	**le bâtiment**	ler bahteemahng
business district	**le quartier des affaires**	ler kahrtyay day zahfehr
castle	**le château**	ler shahtoa
catacombs	**les catacombes**	lay kahtahkawngb
cathedral	**la cathédrale**	lah kahtaydrahl
cave	**la grotte**	lah grot
cemetery	**le cimetière**	ler seemertyehr
city centre	**le centre (de la ville)**	ler sahngtr (der lah veel)
chapel	**la chapelle**	lah shahpehl
church	**l'église**	laygleez
concert hall	**la salle de concert**	lah sahl der kawngssehr
convent	**le couvent**	ler koovahng
court house	**le palais de justice**	ler pahleh der zhewsteess
downtown area	**le centre (de la ville)**	ler sahngtr (der lah veel)
embankment	**le quai**	ler kay
exhibition	**l'exposition**	lehxpozeessyawng
factory	**l'usine**	lewzeen
fair	**la foire**	lah fwahr
flea market	**le marché aux puces**	ler mahrshay oa pewss
fortress	**la forteresse**	lah forterrehss
fountain	**la fontaine**	lah fawngtehn
gardens	**le jardin public**	ler zhahrdang pewbleek
harbour	**le port**	ler por
lake	**le lac**	ler lahk
library	**la bibliothèque**	lah beebleeyotehk
market	**le marché**	ler mahrshay
memorial	**le monument**	ler monewmahng
monastery	**le monastère**	ler monahstehr
monument	**le monument**	ler monewmahng
museum	**le musée**	ler mewzay
old town	**la vieille ville**	lah vyehy veel
opera house	**l'opéra**	lopayrah
palace	**le palais**	ler pahleh
park	**le parc**	ler pahrk
parliament building	**le Parlement**	ler pahrlermahng
planetarium	**le planétarium**	ler plahnaytahryom
royal palace	**le palais royal**	ler pahleh rwahyahl
ruins	**les ruines**	lay rween

shopping area	**le quartier commerçant**	ler kahrtyay kommehrssahng
stadium	**le stade**	ler stahd
statue	**la statue**	lah stahtew
stock exchange	**la bourse**	lah boors
theatre	**le théâtre**	ler tayahtr
tomb	**la tombe**	lah tawngb
tower	**la tour**	lah toor
town hall	**l'hôtel de ville**	loatehl der veel
university	**l'université**	lewneevehrseetay
zoo	**le jardin zoologique**	ler zhahrdang zoalozheek

Admission *A l'entrée*

Is ... open on Sundays?	**Est-ce que ... est ouvert le dimanche?**	ehss ker ... eh toovehr ler deemahngsh
When does it open?	**A partir de quelle heure est-ce ouvert?**	ah pahrteer der kehl urr ehss oovehr
When does it close?	**Quelle est l'heure de fermeture?**	kehl eh lurr der fermertewr
How much is the entrance fee?	**Combien coûte l'entrée?**	kawngbyang koot lahngtray
Is there any reduction for ...?	**Y a-t-il une réduction pour ...?**	ee ahteel ewn raydewksyawng poor
children	**les enfants**	lay zahngfahng
disabled	**les handicapés**	lay ahngdeekahpay
groups	**les groupes**	lay groop
pensioners	**les retraités**	lay rertrehtay
students	**les étudiants**	lay zaytewdyahng
Have you a guidebook (in English)?	**Avez-vous un guide (en anglais)?**	ahvay voo ang geed (ahng nahnggleh)
Can I buy a catalogue?	**Puis-je acheter un catalogue?**	pweezh ahshtay ang kahtahlog
Is it all right to take pictures?	**Est-il permis de prendre des photos?**	ehteel pehrmee der prahngdr day fotoa

ENTRÉE LIBRE	ADMISSION FREE
INTERDICTION DE PHOTOGRAPHIER	NO CAMERAS ALLOWED

Who–What–When? *Qui – Quoi – Quand?*

What's that building?	**Quel est ce bâtiment?**	kehl eh ser bahteemahng
Who was the ...?	**Qui était ...?**	kee ayteh
architect	**l'architecte**	lahrsheetehkt
artist	**l'artiste**	lahrteest
painter	**le peintre**	ler pangtr
sculptor	**le sculpteur**	ler skewlturr
Who built it?	**Qui l'a construit?**	kee lah kawngstrwee
Who painted that picture?	**Qui est l'auteur de ce tableau?**	kee eh loaturr der ser tahbloa
When did he live?	**A quelle époque vivait-il?**	ah kehl aypok veevehteel
When was it built?	**A quand remonte la construction?**	ah kahng rermawngt lah kawngstrewksyawng
Where's the house where ... lived?	**Où est la maison où vécut ...?**	oo eh lah mehzawng oo vaykew
We're interested in ...	**Nous nous intéressons ...**	noo noo zangtayrehssawng
antiques	**aux antiquités**	oa zahngteekeetay
archaeology	**à l'archéologie**	ah lahrkayolozhee
art	**à l'art**	ah lahr
botany	**à la botanique**	ah lah bottahneek
ceramics	**à la céramique**	ah lah sayrahmeek
coins	**aux monnaies**	oa monneh
fine arts	**aux beaux-arts**	oa boa zahr
furniture	**aux meubles**	oa murbl
geology	**à la géologie**	ah lah zhayolozhee
handicrafts	**à l'artisanat**	ah lahrteezahnah
history	**à l'histoire**	ah leestwahr
medicine	**à la médecine**	ah lah maydsseen
music	**à la musique**	ah lah mewzeek
natural history	**à l'histoire naturelle**	ah leestwahr nahtewrehl
ornithology	**à l'ornithologie**	ah lorneetolozhee
painting	**à la peinture**	ah lah pangtewr
pottery	**à la poterie**	ah lah potterree
religion	**à la religion**	ah lah rerleezhyawng
sculpture	**à la sculpture**	ah lah skewltewr
zoology	**à la zoologie**	ah lah zoalozhee
Where's the ... department?	**Où est le département de ...?**	oo eh ler daypahrtermahng der

It's …	**C'est …**	seh
amazing	**étonnant**	aytonnahng
awful	**horrible**	orreebl
beautiful	**beau**	boa
gloomy	**sombre**	sawngbr
impressive	**impressionnant**	angprehssyonnahng
interesting	**intéressant**	angtayrehssahng
magnificent	**splendide**	splahngdeed
overwhelming	**imposant**	angpoazahng
strange	**étrange**	aytrahngzh
superb	**superbe**	sewpehrb
terrifying	**effrayant**	ehfrayyahng
tremendous	**formidable**	formeedahbl
ugly	**laid**	leh

Religious services *Services religieux*

France is particularly rich in cathedrals and churches worth visiting, while Geneva in Switzerland was the cradle of Calvinism. Most places are open for the public to view, except of course when a service is in progress.

If you're interested in taking photographs, you should obtain permission first.

Is there a … near here?	**Y a-t-il près d'ici …?**	ee ahteel preh deessee
Catholic church	**une église (catholique)**	ewn aygleez (kahtoleek)
Protestant church	**un temple (protestant)**	ang tahngpl (protehstahng)
mosque	**une mosquée**	ewn moskay
synagogue	**une synagogue**	ewn seenahgog
At what time is …?	**A quelle heure commence …?**	ah kehl urr kommahngss
mass/the service	**la messe/le culte**	lah mehss/ler kewlt
Where can I find a … who speaks English?	**Où puis-je trouver un … qui parle anglais?**	oo pweezh troovay ang … kee pahrl ahnggleh
priest/minister/rabbi	**prêtre/pasteur/ rabbin**	prehtr/pahsturr/rahbang
I'd like to visit the church.	**Je voudrais visiter l'église.**	zher voodreh veezeetay laygleez

In the countryside *A la campagne*

Is there a scenic route to ...?	**Y a-t-il une route touristique pour ...?**	ee ahteel ewn root tooreesteek poor
How far is it to ...?	**A quelle distance est-on de ...?**	ah kehl deestahngss ehtawng der
Can we walk?	**Pouvons-nous y aller à pied?**	poovawng noo ee ahlay ah pyay
How high is that mountain?	**Quelle est l'altitude de cette montagne?**	kehl eh lahlteetewd der seht mawngtahñ
What's the name of that ...?	**Quel est le nom de ...?**	kehl eh ler nawng der
animal/bird	**cet animal/cet oiseau**	seht ahneemahl/seht wahzoa
flower/tree	**cette fleur/cet arbre**	seht flurr/seht ahrbr

Landmarks *Points de repère*

bridge	**le pont**	ler pawng
cliff	**la falaise**	lah fahlehz
farm	**la ferme**	lah fehrm
field	**le champ**	ler shahng
footpath	**le sentier**	ler sahngtyay
forest	**la forêt**	lah foreh
garden	**le jardin**	ler zhahrdang
hamlet	**le hameau**	ler ahmoa
hill	**la colline**	lah kolleen
house	**la maison**	lah mehzawng
lake	**le lac**	ler lahk
meadow	**le pré**	ler pray
mountain	**la montagne**	lah mawngtahñ
path	**le chemin**	ler shermang
peak	**le sommet**	ler sommeh
pond	**l'étang**	laytahng
river	**le fleuve/la rivière**	ler flurv/lah reevyehr
road	**la route**	lah root
sea	**la mer**	lah mehr
spring	**la source**	lah soorss
valley	**la vallée**	lah vahlay
village	**le village**	ler veelahzh
vineyard	**le vignoble**	ler veeñobl
wall	**le mur**	ler mewr
waterfall	**la chute d'eau**	lah shewt doa
wood	**le bois**	ler bwah

ASKING THE WAY, see page 76

Relaxing

Cinema (movies)—Theatre *Cinéma – Théâtre*

You can find out what's playing from newspapers and billboards. In Paris ask for the weekly entertainment guides *Pariscope* and *l'Officiel des Spectacles*. In Brussels ask for *Le Bulletin*. Most American and British films are dubbed. However, some cinemas in Paris and Geneva show original versions—usually with French subtitles.

What's showing at the cinema tonight?	**Qu'y a-t-il ce soir au cinéma?**	kee ahteel ser swahr oa seenaymah
What's playing at the ... Theatre?	**Que joue-t-on au théâtre ...?**	ker zhootawng oa tayahtr
What sort of play is it?	**De quel genre de pièce s'agit-il?**	der kehl zhahngr der pyehss sahzhee teel
Who's it by?	**Qui l'a écrite?**	kee lah aykreet
Can you recommend (a) ...?	**Pouvez-vous me conseiller ...?**	poovay voo mer kawngssehyay
good film	**un bon film**	ang bawng feelm
comedy	**une comédie**	ewn komaydee
musical	**une comédie musicale**	ewn komaydee mewseekahl
Where's that new film by ... being shown?	**Dans quel cinéma passe le nouveau film de ...?**	dahng kehl seenaymah pahss ler noovoa feelm der
Who's in it?	**Qui joue?**	kee zhoo
Who's playing the lead?	**Qui tient le rôle principal?**	kee tyang ler roal prangsseepahl
Who's the director?	**Qui en est le metteur en scène?**	kee ahng neh ler mehturr ahng sehn
At what theatre is that new play by ... being performed?	**Dans quel théâtre joue-t-on la nouvelle pièce de ...?**	dahng kehl tayahtr zhootawng lah noovehl pyehss der
Is there a sound-and-light show on somewhere?	**Y a-t-il un spectacle son et lumière?**	ee ahteel ang spehktahkl sawng ay lewmyehr

What time does it begin?	**A quelle heure le spectacle commence-t-il?**	ah kehl urr ler spehktahkl kommahngss teel
Are there any seats for tonight?	**Y a-t-il des places pour ce soir?**	ee ahteel day plahss poor ser swahr
How much are the seats?	**Combien coûtent les places?**	kawngbyang koot lay plahss
I want to reserve 2 seats for the show on Friday evening.	**Je voudrais réserver 2 places pour le spectacle de vendredi soir.**	zher voodreh rayzehrvay 2 plahss poor ler spehktahkl der vahngdrerdee swahr
Can I have a ticket for the matinée on Tuesday?	**Je voudrais un billet pour la matinée de mardi.**	zher voodreh ang beeyeh poor lah mahteenay der mahrdee
I want a seat in the stalls (orchestra).	**Je voudrais une place au parterre.**	zher voodreh ewn plahss oa pahrtehr
Not too far back.	**Pas trop loin.**	pah troa lwang
Somewhere in the middle.	**Vers le milieu.**	vehr ler meelyur
How much are the seats in the circle (mezzanine)?	**Combien coûtent les places au balcon?**	kawngbyang koot lay plahss oa bahlkawng
May I please have a programme?	**Le programme, s'il vous plaît.**	ler prograhm seel voo pleh
Where's the cloakroom?	**Où est le vestiaire?**	oo eh ler vehstyehr

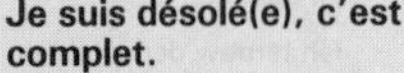

Je suis désolé(e), c'est complet.	I'm sorry, we're sold out.
Il ne reste que quelques places au balcon.	There are only a few seats left in the circle (mezzanine).
Votre billet, s'il vous plaît.	May I see your ticket?
Voici votre place.*	This is your seat.

* It's customary to tip usherettes *(l'ouvreuse)* in most French and Belgian theatres.

DAYS OF THE WEEK, see page 151

Opera—Ballet—Concert *Opéra – Ballet – Concert*

Can you recommend a ...?	**Pouvez-vous me recommander ...?**	poovay voo mer rerkommahngday
ballet	**un ballet**	ang bahlleh
concert	**un concert**	ang kawngssehr
opera	**un opéra**	ang nopayrah
operetta	**une opérette**	ewn opayreht
Where's the opera house/the concert hall?	**Où se trouve l'Opéra/ la salle de concert?**	oo ser troov lopayrah/ lah sahl der kawngssehr
What's on at the opera tonight?	**Que joue-t-on ce soir à l'Opéra?**	ker zhootawng ser swahr ah lopayrah
Who's singing/ dancing?	**Qui chante/danse?**	kee shahngt/dahngss
What orchestra is playing?	**Quel est le nom de l'orchestre?**	kehl eh ler nawng der lorkehstr
What are they playing?	**Que jouera-t-on?**	ker zhoorah tawng
Who's the conductor/ soloist?	**Qui est le chef d'orchestre/le soliste?**	kee eh ler shehf dorkehstr/ ler soleest

Nightclubs *Boîtes de nuit*

Can you recommend a good nightclub?	**Pouvez-vous m'indiquer une bonne boîte de nuit?**	poovay voo mangdeekay ewn bon bwaht der nwee
Is there a floor show?	**Est-ce qu'il y a un spectacle de cabaret?**	ehss keel ee ah ang spehktahkl der kahbahreh
What time does the show start?	**A quelle heure commence le spectacle?**	ah kehl urr kommahngss ler spehktahkl
Is evening dress required?	**La tenue de soirée est-elle exigée?**	lah ternew der swahray ehtehl ehxeezhay

Discos *Discothèques*

Where can we go dancing?	**Où pouvons-nous danser?**	oo poovawng noo dahngssay
Is there a discotheque in town?	**Y a-t-il une discothèque en ville?**	ee ahteel ewn deeskotehk ahng veel
Would you like to dance?	**Voulez-vous danser?**	voolay voo dahngssay

Sports *Sports*

Football (soccer), tennis, boxing, wrestling and bicycle, car and horse racing are among popular spectator sports. If you like sailing, fishing, horseback riding, golf, tennis, hiking, cycling, swimming, golf or trap shooting, you'll find plenty of opportunity to satisfy your recreational bent.

Is there a football (soccer) match anywhere this Saturday?	**Y a-t-il un match de football quelque part ce samedi?**	ee ahteel ang "match" der "football" kehlker pahr ser sahmdee
Which teams are playing?	**Quelles sont les équipes?**	kehl sawng lay zaykeep
Can you get me a ticket?	**Puis-je avoir un billet?**	pweezh ahvwahr ang beeyeh

basketball	**le basket-ball**	ler "basket-ball"
boxing	**la boxe**	lah box
car racing	**les courses d'autos**	lay koors doato
cycling	**le cyclisme**	ler seekleesm
football (soccer)	**le football**	ler "football"
horse racing	**les courses (de chevaux)**	lay koors (der shervoa)
skiing	**le ski**	ler skee
swimming	**la natation**	lah nahtahssyawng
tennis	**le tennis**	ler tehnees
volleyball	**le volley-ball**	ler vollehboal

I'd like to see a boxing match.	**Je voudrais voir un match de boxe.**	zher voodreh vwahr ang "match" der box
What's the admission charge?	**Combien coûte l'entrée?**	kawngbyang koot lahngtray
Where's the nearest golf course?	**Où se trouve le terrain de golf le plus proche?**	oo ser troov ler tehrang der golf ler plew prosh
Where are the tennis courts?	**Où se trouvent les courts de tennis?**	oo ser troov lay koor der tehneess
What's the charge per ...?	**Quel est le tarif par ...?**	kehl eh ler tahreef pahr
day/round/hour	**jour/partie/heure**	zhoor/pahrtee/urr

Can I hire (rent) rackets?	**Puis-je louer des raquettes?**	pweezh looay day rahkeht
Where's the race course (track)?	**Où est le champ de courses?**	oo eh ler shahng der koors
Is there any good fishing around here?	**Y a-t-il un bon endroit pour pêcher dans les environs?**	ee ahteel ang bawng nahngdrwah poor pehshay dahng lay zahngveerawng
Do I need a permit?	**Est-ce que j'ai besoin d'un permis?**	ehss ker zhay berzwang dang pehrmee
Where can I get one?	**Où puis-je m'en procurer un?**	oo pweezh mahng prokewray ang
Can one swim in the lake/river?	**Peut-on nager dans le lac/la rivière?**	purtawng nahzhay dahng ler lahk/lah reevyehr
Is there a swimming pool here?	**Y a-t-il une piscine?**	ee ahteel ewn peesseen
Is it open-air or indoor?	**Est-elle en plein air ou couverte?**	ehtehl ahng plehn ehr oo koovehrt
Is it heated?	**Est-elle chauffée?**	ehtehl shoafay
What's the temperature of the water?	**Quelle est la température de l'eau?**	kehl eh la tahngpayrahtewr der loa
Is there a sandy beach?	**Y a-t-il une plage de sable?**	ee ahteel ewn plahzh der sahbl

On the beach *A la plage*

Is it safe for swimming?	**Peut-on nager sans danger?**	purtawng nahzhay sahng dahngzhay
Is there a lifeguard?	**Y a-t-il un maître nageur?**	ee ahteel ang mehtr nahzhurr
Is it safe for children?	**Est-ce sans danger pour les enfants?**	ehss sahng dahngzhay poor lay zahngfahng
The sea is very calm.	**La mer est très calme.**	lah mehr eh treh kahlm
There are some big waves.	**Il y a de grosses vagues.**	eel ee ah der groass vahg
Are there any dangerous currents?	**Y a-t-il des courants dangereux?**	ee ahteel day koorahng dahngzherrur
What time is high tide/low tide?	**A quelle heure est la marée haute/basse?**	ah kehl urr eh lah mahray oat/bahss

I want to hire a/an/ some ...	**Je voudrais louer ...**	zher voodreh looay
bathing hut (cabana)	**une cabine**	ewn kahbeen
deck-chair	**une chaise longue**	ewn shehz lawngg
motorboat	**un canot à moteur**	ang kahnoa ah moturr
rowing-boat	**une barque à rames**	ewn bahrk ah rahm
sailboard	**une planche à voile**	ewn plahngsh ah vwahl
sailing-boat	**un voilier**	ang vwahlyay
skin-diving equipment	**un équipement de plongée sous-marine**	ang naykeepmahng der plawngzhay soomahreen
sunshade (umbrella)	**un parasol**	ang pahrahssol
surfboard	**une planche de surf**	ewn plahngsh der "surf"
water-skis	**des skis nautiques**	day skee noateek

PLAGE PRIVÉE	PRIVATE BEACH
BAIGNADE INTERDITE	NO SWIMMING

Winter sports *Sports d'hiver*

Is there a skating rink near here?	**Y a-t-il une patinoire près d'ici?**	ee ahteel ewn pahteenwahr preh deessee
I'd like to ski.	**Je voudrais faire du ski.**	zher voodreh fehr dew skee
downhill/cross-country skiing	**ski de piste/ski de fond**	skee der peest/skee der fawng
Are there any ski runs for ...?	**Y a-t-il des pistes pour ...?**	ee ahteel day peest poor
beginners	**débutants**	daybewtahng
average skiers	**skieurs moyens**	skeeurr mwahyang
good skiers	**bons skieurs**	bawng skeeurr
Can I take skiing lessons?	**Puis-je prendre des leçons de ski?**	pweezh prahngdr day lerssawng der skee
Are there ski lifts?	**Y a-t-il des téléskis?**	ee ahteel day taylayskee
I want to hire ...	**Je voudrais louer ...**	zher voodreh looay
poles	**des bâtons**	day bahtawng
skates	**des patins**	day pahtang
ski boots	**des chaussures de ski**	day shoassewr der skee
skiing equipment	**un équipement de ski**	ang naykeepmahng der skee
skis	**des skis**	day skee

Making friends

Introductions *Présentations*

May I introduce ...?	**Puis-je vous présenter ...?**	pweezh voo prayzahngtay
John, this is ...	**Jean, voici ...**	zhahng vwahssee
My name is ...	**Je m'appelle ...**	zher mahpehl
Pleased to meet you.	**Enchanté(e).**	ahngshahngtay
What's your name?	**Comment vous appelez-vous?**	kommahng voo zahperlay voo
How are you?	**Comment allez-vous?**	kommahng tahlay voo
Fine, thanks. And you?	**Très bien, merci. Et vous?**	treh byang mehrsee. ay voo

Follow-up *Pour rompre la glace*

How long have you been here?	**Depuis combien de temps êtes-vous ici?**	derpwee kawngbyang der tahng eht voo zeessee
We've been here a week.	**Nous sommes ici depuis une semaine.**	noo som zeessee derpwee ewn sermehn
Is this your first visit?	**Est-ce la première fois que vous venez?**	ehss lah prermyehr fwah ker voo vernay
No, we came here last year.	**Non, nous sommes déjà venus l'an dernier.**	nawng noo som dayzhah vernew lahng dehrnyay
Are you enjoying your stay?	**Est-ce que vous vous plaisez ici?**	ehss ker voo voo plehzay eessee
Yes, I like it very much.	**Oui, je m'y plais beaucoup.**	wee zher mee pleh boakoo
I like the landscape a lot.	**Ce paysage me plaît beaucoup.**	ser payeezahzh mer pleh boakoo
Do you travel a lot?	**Est-ce que vous voyagez beaucoup?**	ehss ker voo vwahyahzhay boakoo
Where do you come from?	**D'où êtes-vous?**	doo eht voo
I'm from ...	**Je viens de ...**	zher vyang der
What nationality are you?	**Quelle est votre nationalité?**	kehl eh votr nahssyonahleetay

COUNTRIES, see page 146

I'm ...	**Je suis de nationalité ...**	zer swee der nahssyonahleetay
American	**américaine**	ahmayreekehn
British	**britannique**	breetahneek
Canadian	**canadienne**	kahnahdyehn
Irish	**irlandaise**	eerlahngdehz
Where are you staying?	**Où logez-vous?**	oo lozhay voo
Are you on your own?	**Etes-vous seul(e)?**	eht voo surl
I'm with my ...	**Je suis avec ...**	zher swee ahvehk
wife	**ma femme**	mah fahm
husband	**mon mari**	mawng mahree
family	**ma famille**	mah fahmeey
children	**mes enfants**	may zahngfahng
parents	**mes parents**	may pahrahng
boyfriend/girlfriend	**mon ami/amie**	mawng nahmee/nahmee

father/mother	**le père/la mère**	ler pehr/lah mehr
son/daughter	**le fils/la fille**	ler feess/lah feey
brother/sister	**le frère/la sœur**	ler frehr/lah surr
uncle/aunt	**l'oncle/la tante**	lawngkler/lah tahngt
nephew/niece	**le neveu/la nièce**	ler nurvur/lah nyehss
cousin	**le cousin/la cousine**	ler koozang/lah koozeen

Are you married/ single?	**Etes-vous marié(e)/ célibataire?**	eht voo mahryay/ sayleebahtehr
Do you have children?	**Avez-vous des enfants?**	ahvay voo day zahngfahng
What do you think of the country/people?	**Comment trouvez-vous le pays/les gens?**	kommahng troovay voo ler pehee/lay zhahng
What's your occupation?	**Quelle est votre profession?**	kehl eh votr profehssyawng
I'm a student.	**Je suis étudiant(e).**	zher swee zaytewdyahng(t)
What are you studying?	**Qu'étudiez-vous?**	kaytewdyay voo
I'm here on a business trip.	**Je suis en voyage d'affaires.**	zher swee zahng vwahyahzh dahfehr
Do you play cards/ chess?	**Jouez-vous aux cartes/aux échecs?**	zhooay voo oa kahrt/ oa zayshehk

The weather *Le temps*

What a lovely day!	**Quelle belle journée!**	kehl behl zhoornay
What awful weather!	**Quel sale temps!**	kehl sahl tahng
Isn't it cold/ hot today?	**Qu'il fait froid/ Quelle chaleur!**	keel feh frwah/kehl shahlurr
Is it usually as warm as this?	**Fait-il toujours aussi chaud?**	fehteel toozhoor oassee shoa
Do you think it's going to ... tomorrow?	**Pensez-vous qu'il ... demain?**	pahngsay voo keel ... dermang
be a nice day	**fera beau**	ferrah boa
rain	**pleuvra**	plurvrah
snow	**neigera**	nehzherrah
What is the weather forecast?	**Quelles sont les prévisions météo?**	kehl sawng lay prayveezyawng maytayoa

cloud	**le nuage**	ler newahzh
fog	**le brouillard**	ler brooyahr
frost	**le gel**	ler zhehl
ice	**la glace**	lah glahss
lightning	**l'éclair**	layklehr
moon	**la lune**	lah lewn
rain	**la pluie**	lah plwee
sky	**le ciel**	ler syehl
snow	**la neige**	lah nehzh
star	**l'étoile**	laytwahl
sun	**le soleil**	ler solehy
thunder	**le tonnerre**	ler tonnehr
thunderstorm	**l'orage**	lorahzh
wind	**le vent**	ler vahng

Invitations *Invitations*

Would you like to have dinner with us on ...?	**Voudriez-vous dîner avec nous ...?**	voodreeyay voo deenay ahvehk noo
May I invite you for lunch?	**Puis-je vous inviter à déjeuner?**	pweezh voo zangveetay ah dayzhurnay

DAYS OF THE WEEK, see page 151

Can you come over for a drink this evening?	**Pouvez-vous venir prendre un verre chez moi ce soir?**	poovay voo verneer prahngdr ang vehr shay mwah ser swahr
There's a party. Are you coming?	**Il y a une réception. Viendrez-vous?**	eel ee ah ewn rayssehp-syawng. vyangdray voo
That's very kind of you.	**C'est très aimable.**	seh treh zehmahbl
Great. I'd love to come.	**Je viendrai avec plaisir.**	zher vyangdray ahvehk plehzeer
What time shall we come?	**A quelle heure faut-il venir?**	ah kehl urr foateel verneer
May I bring a friend/ a girlfriend?	**Puis-je amener un ami/une amie?**	pweezh ahmernay ang nahmee/ewn ahmee
I'm afraid we've got to leave now.	**Nous devons partir maintenant.**	noo dervawng pahrteer mangternahng
Next time you must come to visit us.	**La prochaine fois, il faudra que vous veniez chez nous.**	lah proshehn fwah eel foadrah ker voo vernyay shay noo
Thanks for the evening. It was great.	**Merci pour la soirée. C'était formidable.**	mehrsee poor lah swahray. sayteh formeedahbl

Dating *Rendez-vous*

Do you mind if I smoke?	**Est-ce que ça vous dérange que je fume?**	ehss ker sah voo dayrahngzh ker zher fewm
Would you like a cigarette?	**Voulez-vous une cigarette?**	voolay voo ewn seegahreht
Do you have a light, please?	**Avez-vous du feu, s'il vous plaît?**	ahvay voo dew fur seel voo pleh
Why are you laughing?	**Pourquoi riez-vous?**	poorkwah reeyay voo
Is my French that bad?	**Mon français est-il si mauvais?**	mawng frahngsseh ehteel see moaveh
Do you mind if I sit down here?	**Me permettez-vous de m'asseoir ici?**	mer pehrmehtay voo der mahsswahr eessee
Can I get you a drink?	**Puis-je vous offrir un verre?**	pweezh voo zoffreer ang vehr
Are you waiting for someone?	**Attendez-vous quelqu'un?**	ahtahngday voo kehlkang

Are you free this evening?	**Etes-vous libre ce soir?**	eht voo leebr ser swahr
Would you like to go out with me tonight?	**Voulez-vous sortir avec moi ce soir?**	voolay voo sorteer ahvehk mwah ser swahr
Would you like to go dancing?	**Aimeriez-vous aller danser?**	ehmerryay voo ahlay dahngssay
I know a good discotheque.	**Je connais une bonne discothèque.**	zher konneh ewn bon deeskotehk
Shall we go to the cinema (movies)?	**Nous pourrions aller au cinéma.**	noo pooryawng ahlay oa seenaymah
Would you like to go for a drive?	**Aimeriez-vous faire un tour en voiture?**	ehmerryay voo fehr ang toor ahng vwahtewr
Where shall we meet?	**Où nous retrouverons-nous?**	oo noo rertrooverrawng noo
I'll pick you up at your hotel.	**Je viendrai vous prendre à votre hôtel.**	zher vyangdray voo prahngdr ah votr oatehl
I'll call for you at 8.	**Je viendrai vous chercher à 8 heures.**	zher vyangdray voo shehrshay ah 8 urr
May I take you home?	**Puis-je vous raccompagner?**	pweezh voo rahkawngpahñay
Can I see you again tomorrow?	**Puis-je vous revoir demain?**	pweezh voo rervwahr dermang
What's your telephone number?	**Quel est votre numéro de téléphone?**	kehl eh votr newmayroa der taylayfon

... and you might answer:

I'd love to, thank you.	**Avec plaisir, merci.**	ahvehk plehzeer mehrsee
Thank you, but I'm busy.	**Merci, mais je suis pris(e).**	mehrsee meh zher swee pree(z)
No, I'm not interested, thank you.	**Non, cela ne m'intéresse pas.**	nawng serlah ner mangtayrehss pah
Leave me alone, please!	**Laissez-moi tranquille!**	lehssay mwah trahngkeel
Thank you, it's been a wonderful evening.	**Merci, j'ai passé une merveilleuse soirée.**	mehrsee zhay pahssay ewn mehrvehyurz swahray
I've enjoyed myself.	**Je me suis bien amusé(e).**	zher mer swee byang nahmewzay

Shopping guide

This shopping guide is designed to help you find what you want with ease, accuracy and speed. It features:

1. a list of all major shops, stores and services (p. 98)
2. some general expressions required when shopping to allow you to be specific and selective (p. 100)
3. full details of the shops and services most likely to concern you. Here you'll find advice, alphabetical lists of items and conversion charts listed under the headings below.

LAUNDRY, see page 29/HAIRDRESSER'S, see page 30

Shops, stores and services *Magasins et services*

Shops usually open at around 9 a.m. and close anytime between 5.30 and 7 p.m. (until 6 in Belgium and until 6.30 in Switzerland). Most businesses close for an hour or two at noon—except department stores. Some shops are open on Sundays and holidays in France. They generally close Saturdays at 5 p.m. in Switzerland. Shopkeepers take a day off during the week—usually Monday.

Where's the nearest ...?	**Où est ... le/la plus proche?**	oo eh ... ler/lah plew prosh
antique shop	**l'antiquaire**	lahngteekehr
art gallery	**la galerie d'art**	lah gahlerree dahr
baker's	**la boulangerie**	lah boolahngzherree
bank	**la banque**	lah bahngk
barber's	**le coiffeur**	ler kwahfurr
beauty salon	**l'institut de beauté**	langsteetew der boatay
bookshop	**la librairie**	lah leebrehree
butcher's	**la boucherie**	lah boosherree
cake shop	**la pâtisserie**	lah pahteesserree
camera shop	**le magasin de photos**	ler mahgahzang der fotoa
chemist's	**la pharmacie**	lah fahrmahssee
confectioner's	**la confiserie**	lah kawngfeezerree
dairy	**la laiterie**	lah lehterree
delicatessen	**la charcuterie/ le traiteur**	lah shahrkewterree/ ler trehturr
dentist	**le dentiste**	ler dahngteest
department store	**le grand magasin**	ler grahng mahgahzang
drugstore	**la pharmacie**	lah fahrmahssee
dry cleaner's	**la teinturerie**	lah tangtewrerree
electrician	**l'électricien**	laylehktreessyang
fishmonger's	**la poissonnerie**	lah pwahssonnerree
flower shop	**le fleuriste**	ler flurreest
furrier's	**le fourreur**	ler foorrurr
greengrocer's	**le primeur**	ler preemurr
grocery	**l'épicerie/le magasin d'alimentation**	laypeesserree/ler mahgahzang dahleemahngtahssyawng
hairdresser's (ladies/men)	**le coiffeur (pour dames/messieurs)**	ler kwahfurr (poor dahm/mehssyur)
hardware store	**la quincaillerie**	lah kangkahyerree
health food shop	**le magasin de diététique**	ler mahgahzang der dyaytayteek

hospital	**l'hôpital**	loapeetahl
ironmonger's	**la quincaillerie**	lah kangkahyerree
jeweller's	**la bijouterie**	lah beezhooterree
launderette	**la laverie automatique**	lah lahverree oatomahteek
library	**la bibliothèque**	lah beebleeyotehk
laundry	**la blanchisserie**	lah blahngsheesserree
market	**le marché**	ler mahrshay
newsagent's	**le marchand de journaux**	ler mahrshahng der zhoornoa
newsstand	**le kiosque à journaux**	ler kyosk ah zhoornoa
optician	**l'opticien**	lopteessyang
pastry shop	**la pâtisserie**	lah pahteesserree
photographer	**le photographe**	ler fotograhf
police station	**le poste de police**	ler post der poleess
post office	**le bureau de poste**	ler bewroa der post
shoemaker's (repairs)	**la cordonnerie**	lah kordonnerree
shoe shop	**le magasin de chaussures**	ler mahgahzang der shoassewr
shopping centre	**le centre commercial**	ler sahngtr kommehrsyahl
souvenir shop	**le magasin de souvenirs**	ler mahgahzang der sooverneer
sporting goods shop	**le magasin d'articles de sport**	ler mahgahzang dahrteekl der spor
stationer's	**la papeterie**	lah pahpehterree
supermarket	**le supermarché**	ler sewpehrmahrshay
tailor's	**le tailleur**	ler tahyurr
telegraph office	**le bureau du télégraphe**	ler bewroa dew taylaygrahf
tobacconist's	**le bureau de tabac**	ler bewroa der tahbah
toy shop	**le magasin de jouets**	ler mahgahzang der zhooeh
travel agency	**l'agence de voyages**	lahzhahngss der vwahyahzh
vegetable store	**le primeur**	ler preemurr
veterinarian	**le vétérinaire**	ler vaytayreenehr
watchmaker's	**l'horlogerie**	lorlozherree
wine merchant	**le marchand de vin**	ler mahrshahng der vang

ENTRÉE	ENTRANCE
SORTIE	EXIT
SORTIE DE SECOURS	EMERGENCY EXIT

General expressions *Expressions générales*

Where? *Où?*

Where's there a good ...?	**Où y a-t-il un bon/ une bonne ...?**	oo ee ahteel ang bawng/ ewn bon
Where can I find a ...?	**Où puis-je trouver ...?**	oo pweezh troovay
Where's the main shopping area?	**Où se trouve le quartier commerçant?**	oo ser troov ler kahrtyay kommehrssahng
Is it far from here?	**Est-ce loin d'ici?**	ehss lwang deessee
How do I get there?	**Comment puis-je m'y rendre?**	kommahng pweezh mee rahngdr

SOLDES SALE

Service *Service*

Can you help me?	**Pourriez-vous m'aider?**	pooryay voo mehday
I'm just looking.	**Je ne fais que regarder.**	zher ner feh ker rergahrday
I want ...	**Je désire ...**	zher dayzeer
Can you show me some ...?	**Pourriez-vous me montrer ...?**	pooryay voo mer mawngtray
Do you have any ...?	**Avez-vous ...?**	ahvay voo
Where's the ... department?	**Où se trouve le rayon ...?**	oo ser troov ler rehyawng
Where is the lift (elevator)/escalator?	**Où est l'ascenseur/ l'escalier mécanique?**	oo eh lahssahngssurr/ lehskahlyay maykahneek
Where do I pay?	**Où est la caisse?**	oo eh lah kehss

That one *Celui-là*

Can you show me ...?	**Pouvez-vous me montrer ...?**	poovay voo mer mawngtray
this/that	**ceci/cela**	serssee/serlah
the one in the window/in the display case	**celui qui est en vitrine/ à l'étalage**	serlwee kee eh ahng veetreen/ah laytahlahzh

Defining the article *Description de l'article*

I'd like a ... one.	**Je désire un ...**	zher dayzeer ang
big	**grand**	grahng
cheap	**bon marché**	bawng mahrshay
dark	**foncé**	fawngssay
good	**bon**	bawng
heavy	**lourd**	loor
large	**grand**	grahng
light (weight)	**léger**	layzhay
light (colour)	**clair**	klehr
oval	**ovale**	ovahl
rectangular	**rectangulaire**	rehktahnggewlehr
round	**rond**	rawng
small	**petit**	pertee
square	**carré**	kahray
sturdy	**solide**	soleed
I don't want anything too expensive.	**Je ne voudrais pas quelque chose de trop cher.**	zher ner voodreh pah kehlker shoaz der troa shehr

Preference *Préférences*

Can you show me some more?	**Pouvez-vous m'en montrer d'autres?**	poovay voo mahng mawngtray doatr
Haven't you anything ...?	**N'auriez-vous pas quelque chose de ...?**	noaryay voo pah kehlker shoaz der
cheaper/better	**meilleur marché/ mieux**	mehyurr mahrshay/myur
larger/smaller	**plus grand/plus petit**	plew grahng/plew pertee

How much? *Combien?*

How much is this?	**Combien coûte ceci?**	kawngbyang koot serssee
How much are they?	**Combien coûtent-ils?**	kawngbyang koot teel
I don't understand.	**Je ne comprends pas.**	zher ner kawngprahng pah
Please write it down.	**Pourriez-vous l'écrire, s'il vous plaît?**	pooryay voo laykreer seel voo pleh
I don't want to spend more than ... francs.	**Je ne veux pas dépenser plus de ... francs.**	zher ner vur pah daypahngssay plew der ... frahng

COLOURS, see page 113

Decision *Décision*

It's not quite what I want.	**Ce n'est pas exactement ce que je veux.**	ser neh pah zehxahktermahng ser ker zher vur
No, I don't like it.	**Non, cela ne me plaît pas.**	nawng serlah ner mer pleh pah
I'll take it.	**Je le prends.**	zher ler prahng

Ordering *Commande*

Can you order it for me?	**Pourriez-vous me le commander?**	pooryay voo mer ler kommahngday
How long will it take?	**Combien de temps cela prendra-t-il?**	kawngbyang der tahng serlah prahngdrah teel

Delivery *Livraison*

I'll take it with me.	**Je l'emporte.**	zher lahngport
Deliver it to the ... Hotel.	**Veuillez le livrer à l'Hôtel ...**	vuryay ler leevray ah loatehl
Please send it to this address.	**Veuillez l'envoyer à cette adresse.**	vuryay lahngvwahyay ah seht ahdrehss
Will I have any difficulty with the customs?	**Aurai-je des difficultés avec la douane?**	oarehzh day deefeekewltay ahvehk lah dwahn

Paying *Paiement*

How much is it?	**Combien vous dois-je?**	kawngbyang voo dwahzh
Can I pay by traveller's cheque?	**Puis-je payer en chèques de voyage?**	pweezh pehyay ahng shehk der vwahyahzh
Do you accept dollars/pounds?	**Acceptez-vous les dollars/livres?**	ahksehptay voo lay dollar/leevr
Do you accept credit cards?	**Acceptez-vous les cartes de crédit?**	ahksehptay voo lay kahrt der kraydee
Do I have to pay the VAT (sales tax)?	**Dois-je payer la T.V.A.?**	dwahzh pehyay lah tay vay ah
Haven't you made a mistake in the bill?	**N'y a-t-il pas une erreur dans la facture?**	nee ahteel pah zewn ehrurr dahng lah fahktewr

Anything else? *Autre chose?*

No, thanks, that's all.	**Non merci, ce sera tout.**	nawng mehrsee ser serrah too
Yes, I want ...	**Oui, je voudrais ...**	wee zher voodreh
Show me ...	**Veuillez me montrer ...**	vuryay mer mawngtray
May I have a bag, please?	**Puis-je avoir un sac, s'il vous plaît?**	pweezh ahvwahr ang sahk seel voo pleh

Dissatisfied? *Mécontent?*

Can you please exchange this?	**Pourriez-vous échanger ceci?**	pooryay voo ayshahngzhay serssee
I want to return this.	**Je voudrais vous rendre ceci.**	zher voodreh voo rahngdr serssee
I'd like a refund. Here's the receipt.	**Je voudrais me faire rembourser. Voici la quittance.**	zher voodreh mer fehr rahngboorsay. vwahssee lah keetahngss

Puis-je vous être utile?	Can I help you?
Que désirez-vous?	What would you like?
Quelle ... désirez-vous?	What ... would you like?
couleur/forme qualité/quantité	colour/shape quality/quantity
Je suis désolé(e), nous n'en avons pas.	I'm sorry, we haven't any.
Notre stock est épuisé.	We're out of stock.
Pouvons-nous le commander?	Shall we order it for you?
Désirez-vous l'emporter ou faut-il vous l'envoyer?	Will you take it with you or shall we send it?
Autre chose?	Anything else?
Cela fera ... francs, s'il vous plaît.	That's ... francs, please.
La caisse se trouve là-bas.	The cashier's over there.

Bookshop—Stationer's *Librairie – Papeterie*

In France, bookshops and stationers' are usually separate shops, though the latter will often sell paperbacks. Newspapers and magazines are sold at newsstands.

Where's the nearest ...?	**Où est ... le/la plus proche?**	oo eh ... ler/lah plew prosh
bookshop	**la librairie**	lah leebrehree
stationer's	**la papeterie**	lah pahpehterree
newsstand	**le kiosque à journaux**	ler kyosk ah zhoornoa
Where can I buy an English-language newspaper?	**Où puis-je acheter un journal en anglais?**	oo pweezh ahshertay ang zhoornahl ahng nahngglеh
Where's the guide-book section?	**Où sont les guides de voyage?**	oo sawng lay geed der vwahyahzh
Where do you keep the English books?	**Où se trouvent les livres en anglais?**	oo ser troov lay leevr ahng nahnggleh
Have you any of ...'s books in English?	**Avez-vous des livres de ... en anglais?**	ahvay voo day leevr der ... ahng nahnggleh
Do you have second-hand books?	**Avez-vous des livres d'occasion?**	ahvay voo day leevr dokahzyawng
I want to buy a/an/some ...	**Je voudrais acheter ...**	zher voodreh ahshertay
address book	**un carnet d'adresses**	ang kahrneh dahdrehss
ball-point pen	**un stylo à bille**	ang steeloa ah beey
book	**un livre**	ang leevr
calendar	**un calendrier**	ang kahlahngdreeyay
carbon paper	**du papier carbone**	dew pahpyay kahrbon
cellophane tape	**du ruban adhésif**	dew rewbahng ahdayzeef
crayons	**des crayons de couleur**	day krehyawng der koolurr
dictionary	**un dictionnaire**	ang deeksyonnehr
French-English	**français-anglais**	frahngsseh ahnggleh
pocket	**de poche**	der posh
drawing paper	**du papier à dessin**	dew pahpyay ah dehssang
drawing pins	**des punaises**	day pewnehz
envelopes	**des enveloppes**	day zahngverlop
eraser	**une gomme**	ewn gom
exercise book	**un cahier**	ang kahyay
felt-tip pen	**un crayon feutre**	ang krehyawng furtr

fountain pen	**un stylo**	ang steeloa
glue	**de la colle**	der lah kol
grammar book	**une grammaire**	ewn grahmehr
guidebook	**un guide**	ang geed
ink	**de l'encre**	der lahngkr
black/red/blue	**noire/rouge/bleue**	nwahr/roozh/blur
(adhesive) labels	**des étiquettes (autocollantes)**	day zayteekeht (oatokollahngt)
magazine	**une revue**	ewn rervew
map	**une carte (géographique)**	ewn kahrt (zhayoagrahfeek)
map of the town	**un plan de ville**	ang plahng der veel
road map of ...	**une carte routière de ...**	ewn kahrt rootyehr der
mechanical pencil	**un porte-mine**	ang port meen
newspaper	**un journal**	ang zhoornahl
American/English	**américain/anglais**	amayreekang/ahnggleh
notebook	**un bloc-notes**	ang blok not
note paper	**du papier à lettres**	dew pahpyay ah lehtr
paintbox	**une boîte de couleurs**	ewn bwaht der koolurr
paper	**du papier**	dew pahpyay
paperback	**un livre de poche**	ang leevr der posh
paperclips	**des trombones**	day trawngbon
paper napkins	**des serviettes en papier**	day sehrvyeht ahng pahpyay
paste	**de la colle**	der lah kol
pen	**une plume**	ewn plewm
pencil	**un crayon**	ang krehyawng
pencil sharpener	**un taille-crayon**	ang tahy krehyawng
playing cards	**des cartes à jouer**	day kahrt ah zhooay
pocket calculator	**une calculatrice de poche**	ewn kahlkewlahtreess der posh
postcard	**une carte postale**	ewn kahrt postahl
propelling pencil	**un porte-mine**	ang port meen
refill (for a pen)	**une recharge (pour stylo)**	ewn rershahrzh (poor steeloa)
rubber	**une gomme**	ewn gom
ruler	**une règle**	ewn rehgl
staples	**des agrafes**	day zahgrahf
string	**de la ficelle**	der lah feessehl
thumbtacks	**des punaises**	day pewnehz
tissue paper	**du papier de soie**	dew pahpyay der swah
typewriter ribbon	**un ruban de machine à écrire**	ang rewbahng der mahsheen ah aykreer
typing paper	**du papier à machine**	dew pahpyay ah mahsheen
writing pad	**un bloc**	ang blok

Camping equipment *Matériel de camping*

I'd like a/an/some ...	**Je voudrais ...**	zher voodreh
bottle-opener	**un ouvre-bouteilles**	ahng noovr bootehy
bucket	**un seau**	ahng soa
butane gas	**du butane**	dew bewtahn
campbed	**un lit de camp**	ang lee der kahng
can opener	**un ouvre-boîtes**	ang noovr bwaht
candles	**des bougies**	day boozhee
(folding) chair	**une chaise (pliante)**	ewn shehz (pleeyahngt)
charcoal	**du charbon de bois**	dew shahrbawng der bwah
clothes pegs	**des pinces à linge**	day pangss ah langzh
compass	**une boussole**	ewn boossol
cool box	**une glacière**	ewn glahssyehr
corkscrew	**un tire-bouchon**	ang toor booshawng
crockery	**de la vaisselle**	der lah vehssehl
cutlery	**des couverts**	day koovehr
deck-chair	**une chaise longue**	ewn shehz lawngg
dishwashing detergent	**du produit (à) vaisselle**	dew prodwee (ah) vehssehl
first-aid kit	**une trousse de premiers secours**	ewn trooss der prermyay serkoor
fishing tackle	**un attirail de pêche**	ang nahteerahy der pehsh
flashlight	**une lampe de poche**	ewn lahngp der posh
food box	**une boîte à conservation**	ewn bwaht ah kawng-ssehrrvahssyawng
frying-pan	**une poêle**	ewn pwahl
groundsheet	**un tapis de sol**	ang tahpee der sol
hammer	**un marteau**	ang mahrtoa
hammock	**un hamac**	ang ahmahk
haversack	**une musette**	ewn mewzeht
ice pack	**une cartouche réfrigérante**	ewn kahrtoosh rayfree-zhayrahngt
kerosene	**du pétrole**	dew paytrol
knapsack	**un sac à dos**	ang sahk ah doa
lamp	**une lampe**	ewn lahngp
lantern	**une lanterne**	ewn lahngtehrn
matches	**des allumettes**	day zahlewmeht
mattress	**un matelas**	ang mahterlah
methylated spirits	**de l'alcool à brûler**	der lahlkol ah brewlay
mosquito net	**une moustiquaire**	ewn moosteekehr
pail	**un seau**	ang soa
paper napkins	**des serviettes en papier**	day sehrvyeht ahng pahpyay
paraffin	**du pétrole**	dew paytrol
penknife	**un canif**	ang kahneef

CAMPING, see page 32

picnic basket	**un panier à pique-nique**	ang pahnyay ah peekneek
plastic bag	**un sac en plastique**	ang sahk ahng plahsteek
rope	**de la corde**	der lah kord
rucksack	**un sac de montagne**	ang sahk der mawngtañ
saucepan	**une casserole**	ewn kahsserrol
scissors	**des ciseaux**	day seezoa
screwdriver	**un tournevis**	ang toornerveess
sleeping bag	**une sac de couchage**	ang sahk der kooshahzh
stew pot	**une marmite**	ewn mahrmeet
(folding) table	**une table (pliante)**	ewn tahbl (pleeyahngt)
tent	**une tente**	ewn tahngt
tent pegs	**des piquets de tente**	day peekeh der tahngt
tent pole	**un montant de tente**	ang mawngtahng der tahngt
tinfoil	**du papier d'aluminium**	dew pahpyay dahlewmeenyom
tin opener	**un ouvre-boîtes**	ang noovr bwaht
tongs	**une pince**	ewn pangss
torch	**une lampe de poche**	ewn lahngp der posh
vacuum flask	**un thermos**	ang tehrmoass
washing powder	**de la lessive**	der lah lehsseev
water flask	**une gourde**	ewn goord
wood alcohol	**de l'alcool à brûler**	der lahlkol ah brewlay

Crockery *Vaisselle*

cups	**des tasses**	day tahss
mugs	**des grosses tasses**	day gross tahss
plates	**des assiettes**	day zahssyeht
saucers	**des soucoupes**	day sookoop
tumblers	**des gobelets**	day goberleh

Cutlery *Couverts*

forks	**des fourchettes**	day foorsheht
knives	**des couteaux**	day kootoa
dessert knives	**des couteaux à dessert**	day kootoa ah dehssehr
spoons	**des cuillères**	day kweeyehr
teaspoons	**des cuillères à café**	day kweeyehr ah kahfay
(made of) plastic	**(en) plastique**	ahng plahsteek
(made of) stainless steel	**(en) inox**	(ahng) eenox

Chemist's (drugstore) *Pharmacie*

You will recognize a chemist's by the sign outside—a green cross, which is lit at night. In the window you'll see a notice telling you where the nearest all-night chemist's is. Go to a *parfumerie* (pahrfewmerree) for perfume and cosmetics. Otherwise, other toilet and household articles can be bought from a *droguerie* (drogerree).

This section is divided into two parts:

1. Pharmaceutical—medicine, first-aid, etc.
2. Toiletry—toilet articles, cosmetics

General *Généralités*

Where's the nearest (all-night) chemist's?	**Où se trouve la pharmacie (de nuit) la plus proche?**	oo ser troov lah fahrmahssee der nwee lah plew prosh
What time does the chemist's open/close?	**A quelle heure ouvre/ferme la pharmacie?**	ah kehl urr oovr/fehrm lah fahrmahssee

1—Pharmaceutical *Médicaments, premiers soins, etc.*

I want something for ...	**Je voudrais quelque chose contre ...**	zher voodreh kehlker shoaz kawngtr
a cold/a cough	**le rhume/la toux**	ler rewm/lah too
hay fever	**le rhume des foins**	ler rewm day fwang
insect bites	**les piqûres d'insectes**	lay peekewr dangsehkt
a hangover	**la gueule de bois**	lah gurl der bwah
sunburn	**les coups de soleil**	lay koo der solehy
travel sickness	**le mal du voyage**	ler mahl dew vwahyahzh
an upset stomach	**les indigestions**	lay zangdeezhehstyawng
Can you make up this prescription for me?	**Pourriez-vous me préparer cette ordonnance?**	pooryay voo mer praypahray seht ordonnahngss
Can I get it without a prescription?	**Puis-je l'obtenir sans ordonnance?**	pweezh lobterneer sahng zordonnahngss
Shall I wait?	**Dois-je attendre?**	dwahzh ahtahngdr

DOCTOR, see page 137

Can I have a/an/ some ...?	**Puis-je avoir ...?**	pweezh ahvwahr
analgesic	**un analgésique**	ang nahnahlzhayzeek
antiseptic cream	**de la pommade antiseptique**	der lah pommahd ahngteessehpteek
aspirin	**de l'aspirine**	der lahspeereen
bandage	**un bandage**	ang bahngdahzh
elastic bandage	**bandage élastique**	bahngdahzh aylahsteek
Band-Aids	**du sparadrap**	dew spahrahdrah
contraceptives	**des contraceptifs**	day kawngtrahssehpteef
corn plasters	**des emplâtres pour les cors**	day zahngplahtr poor lay kor
cotton wool (absorbent cotton)	**du coton hydrophile**	dew kotawng eedrofeel
cough drops	**des pastilles contre la toux**	day pahsteey kawngtr lah too
disinfectant	**un désinfectant**	ang dayzangfehktahng
ear drops	**des gouttes pour les oreilles**	day goot poor lay zorehy
Elastoplast	**du sparadrap**	dew spahrahdrah
eye drops	**des gouttes oculaires**	day goot okewlehr
gauze	**de la gaze**	der lah gahz
insect repellent/ spray	**de la crème anti-insecte/une bombe insecticide**	der lah krehm ahngtee-angssehkt/ewn bawngb angssehkteesseed
iodine	**de la teinture d'iode**	der lah tangtewr dyod
laxative	**un laxatif**	ang lahxahteef
mouthwash	**un gargarisme**	ang gahrgahreezm
nose drops	**des gouttes nasales**	day goot nahzahl
sanitary towels (napkins)	**des serviettes hygiéniques**	day sehrvyeht eezhyayneek
sleeping pills	**un somnifère**	ang somneefehr
suppositories	**des suppositoires**	day sewpoazeetwahr
... tablets	**des comprimés ...**	day kawngpreemay
tampons	**des tampons hygiéniques**	day tahngpawng eezhyayneek
thermometer	**un thermomètre**	ang tehrmomehtr
throat lozenges	**des pastilles pour la gorge**	day pahsteey poor lah gorzh
tranquillizers	**un tranquillisant**	ang trahngkeeleezahng
vitamin pills	**des vitamines**	day veetahmeen

POISON	POISON
POUR USAGE EXTERNE	FOR EXTERNAL USE ONLY

2—Toiletry *Articles de toilette*

I'd like a/an/some ...	**Je voudrais ...**	zher voodreh
after-shave lotion	**de la lotion après rasage**	der lah lossyawng ahpreh rahzahzh
astringent	**un astringent**	ang nahstrangzhahng
bath essence	**du bain de mousse**	dew bang der mooss
bath salts	**des sels de bain**	day sehl der bang
cream	**une crème**	ewn krehm
cleansing cream	**une crème démaquillante**	ewn krehm daymahkeeyahngt
foundation cream	**du fond de teint**	dew fawng der tang
moisturizing cream	**une crème hydratante**	ewn krehm eedrahtahngt
night cream	**une crème de nuit**	ewn krehm der nwee
cuticle remover	**un produit pour enlever les cuticules**	ahng prodwee poor ahnglervay lay kewteekewl
deodorant	**un déodorant**	ang dayodorahng
emery board	**une lime à ongles**	ewn leem ah awnggl
eye liner	**un eye-liner**	ang "eye liner"
eye pencil	**un crayon pour les yeux**	ang krehyawng poor lay zyur
eye shadow	**du fard à paupières**	dew fahr ah poapyehr
face powder	**de la poudre**	der lah poodr
foot cream	**de la crème pour les pieds**	der lah krehm poor lay pyay
hand cream	**de la crème pour les mains**	der lah krehm poor lay mang
lipsalve	**du beurre de cacao**	dew burr der kahkahoa
lipstick	**du rouge à lèvres**	dew roozh ah lehvr
make-up remover pads	**des disques démaquillants**	day deesk daymahkeeyahng
nail brush	**une brosse à ongles**	ewn bross ah awnggl
nail clippers	**un coupe-ongles**	ang koop awnggl
nail file	**une lime à ongles**	ewn leem ah awnggl
nail polish	**du vernis à ongles**	dew vehrnee ah awnggl
nail polish remover	**du dissolvant**	dew deessolvahng
nail scissors	**des ciseaux à ongles**	day seezoa ah awnggl
perfume	**du parfum**	dew pahrfang
powder	**de la poudre**	der lah poodr
powder puff	**une houppette**	ewn oopeht
razor	**un rasoir**	ang rahzwahr
razor blades	**des lames de rasoir**	day lahm der rahzwahr
rouge	**du fard à joues**	dew fahr ah zhoo
safety pins	**des épingles de sûreté**	day zaypanggl der sewrtay

shaving brush	**un blaireau**	ang blehroa
shaving cream	**de la crème à raser**	der lah krehm ah rahzay
soap	**du savon**	dew sahvawng
sponge	**une éponge**	ewn aypawngzh
sun-tan cream	**de la crème solaire**	der lah krehm solehr
sun-tan oil	**de l'huile solaire**	der lweel solehr
talcum powder	**du talc**	dew tahlk
tissues	**des mouchoirs en papier**	day mooshwahr ahng pahpyay
toilet paper	**du papier hygiénique**	dew pahpyay eezhyayneek
toilet water	**de l'eau de toilette**	der loa der twahleht
toothbrush	**une brosse à dents**	ewn bross ah dahng
toothpaste	**du dentifrice**	dew dahngteefreess
towel	**une serviette**	ewn sehrvyeht
tweezers	**une pince à épiler**	ewn pangss ah aypeelay

For your hair *Pour vos cheveux*

bobby pins	**des pinces à cheveux**	day pangss ah shervur
colour shampoo	**un shampooing colorant**	ang shahngpwang kolorahng
comb	**un peigne**	ang pehñ
curlers	**des bigoudis**	day beegoodee
dry shampoo	**un shampooing sec**	ang shahngpwang sehk
dye	**une teinture**	ewn tangtewr
hairbrush	**une brosse à cheveux**	ewn bross ah shervur
hairgrips	**des pinces à cheveux**	day pangss ah shervur
hair lotion	**une lotion capillaire**	ewn lossyawng kahpeelehr
hairpins	**des épingles à cheveux**	day zaypanggl ah shervur
hair spray	**de la laque**	der lah lahk
setting lotion	**un fixatif**	ang feexahteef
shampoo	**du shampooing**	dew shahngpwang
for dry/greasy (oily) hair	**pour cheveux secs/ gras**	poor shervur sehk/ grah
tint	**une coloration**	ewn kolorahssyawng
wig	**une perruque**	ewn pehrewk

For the baby *Pour votre bébé*

baby food	**des aliments pour bébés**	day zahleemahng poor baybay
dummy (pacifier)	**une tétine**	ewn tayteen
feeding bottle	**un biberon**	ang beeberrawng
nappies (diapers)	**des couches**	day koosh

Clothing *Habillement*

If you want to buy something specific, prepare yourself in advance. Look at the list of clothing on page 116. Get some idea of the colour, material and size you want. They're all listed on the next few pages.

General *Généralités*

I'd like ...	**Je voudrais ...**	zher voodreh
I want ... for a 10-year-old boy/girl.	**Je voudrais ... pour un garçon/une fillette de 10 ans.**	zher voodreh ... poor ang gahrsawng/ewn feeyeht der 10 ahng
I want something like this.	**Je voudrais quelque chose dans ce genre.**	zher voodreh kehlker shoaz dahng ser zhahngr
I like the one in the window.	**Celui qui est en vitrine me plaît.**	serlwee kee eh tahng veetreen mer pleh
How much is that per metre?	**Combien coûte le mètre?**	kawngbyang koot ler mehtr

1 centimetre (cm.) = 0.39 in.		1 inch = 2.54 cm.
1 metre (m.) = 39.37 in.		1 foot = 30.5 cm.
10 metres = 32.81 ft.		1 yard = 0.91 m.

Colour *Couleur*

I want something in ...	**Je voudrais quelque chose en ...**	zher voodreh kehlker shoaz ahng
I want a darker/lighter shade.	**Je voudrais un ton plus foncé/plus clair.**	zher voodreh ang tawng plew fawngssay/plew klehr
I want something to match this.	**Je voudrais quelque chose d'assorti à cela.**	zher voodreh kehlker shoaz dahssortee ah serlah
I don't like the colour.	**Je n'aime pas cette couleur.**	zher nehm pah seht koolurr

beige	**beige**	behzh
black	**noir**	nwahr
blue	**bleu**	blur
brown	**brun**	brang
fawn	**fauve**	foav
golden	**doré**	doray
green	**vert**	vehr
grey	**gris**	gree
mauve	**mauve**	moav
orange	**orange**	orahngzh
pink	**rose**	roaz
purple	**violet**	vyoleh
red	**rouge**	roozh
scarlet	**écarlate**	aykahrlaht
silver	**argenté**	ahrzhahngtay
turquoise	**turquoise**	tewrkwahz
white	**blanc**	blahng
yellow	**jaune**	zhoan
light ...	**... clair**	... klehr
dark ...	**... foncé**	... fawngssay

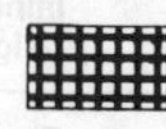

uni (ewnee) | **à rayures** (ah rehyewr) | **à pois** (ah pwah) | **à carreaux** (ah kahroa) | **fantaisie** (fahngtayzee)

Material *Tissus*

Do you have anything in ...?	**Avez-vous quelque chose en ...?**	ahvay voo kehlker shoaz ahng
Is that ...?	**Est-ce ...?**	ehss
handmade	**fait à la main**	feh ah lah mang
imported	**importé**	angportay
made here	**de fabrication locale**	der fahbreekahssyawng lokahl
I want something thinner.	**Je voudrais quelque chose de plus mince.**	zher voodreh kehlker shoaz der plew mangss
Do you have any better quality?	**N'auriez-vous pas une meilleure qualité?**	noaryay voo pah zewn mehyurr kahleetay

What's it made of?	**En quoi est-ce?**	ahng kwah ehss
cambric	**batiste**	bahteest
camel-hair	**poil de chameau**	pwahl der shahmoa
chiffon	**mousseline**	moosserleen
corduroy	**velours côtelé**	verloor koaterlay
cotton	**coton**	kotawng
crepe	**crêpe**	krehp
denim	**toile de coton**	twahl der kotawng
felt	**feutre**	furtr
flannel	**flanelle**	flahnehl
gabardine	**gabardine**	gahbahrdeen
lace	**dentelle**	dahngtehl
leather	**cuir**	kweer
linen	**lin**	lang
poplin	**popeline**	popperleen
satin	**satin**	sahtang
silk	**soie**	swah
suede	**daim**	dang
terrycloth	**tissu-éponge**	teessew aypawngzh
velvet	**velours**	verloor
velveteen	**velours de coton**	verloor der kotawng
wool	**laine**	lehn
worsted	**peigné**	pehñay

Is it ...?	**Est-ce ...?**	ehss
pure cotton/wool	**pur coton/pure laine**	pewr kotawng/pewr lehn
synthetic	**synthétique**	sangtayteek
colour fast	**grand teint**	grahng tang
wrinkle resistant	**infroissable**	angfrwahssahbl
Is it hand washable/ machine washable?	**Peut-on le laver à la main/ à la machine?**	purtawng ler lahvay ah lah mang/ ah lah mahsheen
Will it shrink?	**Est-ce que cela rétrécit au lavage?**	ehss ker serlah raytrayssee oa lahvahzh

Size *Taille*

I take size 38.	**Je porte du 38.**	zher port dew 38
Could you measure me?	**Pouvez-vous prendre mes mesures?**	poovay voo prahngdr may merzewr
I don't know the French sizes.	**Je ne connais pas les tailles françaises.**	zher ner konneh pah lay tahy frahngssehz

Sizes can vary somewhat from one manufacturer to another, so be sure to try on shoes and clothing before you buy.

Women *Dames*

Dresses/Suits						
American	8	10	12	14	16	18
British	10	12	14	16	18	20
Continental	36	38	40	42	44	46

Stockings						
American / British	8	8½	9	9½	10	10½
Continental	0	1	2	3	4	5

Shoes				
American	6	7	8	9
British	4½	5½	6½	7½
Continental	37	38	40	41

Men *Messieurs*

Suits/Overcoats						
American / British	36	38	40	42	44	46
Continental	46	48	50	52	54	56

Shirts				
American / British	15	16	17	18
Continental	38	41	43	45

Shoes									
American / British	5	6	7	8	8½	9	9½	10	11
Continental	38	39	41	42	43	43	44	44	45

A good fit? *Un essayage?*

Can I try it on?	**Puis-je l'essayer?**	pweezh lehssehyay
Where's the fitting room?	**Où est la cabine d'essayage?**	oo eh lah kahbeen dehssehyahzh
Is there a mirror?	**Y a-t-il un miroir?**	ee ahteel ang meerwahr
It fits very well.	**Cela va très bien.**	serlah vah treh byang
It doesn't fit.	**Cela ne me va pas.**	serlah ner mer vah pah

NUMBERS, see page 147

It's too ...	**C'est trop ...**	seh troa
short/long	**court/long**	koor/lawng
tight/loose	**étroit/large**	aytrwah/lahrzh
How long will it take to alter?	**Combien de temps faut-il compter pour la retouche?**	kawngbyang der tahng foateel kawngtay poor lah rertoosh

Clothes and accessories *Vêtements et accessoires*

I would like a/an some ...	**Je voudrais ...**	zher voodreh
anorak	**un anorak**	ang nahnorahk
bathing cap	**un bonnet de bain**	ang bonneh der bang
bathing suit	**un costume de bain**	ang kostewm der bang
bathrobe	**un peignoir (de bain)**	ang pehnwahr (der bang)
blouse	**un chemisier**	ang shermeezyay
bow tie	**un nœud papillon**	ang nur pahpeeyawng
bra	**un soutien-gorge**	ang sootyang gorzh
braces	**des bretelles**	day brertehl
briefs	**un slip**	ang sleep
cap	**une casquette**	ewn kahskeht
cardigan	**un cardigan**	ang kahrdeegahng
coat	**un manteau**	ang mahngtoa
dress	**une robe**	ewn rob
dressing gown	**un peignoir**	ang pehnwahr
evening dress (woman's)	**une robe du soir**	ewn rob dew swahr
girdle	**une gaine**	ewn gehn
gloves	**des gants**	day gahng
handbag	**un sac à main**	ang sahk ah mang
handkerchief	**un mouchoir**	ang mooshwahr
hat	**un chapeau**	ang shahpoa
jacket (man's)	**un veston**	ang vehstawng
jacket (woman's)	**une jaquette**	ewn zhahkeht
jeans	**des jeans**	day "jeans"
jersey	**un tricot**	ang treekoa
jumper (Br.)	**un chandail**	ang shahngdahy
nightdress	**une chemise de nuit**	ewn shermeez der nwee
overalls	**une salopette**	ewn sahlopeht
pair of ...	**une paire de ...**	ewn pehr der
panties	**un slip**	ang sleep
pants (Am.)	**un pantalon**	ang pahngtahlawng
panty girdle	**une gaine-culotte**	ewn gehn kewlot
panty hose	**un collant**	ang kollahng

pullover	**un pull(over)**	ang pewl(ovehr)
roll-neck (turtle-neck)	**à col roulé**	ah kol roolay
round-neck	**à col rond**	ah kol rawng
V-neck	**à col en V**	ah kol ahng vay
with long/short sleeves	**avec manches longues/courtes**	ahvehk mahngsh lawngg/koort
without sleeves	**sans manches**	sahng mahngsh
pyjamas	**un pyjama**	ang peezhahmah
raincoat	**un imperméable**	ang nangpehrmayahbl
scarf	**un foulard**	ang foolahr
shirt	**une chemise**	ewn shermeez
shorts	**un short**	ang short
skirt	**une jupe**	ewn zhewp
slip	**un jupon**	ang zhewpawng
socks	**des chaussettes**	day shoasseht
sports jacket	**une veste de sport**	ewn vehst der spor
stockings	**des bas**	day bah
suit (man's)	**un complet**	ang kawngpleh
suit (woman's)	**un tailleur**	ang tahyurr
suspenders (Am.)	**des bretelles**	day brertehl
sweater	**un chandail**	ang shahngdahy
sweatshirt	**un sweatshirt**	ang ''sweatshirt''
swimming trunks	**un maillot de bain**	ang mahyoa der bang
swimsuit	**un costume de bain**	ang kostewm der bang
T-shirt	**un teeshirt**	ang teeshirt
tie	**une cravate**	ewn krahvaht
tights	**un collant**	ang kollahng
top coat	**un pardessus**	ang pahrderssew
tracksuit	**un survêtement**	ang sewrvehtermahng
trousers	**un pantalon**	ang pahngtahlawng
umbrella	**un parapluie**	ang pahrahplwee
underpants	**un caleçon/slip**	ang kahlssawng/sleep
undershirt	**un maillot de corps**	ang mahyoa der kor
vest (Am.)	**un gilet**	ang zheeleh
vest (Br.)	**un maillot de corps**	ang mahyoa der kor
waistcoat	**un gilet**	ang zheeleh

belt	**une ceinture**	ewn sangtewr
buckle	**une boucle**	ewn bookl
button	**un bouton**	ang bootawng
pocket	**une poche**	ewn posh
press stud (snap fastener)	**un bouton-pression**	ang bootawng prehssyawng
zip (zipper)	**une fermeture-éclair**	ewn fehrmertewr ayklehr

Shoes *Chaussures*

I'd like a pair of ...	**Je voudrais une paire de ...**	zher voodreh ewn pehr der
boots	**bottes**	bot
moccasins	**mocassins**	mokahssang
plimsolls (sneakers)	**tennis**	tehneess
sandals	**sandales**	sahngdahl
shoes	**chaussures**	shoassewr
flat	**à talons plats**	ah tahlawng plah
with a heel	**à talons hauts**	ah tahlawng oa
slippers	**pantoufles**	pahngtoofl
These are too ...	**Ceux-ci sont trop ...**	sursee sawng troa
narrow/wide	**étroits/larges**	aytrwah/lahrzh
large/small	**grands/petits**	grahng/pertee
Do you have a larger/smaller size?	**Avez-vous une pointure plus grande/ plus petite?**	ahvay voo zewn pwangtewr plew grahngd/plew perteet
Do you have the same in black?	**Avez-vous les mêmes en noir?**	ahvay voo lay mehm ang nwahr
cloth	**en toile**	ang twahl
leather	**en cuir**	ang kweer
rubber	**en caoutchouc**	ang kahootshoo
suede	**en daim**	ang dang
Is it genuine leather?	**Est-ce du cuir véritable?**	ehss dew kweer vayreetahbl
I need some shoe polish/shoelaces.	**Je voudrais du cirage/des lacets.**	zher voodreh dew seerahzh/day lahsseh

Shoes worn out? Here's the key to getting them fixed again:

Can you repair these shoes?	**Pouvez-vous réparer ces chaussures?**	poovay voo raypahray say shoassewr
Can you stitch this?	**Pouvez-vous coudre ceci?**	poovay voo koodr serssee
I want new soles and heels.	**Je voudrais un res-semelage complet.**	zher voodreh ang rersser-merlahzh kawngpleh
When will they be ready?	**Quand seront-elles prêtes?**	kahng serrawng tehl preht

COLOURS, see page 113

Electrical appliances *Appareils électriques*

220-volt, 50-cycle A.C. is used almost everywhere in France, Switzerland and Belgium.

What's the voltage?	**Quel est le voltage?**	kehl eh ler voltahzh
Do you have a battery for this?	**Avez-vous une pile pour ceci?**	ahvay voo ewn peel poor serssee
This is broken. Can you repair it?	**Ceci est cassé. Pouvez-vous le réparer?**	serssee eh kahssay. poovay voo ler raypahray
Can you show me how it works?	**Pourriez-vous me montrer comment cela fonctionne?**	pooryay voo mer mawngtray kommahng serlah fawngksyon
I'd like (to hire) a video cassette.	**Je voudrais (louer) une vidéocassette.**	zher voodreh (looay) ewn veedayoakahsseht
I'd like a/an/some ...	**Je voudrais ...**	zher voodreh
adaptor	**une prise de raccordement**	ewn preez der rahkordermang
amplifier	**un amplificateur**	ang nahngpleefeekahturr
bulb	**une ampoule**	ewn ahngpool
clock-radio	**un radio-réveil**	ang rahdyoa rayvehy
electric toothbrush	**une brosse à dents électrique**	ewn bross ah dahng aylehktreek
extension lead (cord)	**un prolongateur**	ang prolawnggahturr
hair dryer	**un sèche-cheveux**	ang sehsh shervur
headphones	**un casque à écouteurs**	ang kahsk ah aykooturr
(travelling) iron	**un fer à repasser (de voyage)**	ang fehr ah rerpahssay (der vwahyahzh)
lamp	**une lampe**	ewn lahngp
plug	**une fiche**	ewn feesh
portable ...	**... portatif**	... portahteef
radio	**un poste de radio**	ang post der rahdyoa
car radio	**un autoradio**	ang noatorahdyoa
record player	**un tourne-disque**	ang toorner deesk
shaver	**un rasoir électrique**	ang rahzwahr aylehktreek
speakers	**des haut-parleurs**	day oa pahrlurr
(cassette) tape recorder	**un magnétophone (à cassettes)**	ang mahñaytofon (ah kahsseht)
(colour) television	**un téléviseur (en couleur)**	ang taylayveezurr (ang koolurr)
transformer	**un transformateur**	ang trahngsformahturr
video-recorder	**un magnétoscope**	ang mahñaytoskop

Grocery *Magasin d'alimentation*

I'd like some bread, please.	**Je voudrais du pain, s'il vous plaît.**	zher voodreh dew pang seel voo pleh
What sort of cheese do you have?	**Quelle sorte de fromage avez-vous?**	kehl sort der fromahzh ahvay voo
A piece of ...	**Un morceau de ...**	ang morsoa der
that one	**celui-là**	serlwee lah
the one on the shelf	**celui sur l'étagère**	serlwee sewr laytahzhehr
I'll have one of those, please.	**Je prendrai un de ceux-là, s'il vous plaît.**	zher prahngdray ang der sur lah seel voo pleh
May I help myself?	**Puis-je me servir?**	pweezh mer sehrveer
I'd like ...	**Je voudrais ...**	zher voodreh
a kilo of apples	**un kilo de pommes**	ang keeloa der pom
half a kilo of tomatoes	**un demi-kilo/une livre de tomates**	ang dermee keeloa/ewn leevr der tomaht
100 grams of butter	**100 grammes de beurre**	sahng grahm der burr
a litre of milk	**un litre de lait**	ang leetr der leh
half a dozen eggs	**une demi-douzaine d'œufs**	ewn dermee doozehn dur
4 slices of ham	**4 tranches de jambon**	4 trahngsh der zhahngbawng
a packet of tea	**un paquet de thé**	ang pahkeh der tay
a jar of jam	**un pot de confiture**	ang poa der kawngfeetewr
a tin (can) of peaches	**une boîte de pêches**	ewn bwaht der pehsh
a tube of mustard	**un tube de moutarde**	ang tewb der mootahrd
a box of chocolates	**une boîte de chocolats**	ewn bwaht der shokolah

1 kilogram or kilo (kg.) = 1000 grams (g.)

100 g. = 3.5 oz.	½ kg. = 1.1 lb.
200 g. = 7.0 oz.	1 kg. = 2.2 lb.

1 oz. = 28.35 g.
1 lb. = 453.60 g.

1 litre (l.) = 0.88 imp. qt. or 1.06 U.S. qt.

1 imp. qt. = 1.14 l.	1 U.S. qt. = 0.95 l.
1 imp. gal. = 4.55 l.	1 U.S. gal. = 3.8 l.

FOOD, see also page 63

Jeweller's—Watchmaker's *Bijouterie–Horlogerie*

Could I please see that?	**Pourrais-je voir ceci, s'il vous plaît?**	poorehzh vwahr serssee seel voo pleh
Do you have anything in gold?	**Avez-vous quelque chose en or?**	ahvay voo kehlker shoaz ahng nor
How many carats is this?	**Combien de carats y a-t-il?**	kawngbyang der kahrah ee ahteel
Is this real silver?	**Est-ce de l'argent véritable?**	ehss der lahrzhahng vayreetahbl
Can you repair this watch?	**Pouvez-vous réparer cette montre?**	poovay voo raypahray seht mawngtr
I'd like a/an/some ...	**Je voudrais ...**	zher voodreh
alarm clock	**un réveil**	ang rayvehy
bangle	**un bracelet**	ang brahsserleh
battery	**une pile**	ewn peel
bracelet	**un bracelet**	ang brahsserleh
chain bracelet	**une gourmette**	ewn goormeht
charm bracelet	**un bracelet à breloques**	ang brahsserleh ah brerlok
brooch	**une broche**	ewn brosh
chain	**une chaînette**	ewn shehneht
charm	**une breloque**	ewn brerlok
cigarette case	**un étui à cigarettes**	ang naytwee ah seegahreht
cigarette lighter	**un briquet**	ang breekeh
clip	**un clip**	ang kleep
clock	**une pendule**	ewn pahngdewl
cross	**une croix**	ewn krwah
cuckoo clock	**un coucou**	ang kookoo
cuff links	**des boutons de manchettes**	day bootawng der mahngsheht
cutlery	**des couverts**	day koovehr
earrings	**des boucles d'oreilles**	day bookl dorehy
gem	**une pierre précieuse**	ewn pyehr prayssyurz
jewel box	**un coffret à bijoux**	ang kofreh ah beezhoo
mechanical pencil	**un porte-mine**	ang port meen
music box	**une boîte à musique**	ewn bwaht ah mewzeek
necklace	**un collier**	ang kollyay
pendant	**un pendentif**	ang pahngdahngteef
pin	**une épingle**	ewn aypanggl
pocket watch	**une montre de gousset**	ewn mawngtr der goosseh

powder compact	**un poudrier**	ang poodreeyay
propelling pencil	**un porte-mine**	ang port meen
ring	**une bague**	ewn bahg
engagement ring	**une bague de fiançailles**	ewn bahg der fyahngssahy
signet ring	**une chevalière**	ewn shervahlyehr
wedding ring	**une alliance**	ewn ahlyahngss
rosary	**un chapelet**	ang shaperleh
silverware	**de l'argenterie**	der lahrzhahngterree
tie clip	**une pince à cravate**	ewn pangss ah krahvaht
tie pin	**une épingle à cravate**	ewn aypanggl ah krahvaht
watch	**une montre**	ewn mawngtr
automatic	**automatique**	oatomahteek
digital	**digitale**	deezheetahl
quartz	**à quartz**	ah kwahrtss
with a second hand	**avec trotteuse**	ahvehk trotturz
watchstrap	**un bracelet de montre**	ang brahsserleh der mawngtr
wristwatch	**une montre-bracelet**	ewn mawngtr brahsserleh

amber	**ambre**	ahngbr
amethyst	**améthyste**	ahmayteest
chromium	**chrome**	kroam
copper	**cuivre**	kweevr
coral	**corail**	korahy
crystal	**cristal**	kreestahl
cut glass	**cristal taillé**	kreestahl tahyay
diamond	**diamant**	dyahmahng
emerald	**émeraude**	aymerroad
enamel	**émail**	aymahy
gold	**or**	or
gold plate	**plaqué or**	plahkay or
ivory	**ivoire**	eevwahr
jade	**jade**	zhahd
onyx	**onyx**	oneeks
pearl	**perle**	pehrl
pewter	**étain**	aytang
platinum	**platine**	plahteen
ruby	**rubis**	rewbee
sapphire	**saphir**	sahfeer
silver	**argent**	ahrzhahng
silver plate	**plaqué argent**	plahkay ahrzhahng
stainless steel	**inox**	eenox
topaz	**topaze**	topahz
turquoise	**turquoise**	tewrkwahz

Optician *Opticien*

I've broken my glasses.	**J'ai cassé mes lunettes.**	zhay kahssay may lewneht
Can you repair them for me?	**Pouvez-vous me les réparer?**	poovay voo mer lay raypahray
When will they be ready?	**Quand seront-elles prêtes?**	kahng serrawng tehl preht
Can you change the lenses?	**Pouvez-vous changer les verres?**	poovay voo shahngzhay lay vehr
I want tinted lenses.	**Je voudrais des verres teintés.**	zher voodreh day vehr tangtay
The frame is broken.	**La monture est cassée.**	lah mawngtewr eh kahssay
I'd like a spectacle case.	**Je voudrais un étui à lunettes.**	zher voodreh ang naytwee ah lewneht
I'd like to have my eyesight checked.	**Je voudrais faire contrôler ma vue.**	zher voodreh fehr kawngtroalay mah vew
I'm short-sighted/ long-sighted.	**Je suis myope/ presbyte.**	zher swee myop/prehsbeet
I want some contact lenses.	**Je voudrais des verres de contact.**	zher voodreh day vehr der kawngtahkt
I've lost one of my contact lenses.	**J'ai perdu un verre de contact.**	zhay pehrdew ang vehr der kawngtahkt
Could you give me another one?	**Pouvez-vous m'en donner un autre?**	poovay voo mahng donnay ang noatr
I have hard/soft lenses.	**J'ai des verres de contact durs/ souples.**	zhay day vehr der kawngtahkt dewr/soopl
Have you any con-tact-lens liquid?	**Avez-vous un liquide pour verres de contact?**	ahvay voo ang leekeed poor vehr der kawngtahkt
I'd like to buy a pair of sunglasses.	**Je voudrais acheter une paire de lunettes de soleil.**	zher voodreh ahshtay ewn pehr der lewneht der solehy
May I look in a mirror?	**Puis-je me voir dans un miroir?**	pweezh mer vwahr dahng zang meerwahr
I'd like to buy a pair of binoculars.	**Je voudrais acheter des jumelles.**	zher voodreh ahshtay day zhewmehl

Photography *Photographie*

I want a(n) ... camera.	**Je voudrais un appareil de photo ...**	zher voodreh ang nahpahrehy der fotoa
automatic	**automatique**	oatomahteek
inexpensive	**bon marché**	bawng mahrshay
simple	**simple**	sangpl
Show me some cine (movie) cameras, please.	**Veuillez me montrer des caméras, s'il vous plaît.**	vuryay mer mawngtray day kahmayrah seel voo pleh
I'd like to have some passport photos taken.	**Je voudrais me faire faire des photos d'identité.**	zher voodreh mer fehr fehr day fotoa deetahngteetay

Film *Film*

I'd like a film for this camera.	**Je voudrais un film pour cet appareil.**	zher voodreh ang feelm poor seht ahpahrehy
black and white	**en noir et blanc**	ang nwahr ay blahng
colour	**en couleurs**	ang koolurr
colour negative	**pour négatifs couleurs**	poor naygahteef koolurr
colour slide	**pour diapositives**	poor dyahpoazeeteev
cartridge	**un chargeur**	ang shahrzhurr
roll film	**une bobine**	ewn bobeen
video cassette	**une vidéocassette**	ewn veedayoakahsseht
24/36 exposures	**vingt-quatre/ trente-six poses**	vangt kahtr/trahngt see poaz
this size	**ce format**	ser formah
this ASA/DIN number	**ce chiffre ASA/DIN**	ser sheefr ahzah/deen
artificial light type	**pour lumière artificielle**	poor lewmyehr ahrteefeessyehl
daylight type	**pour lumière du jour**	poor lewmyehr dew zhoor
fast (high-speed)	**ultrarapide**	ewltrahrahpeed
fine grain	**à grain fin**	ah grang fang

Processing *Développement*

How much do you charge for developing?	**Combien coûte le développement?**	kawngbyang koot ler dayvlopmahng

I want ... prints of each negative.	**Je voudrais ... copies de chaque négatif.**	zher voodreh ... koppee der shahk naygahteef
with a mat finish	**sur papier mat**	sewr pahpyay maht
with a glossy finish	**sur papier brillant**	sewr pahpyay breeyahng
Will you please enlarge this?	**Veuillez agrandir ceci, s'il vous plaît.**	vuryay ahgrahngdeer serssee seel voo pleh
When will the photos be ready?	**Quand les photos seront-elles prêtes?**	kahng lay fotoa serrawng tehl preht

Accessories and repairs *Accessoires et réparations*

I want a/an/some ...	**Je voudrais ...**	zher voodreh
battery	**une pile**	ewn peel
cable release	**un déclencheur**	ang dayklahngshurr
camera case	**un étui (à appareil photo)**	ang naytwee (ah ahpahrehy fotoa)
(electronic) flash	**un flash (électronique)**	ang "flash" (aylehktroneek)
filter	**un filtre**	ang feeltr
for black and white	**pour noir et blanc**	poor nwahr ay blahng
for colour	**pour la couleur**	poor lah koolurr
lens	**un objectif**	ang nobzhehkteef
telephoto lens	**un téléobjectif**	ang taylayobzhehkteef
wide-angle lens	**un grand-angulaire**	ang grahng tahngewlehr
lens cap	**un capuchon (d'objectif)**	ang kahpewshawng (dobzhehkteef)
Can you repair this camera?	**Pouvez-vous réparer cet appareil?**	poovay voo raypahray seht ahpahrehy
The film is jammed.	**Le film est bloqué.**	ler feelm eh blokay
There's something wrong with the ...	**Il y a quelque chose qui ne va pas avec ...**	eel ee ah kehlker shoaz kee ner vah pah ahvehk
exposure counter	**le compte-poses**	ler kawngt poaz
film winder	**le levier d'avancement**	ler lervyay dahvahngssmahng
flash attachment	**la glissière du flash**	lah gleessyehr dew "flash"
lens	**l'objectif**	lobzhehkteef
light meter	**la cellule photoélectrique**	lah sehllewl fotoaylehktreek
rangefinder	**le télémètre**	ler taylaymehtr
shutter	**l'obturateur**	lobtewrahturr

NUMBERS, see page 147

Tobacconist's *Bureau de tabac*

Tobacco is a state monopoly in France. You recognize licensed tobacconist's—cafés, bars and many newsstands—by the conspicuous red cone. In Belgium and Switzerland you can also buy cigarettes in restaurants, supermarkets, etc.

A packet of cigarettes, please.	**Un paquet de cigarettes, s'il vous plaît.**	ang pahkeh der seegahreht seel voo pleh
Do you have any American/English cigarettes?	**Avez-vous des cigarettes américaines/anglaises?**	ahvay voo day seegahreht ahmayreekehn/ahngglehz
I'd like a carton.	**J'en voudrais une cartouche.**	zhahng voodreh ewn kahrtoosh
Give me a/some ..., please.	**Donnez-moi ..., s'il vous plaît.**	donnay mwah ... seel voo pleh
candy	**des bonbons**	day bawngbawng
chewing gum	**du chewing-gum**	dew "chewing gum"
chewing tobacco	**du tabac à chiquer**	dew tahbah ah sheekay
chocolate	**du chocolat**	dew shokolah
cigarette case	**un étui à cigarettes**	ang naytwee ah seegahreht
cigarette holder	**un fume-cigarette**	ang fewm seegahreht
cigarettes	**des cigarettes**	day seegahreht
filter-tipped/ without filter	**avec filtre/ sans filtre**	ahvehk feeltr/ sahng feeltr
light/dark tobacco	**du tabac blond/ brun**	dew tahbah blawng/brang
mild/strong	**légères/fortes**	layzhehr/fort
menthol	**mentholées**	mahngtolay
king-size	**long format**	lawng formah
cigars	**des cigares**	day seegahr
lighter	**un briquet**	ang breekeh
lighter fluid/gas	**de l'essence/ du gaz à briquet**	der lehssahngss/dew gahz ah breekeh
matches	**des allumettes**	day zahlewmeht
pipe	**une pipe**	ewn peep
pipe cleaners	**des nettoie-pipes**	day nehtwah peep
pipe tobacco	**du tabac pour pipe**	dew tahbah poor peep
pipe tool	**un cure-pipe**	ang kewr peep
postcard	**une carte postale**	ewn kahrt postahl
snuff	**du tabac à priser**	dew tahbah ah preezay
stamps	**des timbres**	day tangbr
sweets	**des bonbons**	day bawngbawng
wick	**une mèche**	ewn mehsh

Miscellaneous *Divers*

Souvenirs *Souvenirs*

Here are some suggestions for articles which you might like to bring back as a souvenir or a gift. Some regions of France produce articles which you may be specially interested in, e.g., lace in Brittany, Normandy and Auvergne, porcelain in Limoges and Sèvres, pottery in Brittany, Alsace and Provence.

crystal	**le cristal**	ler kreestahl
cutlery	**la coutellerie**	lah kootehlerree
lace	**les dentelles**	lay dahngtehl
perfume	**le parfum**	ler pahrfang
porcelain	**la porcelaine**	lah porserlehn
pottery	**la poterie**	lah poterree
women's top fashion	**la haute couture**	lah oat kootewr

Lace, crystal and porcelain are also good buys in Belgium. In addition, you might consider buying there:

copperware	**les objets en cuivre**	lay zobzheh ahng kweevr
diamonds	**les diamants**	lay dyahmahng
tapestry	**la tapisserie**	lah tahpeesserree

Some typical products of Switzerland are:

chocolate	**le chocolat**	ler shokolah
cuckoo clock	**le coucou**	ler kookoo
fondue forks	**les fourchettes à fondue**	lay foorsheht ah fawngdew
fondue pot	**le caquelon**	ler kahkerlawng
watch	**la montre**	lah mawngtr

Records – Cassettes *Disques – Cassettes*

Do you have any records by ...?	**Avez-vous des disques de ...?**	ahvay voo day deesk der
I'd like a ...	**Je voudrais ...**	zher voodreh
cassette	**une cassette**	ewn kahsseht
video cassette	**une vidéocassette**	ewn veedayoakahsseht
compact disc	**un disque compact**	ang deesk kawngpahkt

L.P. (33 rpm)	**33 T. (Tours)**	trahngt trwah (toor)
E.P. (45 rpm)	**Super 45 T.**	sewpehr kahrahngt sangk toor
single	**45 T. Simple**	kahrahngt sangk toor sangpl

Have you any songs by ...?	**Avez-vous des chansons de ...?**	ahvay voo day shahngssawng der
Can I listen to this record?	**Puis-je écouter ce disque?**	pweezh aykootay ser deesk
chamber music	**la musique de chambre**	lah mewzeek der shahngbr
classical music	**la musique classique**	lah mewzeek klahsseek
folk music	**la musique folklorique**	lah mewzeek folkloreek
instrumental music	**la musique instrumentale**	lah mewzeek angstrewmahngtahl
jazz	**le jazz**	ler jazz
light music	**la musique légère**	lah mewzeek layzhehr
orchestral music	**la musique symphonique**	lah mewzeek sangfoneek
pop music	**la musique pop**	lah mewzeek pop

Toys *Jouets*

I'd like a toy/game ...	**Je voudrais un jouet/ jeu ...**	zher voodreh ang zhooeh/ zhur
for a boy	**pour un garçon**	poor ang gahrssawng
for a 5-year-old girl	**pour une fillette de 5 ans**	poor ewn feeyeht der 5 ahng
(beach) ball	**un ballon (de plage)**	ang bahlawng (der plahzh)
bucket and spade (pail and shovel)	**un seau et une pelle**	ang soa ay ewn pehl
building blocks (bricks)	**un jeu de construction**	ang zhur der kawngstrewksyawng
card game	**un jeu de cartes**	ang zhur der kahrt
chess set	**un jeu d'échecs**	ang zhur dayshehk
doll	**une poupée**	ewn poopay
electronic game	**un jeu électronique**	ang zhur aylehktroneek
flippers	**des palmes**	day pahlm
roller skates	**des patins à roulettes**	day pahtang ah rooleht
snorkel	**un tuba**	ang tewbah

Your money: banks—currency

In all European French-speaking countries, the basic unit of currency is the *franc* (frahng), divided into 100 *centimes* (sahngteem). However, these various francs have different value. *Franc* is abbreviated to *Fr* or *F*.

In France, there are coins of 5, 10, 20 and 50 centimes and of 1, 2, 5 and 10 francs. Banknotes come in denominations of 20, 50, 100, 200 and 500 francs.

In Switzerland there are coins of 5, 10, 20 and 50 centimes and of 1, 2 and 5 francs. There are banknotes of 10, 20, 50, 100, 500 and 1,000 francs.

Belgium has coins of 50 centimes and of 1, 5, 20 and 50 francs; there are banknotes of 50, 100, 500, 1,000 and 5,000 francs.

Though hours can vary, banks are generally open from 8.30 or 9 a.m. to noon and from 1.30 or 2 to 4.30 or 5 p.m., Monday to Friday. Main branches often remain open during the lunch hours. In all three countries, you will find currency exchange offices *(bureaux de change)* which are often open outside regular banking hours.

Credit cards may be used in an increasing number of hotels, restaurants, shops, etc. Signs are posted indicating which cards are accepted.

Traveller's cheques are accepted by hotels, travel agents and many shops, although the exchange rate is invariably better at a bank. Don't forget to take your passport when going to cash a traveller's cheque. Eurocheques are also accepted.

Where's the nearest bank?	**Où est la banque la plus proche?**	oo eh lah bahngk lah plew prosh
Where's the nearest currency exchange office?	**Où est le bureau de change le plus proche?**	oo eh ler bewroa der shahngzh ler plew prosh

At the bank *A la banque*

I want to change some dollars/pounds.	**Je voudrais changer des dollars/livres.**	zher voodreh shahngzhay day dollahr/leevr
I want to cash a traveller's cheque.	**Je désire toucher ce chèque de voyage.**	zher dayzeer tooshay ser shehk der vwahyahzh
What's the exchange rate?	**Quel est le cours du change?**	kehl eh ler koor dew shahngzh
How much commission do you charge?	**Quelle commission prenez-vous?**	kehl kommeessyawng prernay voo
Can you cash a personal cheque?	**Puis-je toucher un chèque à ordre?**	pweezh tooshay ang shehk ah ordr
Can you telex my bank in London?	**Pouvez-vous envoyer un télex à ma banque à Londres?**	poovay voo ahngvwahyay ang taylehx ah mah bahngk ah lawngdr
I have a/an/some ...	**Je possède ...**	zher possehd
bank card	**une carte d'identité bancaire**	ewn kahrt deedahngteetay bahngkehr
credit card	**une carte de crédit**	ewn kahrt der kraydee
Eurocheques	**des eurocheques**	day zurroshehk
introduction from ...	**une introduction de ...**	ewn angtrodewksyawng der
letter of credit	**une lettre de crédit**	ewn lehtr der kraydee
I'm expecting some money from New York. Has it arrived?	**J'attends de l'argent de New York. Est-il déjà arrivé?**	zhahtahng der lahrzhahng der New York. ehteel dayzhah ahreevay
Please give me ... notes (bills) and some small change.	**Donnez-moi ... billets et de la monnaie, s'il vous plaît.**	donnay mwah ... beeyeh ay der lah monneh seel voo pleh
Give me ... large notes and the rest in small notes.	**Donnez-moi ... grosses coupures, et le reste en petites coupures.**	donnay mwah ... groass koopewr ay ler rehst ahng perteet koopewr

Deposit—Withdrawal *Dépôts – Retraits*

I want to credit this to my account.	**Je voudrais déposer ceci sur mon compte.**	zher voodreh daypoazay serssee sewr mawng kawngt
I want to ...	**Je désire ...**	zher dayzeer
open an account	**ouvrir un compte**	oovreer ang kawngt
withdraw ... francs	**retirer ... francs**	perteeray ... frahng

NUMBERS, see page 147

I want to credit this to Mr...'s account.	**Je voudrais créditer de cette somme le compte de M. ...**	zher voodreh kraydeetay der seht som ler kawngt der mersyur
Where should I sign?	**Où dois-je signer?**	oo dwahzh seeñay

Business terms *Termes d'affaires*

My name is ...	**Je m'appelle ...**	zher mahpehl
Here's my card.	**Voici ma carte.**	vwahssee mah kahrt
I have an appointment with ...	**J'ai rendez-vous avec ...**	zhay rahngday voo ahvehk
Can you give me an estimate of the cost?	**Pouvez-vous me donner une estimation du coût?**	poovay voo mer donnay ewn ehsteemahssyawng dew koo
What's the rate of inflation?	**Quel est le taux d'inflation?**	kehl eh ler toa dangflahssyawng
Can you provide me with an interpreter/ a secretary?	**Pourriez-vous me procurer un interprète/une secrétaire?**	pooryay voo mer prokewray ang nangtehrpreht/ewn serkraytehr
Where can I make photocopies?	**Où puis-je faire des photocopies?**	oo pweezh fehr day fotokopee

amount	**la somme**	lah som
balance	**la position**	lah poazeessyawng
capital	**le capital**	ler kahpeetahl
cheque book	**le carnet de chèques**	ler kahrneh der shehk
contract	**le contrat**	ler kawngtrah
expenses	**les frais**	lay freh
interest	**l'intérêt**	langtayreh
investment	**l'investissement**	langvehsteessmahng
invoice	**la facture**	lah fahktewr
loss	**la perte**	lah pehrt
mortgage	**l'hypothèque**	leepotehk
payment	**le paiement**	ler pehmahng
percentage	**le pourcentage**	ler poorssahngtahzh
profit	**le bénéfice**	ler baynayfeess
purchase	**l'achat**	lahshah
sale	**la vente**	lah vahngt
share	**l'action**	lahksyawng
transfer	**le transfert**	ler trahngsfehr
value	**la valeur**	lah vahlurr

At the post office

Post offices in France bear the sign *Postes et Télécommunications* or *P&T,* and are generally open from 8 a.m. to noon and from 2 to 6.30 p.m. Swiss post offices are recognized by a *PTT* sign and are open from 7.30 a.m. to noon and from 1.45 to 6.30 p.m. In Belgium, post offices are marked *Postes/Posterijen.* Main ones are open from 9 a.m. to 6 p.m. Note that telephone and telegraph services in Belgium are separated from the post office. In all three countries, post offices are open only in the morning on Saturdays.

In France you can buy stamps either at the post office or a tobacco shop. Letter boxes (mailboxes) are painted yellow in France and Switzerland and red in Belgium.

Where's the nearest post office?	**Où se trouve le bureau de poste le plus proche?**	oo ser troov ler bewroa der post ler plew prosh
What time does the post office open/close?	**A quelle heure ouvre/ferme la poste?**	ah kehl urr oovr/fehrm lah post
A stamp for this letter/postcard, please.	**Un timbre pour cette lettre/carte postale, s'il vous plaît.**	ang tangbr poor seht lehtr/kahrt postahl seel voo pleh
I want ... ...-centime stamps.	**Je voudrais ... timbres à ... centimes.**	zher voodreh ... tangbr ah ... sahngteem
What's the postage for a letter to London?	**Quel est le tarif d'une lettre pour Londres?**	kehl eh ler tahreef dewn lehtr poor lawngdr
What's the postage for a postcard to Los Angeles?	**Quel est le tarif d'une carte postale pour Los Angeles?**	kehl eh ler tahreef dewn kahrt postahl poor Los Angeles
Where's the letter box (mailbox)?	**Où se trouve la boîte aux lettres?**	oo ser troov lah bwaht oa lehtr
I want to send this parcel.	**Je voudrais expédier ce colis.**	zher voodreh ehxpaydyay ser kolee

I want to send this by ...	**Je voudrais envoyer ceci ...**	zher voodreh ahngvwahyay serssee
airmail	**par avion**	pahr ahvyawng
express (special delivery)	**par exprès**	pahr ehxprehss
registered mail	**recommandé**	rerkommahngday
At which counter can I cash an international money order?	**A quel guichet puis-je toucher un mandat international?**	ah kehl geesheh pweezh tooshay ang mahngdah angtehrnahssyonahl
Where's the poste restante (general delivery)?	**Où se trouve la poste restante?**	oo ser troov lah post rehstahngt
Is there any mail for me? My name is ...	**Y a-t-il du courrier pour moi? Je m'appelle ...**	ee ahteel dew kooryay poor mwah. zher mahpehl

TIMBRES	STAMPS
COLIS	PARCELS
MANDATS	MONEY ORDERS

Telegrams *Télégrammes*

In France and Switzerland cables and telegrams are dispatched by the post office. In Belgium you must got to a separate *Téléphone/Télégraphe* office.

I want to send a telegram/telex.	**Je voudrais envoyer un télégramme/télex.**	zher voodreh ahngvwahyay ang taylaygrahm/taylehx
May I please have a form?	**Puis-je avoir une formule, s'il vous plaît?**	pweezh ahvwahr ewn formewl seel voo pleh
How much is it per word?	**Quel est le tarif par mot?**	kehl eh ler tahreef pahr moa
How long will a cable to Boston take?	**Combien de temps met un télégramme pour arriver à Boston?**	kawngbyang der tahng meh ang taylaygrahm poor ahreevay ah Boston
How much will this telex cost?	**Combien coûtera ce télex?**	kawngbyang kooterrah ser taylehx

Telephoning *Pour téléphoner*

The telephone system in France, Belgium and Switzerland is virtually entirely automatic. International or long-distance calls can be made from phone boxes, but if you need assistance in placing the call, go to the post office (in Belgium, to the *Téléphone/Télégraphe* office) or ask at your hotel. Local calls in France can also be made from cafés, where you might have to buy a *jeton* (token) to put into the phone.

Telephone numbers are given in pairs in French so that 12 34 56 would be expressed in French, twelve, thirty-four, fifty-six.

Where's the telephone?	**Où se trouve le téléphone?**	oo ser troov ler taylayfon
I would like a telephone token.	**Je voudrais un jeton (de téléphone).**	zher voodreh ang zhertawng (der taylayfon)
Where's the nearest telephone booth?	**Où se trouve la cabine téléphonique la plus proche?**	oo ser troov lah kahbeen taylayfoneek lah plew prosh
May I use your phone?	**Puis-je utiliser votre téléphone?**	pweezh ewteeleezay votr taylayfon
Do you have a telephone directory for Lyons?	**Avez-vous un annuaire télé-phonique de Lyon?**	ahvay voo ang nahnewehr taylayfoneek der lyawng
What's the dialling (area) code for ...?	**Quel est l'indicatif de ...?**	kehl eh langdeekahteef der
How do I get the international operator?	**Comment obtient-on le service inter-national?**	kommahng obtyang tawng ler sehrveess angtehr-nahssyonahl

Operator *Opératrice*

Good morning, I want Geneva 23 45 67.	**Bonjour, je vou-drais le 23 45 67 à Genève.**	bawngzhoor zher voodreh ler 23 45 67 ah zhernehv
Can you help me get this number?	**Pouvez-vous m'aider à obtenir ce numéro?**	poovay voo mehday ah obterneer ser newmayroa

NUMBERS, see page 147

I want to place a personal (person-to-person) call.	**Je voudrais une communication avec préavis.**	zher voodreh ewn kommewneekahssyawng ahvehk prayahvee
I want to reverse the charges.	**Je voudrais téléphoner en P.C.V.**	zher voodreh taylayfonay ahng pay say vay

Speaking *Au téléphone*

Hello. This is ... speaking.	**Allô. C'est ... à l'appareil.**	ahloa. seh ... ah lahpahrehy
I want to speak to ...	**Je désire parler à ...**	zher dayzeer pahrlay ah
I want extension ...	**Je voudrais l'interne ...**	zher voodreh langtehrn
Speak louder/more slowly, please.	**Veuillez parler plus fort/lentement.**	vuryay pahrlay plew for/lahngtmahng

Bad luck *Pas de chance*

Would you please try again later?	**Pourriez-vous rappeler un peu plus tard, s'il vous plaît?**	pooryay voo rahperlay ang pur plew tahr seel voo pleh
Operator, you gave me the wrong number.	**Mademoiselle, vous m'avez donné un faux numéro.**	mahdmwahzehl voo mahvay donnay ang foa newmayroa
Operator, we were cut off.	**Mademoiselle, nous avons été coupés.**	mahdmwahzehl noo zahvawng zaytay koopay

Telephone alphabet *Code d'épellation*

A	**Anatole**	ahnahtol	N	**Nicolas**	neekolah
B	**Berthe**	behrt	O	**Oscar**	oskahr
C	**Célestin**	saylehstang	P	**Pierre**	pyehr
D	**Désiré**	dayzeeray	Q	**Quintal**	kangtahl
E	**Eugène**	urzhehn	R	**Raoul**	rahool
F	**François**	frahngsswah	S	**Suzanne**	sewzahn
G	**Gaston**	gahstawng	T	**Thérèse**	tayrehz
H	**Henri**	ahngree	U	**Ursule**	ewrsewl
I	**Irma**	eermah	V	**Victor**	veektor
J	**Joseph**	zhozehf	W	**William**	veelyahm
K	**Kléber**	klaybehr	X	**Xavier**	ksahvyay
L	**Louis**	looee	Y	**Yvonne**	eevon
M	**Marcel**	mahrssehl	Z	**Zoé**	zoay

Not there *La personne n'est pas là . . .*

When will he/she be back?	**Quand sera-t-il/elle de retour?**	kahng serrah teel/tehl der rertoor
Will you tell him/her I called? My name is . . .	**Veuillez lui dire que j'ai appelé. Je m'appelle . . .**	vuryay lwee deer ker zhay ahperlay. zher mahpehl
Would you ask him/her to call me?	**Pourriez-vous lui demander de me rappeler?**	pooryay voo lwee dermahngday der mer rahperlay
Would you please take a message?	**Pourriez-vous prendre un message, s'il vous plaît?**	pooryay voo prahngdr ang mehssahzh seel voo pleh

Charges *Taxes*

What was the cost of that call?	**Quel est le prix de la communication?**	kehl eh ler pree der lah kommewneekahssyawng
I want to pay for the call.	**Je voudrais payer la communication.**	zher voodreh pehyay lah kommewneekahssyawng

Il y a un appel (téléphonique) pour vous.	There's a telephone call for you.
Quel numéro demandez-vous?	What number are you calling?
Ce n'est pas libre.	The line's engaged.
Il n'y a personne.	There's no answer.
Vous vous êtes trompé(e) de numéro.	You've got the wrong number.
Le téléphone est en dérangement.	The phone is out of order.
Un moment!	Just a moment.
Ne quittez pas!	Hold on, please.
Il/Elle est absent(e) pour le moment.	He's/She's out at the moment.

Doctor

To be at ease, make sure your health insurance policy covers any illness or accident while on holiday. If not, ask your insurance representative, automobile association or travel agent for details of special health insurance.

General *Généralités*

Can you get me a doctor?	**Pouvez-vous m'appeler un médecin?**	poovay voo mahperlay ang maydssang
Is there a doctor here?	**Y a-t-il un médecin ici?**	ee ahteel ang maydssang eessee
I need a doctor, quickly.	**J'ai besoin d'un médecin, vite.**	zhay berzwang dang maydssang veet
Where can I find a doctor who speaks English?	**Où puis-je trouver un médecin qui parle anglais?**	oo pweezh troovay ang maydssang kee pahrl ahnggleh
Where's the surgery (doctor's office)?	**Où est le cabinet de consultation?**	oo eh ler kahbeeneh der kawngssewltahssyawng
What are the surgery (office) hours?	**Quelles sont les heures de consultation?**	kehl sawng lay zurr der kawngssewltahssyawng
Could the doctor come to see me here?	**Le médecin pourrait-il venir me voir?**	ler maydssang pooreh teel verneer mer vwahr
What time can the doctor come?	**A quelle heure peut-il venir?**	ah kehl urr purteel verneer
Can you recommend a/an ...?	**Pouvez-vous m'indiquer ...?**	poovay voo mangdeekay
general practitioner	**un généraliste**	ang zhaynayrahleest
children's doctor	**un pédiatre**	ang paydyahtr
eye specialist	**un oculiste**	ang nokewleest
gynaecologist	**un gynécologue**	ang zheenaykolog
Can I have an appointment ...?	**Puis-je avoir un rendez-vous ...?**	pweezh ahwahr ang rahngday voo
tomorrow	**pour demain**	poor dermang
as soon as possible	**dès que possible**	deh ker posseebl

CHEMIST'S, see page 108

Parts of the body *Parties du corps*

appendix	**l'appendice**	lahpangdeess
arm	**le bras**	ler brah
artery	**l'artère**	lahrtehr
back	**le dos**	ler doa
bladder	**la vessie**	lah vehssee
bone	**l'os**	loss
bowels	**les intestins**	lay zangtehstang
breast	**le sein**	ler sang
chest	**la poitrine**	lah pwahtreen
ear	**l'oreille**	lorehy
eye(s)	**l'œil (les yeux)**	lery (lay zyur)
face	**le visage**	ler veezahzh
finger	**le doigt**	ler dwah
foot	**le pied**	ler pyay
gland	**la glande**	lah glahngd
hand	**la main**	lah mang
head	**la tête**	lah teht
heart	**le cœur**	ler kurr
jaw	**la mâchoire**	lah mahshwahr
joint	**l'articulation**	lahrteekewlahssyawng
kidney	**le rein**	ler rang
knee	**le genou**	ler zhernoo
leg	**la jambe**	lah zhahngb
lip	**la lèvre**	lah lehvr
liver	**le foie**	ler fwah
lung	**le poumon**	ler poomawng
mouth	**la bouche**	lah boosh
muscle	**le muscle**	ler mewskl
neck	**le cou**	ler koo
nerve	**le nerf**	ler nehr
nervous system	**le système nerveux**	ler seestehm nehrvur
nose	**le nez**	ler nay
rib	**la côte**	lah koat
shoulder	**l'épaule**	laypoal
skin	**la peau**	lah poa
spine	**la colonne vertébrale**	lah kolon vehrtaybrahl
stomach	**l'estomac**	lehstomah
tendon	**le tendon**	ler tahngdawng
thigh	**la cuisse**	lah kweess
throat	**la gorge**	lah gorzh
thumb	**le pouce**	ler pooss
toe	**l'orteil**	lortehy
tongue	**la langue**	lah lahngg
tonsils	**les amygdales**	lay zahmeedahl
vein	**la veine**	lah vehn

Accident—Injury *Accidents – Blessures*

There has been an accident.	**Il est arrivé un accident.**	eel eh tahreevay ang nahkseedahng
My child has had a fall.	**Mon enfant a fait une chute.**	mawng nahngfahng ah feh ewn shewt
He/She has hurt his/her head.	**Il/Elle s'est blessé(e) à la tête.**	eel/ehl seh blehssay ah lah teht
He's/She's unconscious.	**Il/Elle s'est évanoui(e).**	eel/ehl seh tayvahnooee
He's/She's bleeding (heavily).	**Il/Elle saigne (abondamment).**	eel/ehl sehñ (ahbawngdahmmahng)
He's/She's (seriously) injured.	**Il/Elle s'est (grièvement) blessé(e).**	eel/ehl seh (gryehvmahng) blehssay
His/Her arm is broken.	**Il/Elle s'est cassé le bras.**	eel/ehl seh kahssay ler brah
His/Her ankle is swollen.	**Sa cheville est enflée.**	sah sherveey eh tahngflay
I've been stung.	**Quelque chose m'a piqué.**	kehlker shoaz mah peekay
I've got something in my eye.	**J'ai reçu quelque chose dans l'œil.**	zhay rerssew kehlker shoaz dahng lery
I've got a/an ...	**J'ai ...**	zhay
blister	**une ampoule**	ewn ahngpool
boil	**un furoncle**	ang fewrawngkl
bruise	**une contusion**	ewn kawngtewzyawng
burn	**une brûlure**	ewn brewlewr
cut	**une coupure**	ewn koopewr
graze	**une éraflure**	ewn ayrahflewr
insect bite	**une piqûre d'insecte**	ewn peekewr dangssehkt
lump	**une bosse**	ewn boss
rash	**une éruption**	ewn ayrewpsyawng
sting	**une piqûre**	ewn peekewr
swelling	**une enflure**	ewn ahngflewr
wound	**une blessure**	ewn blehssewr
Could you have a look at it?	**Pourriez-vous l'examiner?**	pooryay voo lehxahmeenay
I can't move my ...	**Je ne peux pas bouger le/la/les ...**	zher ner pur pah boozhay ler/lah/lay ...
It hurts.	**Cela me fait mal.**	serlah mer feh mahl

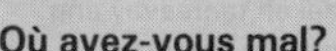

Où avez-vous mal?	Where does it hurt?
Quel genre de douleur éprouvez-vous?	What kind of pain is it?
sourde/aiguë/lancinante persistante/intermittente	dull/sharp/throbbing constant/on and off
C'est ...	It's ...
cassé/foulé déboîté/déchiré	broken/sprained dislocated/torn
Il faut vous faire une radio	I want you to have an X-ray taken.
Il faudra vous mettre un plâtre.	You'll get a plaster.
C'est infecté.	It's infected.
Etes-vous vacciné(e) contre le tétanos?	Have you been vaccinated against tetanus?
Je vais vous donner un antiseptique/calmant.	I'll give you an antiseptic/ a painkiller.

Illness *Maladies*

I'm not feeling well.	**Je ne me sens pas bien.**	zher ner mer sahng pah byang
I'm ill.	**Je suis malade.**	zher swee mahlahd
I feel ...	**J'ai ...**	zhay
dizzy nauseous shivery	**des vertiges** **des nausées** **des frissons**	day vehrteezh day noazay day freessawng
I've got a fever.	**J'ai de la fièvre.**	zhay der lah fyehvr
My temperature is 38 degrees.	**J'ai 38 de fièvre.**	zhay 38 de fyehvr
I've been vomiting.	**J'ai eu des vomissements.**	zhay ew day voameessmahng
I'm constipated/ I've got diarrhoea.	**Je suis constipé(e)/ J'ai la diarrhée.**	zher swee kawngsteepay/ zhay la dyahray
My ... hurt(s).	**J'ai mal à ...**	zhay mahl ah

I've got (a/an) ...	**J'ai ...**	zhay
asthma	**de l'asthme**	der lahsm
backache	**mal aux reins**	mahl oa rang
cold	**un rhume**	ang rewm
cough	**la toux**	lah too
cramps	**des crampes**	day krahngp
earache	**mal aux oreilles**	mahl oa zorehy
hay fever	**le rhume des foins**	ler rewm day fwang
headache	**mal à la tête**	zhay mahl ah lah teht
indigestion	**une indigestion**	ewn angdeezhehstyawng
nosebleed	**des saignements de nez**	day sehñmahng der nay
palpitations	**des palpitations**	day pahlpeetahssyawng
rheumatism	**des rhumatismes**	day rewmahteezm
sore throat	**mal à la gorge**	mahl ah lah gorzh
stiff neck	**un torticolis**	ang torteekolee
stomach ache	**mal à l'estomac**	mahl ah lehstomah
sunstroke	**une insolation**	ewn angsolahssyawng
I have difficulties breathing.	**J'ai de la peine à respirer.**	zhay der lah pehn ah rehspeeray
I have a pain in my chest.	**Je ressens une douleur dans la poitrine.**	zher rersahng ewn doolurr dahng lah pwahtreen
I had a heart attack ... years ago.	**J'ai eu une crise cardiaque il y a ... ans.**	zhay ew ewn kreez kahrdyahk eel ee ah ... ahng
My blood pressure is too high/too low.	**Ma tension est trop élevée/basse.**	mah tahngssyawng eh troa paylervay/bahss
I'm allergic to ...	**Je suis allergique à ...**	zher swee zahlehrzheek ah
I'm a diabetic.	**Je suis diabétique.**	zher swee dyahbayteek

Women's section *Typiquement féminin ...*

I have period pains.	**J'ai des règles douloureuses.**	zhay day rehgl dooloorurz
I have a vaginal infection.	**J'ai une infection vaginale.**	zhay ewn angfehksyawng vahzheenahl
I'm on the pill.	**Je prends la pilule.**	zher prahng lah peelewl
I haven't had my period for 2 months.	**Je n'ai pas eu mes règles depuis 2 mois.**	zher nay pah ew may rehgl derpwee 2 mwah
I'm (3 months) pregnant.	**Je suis enceinte (de 3 mois).**	zher swee zahngssangt (der 3 mwah)

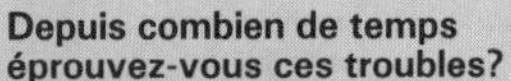

Depuis combien de temps éprouvez-vous ces troubles?	How long have you been feeling like this?
Est-ce la première fois que vous en souffrez?	Is this the first time you've had this?
Je vais prendre votre température/tension.	I'll take your temperature/ blood pressure.
Relevez votre manche.	Roll up your sleeve, please.
Déshabillez-vous (jusqu'à la ceinture), s'il vous plaît.	Please undress (down to the waist).
Etendez-vous là, s'il vous plaît.	Please lie down over here.
Ouvrez la bouche.	Open your mouth.
Respirez à fond.	Breathe deeply.
Toussez, s'il vous plaît.	Cough, please.
Où avez-vous mal?	Where do you feel the pain?
Vous avez ...	You've got (a/an) ...
l'appendicite	appendicitis
une cystite	cystitis
une gastrite	gastritis
la grippe	flu
une inflammation de ...	inflammation of ...
une intoxication alimentaire	food poisoning
la jaunisse	jaundice
une maladie vénérienne	venereal disease
une pneumonie	pneumonia
la rougeole	measles
Je vais vous faire une piqûre.	I'll give you an injection.
Je voudrais un prélèvement de votre sang/de vos selles/ de votre urine.	I want a specimen of your blood/stools/urine.
Vous devrez garder le lit ... jours.	You must stay in bed for ... days.
Vous devriez consulter un spécialiste.	I want you to see a specialist.
Je désire que vous alliez à l'hôpital vous faire faire un bilan (de santé).	I want you to go to the hospital for a general check-up.

Prescription—Treatment *Ordonnance – Traitement*

This is my usual medicine.	**Voici mon médicament habituel.**	vwahssee mawng maydeekahmahng ahbeetewehl
Can you give me a prescription for this?	**Pouvez-vous me donner une ordonnance pour cela?**	poovay voo mer donnay ewn ordonnahngss poor serlah
Can you prescribe a/an/some ...?	**Pourriez-vous me prescrire ...?**	pooryay voo mer prehskreer
antidepressant	**un remontant**	ang rermawngtahng
sleeping pills	**un somnifère**	ang somneefehr
tranquillizer	**un tranquillisant**	ang trahngkeeleezahng
I'm allergic to antibiotics/penicilline.	**Je suis allergique aux antibiotiques/ à la pénicilline.**	zher swee zahlehrzheek oa zahngteebyoteek/ ah lah payneesseeleen
I don't want anything too strong.	**Je ne veux pas quelque chose de trop fort.**	zher ner vur pah kehlker shoaz der troa for
How many times a day should I take it?	**Combien de fois par jour faut-il le prendre?**	kawngbyang der fwah pahr zhoor foateel ler prahngdr
Must I swallow them whole?	**Dois-je les avaler?**	dwahzh lay zahvahlay

Quel traitement suivez-vous?	What treatment are you having?
Quel médicament prenez-vous?	What medicine are you taking?
En injection ou par voie orale?	Injection or oral?
Prenez ... cuillères à café de ce médicament ...	Take ... teaspoons of this medicine ...
Prenez une pilule avec un verre d'eau ...	Take one pill with a glass of water ...
toutes les ... heures	every ... hours
... fois par jour	... times a day
avant/après les repas	before/after each meal
le matin/le soir	in the morning/at night
en cas de douleurs	in case of pain
pendant ... jours	for ... days

CHEMISTS'S, see p. 108

Fee *Honoraires*

How much do I owe you?	**Combien vous dois-je?**	kawngbyang voo dwahzh
May I have a receipt for my health insurance?	**Puis-je avoir une quittance pour mon assurance maladie?**	pweezh ahvwahr ewn keettahngss poor mawng nahssewrahngss mahlahdee
Can I have a medical certificate?	**Puis-je avoir un certificat médical?**	pweezh ahvwahr ang sehrteefeekah maydeekahl
Would you fill in this health insurance form, please?	**Ayez l'obligeance de remplir cette feuille maladie.**	ehyay lobleezhahngss der rahngpleer seht fury mahlahdee

Hospital *Hôpital*

What are the visiting hours?	**Quelles sont les heures de visite?**	kehl sawng lay zurr der veezeet
When can I get up?	**Quand pourrai-je me lever?**	kahng poorehzh mer lervay
When will the doctor come?	**Quand le médecin doit-il passer?**	kahng ler maydssang dwahteel pahssay
I'm in pain.	**J'ai mal.**	zhay mahl
I can't eat/sleep.	**Je ne peux pas manger/dormir.**	zher ner pur pah mahngzhay/dormeer
Can I have a pain-killer/some sleeping pills?	**Puis-je avoir un calmant/somnifère?**	pweezh ahwahr ang kahlmahng/somneefehr
Where is the bell?	**Où est la sonnette?**	oo eh lah sonneht

nurse	**l'infirmière**	langfeermyehr
patient	**le patient/la patiente**	ler pahssyahng/ lah pahssyahngt
anaesthetic	**l'anesthésique**	lahnehstayzeek
blood transfusion	**la transfusion (sanguine)**	lah trahngsfewzyawng (sahnggeen)
injection	**la piqûre**	lah peekewr
operation	**l'opération**	lopayrahssyawng
bed	**le lit**	ler lee
bedpan	**le bassin**	ler bahssang
thermometer	**le thermomètre**	ler tehrmomehtr

Dentist *Dentiste*

Can you recommend a good dentist?	**Pouvez-vous m'indiquer un bon dentiste?**	poovay voo mangdeekay ang bawng dahngteest
Can I make an (urgent) appointment to see Dr...?	**Puis-je prendre un rendez-vous (urgent) avec le docteur ...?**	pweezh prahngdr ang rahngday voo (ewrzhahng) ahvehk ler dokturr
Can't you possibly make it earlier than that?	**Ne pourriez-vous pas me prendre plus tôt?**	ner pooryay voo pah mer prahngdr plew toa
I have a broken tooth.	**Je me suis cassé une dent.**	zher mer swee kahssay ewn dahng
I have a toothache.	**J'ai mal aux dents.**	zhay mahl oa dahng
I have an abscess.	**J'ai un abcès.**	zhay ang nahbseh
This tooth hurts.	**Cette dent me fait mal.**	seht dahng mer feh mahl
at the top	**en haut**	ahng oa
at the bottom	**en bas**	ahng bah
in the front	**devant**	dervahng
at the back	**au fond**	oa fawng
Can you fix it temporarily?	**Pouvez-vous faire un traitement provisoire?**	poovay voo fehr ang trehtmahng proveezwahr
I don't want it extracted.	**Je ne voudrais pas me la faire arracher.**	zher ner voodreh pah mer lah fehr ahrahshay
Could you give me an anaesthetic?	**Pouvez-vous faire une anesthésie locale?**	poovay voo fehr ewn ahnehstayzee lokahl
I've lost a filling.	**J'ai perdu un plombage.**	zhay pehrdew ang plawngbahzh
The gum ...	**La gencive ...**	lah zhahngsseev
is very sore	**est très douloureuse**	eh treh dooloorurz
is bleeding	**saigne**	sehñ
I've broken this denture.	**J'ai cassé mon dentier.**	zhay kahssay mawng dahngtyay
Can you repair this denture?	**Pouvez-vous réparer ce dentier?**	poovay voo raypahray ser dahngtyay
When will it be ready?	**Quand sera-t-il prêt?**	kahng serrah teel preh

Reference section

Where do you come from? *D'où venez-vous?*

Africa	**l'Afrique**	lahfreek
Asia	**l'Asie**	lahzee
Australia	**l'Australie**	loastrahlee
Europe	**l'Europe**	lurrop
North America	**l'Amérique du Nord**	lahmayreek dew nor
South America	**l'Amérique du Sud**	lahmayreek dew sewd
Algeria	**l'Algérie**	lahlzhayree
Austria	**l'Autriche**	loatreesh
Belgium	**la Belgique**	lah behlzheek
Canada	**le Canada**	ler kahnahdah
China	**la Chine**	lah sheen
Denmark	**le Danemark**	ler dahnmahrk
England	**l'Angleterre**	lahngglertehr
Finland	**la Finlande**	lah fanglahngd
France	**la France**	lah frahngss
Germany	**l'Allemagne**	lahlmahñ
Great Britain	**la Grande-Bretagne**	lah grahngd brertañ
Greece	**la Grèce**	lah grehss
India	**l'Inde**	langd
Ireland	**l'Irlande**	leerlahngd
Israel	**Israël**	eesrahehl
Italy	**l'Italie**	leetahlee
Japan	**le Japon**	ler zhahpawng
Luxembourg	**le Luxembourg**	ler lewxahngboor
Morocco	**le Maroc**	ler mahrok
Netherlands	**les Pays-Bas**	lay peheebah
New Zealand	**la Nouvelle-Zélande**	lah noovehl zaylahngd
Norway	**la Norvège**	lah norvehzh
Portugal	**le Portugal**	ler portewgahl
Scotland	**l'Ecosse**	laykoss
South Africa	**l'Afrique du Sud**	lahfreek dew sewd
Soviet Union	**l'Union soviétique**	lewnyawng sovyayteek
Spain	**l'Espagne**	lehspañ
Sweden	**la Suède**	lah swehd
Switzerland	**la Suisse**	lah sweess
Tunisia	**la Tunisie**	lah tewneezee
Turkey	**la Turquie**	lah tewrkee
United States	**les Etats-Unis**	lay zaytah zewnee
Wales	**le Pays de Galles**	ler pehee der gahl
Yugoslavia	**la Yougoslavie**	lah yoogoslahvee

Numbers *Nombres*

0	**zéro**	zayroa
1	**un, une**	ang ewn
2	**deux**	dur
3	**trois**	trwah
4	**quatre**	kahtr
5	**cinq**	sangk
6	**six**	seess
7	**sept**	seht
8	**huit**	weet
9	**neuf**	nurf
10	**dix**	deess
11	**onze**	awngz
12	**douze**	dooz
13	**treize**	trehz
14	**quatorze**	kahtorz
15	**quinze**	kangz
16	**seize**	sehz
17	**dix-sept**	deess seht
18	**dix-huit**	deez weet
19	**dix-neuf**	deez nurf
20	**vingt**	vang
21	**vingt et un**	vang tay ang
22	**vingt-deux**	vangt dur
23	**vingt-trois**	vangt trwah
24	**vingt-quatre**	vangt kahtr
25	**vingt-cinq**	vangt sangk
26	**vingt-six**	vangt seess
27	**vingt-sept**	vangt seht
28	**vingt-huit**	vangt weet
29	**vingt-neuf**	vangt nurf
30	**trente**	trahngt
31	**trente et un**	trahngt ay ang
32	**trente-deux**	trahngt dur
33	**trente-trois**	trahngt trwah
40	**quarante**	kahrahngt
41	**quarante et un**	kahrahngt ay ang
42	**quarante-deux**	kahrahngt dur
43	**quarante-trois**	kahrahngt trwah
50	**cinquante**	sangkahngt
51	**cinquante et un**	sangkahngt ay ang
52	**cinquante-deux**	sangkahngt dur
53	**cinquante-trois**	sangkahngt trwah
60	**soixante**	swahssahngt
61	**soixante et un**	swahssahngt ay ang
62	**soixante-deux**	swahssahngt dur

63	**soixante-trois**	swahssahngt trwah
70*	**soixante-dix**	swahssahngt deess
71	**soixante et onze**	swahssahngt ay awngz
72	**soixante-douze**	swahssahngt dooz
73	**soixante-treize**	swahssahngt trehz
80*	**quatre-vingts**	kahtrer vang
81	**quatre-vingt-un**	kahtrer vang ang
82	**quatre-vingt-deux**	kahtrer vang dur
83	**quatre-vingt-trois**	kahtrer vang trwah
90*	**quatre-vingt-dix**	kahtrer vang deess
91	**quatre-vingt-onze**	kahtrer vang awngz
92	**quatre-vingt-douze**	kahtrer vang dooz
93	**quatre-vingt-treize**	kahtrer vang trehz
100	**cent**	sahng
101	**cent un**	sahng ang
102	**cent deux**	sahng dur
110	**cent dix**	sahng deess
120	**cent vingt**	sahng vang
130	**cent trente**	sahng trahngt
140	**cent quarante**	sahng kahrahngt
150	**cent cinquante**	sahng sangkahngt
160	**cent soixante**	sahng swahssahngt
170	**cent soixante-dix**	sahng swahssahngt deess
180	**cent quatre-vingts**	sahng kahtrer vang
190	**cent quatre-vingt-dix**	sahng kahtrer vang deess
200	**deux cents**	dur sahng
300	**trois cents**	trwah sahng
400	**quatre cents**	kahtrer sahng
500	**cinq cents**	sang sahng
600	**six cents**	seess sahng
700	**sept cents**	seht sahng
800	**huit cents**	wee sahng
900	**neuf cents**	nurf sahng
1000	**mille**	meel
1100	**mille cent**	meel sahng
1200	**mille deux cents**	meel dur sahng
2000	**deux mille**	dur meel
5000	**cinq mille**	sang meel
10,000	**dix mille**	dee meel
50,000	**cinquante mille**	sangkahngt meel
100,000	**cent mille**	sahng meel
1,000,000	**un million**	ang meelyawng
1,000,000,000	**un milliard**	ang meelyahr

* In certain areas, particularly in Belgium and Switzerland, older forms are still in use: 70 = **septante** (sehptahngt), 80 = **huitante** (weetahngt), 90 = **nonante** (nonahngt).

first	**premier (1er)**	prermyay
second	**deuxième (2e)**	durzyehm
third	**troisième (3e)**	trwahzyehm
fourth	**quatrième**	kahtreeyehm
fifth	**cinquième**	sangkyehm
sixth	**sixième**	seezyehm
seventh	**septième**	sehtyehm
eighth	**huitième**	weetyehm
ninth	**neuvième**	nurvyehm
tenth	**dixième**	deezyehm
once/twice	**une fois/deux fois**	ewn fwah/dur fwah
three times	**trois fois**	trwah fwah
a half	**une moitié**	ewn mwahtyay
half a ...	**un/une demi-**	ang/ewn dermee
half of ...	**la moitié de ...**	lah mwahtyay der
half (adj.)	**un/une demi-**	ang/ewn dermee
a quarter/one third	**un quart/un tiers**	ang kahr/ang tyehr
a pair of	**une paire de**	ewn pehr der
a dozen	**une douzaine**	ewn doozehn
one per cent	**un pour cent**	ang poor sahng
3.4%	**3,4%**	trwah veergewl kahtr poor sahng
1981	**mille neuf cent quatre-vingt-un**	meel nurf sahng kahtr vang ang
1992	**mille neuf cent quatre-vingt-douze**	meel nurf sahng kahtr vang dooz
2003	**deux mille trois**	dur meel trwah

Year and age *Année et âge*

year	**l'an/l'année**	lahng/lahnay
leap year	**l'année bissextile**	lahnay beessehxteel
decade	**la décennie**	lah dayssehnee
century	**le siècle**	ler syehkl
this year	**cette année**	seht ahnay
last year	**l'année dernière**	lahnay dehrnyehr
next year	**l'année prochaine**	lahnay proshehn
each year	**chaque année**	shahk ahnay
2 years ago	**il y a 2 ans**	eel ee ah 2 zahng
in one year	**dans un an**	dahng zang nahng
in the eighties	**dans les années quatre-vingts**	dahng lay zahnay kahtr vang
the 16th century	**le seizième siècle**	ler sehzyehm syehkl
in the 20th century	**au vingtième siècle**	oa vangtyehm syehkl

How old are you?	**Quel âge avez-vous?**	kehl ahzh ahvay voo
I'm 30 years old.	**J'ai trente ans.**	zhay trahngt ahng
He/She was born in 1960.	**Il/Elle est né(e) en mille neuf cent soixante.**	eel/ehl eh nay ahng meel nurf sahng swahssahngt
What is his/her age?	**Quel âge a-t-il/elle?**	kehl ahzh ahteel/ehl
Children under 16 are not admitted.	**Les enfants de moins de seize ans ne sont pas admis.**	lay zahngfahng der mwang der sehz ahng ner sawng pah zahdmee

Seasons *Saisons*

spring/summer	**le printemps/l'été**	ler prangtahng/laytay
autumn/winter	**l'automne/l'hiver**	loaton/leevehr
in spring	**au printemps**	oa prangtahng
during the summer	**pendant l'été**	pahngdahng laytay
in autumn	**en automne**	ahng noaton
during the winter	**pendant l'hiver**	pahngdahng leevehr
high season	**haute saison**	oat sehzawng
low season	**basse saison**	bahss sehzawng

Months *Mois*

January	**janvier***	zhahngvyay
February	**février**	fayvreeyay
March	**mars**	mahrs
April	**avril**	ahvreel
May	**mai**	may
June	**juin**	zhwang
July	**juillet**	zhweeyeh
August	**août**	oot
September	**septembre**	sehptahngbr
October	**octobre**	oktobr
November	**novembre**	novahngbr
December	**décembre**	dayssahngbr
in September	**en septembre**	ahng sehptahngbr
since October	**depuis octobre**	derpwee oktobr
the beginning of January	**le début (de) janvier**	ler daybew (der) zhahngvyay
the middle of February	**la mi-février**	lah mee fayvreeyay
the end of March	**la fin (de) mars**	lah fang (der) mahrs

* The names of months aren't capitalized in French.

Days and Date *Jours et date*

What day is it today?	**Quel jour sommes-nous?**	kehl zhoor som noo
Sunday	**dimanche***	deemahngsh
Monday	**lundi**	langdee
Tuesday	**mardi**	mahrdee
Wednesday	**mercredi**	mehrkrerdee
Thursday	**jeudi**	zhurdee
Friday	**vendredi**	vahngdrerdee
Saturday	**samedi**	sahmdee
It's ...	**Nous sommes ...**	noo som
July 1	**le 1er juillet**	ler prermyay zhweeyeh
March 10	**le 10 mars**	ler dee mahrs
in the morning	**le matin**	ler mahtang
during the day	**pendant la journée**	pahngdahng lah zhoornay
in the afternoon	**l'après-midi**	lahpreh meedee
in the evening	**le soir**	ler swahr
at night	**la nuit**	lah nwee
the day before yesterday	**avant-hier**	ahvahng tyehr
yesterday	**hier**	yehr
today	**aujourd'hui**	oazhoordwee
tomorrow	**demain**	dermang
the day after tomorrow	**après-demain**	ahpreh dermang
the day before	**la veille**	lah vehy
the next day	**le lendemain**	ler lahngdermang
two days ago	**il y a deux jours**	eel ee ah dur zhoor
in three days' time	**dans trois jours**	dahng trwah zhoor
last week	**la semaine passée**	lah sermehn pahssay
next week	**la semaine prochaine**	lah sermehn proshehn
for a fortnight (two weeks)	**pendant quinze jours**	pahngdahng kangz zhoor
birthday	**l'anniversaire**	lahneevehrsehr
day off	**le jour de congé**	ler zhoor der kawngzhay
holiday	**le jour férié**	ler zhoor fayryay
holidays/vacation	**les vacances**	lay vahkahngss
week	**la semaine**	lah sermehn
weekend	**le week-end**	ler "weekend"
working day	**le jour ouvrable**	ler zhoor oovrahbl

* The names of days aren't capitalized in French.

Public holidays *Jours fériés*

While there may be additional regional holidays, only national holidays in France (F), Belgium (B) and Switzerland (CH) are cited below.

January 1	**Nouvel An**	New Year's Day	F	CH	B
January 2				CH*	
May 1	**Fête du Travail**	Labour Day	F		B
July 14	**Fête Nationale**	Bastille Day	F		
July 21	**Fête Nationale**	National Day			B
August 1	**Fête Nationale**	National Day		CH*	
August 15	**Assomption**	Assumption Day	F		B
November 1	**Toussaint**	All Saints Day	F		B
November 11	**Armistice**	Armistice Day	F		B
December 25	**Noël**	Christmas	F	CH	B
December 26	**Saint-Etienne**	St. Stephen's Day		CH*	
Movable dates:	**Vendredi-Saint**	Good Friday	F	CH*	
	Lundi de Pâques	Easter Monday	F	CH*	B
	Ascension	Ascension Thursday	F	CH	B
	Lundi de Pentecôte	Whit Monday	F	CH	B

* Most cantons.

Merry Christmas!	**Joyeux Noël!**	zhwahyur noehl
Happy New Year!	**Bonne année!**	bon ahnay
Happy Easter!	**Joyeuses Pâques!**	zhwahyurz pahk
Happy birthday!	**Bon anniversaire!**	bawng nahneevehrsehr
Best wishes!	**Mes/Nos meilleurs vœux!**	may/noa mehyurr vur
Congratulations!	**Félicitations!**	fayleesseetahssyawng
Good luck/ All the best!	**Bonne chance!**	bon shahngss
Have a good trip!	**Bon voyage!**	bawng vwahyahzh
Have a good holiday!	**Bonnes vacances!**	bon vahkahngss
Best regards from ...	**Meilleures salutations de ...**	mehyurr sahlewtahssyawng der
My regards to ...	**Mes amitiés à ...**	may zahmeetyay ah

What time is it? *Quelle heure est-il?*

Excuse me. Can you tell me the time?	**Pardon. Pouvez-vous m'indiquer l'heure?**	pahrdawng. poovay voo mangdeekay lurr
It's ...	**Il est ...**	eel eh
five past one	**une heure cinq***	ewn urr sangk
ten past two	**deux heures dix**	dur zurr deess
a quarter past three	**trois heures un quart**	trwah zurr ang kahr
twenty past four	**quatre heures vingt**	kahtr urr vang
twenty-five past five	**cinq heures vingt-cinq**	sangk urr vangt sangk
half past six	**six heures et demie**	see zurr ay dermee
twenty-five to seven	**sept heures moins vingt-cinq**	seht urr mwang vangt sangk
twenty to eight	**huit heures moins vingt**	weet urr mwang vang
a quarter to nine	**neuf heures moins un quart**	nurv urr mwang zang kahr
ten to ten	**dix heures moins dix**	dee zurr mwang deess
five to eleven	**onze heures moins cinq**	awngz urr mwang sangk
twelve o'clock (noon/midnight)	**douze heures (midi/minuit)**	dooz urr (meedee/meenwee)
in the morning	**du matin**	dew mahtang
in the afternoon	**de l'après-midi**	der lahpreh meedee
in the evening	**du soir**	dew swahr
The train leaves at ...	**Le train part à ...**	ler trang pahr ah
13.04 (1.04 p.m.)	**treize heures quatre***	trehz urr kahtr
0.40 (0.40 a.m.)	**zéro heure quarante**	zayroa urr kahrahngt
in five minutes	**dans cinq minutes**	dahng sank meenewt
in a quarter of an hour	**dans un quart d'heure**	dahng zang kahr durr
half an hour ago	**il y a une demi-heure**	eel ee ah ewn dermee urr
about two hours	**environ deux heures**	ahngveerawng dur zurr
more than 10 minutes	**plus de dix minutes**	plew der dee meenewt
less than 30 seconds	**moins de trente secondes**	mwang der trahngt sergawngd
The clock is fast/ slow.	**L'horloge avance/ a du retard.**	lorlozh ahvahngss/ah dew rertahr

*In ordinary conversation, time is expressed as shown here. However, official time uses a 24-hour clock which means that after noon hours are counted from 13 to 24.

Common abbreviations *Abréviations courantes*

apr. J.-C.	**après Jésus-Christ**	A.D.
av. J.-C.	**avant Jésus-Christ**	B.C.
bd, boul.	**boulevard**	boulevard
c.-à-d.	**c'est-à-dire**	that is to say, i.e.
c/c	**compte courant**	current account
CCP	**compte de chèques postaux**	postal account
CEE	**Communauté Economique Européenne**	European Economic Community
CFF	**Chemins de Fer Fédéraux**	Swiss Federal Railways
ch	**chevaux vapeur**	horsepower
Cie, Co.	**Compagnie**	Co.
CRS	**Compagnies Républicaines de Sécurité**	French order and riot police
CV	**chevaux-vapeur**	horsepower
E.U.	**Etats-Unis**	U.S.A.
exp.	**expéditeur**	sender
h	**heure**	hour, o'clock
hab.	**habitants**	inhabitants, population
M./MM.	**Monsieur/Messieurs**	Mr./Messrs.
Mlle	**Mademoiselle**	Miss
Mme	**Madame**	Mrs.
ONU	**Organisation des Nations Unies**	United Nations Organization
PDG	**président-directeur général**	chairman (president) of the board
p.ex.	**par exemple**	for instance, e.g.
p.p.	**port payé**	postage paid
RATP	**Régie Autonome des Transports Parisiens**	Paris transport authority
RN	**route nationale**	national road
s/	**sur**	on
SA	**société anonyme**	Ltd., Inc.
S.à.R.L.	**société à responsabilité limitée**	limited liability company
SI	**Syndicat d'Initiative**	tourist office (France)
SNCB	**Société Nationale des Chemins de Fer Belges**	Belgian National Railways
SNCF	**Société Nationale des Chemins de Fer Français**	French National Railways
s.v.p.	**s'il vous plaît**	please
T.T.C.	**Toutes taxes comprises**	all taxes included
T.V.A.	**Taxe à la Valeur Ajoutée**	VAT, value-added tax

Signs and notices *Ecriteaux*

A louer	For hire/For rent/To let
Ascenseur	Lift (elevator)
Attention	Caution
Attention au chien	Beware of the dog
A vendre	For sale
Caisse	Cash desk
Chaud	Hot
Chemin privé	Private road
Chiens interdits	Dogs not allowed
Complet	Full/No vacancies
Dames	Ladies
Danger (de mort)	Danger (of death)
Défense de ...	... forbidden
Défense d'entrer sous peine d'amende	Trespassers will be prosecuted
Défense de fumer	No smoking
Entrée	Entrance
Entrée interdite	No entrance
Entrée libre	Admission free
Entrez sans frapper	Enter without knocking
Fermé	Closed
Fermez la porte	Close the door
Froid	Cold
Fumeurs	Smoking allowed
Haute tension	High voltage
Hommes	Men
Hors service	Out of order
Libre	Vacant
Messieurs	Gentlemen
Ne pas déranger	Do not disturb
Ne pas toucher, s.v.p.	Do not touch
Occupé	Occupied
Ouvert de ... à ...	Open from ... to ...
Peinture fraîche	Wet paint
Piste cyclable	Cycle path
Poussez	Push
Privé	Private
Renseignements	Information
Réservé	Reserved
Soldes	Sale
Sonnez, s'il vous plaît	Please ring
Sortie	Exit
Sortie de secours	Emergency exit
Tirez	Pull

Emergency *Urgences*

Call the police	**Appelez la police**	ahperlay lah poleess
DANGER	**DANGER**	dahngzhay
FIRE	**AU FEU**	oa fur
Gas	**Gaz**	gahz
Get a doctor	**Appelez un médecin**	ahperlay ang maydssang
Go away	**Allez-vous-en**	ahlay voo zahng
HELP	**AU SECOURS**	oa serkoor
Get help quickly	**A l'aide, vite**	ah lehd veet
I'm ill	**Je suis malade**	zher swee mahlahd
I'm lost	**Je me suis perdu(e)**	zher mer swee pehrdew
Leave me alone	**Laissez-moi tranquille**	lehssay mwah trahngkeel
LOOK OUT	**ATTENTION**	ahtahngssyawng
POLICE	**POLICE**	poleess
Quick	**Vite**	veet
STOP	**ARRÊTEZ**	ahrehtay
Stop that man/ woman	**Arrêtez cet homme/ cette femme**	ahrehtay seht om/ seht fahm
STOP THIEF	**AU VOLEUR**	oa volurr

Emergency telephone numbers *Numéros d'urgence*

	Belgium	France	Switzerland
Fire	900	18	118
Ambulance	900	17	117
Police	901	17	117

Lost! *En cas de perte ou de vol*

Where's the ...?	**Où est ...?**	oo eh
lost property (lost and found) office?	**le bureau des objets trouvés**	ler bewroa day zobzheh troovay
police station	**le poste de police**	ler post der poleess
I want to report a theft.	**Je voudrais déclarer un vol.**	zher voodreh dayklahray ang vol
My ... has been stolen.	**On m'a volé ...**	awng mah volay
I've lost my ...	**J'ai perdu ...**	zhay pehrdew
handbag	**mon sac à main**	mawng sahk ah mang
passport	**mon passeport**	mawng pahsspor
wallet	**mon portefeuille**	mawng portfury

CAR ACCIDENTS, see page 78

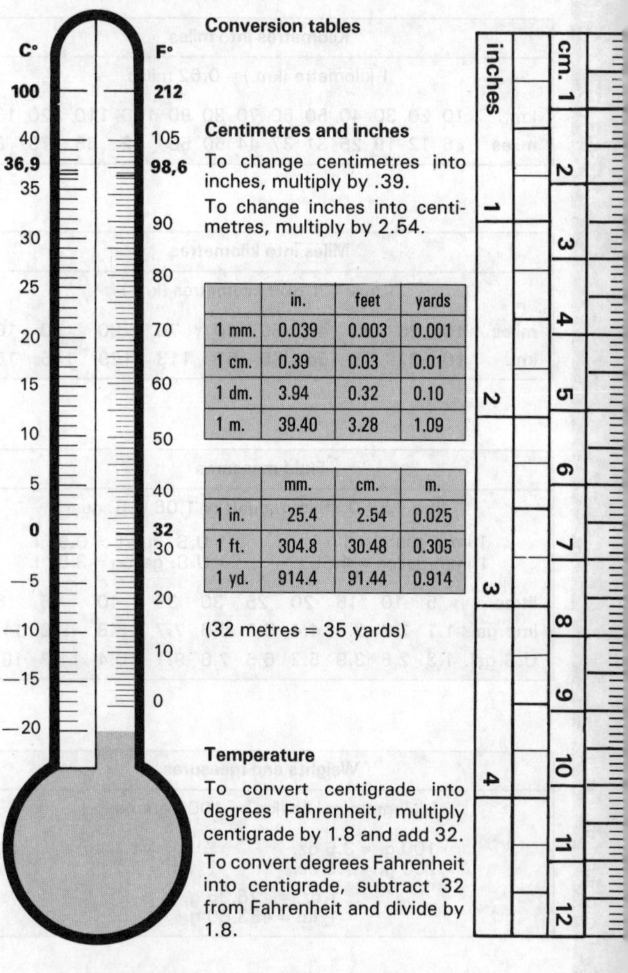

Conversion tables

Centimetres and inches

To change centimetres into inches, multiply by .39.

To change inches into centimetres, multiply by 2.54.

	in.	feet	yards
1 mm.	0.039	0.003	0.001
1 cm.	0.39	0.03	0.01
1 dm.	3.94	0.32	0.10
1 m.	39.40	3.28	1.09

	mm.	cm.	m.
1 in.	25.4	2.54	0.025
1 ft.	304.8	30.48	0.305
1 yd.	914.4	91.44	0.914

(32 metres = 35 yards)

Temperature

To convert centigrade into degrees Fahrenheit, multiply centigrade by 1.8 and add 32.

To convert degrees Fahrenheit into centigrade, subtract 32 from Fahrenheit and divide by 1.8.

Kilometres into miles

1 kilometre (km.) = 0.62 miles

km.	10	20	30	40	50	60	70	80	90	100	110	120	130
miles	6	12	19	25	31	37	44	50	56	62	68	75	81

Miles into kilometres

1 mile = 1.609 kilometres (km.)

miles	10	20	30	40	50	60	70	80	90	100
km.	16	32	48	64	80	97	113	129	145	161

Fluid measures

1 litre (l.) = 0.88 imp. quart or 1.06 U.S. quart

1 imp. quart = 1.14 l.
1 imp. gallon = 4.55 l.

1 U.S. quart = 0.95 l.
1 U.S. gallon = 3.8 l.

litres	5	10	15	20	25	30	35	40	45	50
imp. gal.	1.1	2.2	3.3	4.4	5.5	6.6	7.7	8.8	9.9	11.0
U.S. gal.	1.3	2.6	3.9	5.2	6.5	7.8	9.1	10.4	11.7	13.0

Weights and measures

1 kilogram or kilo (kg.) = 1000 grams (g.)

100 g. = 3.5 oz.
200 g. = 7.0 oz.

½ kg. = 1.1 lb.
1 kg. = 2.2 lb.

1 oz. = 28.35 g.
1 lb. = 453.60 g.

CLOTHING SIZES, see page 115/YARDS AND INCHES, see page 112

Basic Grammar

Articles *Articles*

All nouns in French are either masculine or feminine.

1. **Definite article** (the):

masc. *le* **train**	the train	fem. *la* **voiture**	the car

Le and **la** are contracted to **l'** when followed by a vowel or a silent **h***.

l'avion	the plane	**l'hôtel**	the hotel

Plural (masc. and fem.):

les **trains** *les* **voitures** *les* **avions**

2. **Indefinite article** (a/an):

masc. *un* **timbre**	a stamp	fem. *une* **lettre**	a letter

Plural (masc. and fem.):

des **timbres**	stamps	*des* **lettres**	letters

3. **Some/any** (partitive)

Expressed by **de, du, de la, de l', des** as follows:

masc. **du** (= **de** + **le**)
fem. **de la**

de l' when followed by a vowel or a silent **h***

Plural (masc. and fem.): **des** (= **de** + **les**)

du **sel**	some salt	*de la* **moutarde**	some mustard
*de l'***ail**	some garlic	*des* **oranges**	some oranges

In negatives sentences, **de** is generally used.

Il n'y a pas *de* taxis.	There aren't any taxis.
Je n'ai pas *d'*argent.	I haven't any money.

Note the concentration **d'** before a vowel.

*In French the letter *h* at the beginning of a word is not pronounced. However, in several words the *h* is what is called "aspirate", i.e., no liaison is made with the word preceding it. E.g., *le héros*.

Nouns *Noms*

1. As already noted, nouns are either masculine or feminine. There are no short cuts for determining gender (though, note that most nouns ending in **-e, -té, -tion** are feminine). So always learn a noun together with its accompanying article.

2. The plural of the majority of nouns is formed by adding s to the singular. (The final s is not pronounced.)

3. To show possession, use the preposition **de** (of).

la fin *de* **la semaine**	the end of the week
le début *du* **mois**	the beginning of the month
le patron *de* **l'hôtel**	the owner of the hotel
les valises *des* **voyageurs**	the traveller's luggage
la chambre *de* **Robert**	Robert's room

Adjectives *Adjectifs*

1. Adjectives agree with the noun in gender and number. Most of them form the feminine by adding **e** to the masculine (unless the word already ends in **e**). For the plural, add **s**.

a. **un grand magasin**	a big shop	**des grands magasins**
b. **une auto anglaise**	an English car	**des autos anglaises**

2. As can be seen from the above, adjectives can come (a) before the noun or (b) after the noun. Since it is basically a question of sound and idiom, rules are difficult to formulate briefly; but adjectives more often follow nouns.

3. **Demonstrative adjectives:**

this/that	**ce** *(masc.)*
	cet *(masc. before a vowel or silent* **h***)*
	cette *(fem.)*
these/those	**ces** *(masc. and fem.)*

4. **Possessive adjectives:** These agree in number and gender with *the noun they modify,* i.e., with the thing possessed and not the possessor.

	masc.	fem.	plur.
my	**mon**	**ma**	**mes**
your	**ton**	**ta**	**tes**
his/her/its	**son**	**sa**	**ses**
our	**notre**	**notre**	**nos**
your	**votre**	**votre**	**vos**
their	**leur**	**leur**	**leurs**

Thus, depending on the context:

son **fils**	can mean *his* son or *her* son
sa **chambre**	can mean *his* room or *her* room
ses **vêtements**	can mean *his* clothes or *her* clothes

Personal pronouns *Pronoms personnels*

	Subject	Direct object	Indirect object	After a preposition
I	**je**	**me**	**me**	**moi**
you	**tu**	**te**	**te**	**toi**
he/it (masc.)	**il**	**le**	**lui**	**lui**
she/it (fem.)	**elle**	**la**	**lui**	**elle**
we	**nous**	**nous**	**nous**	**nous**
you	**vous**	**vous**	**vous**	**vous**
they (masc.)	**ils**	**les**	**leur**	**eux**
they (fem.)	**elles**	**les**	**leur**	**elles**

Note: There are two forms for "you" in French: **tu** is used when talking to relatives, close friends and children (and between young people); **vous** is used in all other cases, and is also the plural form of **tu.**

Prepositions *Prépositions*

There is a list of prepositions on page 15. Be careful with **à** (to, at) and **de** (of, from).

à + le = au	**de + le = du**
à + les = aux	**de + les = des**

Adverbs *Adverbes*

Adverbs are generally formed by adding **-ment** to the feminine form of the adjective.

masc.:	fem.:	adverb:
lent (slow)	**lente**	**lentement**
sérieux (serious)	**sérieuse**	**sérieusement**

Verbs *Verbes*

Here we are concerned only with the infinitive and the present tense.

Learn these two **auxiliary verbs:**

être (to be)	**avoir** (to have)
je suis *(I am)*	**j'ai** *(I have)*
tu es *(you are)*	**tu as** *(you have)*
il/elle est *(he, she, it is)*	**il/elle a** *(he, she, it has)*
nous sommes *(we are)*	**nous avons** *(we have)*
vous êtes *(you are)*	**vous avez** *(you have)*
ils/elles sont *(they are)*	**ils/elles ont** *(they have)*

Il y a is equivalent to "there is/there are":

Il y a une lettre pour vous.	There's a letter for you.
Il y a trois colis pour elle.	There are three parcels for her.
Y a-t-il du courrier pour moi?	Is there any post for me?
Il n'y pas de lettres pour vous.	There are no letters for you.

Regular verbs follow one of three patterns (conjugations) depending on the ending of the infinitive.

Infinitive	1 ends in **-er**	2 ends in **-ir**	3 ends in **-re**
	parler (to speak)	**finir** (to finish)	**attendre** (to wait)
je	**parle**	**finis**	**attends***
tu	**parles**	**finis**	**attends**
il/elle	**parle**	**finit**	**attend**
nous	**parlons**	**finissons**	**attendons**
vous	**parlez**	**finissez**	**attendez**
ils/elles	**parlent**	**finissent**	**attendent**
Imperative	**parlez**	**finissez**	**attendez**

* **j'attends: je** is contracted before the following vowel

Irregular verbs: As in all languages, these have to be learned. Here are four you'll find useful.

Infinitive	**pouvoir** (to be able)	**aller** (to go)	**voir** (to see)	**faire** (to do/make)
je	**peux**	**vais**	**vois**	**fais**
tu	**peux**	**vas**	**vois**	**fais**
il/elle	**peut**	**va**	**voit**	**fait**
nous	**pouvons**	**allons**	**voyons**	**faisons**
vous	**pouvez**	**allez**	**voyez**	**faites**
ils/elles	**peuvent**	**vont**	**voient**	**font**
Imperative	–	**allez**	**voyez**	**faites**

Negatives *Négations*

Negatives are generally formed by putting **ne** before the verb and **pas** after it (**ne** is contracted to **n'** before a following vowel or a silent **h**).

Je parle français.	I speak French.
Je *ne* parle *pas* français.	I don't speak French.
Elle est riche.	She is rich.
Elle *n'*est *pas* riche.	She isn't rich.

Questions *Questions*

Questions may be formed in one of two ways:

1. by inverting the subject and the verb (putting the verb first, the subject second):

Est-elle riche?	Is she rich?
Avez-vous des enfants?	Have you any children?
Parle-t-il français?*	Does he speak French?

2. by using the expression "**est-ce que**" + the affirmative word order.

Est-ce que vous parlez français?	Do you speak French?

* t is inserted between the two vowels

Dictionary
and alphabetical index

English–French

f feminine *m* masculine *pl* plural

a un, une 159
abbey abbaye *f* 81
abbreviation abréviation *f* 154
able, to be pouvoir 163
about *(approximately)* environ 153
above au-dessus (de) 15, 63
abscess abcès *m* 145
absent absent(e) 136
absorbent cotton coton hydrophile *m* 109
accept, to accepter 62, 102
accessories accessoires *m/pl* 116, 125
accident accident *m* 78, 139
accommodation logement *m* 22
account compte *m* 130, 131
ache douleur *f* 141
adaptor prise de raccordement *f* 119
address adresse *f* 21, 31, 76, 79, 102
address book carnet d'adresses *m* 104
adhesive autocollant(e) 105
admission entrée *f* 82, 89, 155
admitted admis(e) 150
Africa Afrique *f* 146
after après 15; au-delà de 77
afternoon après-midi *m* 151, 153
after-shave lotion lotion après rasage *f* 110
age âge *m* 149, 150
ago il y a 149, 151
air conditioner climatiseur *m* 28
air conditioning climatisation *f* 23
airmail par avion 133
airplane avion *m* 65
airport aéroport *f* 16, 21, 65
alarm clock réveil *m* 121
alcoholic alcoolisé 59
Algeria Algérie *f* 146
allergic allergique 141, 143
allow, to autoriser 79
almond amande *f* 54
alphabet alphabet *m* 9
also aussi 15
alter, to *(garment)* retoucher 116
amazing étonnant 84
amber ambre *m* 122
ambulance ambulance *f* 79
American américain(e) 93, 105, 126
American plan pension complète *f* 24
amethyst améthyste *f* 122
amount montant *m* 62; somme *f* 131
amplifier amplificateur *m* 119
anaesthetic anesthésique *m* 144, 145
analgesic analgésique *m* 109
anchovy anchois *m* 44
and et 15
animal animal *m* 85
aniseed anis *m* 50
ankle cheville *f* 139
anorak anorak *m* 116
answer réponse *f* 136
antibiotic antibiotique *m* 143
antidepressant remontant *m* 143
antiques antiquités *f/pl* 83
antique shop antiquaire *m* 98
antiseptic antiseptique 109
antiseptic antiseptique *m* 140
any de, de la, du (*pl* des) 15
anyone quelqu'un 12
anything quelque chose 17, 25, 113
anywhere quelque part 89
aperitif apéritif *m* 56

appendicitis appendicite *f* 142
appendix appendice *m* 138
appetizer hors-d'œuvre *m* 41
apple pomme *f* 54, 63
apple juice jus de pomme *m* 60
appliance appareil *m* 119
appointment rendez-vous *m* 30, 131, 137, 145
apricot abricot *m* 54
April avril *m* 150
archaeology archéologie *f* 83
architect architecte *m* 83
area code indicatif *m* 134
arm bras *m* 138, 139
arrival arrivée *f* 16, 65
arrive, to arriver 65, 68, 130
art art *m* 83
artery artère *f* 138
art gallery galerie d'art *f* 81, 98
artichoke artichaut *m* 49
artificial artificiel(le) 124
artist artiste *m/f* 83
ashtray cendrier *m* 27, 36
Asia Asie *f* 146
ask, to demander 25, 61, 136
asparagus asperge *f* 49
aspirin aspirine *f* 109
assorted varié(e) 41
asthma asthme *m* 141
at à 15
at least au moins 24
at once immédiatement 31
August août *m* 150
aunt tante *f* 93
Australia Australie *f* 146
automatic automatique 20, 122, 124
autumn automne *m* 150
available disponible 40
average moyen(ne) 91
awful horrible 84

B

baby bébé *m* 24, 111
baby food aliments pour bébés *m/pl* 111
babysitter garde d'enfants *f* 27
back dos *m* 138
backache mal de reins *m* 141
bacon bacon *m* 38; lard *m* 46
bacon and eggs œufs au bacon *m/pl* 38
bad mauvais(e) 14, 95
bag sac *m* 18, 103
baggage bagages *m/pl* 18, 26, 31, 71
baggage cart chariot à bagages *m* 18, 71
baggage check consigne *f* 67, 71
baggage locker consigne automatique *f* 18, 67, 71
baked au four 45, 47
baker's boulangerie *f* 98
balance *(account)* position *f* 131
balcony balcon *m* 23
ball *(inflated)* ballon *m* 128
ballet ballet *m* 88
ball-point pen stylo à bille *m* 104
banana banane *f* 54, 63
bandage bandage *m* 109
Band-Aid sparadrap *m* 109
bangle bracelet *m* 121
bangs frange *f* 30
bank *(finance)* banque *f* 98, 129
bank card carte d'identité bancaire *f* 130
banknote billet *m* 130; coupure *m* 130
bar bar *m* 33, 67; *(chocolate)* plaque *f* 64
barber's coiffeur *m* 30, 98
bass *(fish)* bar *m* 44
bath *(hotel)* salle de bains *f* 23, 25, 27
bath essence bain de mousse *m* 110
bathing cap bonnet de bain *m* 116
bathing hut cabine *f* 91
bathing suit costume de bain *m* 116
bathrobe peignoir (de bain) *m* 116
bathroom salle de bains *f* 27
bath salts sels de bain *m/pl* 110
bath towel serviette de bain *f* 27
battery pile *f* 119, 121, 125; *(car)* batterie *f* 75, 78
bay leaf laurier *m* 50
be, to être 161; se trouver 11
beach plage *f* 90
beach ball ballon de plage *m* 128
bean haricot *m* 49
beard barbe *f* 31
beautiful beau, belle 14, 84
beauty salon salon de beauté *m* 30; institut de beauté *m* 98
bed lit *m* 24, 144
bed and breakfast chambre avec petit déjeuner *f* 24
bedpan bassin *m* 144
beef bœuf *m* 46
beer bière *f* 56, 63
beet(root) betterave *f* 49

before *(place)* devant 15; *(time)* avant 15, 151
begin, to commencer 80, 87, 88
beginner débutant(e) *m/f* 91
beginning début *m* 150
behind derrière 15, 77
beige beige 113
Belgian belge 18
Belgium Belgique *f* 146
bell *(electric)* sonnette *f* 144
bellboy chasseur *m* 26
below au-dessous (de) 15
belt ceinture *f* 117
bend *(road)* virage *m* 79
berth couchette *f* 69, 70, 71
best meilleur(e) 152
better meilleur(e) 14, 113; mieux 25, 101
between entre 15
bicycle bicyclette *f* 74
big grand(e) 14, 101
bilberry myrtille *f* 54
bill note *f* 31; addition *f* 62; facture *f* 102; *(banknote)* billet *m* 130; coupure *m* 130
billion *(Am.)* milliard *m* 148
binoculars jumelles *f/pl* 123
bird oiseau *m* 85
birth naissance *f* 25
birthday anniversaire *m* 151, 152
biscuit *(Br.)* biscuit *m* 63
bitter amer, amère 61
black noir(e) 113
blackberry mûre *f* 54
blackcurrant cassis *m* 54
bladder vessie *f* 138
blade lame *f* 110
blanket couverture *f* 27
bleach décoloration *f* 30
bleed, to saigner 139, 145
blind (window) store *m* 29
blister ampoule *f* 139
block, to boucher 28
blood sang *m* 142
blood pressure tension *f* 141
blood transfusion transfusion (sanguine) *f* 144
blouse chemisier *m* 116
blow-dry brushing *m* 30
blue bleu(e) 113
blueberry myrtille *f* 54
boar *(wild)* sanglier *m* 48; *(young)* marcassin *m* 48
boarding house pension *f* 19, 22
boat bateau *m* 74
bobby pin pince à cheveux *f* 111
body corps *m* 138
boil furoncle *m* 139
boiled bouilli(e) 47
boiled egg œuf à la coque *m* 38
bone os *m* 138
book livre *m* 12, 104
book, to réserver 69
booking office bureau de réservation *m* 19, 67
booklet carnet *m* 72
bookshop librairie *f* 98, 104
boot botte *f* 118
born né(e) 150
botanical gardens jardin botanique *m* 81
botany botanique *f* 83
bottle bouteille *f* 17, 59
bottle-opener ouvre-bouteilles *m* 106
bottom bas *m* 145
bowels intestins *m/pl* 138
bow tie nœud papillon *m* 116
box boîte *f* 120
boxing boxe *f* 89
boy garçon *m* 112, 128
boyfriend ami *m* 93
bra soutien-gorge *m* 116
bracelet bracelet *m* 121
braces *(suspenders)* bretelles *f/pl* 116
braised braisé 47
brake frein *m* 78
brandy cognac *m* 60
bread pain *m* 36, 38, 64
break, to casser 29, 119, 123, 145; se casser 139, 145
break down, to être en panne 78
breakdown panne *f* 78
breakdown van dépanneuse *f* 78
breakfast petit déjeuner *m* 24, 34, 38
breast sein *m* 138
breathe, to respirer 141
bridge pont *m* 85
briefs slip *m* 116
brill barbue *f* 44
bring, to apporter 13
bring down, to descendre 31
British britannique 93
broken cassé(e) 29, 119, 140
brooch broche *f* 121
brother frère *m* 93
brown brun(e) 113
bruise contusion *f* 139
brush brosse *f* 111

Brussels sprouts choux de Bruxelles *m/pl* 49
bucket seau *m* 106, 128
buckle boucle *f* 117
build, to construire 83
building bâtiment *m* 81, 83
bulb ampoule *f* 28, 75, 119
burn brûlure *f* 139
burn out, to *(bulb)* sauter 28
bus bus *m* 18, 19, 65, 72, 73
business affaires *f/pl* I6, 131
business trip voyage d'affaires *m* 93
bus stop arrêt de bus *m* 72, 73
busy occupé(e) 96
butane gas butane *m* 32, 106
butcher's boucherie *f* 98
butter beurre *m* 36, 38, 64
button bouton *m* 29, 117
buy, to acheter 82, 104

C

cabana cabine *f* 91
cabbage chou *m* 49
cabin cabine *f* 74
cable télégramme *m* 133
cable car télécabine *f* 74
cable release déclencheur *m* 125
caffein-free décaféiné 38, 60
cake gâteau *m* 55, 64
calculator calculatrice *f* 105
calendar calendrier *m* 104
call *(phone)* appel *m* 135; communication *f* 136
call, to appeler 11, 78, 136, 156
call back, to rappeler 136
calm calme 90
cambric batiste *m* 114
camel-hair poil de chameau *m* 114
camera appareil de photo *m* 124, 125
camera case étui à appareil photo *m* 125
camera shop magasin de photos *m* 98
camp, to camper 32
campbed lit de camp *m* 106
camping camping *m* 32
camping equipment matériel de camping *m* 106
camp site camping *m* 32
can *(of peaches)* boîte *f* 120
can *(to be able)* pouvoir 12, 163
Canada Canada *m* 146
Canadian canadien(ne) 93
cancel, to annuler 65
candle bougie *f* 106
candy bonbon *m* 126
can opener ouvre-boîtes *m* 106
cap casquette *f* 116
caper câpre *f* 50
capital *(finance)* capital *m* 131
car voiture *f* 19, 20, 75, 76, 78
carat carat *m* 121
caravan caravane *f* 32
caraway cumin *m* 50, 64
carbon paper papier carbone *m* 104
carbonated gazeux(euse) 60
carburetor carburateur *m* 78
card carte *f* 93, 131
card game jeu de cartes *m* 128
cardigan cardigan *m* 116
car hire location de voitures *f* 20
carp carpe *f* 44
car park parking *m* 77
car racing courses d'autos *m/pl* 89
car radio autoradio *m* 119
car rental location de voitures *f* 20
carrot carotte *f* 49
carry, to porter 21
cart chariot *m* 18
carton *(of cigarettes)* cartouche (de cigarettes) *f* 17
cartridge *(camera)* chargeur *m* 124
case *(instance)* cas *m* 143; *(cigarettes etc)* étui *m* 121, 123, 125
cash, to toucher 130, 133
cash desk caisse *f* 155
cashier caissier *m* 103
cassette cassette *f* 119, 127
castle château *m* 81
catacomb catacombe *f* 81
catalogue catalogue *m* 82
cathedral cathédrale *f* 81
Catholic catholique 84
cauliflower chou-fleur *m* 49
caution attention *f* 79, 155
cave grotte *f* 81
cellophane tape ruban adhésif *m* 104
cemetery cimetière *m* 81
centimetre centimètre *m* 112
centre centre *m* 19, 21, 76, 81
century siècle *m* 149
ceramics céramique *f* 83
cereal céréales *f/pl* 38
certificate certificat *m* 144
chain *(jewellery)* chaînette *f* 121
chain bracelet gourmette *f* 121
chair chaise *f* 106
chamber music musique de chambre *f* 128

change *(money)* monnaie *f* 62, 77, 130
change, to changer 61, 65, 68, 73, 75, 123; *(money)* 18, 130
chapel chapelle *f* 81
charcoal charbon de bois *m* 106
charge tarif *m* 20, 32, 77, 89; note *f* 28; taxe *f* 136
charge, to faire payer 24; *(commission)* prendre 130
charm *(trinket)* breloque *f* 121
charm bracelet bracelet à breloques *m* 121
cheap bon marché 14, 24, 25, 101
check chèque *m* 130; *(restaurant)* addition *f* 62
check, to contrôler 75, 123; vérifier 75; *(luggage)* faire enregistrer 71
check book carnet de chèques *m* 131
check in, to *(airport)* enregistrer 65
check out, to partir 31
checkup *(medical)* bilan de santé *m* 142
cheers! à votre santé! 56
cheese fromage *m* 53, 64
chemist's pharmacie *f* 98, 108
cheque chèque *m* 130
cheque book carnet de chèques *m* 131
cherry cerise *f* 54
chervil cerfeuil *m* 50
chess échecs *m/pl* 93
chess set jeu d'échecs *m* 128
chest poitrine *f* 138, 141
chestnut marron *m* 54
chewing gum chewing-gum *m* 126
chewing tobacco tabac à chiquer *m* 126
chicken poulet *m* 48, 63
chicken breast suprême de volaille *m* 49
chicory endive *f* 49; *(Am.)* chicorée *f* 49
chiffon mousseline *f* 114
child enfant *m/f* 24, 61, 82, 93, 139, 150
children's doctor pédiatre *m/f* 137
China Chine *f* 146
chips (pommes) frites *f/pl* 51, 63; *(Am.)* chips *m/pl* 51, 64
chives ciboulette *f* 50
chocolate chocolat *m* 120, 126, 127; *(hot)* chocolat chaud *m* 38, 60
chocolate bar plaque de chocolat *f* 64
choice choix *m* 40
chop côtelette *f* 46
Christmas Noël *m* 152
chromium chrome *m* 122
church église *f* 81, 84; *(Protestant)* temple *m* 84
cigar cigare *m* 126
cigarette cigarette *f* 17, 95, 126
cigarette case étui à cigarettes *m* 121, 126
cigarette holder fume-cigarette *m* 126
cigarette lighter briquet *m* 121
cine camera caméra *f* 124
cinema cinéma *m* 86, 96
cinnamon cannelle *f* 50
circle *(theatre)* balcon *m* 87
city ville *f* 81
clam palourde *f* 45
classical classique 128
clean propre 61
clean, to nettoyer 29, 76
cleansing cream crème démaquillante *f* 110
clear, to *(cheque)* vérifier 130
cliff falaise *f* 85
cloakroom vestiaire *m* 87
clock pendule *f* 121; horloge *f* 153
clock-radio radio-réveil *m* 119
close *(near)* proche 78, 98
close, to fermer 11, 82, 108, 132
closed fermé(e) 155
cloth toile *f* 118
clothes vêtements *m/pl* 29, 116
clothes peg pince à linge *f* 106
clothing habillement *m* 112
cloud nuage *m* 94
clove clou de girofle *m* 50
coach *(bus)* car *m* 72
coat manteau *m* 116
coconut noix de coco *f* 54
cod morue *f* 45; *(fresh)* cabillaud *m* 44
coffee café *m* 38, 60, 64
coin monnaie *f* 83
cold froid(e) 14, 25, 61, 94
cold *(illness)* rhume *m* 108, 141
cold cuts charcuterie *f* 64
colour couleur *f* 103, 112, 124, 125
colour fast grand teint 114
colour negative négatif couleurs *m* 124
colour rinse coloration *f* 30
colour shampoo shampooing colorant *m* 111
comb peigne *m* 111
come, to venir 36, 92, 95, 137, 146

comedy comédie *f* 86
commission commission *f* 130
common *(frequent)* courant(e) 154
compact disc disque compact *m* 127
compartment compartiment *m* 70
compass boussole *f* 106
complaint réclamation *f* 61
concert concert *m* 88
concert hall salle de concert *f* 81, 88
conductor *(orchestra)* chef d'orchestre *m* 88
confectioner's confiserie *f* 98
confirm, to confirmer 65
confirmation confirmation *f* 23
congratulation félicitation *f* 152
connection *(train)* correspondance *f* 65, 68
constipated constipé(e) 140
contact lens verre de contact *m* 123
contain, to contenir 37
contraceptive contraceptif *m* 109
control contrôle *m* 16
convent couvent *m* 81
cookie biscuit *m* 64
cool box glacière *f* 106
copper cuivre *m* 122
copperware objets en cuivre *m/pl* 127
coral corail *m* 122
corduroy velours côtelé *m* 114
cork bouchon *m* 61
corkscrew tire-bouchons *m* 106
corn *(Am.)* maïs *m* 50; *(foot)* cor *m* 109
corner angle *m* 36; *(street)* coin de rue *m* 21, 77
corn plaster emplâtre pour les cors *m* 109
cost coût *m* 131; prix *m* 136
cost, to coûter 11, 133
cotton coton *m* 114
cotton wool coton hydrophile *m* 109
cough toux *f* 108, 141
cough, to tousser 142
cough drops pastilles contre la toux *f/pl* 109
counter guichet *m* 133
country pays *m* 93
countryside campagne *f* 85
court house palais de justice *m* 81
cousin cousin(e) *m/f* 93
cover charge couvert *m* 62
crab crabe *m* 44
cracker biscuit salé *m* 64
cramp crampe *f* 141
crayfish écrevisse *f* 44
crayon crayon de couleur *m* 104
cream crème *f* 55, 60, 110
credit crédit *m* 130
credit, to créditer 130, 131
credit card carte de crédit *f* 20, 31, 62, 102, 130
crepe crèpe *m* 114
crisps chips *m/pl* 51, 64
crockery vaisselle *f* 106, 107
cross croix *f* 121
cross-country skiing ski de fond *m* 91
crossing *(by sea)* traversée *f* 74
crossroads carrefour *m* 77
cruise croisière *f* 74
crystal cristal *m* 122, 127
cuckoo clock coucou *m* 121, 127
cucumber concombre *m* 49
cuff link bouton de manchette *m* 121
cup tasse *f* 36, 60, 107
curler bigoudi *m* 111
currency monnaie *f* 129
currency exchange office bureau de change *m* 18, 67, 129
current courant *m* 90
curtain rideau *m* 28
curve *(road)* virage *m* 79
customs douane *f* 16, 102
cut *(wound)* coupure *f* 139
cut, to couper 135
cut glass cristal taillé *m* 122
cuticle remover produit pour enlever les cuticules *m* 110
cutlery couverts *m/pl* 106, 107, 121; coutellerie *f* 127
cutlet escalope *f* 46
cycling cyclisme *m* 89
cystitis cystite *f* 142

D

dairy laiterie *f* 98
dance, to danser 88, 96
danger danger *m* 155, 156
dangerous dangereux(euse) 90
dark sombre 25; foncé(e) 101, 112, 113
date date *f* 25, 151; *(fruit)* datte *f* 54
daughter fille *f* 93
day jour *m* 16, 20, 24, 32, 80, 151; journée *f* 151
daylight lumière du jour *f* 124
day off jour de congé *m* 151
death mort *f* 155
decade décennie *f* 149

December décembre *m* 150
decision décision *f* 25, 102
deck *(ship)* pont *m* 74
deck-chair chaise longue *f* 91, 106
declare, to déclarer 17
delay retard *m* 69
delicatessen charcuterie *f*, traiteur *m* 98
delicious délicieux 62
deliver, to livrer 102
delivery livraison *f* 102
denim toile de coton *f* 114
dentist dentiste *m/f* 98, 145
denture dentier *m* 145
deodorant déodorant *m* 110
department *(museum)* département *m* 83; *(shop)* rayon *m* 100
department store grand magasin *m* 98
departure départ *m* 65
deposit *(car hire)* caution *f* 20; *(bank)* depôt *m* 130
deposit, to *(bank)* déposer 130
dessert dessert *m* 37, 55
detour *(traffic)* déviation *f* 79
develop, to développer 124
diabetic diabétique 141
diabetic diabétique *m/f* 37
dialling code indicatif *m* 134
diamond diamant *m* 122, 127
diaper couche *f* 111
diarrhoea diarrhée *f* 140
dictionary dictionnaire *m* 104
diesel gas-oil *m* 75
diet régime *m* 37
difficult difficile 14
difficulty difficulté *f* 28, 102, 141; peine *f* 141
digital digital(e) 122
dining-car wagon-restaurant *m* 66, 68, 71
dining-room salle à manger *f* 27
dinner dîner *m* 34, 94
direct direct(e) 65
direct, to indiquer 13
direction direction *f* 76
director *(theatre)* metteur en scène *m* 86
directory *(phone)* annuaire *m* 134
disabled handicapé(e) 82
disc disque *m* 77, 127
discotheque discothèque *f* 88, 96
disease maladie *f* 142
dish plat *m* 37
dishwashing detergent produit (à) vaisselle *m* 106
disinfectant désinfectant *m* 109
dislocate, to disloquer 140
display case étalage *m* 100
dissatisfied mécontent(e) 103
district *(town)* quartier *m* 81
disturb, to déranger 155
diversion *(traffic)* déviation *f* 79
dizzy pris(e) de vertige 140
do, to faire 163
doctor médecin *m* 79, 137, 144; docteur *m* 145
doctor's office cabinet (de consultation) *m* 137
dog chien *m* 155
doll poupée *f* 128
dollar dollar *m* 18, 130
door porte *f* 155
double bed grand lit *m* 23
double room chambre pour deux personnes *f* 19, 23
down en bas 15
downhill skiing ski de piste *m* 91
downstairs en bas 15
down there là-bas 77
downtown centre *m* 81
dozen douzaine *f* 120, 149
draught beer bière pression *f* 56
drawing paper papier à dessin *m* 104
drawing pin punaise *f* 104
dress robe *f* 116
dressing gown peignoir *m* 116
drink boisson *f* 40, 59, 60, 61; verre *m* 95
drink, to boire 35, 36
drinking water eau potable *f* 32
drip, to *(tap)* fuire 28
drive, to conduire 21, 76
driving licence permis de conduire *m* 20, 79
drop *(liquid)* goutte *f* 109
drugstore pharmacie *m* 98, 108
dry sec, sèche 30, 59, 111
dry cleaner's teinturerie *f* 29, 98
dry shampoo shampooing sec *m* 111
Dublin bay prawn langoustine *f* 44
duck canard *m* 48
duckling caneton *m* 48
dull *(pain)* sourd(e) 140
dummy tétine *f* 111
during pendant 15, 150, 151
duty *(customs)* droits de douane *m/pl* 17

duty-free shop magasin hors-taxe *m* 19
dye teinture *f* 30, 111

E

each chaque 149
ear oreille *f* 138
earache mal aux oreilles *m* 141
ear drops gouttes pour les oreilles *f/pl* 109
early tôt 14
earring boucle d'oreille *f* 121
east est *m* 77
Easter Pâques *f/pl* 152
easy facile 14
eat, to manger 36, 144
eat out, to aller au restaurant 33
eel anguille *f* 44
egg œuf *m* 38, 64, 120
eggplant aubergine *f* 49
eight huit 147
eighteen dix-huit 147
eighth huitième 149
eighty quatre-vingts 148
elastic élastique 109
elastic bandage bandage élastique *m* 109
Elastoplast sparadrap *m* 109
electrical électrique 119
electrical appliance appareil électrique *m* 119
electrician électricien *m* 98
electricity électricité *f* 32
electronic électronique 125, 128
elevator ascenseur *m* 27, 100
eleven onze 147
embankment *(river)* quai *m* 81
embarkation embarquement *m* 74
emerald émeraude *f* 122
emergency urgence *f* 156
emergency exit sortie de secours *f* 27, 99, 155
emery board lime à ongles *f* 110
empty vide 14
enamel émail *m* 122
end fin *f* 150
endive chicorée *f* 49; *(Am.)* endive *f* 49
engine *(car)* moteur *m* 78
England Angleterre *f* 146
English anglais(e) 12, 80, 84, 104
enjoyable agréable 31
enjoy oneself, to s'amuser 96
enlarge, to agrandir 125
enough assez 15
enter, to entrer 155
entrance entrée *f* 67, 99, 155
entrance fee entrée *f* 82
envelope enveloppe *f* 27, 105
equipment équipement *m* 91; matériel *m* 106
eraser gomme *f* 105
escalator escalier mécanique *m* 100
espresso coffee express *m* 60
estimate estimation *f* 131
Europe Europe *f* 146
evening soir *m* 87, 95, 96, 151, 153; soirée *f* 95
evening dress tenue de soirée *f* 88; *(woman)* robe du soir *f* 116
everything tout 31
examine, to examiner 139
exchange, to échanger 103
exchange rate cours du change *m* 18, 130
excursion excursion *f* 80
excuse, to excuser 11
exercise book cahier *m* 105
exhaust pipe pot d'échappement *m* 78
exhibition exposition *f* 81
exit sortie *f* 67, 79, 99, 155
expect, to attendre 130
expensive cher, chère 14, 19, 24, 101
exposure *(photography)* pose *f* 124
exposure counter compte-poses *m* 125
express par exprès 133
expression expression *f* 10
expressway autoroute *f* 76
extension cord/lead prolongateur *m* 119
external externe 109
extra supplémentaire 27
extract, to *(tooth)* arracher 145
eye œil *m* (*pl* yeux) 138, 139
eye drops gouttes oculaires *f* 109
eye pencil crayon pour les yeux *m* 110
eye shadow fard à paupières *m* 110
eyesight vue *f* 123
eye specialist oculiste *m/f* 137

F

face visage *m* 138
face-pack masque de beauté *m* 30
face powder poudre *f* 110
factory usine *f* 81
fair foire *f* 81

fall chute *f* 139; *(autumn)* automne *m* 150
family famille *f* 93,
fan ventilateur *m* 28
fan belt courroie de ventilateur *f* 75
far loin 14, 100
fare tarif *m* 21; prix *m* 68, 73
farm ferme *f* 85
fashion mode *f* 127
fast *(film)* ultrarapide 124
fat *(meat)* gras *m* 37
father père *m* 93
faucet robinet *m* 28
fawn fauve 113
February février *m* 150
fee *(doctor)* honoraires *m/pl* 144
feeding bottle biberon *m* 111
feel, to *(physical state)* se sentir 140
felt feutre *m* 114
felt-tip pen crayon feutre *m* 105
fennel fenouil *m* 50
ferry ferry *m* 74
fever fièvre *f* 140
few peu de 14; *(a)* quelques 14
field champ *m* 85
fifteen quinze 147
fifth cinquième 149
fifty cinquante 147
fig figue *f* 54
file *(tool)* lime *f* 110
fill in, to remplir 26, 144
filling *(tooth)* plombage *m* 145
filling station station-service *f* 75
film film *m* 86, 124, 125
film winder levier d'avancement *m* 125
filter filtre *m* 125
filter-tipped avec filtre 126
find, to trouver 11, 12, 100, 137
fine *(OK)* d'accord 25
fine arts beaux-arts *m/pl* 83
finger doigt *m* 138
finish, to finir 162
fire feu *m* 156
first premier(ère) 68, 73, 149
first-aid kit trousse de premiers secours *f* 106
first class première classe *f* 69
first course entrée *f* 40
first name prénom *m* 25
fish poisson *m* 44
fish, to pêcher 90
fishing pêche *f* 90
fishing tackle attirail de pêche *m* 106
fishmonger's poissonnerie *f* 98
fit, to aller 115, 116
fitting room cabine d'essayage *f* 115
five cinq 147
fix, to réparer 75, 145
fizzy *(mineral water)* gazeux(euse) 60
flannel flanelle *f* 114
flash *(photography)* flash *m* 125
flash attachment glissière du flash *f* 125
flashlight lampe de poche *f* 106
flat plat(e) 118
flat tyre crevaison *f* 75, 78
flea market marché aux puces *m* 81
flight vol *m* 65
flight number numéro de vol *m* 65
flippers palmes *f/pl* 128
floor étage *m* 27
floor show spectacle de cabaret *m* 88
flour farine *f* 37
flower fleur *f* 85
flower shop fleuriste *m* 98
flu grippe *f* 142
fluid liquide *m* 75
fog brouillard *m* 94
folding chair chaise pliante *f* 106
folding table table pliante *f* 107
folk music musique folklorique *f* 128
food nourriture *f* 37; aliment *m* 111
food box boîte à conservation *f* 106
food poisoning intoxication alimentaire *f* 142
foot pied *m* 138
football football *m* 89
foot cream crème pour les pieds *f* 110
footpath sentier *m* 85
for pour 15; pendant 143
forbid, to défendre 155
forecast prévision *f* 94
foreign étranger(ère) 56
forest forêt *f* 85
forget, to oublier 61
fork fourchette *f* 36, 61, 107, 127
form *(document)* formule *f* 133; fiche *f* 25, 26
fortnight quinze jours *m/pl* 151
fortress forteresse *f* 81
forty quarante 147
foundation cream fond de teint *m* 110
fountain fontaine *f* 81
fountain pen stylo *m* 105
four quatre 147
fourteen quatorze 147
fourth quatrième 149

fowl volaille *f* 49
frame *(glasses)* monture *f* 123
France France *f* 146
free libre 14, 70, 82, 96, 155
French français(e) 11, 18, 95, 114
French bean haricot vert *m* 49
french fries (pommes) frites *f/pl* 51, 63
fresh frais, fraîche 54, 61
Friday vendredi *m* 151
fried frit(e) 45, 47
fried egg œuf au plat *m* 38
friend ami(e) *m/f* 93, 95
fringe frange *f* 30
frog grenouille *f* 44
from de 15
front avant 75
frost gel *m* 94
fruit fruit *m* 54
fruit cocktail salade de fruits *f* 54
fruit juice jus de fruits *m* 38, 60
frying-pan poêle *f* 106
full plein(e) 14; complet(ète) 155
full board pension complète *f* 24
full insurance assurance tous risques *f* 20
furniture meubles *m/pl* 83
furrier's fourreur *m* 98

G

gabardine gabardine *f* 114
gallery galerie *f* 81, 98
game jeu *m* 128; *(food)* gibier *m* 48
garage garage *m* 26, 78
garden jardin *m* 85
gardens jardin public *m* 81
garlic ail *m* 50
gas gaz *m* 156
gasoline essence *f* 75, 78
gastritis gastrite *f* 142
gauze gaze *f* 109
gem pierre précieuse *f* 121
general général(e) 27, 100
general delivery poste restante *f* 133
general practitioner généraliste *m/f* 137
gentleman monsieur *m* 155
genuine véritable 118
geology géologie *f* 83
Germany Allemagne *f* 146
get, to *(find)* trouver 11, 19, 21, 32; *(call)* appeler 31, 137; *(obtain)* obtenir 108, 134; se procurer 90; *(go)* se rendre 100
get back, to être de retour 80
get off, to descendre 73
get to, to aller à 19; arriver à 70
get up, to se lever 144
gherkin cornichon *m* 49, 64
gin and tonic gin-tonic *m* 60
ginger gingembre *m* 50
girdle gaine *f* 116
girl fille *f* 112; *(child)* fillette *f* 128
girlfriend amie *f* 93, 95
give, to donner 13, 123, 135
give way, to *(traffic)* céder le passage 79
glad *(to know you)* enchanté(e) 92
gland glande *f* 138
glass verre *m* 36, 59, 60, 61, 143
glasses lunettes *f/pl* 123
gloomy sombre 84
glossy *(finish)* brillant(e) 125
glove gant *m* 116
glue colle *m* 105
go, to aller 96, 162
go away, to s'en aller 156
gold or *m* 121, 122
golden doré(e) 113
gold plate plaqué or *m* 122
golf golf *m* 89
golf course terrain de golf *m* 89
good bon(ne) 14, 101
good-bye au revoir 10
Good Friday Vendredi-Saint *m* 152
goods articles *m/pl* 16
goose oie *f* 48
gooseberry groseille à maquereau *f* 54
gram gramme *m* 120
grammar book grammaire *f* 105
grape raisin *m* 54, 64
grapefruit pamplemousse *m* 54
grapefruit juice jus de pamplemousse *m* 38, 60
gray gris(e) 113
graze éraflure *f* 139
greasy gras(se) 30, 111
great *(excellent)* formidable 95
Great Britain Grande-Bretagne *f* 146
green vert(e) 113
green bean haricot vert *m* 49
greengrocer's primeur *m* 98
green salad salade verte *f* 42
greeting salutation *f* 10
grey gris(e) 113
grilled grillé(e) 45, 47

grocery magasin d'alimentation *m* 98, 120; épicerie *f* 98
groundsheet tapis de sol *m* 106
group groupe *m* 82
guide guide *m/f* 80
guidebook guide (de voyage) *m* 82, 104
guinea fowl pintade *f* 48
gum *(teeth)* gencive *f* 145
gynaecologist gynécologue *m/f* 137

H

haddock aiglefin *m* 44
hair cheveux *m/pl* 30, 111
hairbrush brosse à cheveux *f* 111
haircut coupe de cheveux *f* 30
hairdresser's coiffeur *m* 30, 98; salon de coiffure *m* 27
hair dryer sèche-cheveux *m* 119
hairgrip pince à cheveux *f* 111
hair lotion lotion capillaire *f* 111
hairpin èpingle à cheveux *f* 111
hairspray laque *f* 30, 111
half moitié *f* 149
half a day demi-journée *f* 80
half a dozen demi-douzaine *f* 120
half an hour demi-heure *f* 153
half board demi-pension *f* 24
half price *(ticket)* demi-tarif *m* 69
hall *(large room)* salle *f* 81, 88
hall porter concierge *m* 26
ham jambon *m* 38, 46, 63, 64
ham and eggs œufs au jambon *m/pl* 38
hamlet hameau *m* 85
hammer marteau *m* 106
hammock hamac *m* 106
hand main *f* 138
handbag sac à main *m* 116, 156
hand cream crème pour les mains *f* 110
handicrafts artisanat *m* 83
handkerchief mouchoir *m* 116
handmade fait(e) à la main 113
hanger cintre *m* 27
hangover gueule de bois *f* 108
happy heureux 152
harbour port *m* 81
hard dur(e) 123
hard-boiled *(egg)* dur 38
hardware shop quincaillerie *f* 98
hare lièvre *m* 48
hat chapeau *m* 116
have, to avoir 161; posséder 130; *(meal)* prendre 38
haversack musette *f* 106
hayfever rhume des foins *m* 108, 141
hazelnut noisette *f* 54
he il 161
head tête *f* 138, 139
headache mal de tête *m* 141
headlight phare *m* 79
headphones casque à écouteurs *m* 119
head waiter maître d'hôtel *m* 61
health santé *f* 56
health food shop magasin de diététique *m* 98
health insurance assurance maladie *f* 144
health insurance form feuille maladie *f* 144
heart cœur *m* 138
heart attack crise cardiaque *f* 141
heat, to chauffer 90
heating chauffage *m* 23, 28
heavy lourd(e) 14, 101
heel talon *m* 118
helicopter hélicoptère *m* 74
hello! *(phone)* allô! 135
help aide *m* 156
help! au secours! 156
help, to aider 13, 21, 71, 100, 134; *(oneself)* se servir 120
her son, sa *(pl* ses*)* 161
herbs fines herbes *f/pl* 50
herb tea tisane *f* 60
here ici 14; voici 14
herring hareng *m* 44
high haut(e) 90; *(blood pressure)* élevé(e) 141
high season haute saison *f* 150
high-speed ultrarapide 124
high tide marée haute *f* 90
hill colline *f* 85
hire location *f* 20, 74
hire, to louer 19, 20, 74, 90, 91, 119, 155
his son, sa *(pl* ses*)* 161
history histoire *f* 83
hitchhike, to faire l'auto-stop 74
hold on! *(phone)* ne quittez pas! 136
hole trou *m* 29
holiday jour férié *m* 151
holidays vacances *f/pl* 16, 151
home address lieu de domicile *m* 25
honey miel *m* 38
horse racing courses (de chevaux) *f/pl* 89
horseradish raifort *m* 50

hospital hôpital *m* 99, 144
hot chaud(e) 14, 25, 38, 94
hotel hôtel *m* 19, 21, 22
hotel guide guide des hôtels *m* 19
hotel reservation réservation d'hôtel *f* 19
hot water eau chaude *f* 23, 28
hot-water bottle bouillotte *f* 27
hour heure *f* 153
house maison *f* 83, 85
hovercraft aéroglisseur *m* 74
how comment 11
how far à quelle distance 11, 76, 85
how long combien de temps 11, 24
how many combien 11
how much combien 11, 24, 101
hundred cent 148
hungry, to be avoir faim 13, 35
hurry *(to be in a)* être pressé(e) 21
hurry up! dépêchez-vous! 13
hurt, to faire mal 139, 145; *(oneself)* se blesser 139
husband mari *m* 93
hydrofoil hydroptère *m* 74

I

I je 161
ice glace *f* 94
ice-cream glace *f* 55, 64
ice cube glaçon *m* 27
iced tea thé glacé *m* 60
ice pack cartouche réfrigérante *f* 106
ill malade 140, 156
illness maladie *f* 140
important important(e) 13
imported importé(e) 113
impressive impressionnant(e) 84
in dans 15
include, to comprendre 20, 24, 31, 32, 62, 80
included compris(e) 40, 62
India Inde *f* 146
indigestion indigestion *f* 141
inexpensive bon marché 35, 124
infect, to infecter 140
infection infection *f* 141
inflammation inflammation *f* 142
inflation inflation *f* 131
inflation rate taux d'inflation *m* 131
influenza grippe *f* 142
information renseignement *m* 67, 155
injection piqûre *f* 142, 144
injure, to blesser 139
injured blessé(e) 79, 139
injury blessure *f* 139
ink encre *f* 105
inn auberge *f* 22, 33
inquiry renseignement *m* 68
insect bite piqûre d'insecte *f* 108, 139
insect repellent crème anti-insecte *f* 109
insect spray bombe insecticide *f* 109
inside dedans 15
instead à la place 37
instrumental *(music)* instrumental(e) 128
insurance assurance *f* 20, 79, 144
interest intérêt *m* 80, 131
interested, to be s'intéresser 83, 96
interesting intéressant(e) 84
international international 133, 134
interpreter interprète *m* 131
intersection carrefour *m* 77
introduce, to présenter 92
introduction présentation *f* 92, introduction *f* 130
investment investissement *m* 131
invitation invitation *f* 94
invite, to inviter 94
invoice facture *f* 131
iodine teinture d'iode *f* 109
Ireland Irlande *f* 146
Irish irlandais(e) 92
iron *(laundry)* fer à repasser *m* 119
iron, to repasser 29
ironmonger's quincaillerie *f* 99
Italy Italie *f* 146
its son, sa *(pl ses)* 161
ivory ivoire *m* 122

J

jacket veston *m* 116
jam confiture *f* 38, 63
jam, to coincer 28; bloquer 125
January janvier *m* 150
jar pot *m* 120
jaundice jaunisse *f* 142
jaw mâchoire *f* 138
jeans jeans *m/pl* 116
jersey tricot *m* 116
jewel bijou *m* 121
jewel box coffret à bijoux *m* 121
jeweller's bijouterie *f* 99, 121
joint articulation *f* 138
journey trajet *m* 72
juice jus *m* 38, 41, 60
July juillet *m* 150
jumper *(sweater)* chandail *m* 116
June juin *m* 150

K

keep, to garder 62
kerosene pétrole *m* 106
key clé *f* 27
kidney rein *m* 138
kilogram kilogramme *m* 120
kilometre kilomètre *m* 20, 78
kind aimable 95
kind *(type)* genre *m* 140
knapsack sac à dos *m* 106
knee genou *m* 138
knife couteau *m* 36, 61, 107
knock, to frapper 155
know, to savoir 16, 24; connaître 96, 114

L

label étiquette *f* 105
lace dentelle *f* 114, 127
lady dame *f* 155
lake lac *m* 81, 85, 90
lamb agneau *m* 46
lamp lampe *f* 29, 106, 119
landmark point de repère *m* 85
landscape paysage *m* 92
lane *(traffic)* piste *f* 79
lantern lanterne *f* 106
large grand(e) 101, 118; gros(se) 130
lark alouette *f* 48
last dernier(ère) 14, 68, 73, 149; passé(e) 151
last name nom (de famille) *m* 25
late tard 14
laugh, to rire 95
launderette laverie automatique *f* 99
laundry *(place)* blanchisserie *f* 29, 99; *(clothes)* linge *m* 29
laundry service blanchisserie *f* 23
laxative laxatif *m* 109
leap year année bissextile *f* 149
leather cuir *m* 114, 118
leave, to partir 31, 68, 74, 95; laisser 156; *(deposit)* déposer 26, 71
leek poireau *m* 50
left gauche 21, 63, 69, 77
left-luggage office consigne *f* 67, 71
leg jambe *f* 138
lemon citron *m* 37, 38, 54, 60, 64
lemonade limonade *f* 60
lemon juice citron pressé *m* 60
lens *(glasses)* verre *m* 123; *(camera)* objectif *m* 125
lens cap capuchon d'objectif *m* 125
lentil lentille *f* 50
less moins 15
lesson leçon *f* 91
let, to *(hire out)* louer 155
letter lettre *f* 132
letter box boîte aux lettres *f* 132
lettuce laitue *f* 50
level crossing passage à niveau *m* 79
library bibliothèque *f* 81, 99
licence *(permit)* permis *m* 20, 79
lie down, to s'étendre 142
life belt ceinture de sauvetage *f* 74
life boat canot de sauvetage *m* 74
lifeguard maître nageur *m* 90
lift ascenseur *m* 27, 100
light lumière *f* 28, 124; *(cigarette)* feu *m* 95
light léger(ère) 14, 55, 59, 101, 128; *(colour)* clair(e) 101, 112, 113
lighter briquet *m* 126
lighter fluid essence à briquet *f* 126
lighter gas gaz à briquet *m* 126
light meter cellule photoélectrique *f* 125
lightning éclair *m* 94
like, to vouloir 13, 20, 23; aimer 61, 96, 112; désirer 103; plaire 25, 92, 102
line ligne *f* 73
linen *(cloth)* lin *m* 114
lip lèvre *f* 138
lipsalve beurre de cacao *m* 110
lipstick rouge à lèvres *m* 110
liqueur liqueur *f* 60
liquid liquide *m* 123
listen, to écouter 128
litre litre *m* 59, 75, 120
little *(a)* un peu 14
live, to vivre 83
liver foie *m* 46, 138
lobster homard *m* 44
local local(e) 36, 59
London Londres *m* 130
long long(ue) 116, 117
long-sighted presbyte 123
look, to regarder 100; voir 123
look for, to chercher 13
look out! attention! 156
loose *(clothes)* large 116
lorry camion *m* 79
lose, to perdre 123, 156
loss perte *f* 131
lost perdu(e) 13, 156
lost and found office bureau des objets trouvés *m* 67, 156

lost property office bureau des objets trouvés *m* 67, 156
lot *(a)* beaucoup 14
lotion lotion *f* 110
loud *(voice)* fort(e) 135
love, to aimer 95
lovely beau, belle 94
low bas(se) 90, 141
lower inférieur(e) 69, 71
low season basse saison *f* 150
low tide marée basse *f* 90
luck chance *f* 135, 152
luggage bagages *m/pl* 18, 26, 31, 71
luggage locker consigne automatique *f* 18, 67, 71
luggage trolley chariot à bagages *m* 18, 71
lump *(bump)* bosse *f* 139
lunch déjeuner *m* 34, 80, 94
lung poumon *m* 138

M

machine machine *f* 114
mackerel maquereau *m* 45
magazine revue *f* 105
magnificent splendide 84
maid femme de chambre *f* 26
mail, to mettre à la poste 28
mail courrier *m* 28, 133
mailbox boîte aux lettres *f* 132
make, to faire 131, 162
make up, to faire 28; préparer 108
make-up remover pad disque démaquillant *m* 110
man homme *m* 115, 155
manager directeur *m* 26
manicure manucure *f* 30
many beaucoup de 15
map carte *f* 76, 105; plan *m* 105
March mars *m* 150
marinated mariné(e) 45
market marché *m* 81, 99
marmalade marmelade *f* 38
married marié(e) 93
mass *(church)* messe *f* 84
mat *(finish)* mat(e) 125
match allumette *f* 106, 126; *(sport)* match *m* 89
match, to *(colour)* s'assortir à 112
material *(cloth)* tissu *m* 113
mattress matelas *m* 106
May mai *m* 150
may *(can)* pouvoir 12, 163
meadow pré *m* 85
meal repas *m* 24, 34, 62, 143
mean, to vouloir dire 11; signifier 26
measles rougeole *f* 142
measure, to prendre les mesures 114
meat viande *f* 46, 47, 61
meatball boulette *f* 46
mechanic mécanicien *m* 78
mechanical pencil porte-mine *m* 105, 121
medical médical(e) 144
medicine médecine *f* 83; *(drug)* médicament *m* 143
medium *(meat)* à point 47
medium-sized moyen(ne) 20
meet, to rencontrer 96
melon melon *m* 54
memorial monument *m* 81
mend, to réparer 75; *(clothes)* raccommoder 29
menthol *(cigarettes)* mentholé(e) 126
menu menu *m* 37, 39; *(printed)* carte *f* 36, 39, 40
merry joyeux(euse) 152
message message *m* 28, 136
methylated spirits alcool à brûler *m* 106
metre mètre *m* 112
mezzanine *(theatre)* balcon *m* 87
middle milieu *m* 69, 87, 150
midnight minuit *m* 153
mileage kilomètrage *m* 20
milk lait *m* 38, 60, 64
milkshake frappé *m* 60
million million *m* 148
mineral water eau minérale *f* 60
minister *(religion)* pasteur *m* 84
mint menthe *f* 50
minute minute *f* 153
mirror miroir *m* 115, 123
miscellaneous divers(e) 127
Miss Mademoiselle *f* 10
miss, to manquer 18, 29, 61
mistake erreur *f* 31, 61, 62, 102
mixed salad salade mêlée *f* 42
modified American plan demi-pension *f* 24
moisturizing cream crème hydratante *f* 110
moment moment *m* 136
monastery monastère *m* 81
Monday lundi *m* 151
money argent *m* 129, 130, 156
money order mandat *m* 133

DICTIONARY

Dictionnaire

month mois *m* 16, 150
monument monument *m* 81
moon lune *f* 94
moped vélomoteur *m* 74
more plus 15
morning matin *m* 151, 153
Morocco Maroc *m* 146
mortgage hypothèque *f* 131
mosque mosquée *f* 84
mosquito net moustiquaire *f* 106
mother mère *f* 93
motorbike moto *f* 74
motorboat canot à moteur *m* 91
motorway autoroute *f* 76
mountain montagne *f* 85
moustache moustache *f* 31
mouth bouche *f* 138
mouthwash gargarisme *m* 109
move, to bouger 139
movie film *m* 86
movie camera caméra *f* 124
movies cinéma *m* 86, 96
Mr. Monsieur *m* 10
Mrs. Madame *f* 10
much beaucoup 14
mug grosse tasse *f* 107
mulberry mûre *f* 54
muscle muscle *m* 138
museum musée *m* 81
mushroom champignon *m* 49
music musique *f* 83, 128
musical comédie musicale *f* 86
music box boîte à musique *f* 121
mussel moule *f* 45
must, to devoir 31, 37, 61; falloir 95
mustard moutarde *f* 37, 50, 64
my mon, ma *(pl mes)* 161

N

nail *(human)* ongle *m* 110
nail brush brosse à ongles *f* 110
nail clippers coupe-ongles *m* 110
nail file lime à ongles *f* 110
nail polish vernis à ongles *m* 110
nail polish remover dissolvant *m* 110
nail scissors ciseaux à ongles *m/pl* 110
name nom *m* 23, 25, 79, 85, 92
napkin serviette *f* 36, 105, 106
nappy couche *f* 111
narrow étroit(e) 118
nationality nationalité *f* 25, 92
natural naturel(le) 83
nauseous nauséeux(euse) 140
near près 14; près de 15
nearby à proximité 77
nearest le(a) plus proche 78, 98
neat *(drink)* sec 56, 60
neck cou *m* 138; *(nape)* nuque *f* 30
necklace collier *m* 121
need, to avoir besoin de 90; falloir 29
needle aiguille *f* 27
negative négatif *m* 125
nephew neveu *m* 93
nerve nerf *m* 138
nervous nerveux(euse) 138
nervous system système nerveux *m* 138
Netherlands Pays-Bas *m/pl* 146
never ne ... jamais 15
new nouveau, nouvelle 14
newspaper journal *m* 104, 105
newsstand kiosque à journaux *m* 19, 67, 99, 104
New Year Nouvel An *m* 152
New Zealand Nouvelle-Zélande *f* 146
next prochain(e) 14, 65, 68, 73, 76, 149, 151
next time la prochaine fois 95
next to à côté de 15, 77
nice beau, belle 94
niece nièce *f* 93
night nuit *f* 24, 151
nightclub boîte de nuit *f* 88
night cream crème de nuit *f* 110
nightdress chemise de nuit *f* 116
nine neuf 147
nineteen dix-neuf 147
ninety quatre-vingt-dix 148
ninth neuvième 149
no non 10
noisy bruyant(e) 25
nonalcoholic sans alcool 60
none aucun(e) 15
nonsmoker non-fumeurs *m/pl* 36, 70
noodle nouille *f* 51
noon midi *m* 31, 153
normal normal(e) 30
north nord *m* 77
North America Amérique du Nord *f* 146
nose nez *m* 138
nosebleed saignement de nez *m* 141
nose drops gouttes nasales *f/pl* 109
not ne ... pas 15, 163
note *(banknote)* billet *m* 130; coupure *f* 130
notebook bloc-notes *m* 105

note paper papier à lettres *m* 105
nothing rien 15, 17
notice *(sign)* écriteau *m* 155
November novembre *m* 150
now maintenant 15
number numéro *m* 26, 65, 135, 136; nombre *m* 147
nurse infirmière *f* 144
nutmeg (noix) muscade *f* 50

O

occupation profession *f* 93
occupied occupé(e) 14, 70, 155
October octobre *m* 150
octopus poulpe *f* 45
offer, to offrir 95
office bureau *m* 19, 67, 99, 132, 133, 156
oil huile *f* 37, 75, 111
oily gras(se) 30, 111
old vieux, vieille 14; ancien(ne) 14
old town vieille ville *f* 81
olive olive *f* 41
omelet omelette *f* 42
on sur 15
once une fois 149
one un, une 147
one-way *(ticket)* aller *m* 65, 69
on foot à pied 76
onion oignon *m* 50
on request sur demande 73
on time à l'heure 68
only seulement 80
onyx onyx *m* 122
open ouvert(e) 14, 82, 155
open, to ouvrir 11, 17, 82, 108, 131, 132, 142
open-air en plein air 90
opera opéra *m* 88
opera house opéra *m* 81, 88
operation opération *f* 144
operator opérateur m, opératrice *f* 134
operetta opérette *f* 88
opposite en face (de) 77
optician opticien(ne) *m/f* 99, 123
or ou 15
orange orange 113
orange orange *f* 54, 64
orange juice jus d'orange *m* 38, 60
orchestra orchestre *m* 88; *(seats)* parterre *m* 87
orchestral music musique symphonique *f* 128
order *(goods, meal)* commande *f* 40, 102
order, to *(goods, meal)* commander 61, 102, 103
oregano origan *m* 50
ornithology ornithologie *f* 83
our notre *(pl* nos*)* 161
out of order hors service 155
out of stock épuisé(e) 103
outlet *(electric)* prise *f* 27
outside dehors 15, 36
oval ovale 101
overalls salopette *f* 116
overdone trop cuit(e) 61
overheat, to *(engine)* chauffer 78
overnight *(stay)* d'une nuit 24
overtake, to doubler 79
owe, to devoir 144
owerwhelming imposant(e) 84
oyster huître *f* 44

P

pacifier tétine *f* 111
packet paquet *m* 120, 126
page *(hotel)* chasseur *m* 26
pail seau *m* 106, 128
pain douleur *f* 140, 141, 144
painkiller calmant *m* 140, 144
paint peinture *f* 155
paint, to peindre 83
paintbox boîte de couleurs *f* 105
painter peintre *m* 83
painting peinture *f* 83
pair paire *f* 116, 118, 149
pajamas pyjama *m* 116
palace palais *m* 81
pancake crêpe *f* 63
panties slip *m* 116
pants *(trousers)* pantalon *m* 116
panty girdle gaine-culotte *f* 116
panty hose collant *m* 116
paper papier *m* 105
paperback livre de poche *m* 105
paperclip trombone *f* 105
paper napkin serviette en papier *f* 105, 106
paraffin *(fuel)* pétrole *m* 106
parcel colis *m* 132
parents parents *m/pl* 93
park parc *m* 81
park, to garer 26, 77
parking stationnement *m* 77, 79
parking disc disque de stationnement *m* 77

parking meter parcomètre *m* 77
parliament parlement *m* 81
parsley persil *m* 50
part partie *f* 138
partridge perdrix *f* 48
party *(social gathering)* réception *f* 95
pass, to *(car)* doubler 79
passport passeport *m* 16, 17, 25, 26, 156
passport photo photo d'identité *f* 124
pass through, to être de passage 16
pasta pâtes *f/pl* 51
paste *(glue)* colle *f* 105
pastry pâtisserie *f* 64
pastry shop pâtisserie *f* 99
patch, to *(clothes)* rapiécer 29
path chemin *m* 85
patient patient *m* 144
pay, to payer 31, 62, 102
payment paiement *m* 102, 131
pea petit pois *m* 50
peach pêche *f* 54
peak sommet *m* 85
peanut cacahouète *f* 54
pear poire *f* 54
pearl perle *f* 122
pedestrian piéton *m* 79
peg *(tent)* piquet *m* 107
pen plume *f* 105
pencil crayon *m* 105
pencil sharpener taille-crayon *m* 105
pendant pendentif *m* 121
penicilline pénicilline *f* 143
penknife canif *m* 106
pensioner retraité(e) *m/f* 82
people gens *m/pl* 93
pepper poivre *m* 37, 38, 51, 64
per cent pour cent 149
perch perche *f* 45
per day par jour 20, 32, 89
perfume parfum *m* 110, 127
perfume shop parfumerie *f* 108
perhaps peut-être 15
per hour horaire 77; par heure 89
period *(monthly)* règles *f/pl* 141
period pains règles douloureuses *f/pl* 141
permanent wave permanente *f* 30
permit permis *m* 90
per night par nuit 24
per person par personne 32
person personne *f* 32, 36
personal personnel(le) 17
personal call communication avec préavis *f* 135
personal cheque chèque à ordre *m* 130
person-to-person call communication avec préavis *f* 135
per week par semaine 20, 24
petrol essence *f* 75, 78
pewter étain *m* 122
pheasant faisan *m* 48
phone téléphone *m* 28, 78, 79, 134
phone, to téléphoner 134
phone booth cabine téléphonique *f* 134
phone call appel *m* 135; communication *f* 136
phone number numéro de téléphone *m* 96, 134, 135
photo photo *f* 82, 124, 125
photocopy photocopie *f* 104, 131
photograph, to photographier, prendre des photos 82
photographer photographe *m/f* 99
photography photographie *f* 124
phrase expression *f* 12
pick up, to prendre 80, 96
picnic pique-nique *m* 63
picture tableau *m* 83; *(photo)* photo *f* 82
piece morceau *m* 120
pig cochon *m* 46
pigeon pigeon *m* 48
pike brochet *m* 44
pill pilule *f* 141, 143
pillow oreiller *m* 27
pin épingle *f* 110, 111, 121
pineapple ananas *m* 54
pink rose 113
pipe pipe *f* 126
pipe cleaner nettoie-pipe *m* 126
pipe tool cure-pipe *m* 126
place place *m* 25; endroit *m* 76
place of birth lieu de naissance *m* 25
plaice carrelet *m* 44; plie *f* 45
plane avion *m* 65
planetarium planétarium *m* 81
plaster plâtre *m* 140
plastic plastique *m* 107
plastic bag sac en plastique *m* 107
plate assiette *f* 36, 61, 107
platform quai *m* 67, 68, 69, 70
platinum platine *m* 122
play *(theatre)* pièce *f* 86
play, to jouer 86, 88, 89, 93

playground terrain de jeu *m* 32
playing card carte à jouer *f* 105
please s'il vous plaît 10
plimsolls tennis *m/pl* 118
plug *(electric)* fiche *f* 29
plum prune *f* 54
pneumonia pneumonie *f* 142
poached poché(e) 45
pocket poche *f* 117
point, to *(show)* montrer 12
poison poison *m* 109
poisoning intoxication *f* 142
pole *(ski)* bâton *m* 91
police police *f* 78, 156
police station poste de police *m* 99, 156
polish *(nails)* vernis *m* 110
pond étang *m* 85
pop music musique pop *f* 128
poplin popeline *f* 114
poppy pavot *m* 64
porcelain porcelaine *f* 127
pork porc *m* 46
port port *m* 74; *(wine)* porto *m* 60
portable portatif(ive) 119
porter porteur *m* 18, 71; *(hotel)* bagagiste *m* 26
portion portion *f* 37, 55, 61
possible possible 137
post *(letters)* courrier *m* 28, 133
post, to mettre à la poste 28
postage tarif (d'affranchissement) *m* 132
postage stamp timbre *m* 28, 126, 132
postcard carte postale *f* 105, 126, 132
post office bureau de poste *m* 99, 132
potato pomme de terre *f* 51
pothole nid de poule *m* 79
pottery poterie *f* 83, 127
poultry volaille *f* 48
pound *(money)* livre *f* 18, 130; *(weight)* livre *f* 120
powder poudre *f* 110
powder compact poudrier *m* 122
powder puff houppette *f* 110
prawns scampi *m/pl* 45
preference préférence *f* 101
pregnant enceinte 141
premium *(gasoline)* super *m* 75
preparation préparation *f* 51
prescribe, to prescrire 143
prescription ordonnance *f* 108, 143
press, to *(iron)* repasser à la vapeur 29
press stud bouton-pression *m* 117
pressure pression *f* 75
price prix *m* 24
priest prêtre *m* 84
print *(photo)* copie *f* 125
private privé(e) 91, 155
processing *(photo)* développement *m* 124
profession profession *f* 25
profit bénéfice *m* 131
programme programme *m* 87
prohibit, to interdire 79
pronunciation prononciation *f* 6
propelling pencil porte-mine *m* 105, 122
propose, to proposer 40
Protestant protestant(e) 84
provide, to procurer 131
prune pruneau *m* 54
public holiday jour férié *m* 152
pull, to tirer 155
pullover pull(over) *m* 117
puncture crevaison *f* 75
purchase achat *m* 131
pure pur(e) 114
purple violet(te) 113
push, to pousser 155
put, to mettre 24
pyjamas pyjama *m* 117

Q

quail caille *f* 48
quality qualité *f* 103, 113
quantity quantité *f* 14, 103
quarter quart *m* 149; *(part of town)* quartier *m* 81
quarter of an hour quart d'heure *m* 153
question question *f* 11
quick rapide 14; vite 156
quickly vite 137, 156
quiet tranquille 23, 25

R

rabbi rabbin *m* 84
rabbit lapin *m* 48
race course/track champ de courses *m* 90
racket *(sport)* raquette *f* 90
radiator radiateur *m* 78
radio *(set)* poste de radio *m* 23, 119; radio *f* 28
radish radis *m* 50
railroad crossing passage à niveau *m* 79

DICTIONARY Dictionnaire

railway chemin de fer *m* 154
railway station gare *f* 19, 21, 67, 70
rain pluie *f* 94
rain, to pleuvoir 94
raincoat imperméable *m* 117
raisin raisin sec *m* 54
rangefinder télémètre *m* 125
rare *(meat)* saignant(e) 47, 61
rash éruption *f* 139
raspberry framboise *f* 54
rate tarif *m* 20; taux *m* 131
razor rasoir *m* 110
razor blade lame de rasoir *f* 110
reading-lamp lampe de chevet *f* 27
ready prêt(e) 29, 118, 123, 125, 145
real véritable 121
rear arrière 75
receipt quittance *f* 103, 144
reception réception *f* 23
receptionist réceptionnaire *m* 26
recommend, to recommander 35, 36; indiquer 35, 88, 137, 145; conseiller 80, 86
record *(disc)* disque *m* 127, 128
record player tourne-disque *m* 119
rectangular rectangulaire 101
red rouge 59, 113
redcurrant groseille *f* 54
red mullet rouget *m* 45
reduction réduction *f* 24, 82
refill recharge *f* 105
refund remboursement *m* 103
regards salutations f/pl, amitiés *f/pl* 152
register, to *(luggage)* faire enregistrer 71
registered mail recommandé(e) 133
registration enregistrement *m* 25
registration form fiche *f* 25, 26
regular *(petrol)* normale *f* 75
religion religion *f* 83
religious service service religieux *m*, culte *m* 84
rent, to louer 19, 20, 74, 90, 91, 119, 155
rental location *f* 20, 74
repair réparation *f* 125
repair, to réparer 29, 118, 119, 121, 123, 125, 145
repeat, to répéter 12
report, to déclarer 156
require, to exiger 88
reservation réservation *f* 19, 23, 65, 69
reservations office bureau de réservation *m* 19, 67
reserve, to réserver 19, 23, 36, 87
restaurant restaurant *m* 19, 32, 34, 35, 67
return *(ticket)* aller-retour *m* 65, 69
return, to *(give back)* rendre 103
reverse the charges, to téléphoner en P.C.V. 135
rheumatism rhumatisme *m* 141
rhubarb rhubarbe f 54
rib côte *f* 46, 138
ribbon ruban *m* 105
rice riz *m* 51
right droite 21, 63, 69, 77; *(correct)* juste 14
ring *(on finger)* bague *f* 122
ring, to sonner 155; téléphoner 134
river rivière *f* 85, 90; *(major)* fleuve *m* 85
road route *f* 76, 77, 85
road assistance assistance routière *f* 78
road map carte routière *f* 105
road sign panneau routier *m* 79
roast rôti(e) 47
roast beef rosbif *m* 46
roll *(bread)* petit pain *m* 38, 64
roller skate patin à roulettes *m* 128
roll film bobine *f* 124
roll-neck à col roulé 117
room chambre *f* 19, 23, 24, 25, 28; *(space) place f* 32
room service service d'étage *m* 23
rope corde *f* 107
rosary chapelet *m* 122
rosemary romarin *m* 51
rouge fard à joues *m* 110
round rond(e) 101
round *(golf)* partie *f* 89
round-neck à col rond 117
roundtrip *(ticket)* aller-retour *m* 65, 69
rowing-boat barque à rames *f* 91
royal royal(e) 82
rubber *(material)* caoutchouc *m* 118; *(eraser)* gomme *f* 105
ruby rubis *m* 122
rucksack sac de montagne *m* 107
ruin ruine *f* 81
ruler *(for measuring)* règle *f* 105
rum rhum *m* 60
running water eau courante *f* 23
rye seigle *m* 64

S

saddle selle *f* 46
safe *(not dangerous)* sans danger 90
safe coffre-fort *m* 26
safety pin épingle de sûreté *f* 110
saffron safran *m* 51
sage sauge *f* 51
sailing-boat voilier *m* 91
salad salade *f* 42
sale vente *f* 131; *(bargains)* soldes *m/pl* 100
sales tax T.V.A. *f* 24, 102
salmon saumon *m* 45
salt sel *m* 37, 38, 64
salty salé(e) 61
sand sable *m* 90
sandal sandale *f* 118
sanitary towel/napkin serviette hygiénique *f* 109
sapphire saphir *m* 122
Saturday samedi *m* 151
sauce sauce *f* 51
saucepan casserole *f* 107
saucer soucoupe *f* 107
sauerkraut choucroute *f* 47
sausage saucisse *f* 46, 64
sautéed sauté(e) 45, 47
scallop coquille St-Jacques *f* 45; *(meat)* escalope *f* 46
scampi langoustines *f/pl* 44
scarf foulard *m* 117
scarlet écarlate 113
scenic route route touristique *f* 85
school école *f* 79
scissors ciseaux *m/pl* 107, 110
Scotland Ecosse *f* 146
scrambled egg œuf brouillé *m* 38
screwdriver tournevis *m* 107
sculptor sculpteur *m* 83
sculpture sculpture *f* 83
sea mer *f* 23, 85, 90
sea bream daurade *f* 44
seafood fruits de mer *m/pl* 44
season saison *f* 40, 150
seasoning condiments *m/pl* 37
seat place *f* 69, 70, 87
seat belt ceinture de sécurité *f* 75
second deuxième 149
second seconde *f* 153
second class deuxième classe *f* 69
second hand trotteuse *f* 122
second-hand d'occasion 104
secretary secrétaire *m/f* 27, 131
see, to voir 12, 163
send, to envoyer 102, 103, 133; expédier 132
send up, to faire monter 26
sentence phrase *f* 12
separately séparément 62
September septembre *m* 150
seriously *(wounded)* grièvement 139
service service *m* 24, 62, 98, 100; *(religion)* culte *m* 84
serviette serviette *f* 36
set *(hair)* mise en plis *f* 30
set menu menu (à prix fixe) *m* 36, 40
setting lotion fixatif *m* 30, 111
seven sept 147
seventeen dix-sept 147
seventh septième 149
seventy soixante-dix 148
sew, to coudre 29
shade *(colour)* ton *m* 112
shallot échalote *f* 50
shampoo shampooing *m* 30, 111
shape forme *f* 103
share *(finance)* action *f* 131
sharp *(pain)* aigu(e) 140
shave, to raser 31
shaver rasoir (électrique) *m* 27, 119
shaving brush blaireau *m* 111
shaving cream crème à raser *f* 111
she elle 161
shelf étagère *f* 120
ship navire *m* 74
shirt chemise *f* 117
shivery pris(e) de frissons 140
shoe chaussure *f* 118
shoelace lacet *m* 118
shoemaker's cordonnerie *f* 99
shoe polish cirage *m* 118
shoe shop magasin de chaussures *m* 99
shop magasin *m* 98
shopping achats *m/pl* 97
shopping area quartier commerçant *m* 82, 100
shopping centre centre commercial *m* 99
short court(e) 30, 116, 117
shorts short *m* 117
short-sighted myope 123
shoulder épaule *f* 46, 138
shovel pelle *f* 128
show spectacle *m* 86, 87, 88
show, to montrer 13, 76, 100, 101, 103, 119, 124; indiquer 12
shower douche *f* 23, 32

shrimp crevette *f* 44
shrink, to rétrécir 114
shut fermé(e) 14
shutter *(window)* volet *m* 29; *(camera)* obturateur *m* 125
sick *(ill)* malade 140, 156
sickness *(illness)* maladie *f* 140
side côté *m* 30
sideboards/burns favoris *m/pl* 31
sightseeing visite touristique *f* 80
sightseeing tour visite guidée *f* 80
sign *(notice)* écriteau *m* 155; *(road)* panneau *m* 79
sign, to signer 26, 131
signature signature *f* 25
signet ring chevalière *f* 122
silk soie *f* 114
silver argenté(e) 113
silver argent *m* 121, 122
silver plate plaqué argent *m* 122
silverware argenterie *f* 122
since depuis 15, 150
sing, to chanter 88
single célibataire 93
single *(ticket)* aller *m* 65, 69
single room chambre pour une personne *f* 19, 23
sister sœur *f* 93
sit down, to s'asseoir 95
six six 147
sixteen seize 147
sixth sixième 149
sixty soixante 147
size format *m* 124; *(clothes)* taille *f* 114; *(shoes)* pointure *f* 118
skate patin *m* 91
skating rink patinoire *f* 91
ski ski *m* 91
ski, to faire du ski 91
ski boot chaussure de ski *f* 91
skiing ski *m* 89, 91
ski lift remonte-pente *m* 91
skin peau *f* 138
skin-diving plongée sous-marine *f* 91
skirt jupe *f* 117
ski run piste de ski *f* 91
sky ciel *m* 94
sled luge *f* 91
sleep, to dormir 144
sleeping bag sac de couchage *m* 107
sleeping-car wagon-lit *m* 66, 68, 69, 70
sleeping pill somnifère *m* 109, 143, 144
sleeve manche *f* 117
slice tranche *f* 120
slide *(photo)* diapositive *f* 124
slip jupon *m* 117
slipper pantoufle *f* 118
slow lent(e) 12, 14, 135
slow down, to ralentir 79
small petit(e) 14, 25, 101, 118, 130
smoke, to fumer 95
smoked fumé(e) 45
smoker fumeurs *m/pl* 70
snack casse-croûte *m* 63
snack bar buffet-express *m* 34, 67
snail escargot *m* 44
snap fastener bouton-pression *m* 117
sneakers tennis *m/pl* 118
snorkel tuba *m* 128
snow neige *f* 94
snow, to neiger 94
snuff tabac à priser *m* 126
soap savon *m* 27, 111
soccer football *m* 89
sock chaussette *f* 117
socket *(outlet)* prise *f* 27
soft drink boisson non alcoolisée *f* 64
soft-boiled *(egg)* mollet 28
sold out *(theatre)* complet 87
sole semelle *f* 118; *(fish)* sole *f* 45
soloist soliste *m/f* 88
some de, de la, du *(pl* des*)* 15
someone quelqu'un 95
something quelque chose 36, 55, 108, 112, 113, 125, 139
son fils *m* 93
song chanson *f* 128
soon bientôt 15
sore *(painful)* douloureux(euse) 145
sore throat mal de gorge *m* 141
sorry désolé(e) 11, 87; *(I'm)* excusez-moi 16
sort genre *m* 86; sorte *f* 120
sound-and-light show spectacle son et lumière *m* 86
soup soupe *f*, potage *m* 43
south sud *m* 77
South Africa Afrique du Sud *f* 146
souvenir souvenir *m* 127
souvenir shop magasin de souvenirs *m* 99
Soviet Union Union soviétique *f* 146
spade pelle *f* 128
Spain Espagne *f* 146
spare tyre roue de secours *f* 75
sparking plug bougie *f* 76
sparkling *(wine)* mousseux(euse) 59

spark plug bougie *f* 76
speak, to parler 12, 135, 162
speaker *(loudspeaker)* haut-parleur *m* 119
special spécial(e) 20, 37
special delivery par exprès 133
specialist spécialiste *m/f* 142
speciality specialité *f* 40, 59
specimen *(medical)* prélèvement *m* 142
spectacle case étui à lunettes *m* 123
spell, to épeler 12
spend, to dépenser 101
spice épice *f* 50
spinach épinard *m* 49
spine colonne vertébrale *f* 138
spiny lobster langouste *f* 44
sponge éponge *f* 111
spoon cuillère *f* 36, 61, 107
sport sport *m* 89
sporting goods shop magasin d'articles de sport *m* 99
sports jacket veste de sport *f* 117
sprain, to fouler 140
spring *(season)* printemps *m* 150; *(water)* source *f* 85
square carré(e) 101
squid calmar *m* 44
stadium stade *m* 82
staff personnel *m* 26
stain tache *f* 29
stainless steel inox *m* 107, 122
stalls *(theatre)* parterre *m* 87
stamp *(postage)* timbre *m* 28, 126, 132
staple agrafe *f* 105
star étoile *f* 94
start, to commencer 80, 87, 88; *(car)* démarrer 78
starters hors-d'œuvre *m* 41
station *(railway)* gare *f* 19, 21, 67, 70; *(underground, subway)* station *f* 73
stationer's papeterie *f* 99, 104
statue statue *f* 82
stay séjour *m* 31, 92
stay, to rester 16, 24, 26; loger 93
steal, to voler 156
steamed cuit(e) à la vapeur 45
stew ragoût *m* 47
stewed à l'étouffée 47
stew pot marmite *f* 107
stiff neck torticolis *m* 141
still *(mineral water)* non gazeux (euse) 60
sting piqûre *f* 139
sting, to piquer 139
stitch, to *(clothes)* recoudre 29; *(shoes)* coudre 118
stock *(in shop)* stock *m* 103
stock exchange bourse *f* 82
stocking bas *m* 117
stomach estomac *m* 138
stomach ache maux d'estomac *m/pl* 141
stools selles *f/pl* 142
stop *(bus)* arrêt *m* 72, 73
stop, to s'arrêter 21, 68, 70, 72
stop thief! au voleur! 156
store magasin m 98
straight *(drink)* sec 56, 60
straight ahead tout droit 21, 77
strange étrange 84
strawberry fraise *f* 54
street rue *f* 25
streetcar tram *m* 72
street map plan de ville *m* 19, 105
string ficelle *f* 105
strong fort(e) 143
student étudiant(e) *m/f* 82, 93
study, to étudier 93
stuffed farci(e) 41
sturdy solide 101
subway *(railway)* métro *m* 73
suede daim *m* 114, 118
sugar sucre *m* 37, 63, 64
suit *(man)* complet *m* 117; *(woman)* tailleur *m* 117
suitcase valise *f* 18
summer été *m* 150
sun soleil *m* 94
sunburn coup de soleil *m* 108
Sunday dimanche *m* 151
sunglasses lunettes de soleil *f/pl* 123
sunny ensoleillé(e) 94
sunshade *(beach)* parasol *m* 91
sunstroke insolation *f* 141
sun-tan cream crème solaire *f* 111
sun-tan oil huile solaire *f* 111
super *(petrol)* super *m* 75
superb superbe 84
supermarket supermarché *m* 99
supplement supplément *m* 40
suppository suppositoire *m* 109
surfboard planche de surf *f* 91
surgery *(consulting room)* cabinet (de consultation) *m* 137
surname nom (de famille) *m* 25
surroundings environs *m/pl* 35

suspenders *(Am.)* bretelles *f/pl* 117
swallow, to avaler 143
sweater chandail *m* 117
sweatshirt sweatshirt *m* 117
sweet *(food)* sucré(e) 61; *(wine)* doux, douce 59
sweet bonbon *m* 126
sweet corn maïs *m* 50
sweetener édulcorant *m* 37
swell, to enfler 139
swelling enflure *f* 139
swim, to nager, se baigner 90
swimming natation *f* 89; baignade *f* 91
swimming pool piscine *f* 32, 90
swimming trunks maillot de bain *m* 117
swimsuit costume de bain *m* 117
Swiss suisse 18
switch interrupteur *m* 29
switchboard operator standardiste *m/f* 26
switch on, to *(light)* allumer 79
Switzerland Suisse *f* 146
swollen enflé(e) 139
synagogue synagogue *f* 84
synthetic synthétique 114
system système *m* 138

T

table table *f* 36, 107
tablet comprimé *m* 109
tailor's tailleur *m* 99
take, to prendre 18, 25, 72, 73, 102; porter 114
take away, to *(carry)* emporter 63, 102
talcum powder talc *m* 111
tampon tampon hygiénique *m* 109
tangerine mandarine *f* 54
tap *(water)* robinet *m* 28
tape recorder magnétophone m 119
tapestry tapisserie *f* 127
tarragon estragon *m* 50
tart tarte f, tartelette *f* 55
taxi taxi *m* 19, 21, 31
tea thé *m* 38, 60, 64
team équipe *f* 89
tear, to déchirer 140
tearoom salon de thé *m* 34
teaspoon cuillère à café *f* 107, 143
telegram télégramme *m* 133
telegraph office bureau du télégraphe *m* 99, 133
telephone téléphone *m* 28, 78, 79, 134
telephone, to téléphoner 134
telephone booth cabine téléphonique *f* 134
telephone call appel *m* 135; communication *f* 136
telephone directory annuaire téléphonique *m* 134
telephone number numéro de téléphone *m* 96, 135, 136
telephoto lens téléobjectif *m* 125
television *(set)* poste de télévision *m* 23; télévision *f* 28; téléviseur *m* 119
telex télex *m* 133
telex, to envoyer un télex 130
tell, to dire 13, 73, 136; indiquer 76, 153
temperature température *f* 90, 142; *(fever)* fièvre *f* 140
temporary provisoire 145
ten dix 147
tendon tendon *m* 138
tennis tennis *m* 89
tennis court court de tennis *m* 89
tennis racket raquette de tennis *f* 90
tent tente *f* 32, 107
tenth dixième 149
tent peg piquet de tente *m* 107
tent pole montant de tente *m* 107
term *(word)* terme *m* 131
terrace terrasse *f* 36
terrifying effrayant 84
terrycloth tissu-éponge *m* 114
tetanus tétanos *m* 140
than que 15
thank you merci 10
that ce, cette 160; cela 11, 100
the le, la *(pl* les*)* 159
theatre théâtre *m* 82, 86
theft vol *m* 156
their leur *(pl* leurs*)* 161
then ensuite 15
there là 14; voilà 14
thermometer thermomètre *m* 109, 144
these ces 160; ceux-ci 63
they ils, elles 161
thief voleur *m* 156
thigh cuisse *f* 138
thin mince 113
think, to penser 94; croire 62
third troisième 149
third tiers *m* 149
thirsty, to be avoir soif 13, 35
thirteen treize 147

thirty trente 147
this ce, cette 160, ceci 11, 100
those ces 160; ceux-là 63, 120
thousand mille 148
thread fil *m* 27
three trois 147
throat gorge f 138, 141
throat lozenge pastille pour la gorge *f* 109
through à travers 15
through train train direct *m* 68, 69
thumb pouce *m* 138
thumbtack punaise *f* 105
thunder tonnerre *m* 94
thunderstorm orage *m* 94
Thursday jeudi *m* 151
thyme thym *m* 51
ticket billet *m* 65, 69, 87, 89, 156; *(bus)* ticket *m* 72
ticket office guichet *m* 67
tide marée *f* 90
tie cravate *f* 117
tie clip pince à cravate *f* 122
tight *(clothes)* étroit(e) 116
tights collant *m* 117
time temps *m* 80; *(clock)* heure *f* 137, 153; *(occasion)* fois *f* 143
timetable horaire *m* 68
tin *(can)* boîte *f* 120
tinfoil papier d'aluminium *m* 107
tin opener ouvre-boîtes *m* 107
tint coloration *f* 111
tinted teinté 123
tire pneu *m* 75, 76
tired fatigué(e) 13
tissue *(handkerchief)* mouchoir en papier *m* 111
to à 15
toast pain grillé *m* 38
tobacco tabac *m* 126
tobacconist's bureau de tabac *m* 99, 126
today aujourd'hui 29, 151
toe orteil *m* 138
toilet paper papier hygiénique *m* 111
toiletry articles de toilette *m/pl* 110
toilets toilettes *f/pl* 27, 32, 37, 67
toilet water eau de toilette *f* 111
toll péage *m* 75, 79
tomato tomate *f* 50
tomato juice jus de tomate *m* 41, 60
tomb tombe *f* 82
tomorrow demain 29, 151
tongs pince *f* 107
tongue langue *f* 46, 138
tonic water Schweppes *m* 60
tonight ce soir 29, 86, 87, 96
tonsil amygdale *f* 138
too trop 15; *(also)* aussi 15
tooth dent *f* 145
toothache mal de dents *m* 145
toothbrush brosse à dents *f* 111, 119
toothpaste dentifrice *m* 111
top haut *m* 30, 145
torch *(flashlight)* lampe de poche *f* 107
torn déchiré(e) 140
touch, to toucher 155
tough dur(e) 61
tourist office syndicat d'initiative *m* 22, 80; office du tourisme *m* 80
tourist tax taxe de séjour *f* 32
towards vers 15
towel serviette *f* 27, 111
tower tour *f* 82
town ville *f* 19, 21, 76, 93, 105
town hall mairie *f* 82
tow truck dépanneuse *f* 78
toy jouet *m* 128
toy shop magasin de jouets *m* 99
tracksuit survêtement *m* 117
traffic circulation *f* 79
traffic light feu *m* 77
trailer caravane *f* 32
train train *m* 66, 68, 69, 70; *(underground, subway)* rame *f* 73
tram tram *m* 72
tranquillizer tranquillisant *m* 109, 143
transfer *(bank)* transfert *m* 131
transformer transformateur *m* 119
translate, to traduire 12
transport transport *m* 74
travel, to voyager 92
travel agency agence de voyages *f* 99
traveller's cheque chèque de voyage *m* 18, 62, 102, 130
travelling bag sac de voyage *m* 18
travel sickness mal du voyage *m* 108
treatment traitement *m* 143
tree arbre *m* 85
tremendous formidable 84
trim, to *(beard)* rafraîchir 31
trip voyage *m* 93, 152; trajet *m* 72
tripe tripes *f/pl* 47
trolley chariot *m* 18, 71
trousers pantalon *m* 117
trout truite *f* 45

truck camion *m* 79
truffle truffe *f* 50
try, to essayer 115; *(sample)* goûter 60
T-shirt teeshirt *m* 117
tube tube *m* 120
Tuesday mardi *m* 151
tuna thon *m* 45
Tunisia Tunisie *f* 146
tunny thon *m* 45
turbot turbot *m* 45
turkey dinde *f* 48
turn, to tourner 21, 77
turnip navet *m* 50
turquoise turquoise *f* 122
turtleneck à col roulé 117
tweezers pince à épiler *f* 111
twelve douze 147
twenty vingt 147
twice deux fois 149
twin bed lits jumeaux *m/pl* 23
two deux 147
typewriter machine à écrire *f* 27, 105
typing paper papier à machine *m* 105
tyre pneu *m* 75, 76

U

ugly laid (e) 14, 84
umbrella parapluie *m* 117; *(beach)* parasol *m* 91
uncle oncle *m* 93
unconscious évanoui(e) 139
under sous 15
underdone *(meat)* saignant(e) 47; pas assez cuit(e) 61
underground *(railway)* métro *m* 73
underpants caleçon *m*, slip *m* 117
undershirt maillot de corps *m* 117
understand, to comprendre 12, 16
undress, to déshabiller 142
United States Etats-Unis *m/pl* 146
university université *f* 82
unleaded sans plomb 75
until jusqu'à 15
up en haut 15
upper supérieur(e) 69
upset stomach indigestion *f* 108
upstairs en haut 15
urgent urgent(e) 13, 145
urine urine *f* 142
use usage *m* 17, 109
use, to utiliser 134; se servir de 78
useful utile 15
usual habituel(le) 143

V

vacancy chambre disponible *f* 23
vacant libre 14, 155
vacation vacances *f/pl* 151
vaccinate, to vacciner 140
vacuum flask thermos *m* 107
vaginal vaginal(e) 141
valley vallée *f* 85
value valeur *f* 131
value-added tax T.V.A. *f* 24, 102, 154
vanilla vanille *f* 55
VAT *(sales tax)* T.V.A. *f* 24, 102, 154
veal veau *m* 46
vegetable légume *m* 49
vegetarian végétarien *m* 37
vein veine *f* 138
velvet velours *m* 114
velveteen velours de coton *m* 114
venereal disease maladie vénérienne *f* 142
venison cerf *m*, chevreuil *m* 48
very très 15
vest maillot de corps *m* 117; *(Am.)* gilet *m* 117
video cassette vidéocassette *f* 119, 124, 127
video recorder magnétoscope *m* 119
view vue *f* 23, 25
village village *m* 76, 85
vinegar vinaigre *m* 37
vineyard vignoble *m* 85
visit visite *f* 92
visit, to visiter 84
visiting hours heures de visite *f/pl* 144
vitamin pills vitamines *f/pl* 109
V-neck à col en V 117
volleyball volley-ball *m* 89
voltage voltage *m* 27, 119
vomit, to vomir 140

W

waistcoat gilet *m* 117
wait, to attendre 21, 95, 162
waiter garçon *m* 26, 36
waiting-room salle d'attente *f* 67
waitress serveuse *f* 26; mademoiselle *f* 36
wake, to réveiller 27, 71
Wales Pays de Galles *m* 146
walk, to marcher 74; aller à pied 85
wall mur *m* 85
wallet portefeuille *m* 156
walnut noix *f* 54

want, to *(wish)* vouloir, désirer 13
warm chaud(e) 94
wash to laver 29, 114
washable lavable 114
wash-basin lavabo *m* 28
washing powder lessive *f* 107
watch montre *f* 121, 122, 127
watchmaker's horlogerie *f* 99, 121
watchstrap bracelet de montre *m* 122
water eau *f* 23, 28, 32, 38, 75, 90
watercress cresson *m* 49
waterfall chute d'eau *f* 85
water flask gourde *f* 107
watermelon pastèque *f* 54
water-ski ski nautique *m* 91
wave vague *f* 90
way route *f*, chemin *m* 76
we nous 161
weather temps *m* 93
weather forecast prévisions météo *f/pl* 94
wedding ring alliance *f* 122
Wednesday mercredi *m* 151
week semaine *f* 16, 20, 24, 80, 151
weekend week-end *m* 151
well *(healthy)* bien 10, 140
well-done *(meat)* bien cuit(e) 47
west ouest *m* 77
what quoi, que, comment 11; quel(e) 20, 21
wheel roue *f* 78
when quand, à quelle heure 11
where où 11
which lequel, laquelle 11
whipped cream crème Chantilly *f* 55
whisky whisky *m* 17, 60
white blanc, blanche 59, 113
whitebait blanchaille *f* 44
whiting merlan *m* 45
Whit Sunday Pentecôte *f* 152
who qui 11
why pourquoi 11
wick mèche *f* 126
wide large 118
wide-angle lens grand-angulaire *m* 125
wife femme *f* 93
wig perruque *f* 111
wild boar sanglier *m* 48; *(young)* marcassin *m* 48
wind vent *m* 94
window fenêtre *f* 28, 36, 69; *(shop)* vitrine *f* 100, 112
windscreen/shield pare-brise *m* 76
wine vin *m* 57, 59, 61
wine list carte des vins *f* 59
wine merchant marchand de vin *m* 99
winter hiver *m* 150
winter sports sports d'hiver *m/pl* 91
wiper essuie-glace *m* 76
wish vœu *m* 152
with avec 15
withdraw, to *(bank)* retirer 131
without sans 15
woman femme *f* 115
wonderful merveilleux(euse) 96
wood bois *m* 85
wood alcohol alcool à brûler *m* 107
woodcock bécasse *f* 48
woodgrouse coq de bruyère *m* 48
wool laine *f* 114
word mot *m* 12, 15, 133
work, to *(function)* fonctionner 28, 119
working day jour ouvrable *m* 151
worse pire 14
worsted peigné *m* 114
wound blessure *f* 139
wrinkle resistant infroissable 114
write, to écrire 12, 101
writing pad bloc *m* 105
writing-paper papier à lettres *m* 27
wrong faux, fausse 14, 135

X

X-ray *(photo)* radio *f* 140

Y

year an *m*, année *f* 149
yellow jaune 113
yes oui 10
yesterday hier 151
yet encore 15
yield, to *(traffic)* céder le passage 79
yoghurt yaourt m, yoghourt *m* 38, 64
you tu, vous 161
young jeune 14
your ton, ta *(pl* tes*)* 161; votre *(pl* vos*)* 161
youth hostel auberge de jeunesse *f* 22, 32

Z

zero zéro *m* 147
zip(per) fermeture-éclair *f* 117
zoo jardin zoologique *m* 82
zoology zoologie *f* 83
zucchini courgette f 49

Index français

UNITED KINGDOM
NETHERLANDS
Rhine
Bruxelles
BELGIQUE
(Belgium)
Calais
Lille
GERMANY
ENGLISH CHANNEL
Cherbourg
LUXEMBOURG
Le Havre
Rouen
Reims
Deauville
PARIS
Nancy
Brest
Saint-Malo
Versailles
Strasbourg
Seine
Orléans
Angers
Tours
Dijon
Nantes
FRANCE
Saône
SUISS
(Switzerla
Loire
Poitiers
La Rochelle
ATLANTIC
OCEAN
Clermont-Ferrand
Lyon
Genève
Limoges
Grenoble
Bordeaux
Dordogne
Rhône
ITA
Garonne
Avignon
Monac
Nice
Biarritz
Toulouse
Marseille
Perpignan
Andorra
Corse
(Corsica)
SPAIN
MEDITERRANEAN SEA